BEHIND VALKYRIE

BEHIND VALKYRIE

GERMAN RESISTANCE TO HITLER

Documents

Edited by Peter Hoffmann

McGill-Queen's University Press
Montreal & Kingston | London | Ithaca

Translation by Peter Hoffmann, with assistance from Kyle Jantzen,
Kenneth Reynolds, Katharine Sams, and Andrew Szanajda

This edition © McGill-Queen's University Press 2011
ISBN 978-0-7735-3769-9 (cloth)
ISBN 978-0-7735-3770-5 (paper)

Legal deposit first quarter 2011
Bibliothèque nationale du Québec

Printed in Canada on acid-free paper that is 100% ancient forest free
(100% post-consumer recycled), processed chlorine free

McGill-Queen's University Press acknowledges the support of the
Canada Council for the Arts for our publishing program. We also
acknowledge the financial support of the Government of Canada
through the Canada Book Fund for our publishing activities.

LIBRARY AND ARCHIVES CANADA
CATALOGUING IN PUBLICATION

Behind Valkyrie : German resistance to Hitler : documents / edited by
Peter Hoffmann.

Includes bibliographical references and index.
ISBN 978-0-7735-3769-9 (bound).
ISBN 978-0-7735-3770-5 (pbk.)

1. Anti-Nazi movement – Germany – History – Sources.
2. Government, Resistance to – Germany – History – 20th century –
Sources.   3. Germany – Politics and government – 1933–1945 – Sources.
I. Hoffmann, Peter

DD256.3.B45 2010   943.086   C2010-905415-6

Set in 9.7/13 Calluna and 9.7/13 Baskerville 10 with Futura
Book design & typesetting by Garet Markvoort, zijn digital

To My Students

CONTENTS

ACRONYMS

BDM	Bund Deutscher Mädel | Federation of German Girls
DC	Deutsche Christen | German Christians
DNVP	Deutschnationale Volkspartei | German National People's Party
HJ	Hitler Jugend | Hitler Youth
NSDAP	Nationalsozialistische Deutsche Arbeiterpartei | Nationalist Socialist German Workers' Party, "Nazi" Party
NSFK	Nationalsozialistisches Fliegerkorps | National Socialist Flying Corps
NSKK	Nationalsozialistisches Kraftfahrkorps | National Socialist Motoring Corps
NSV	Nationalsozialistische Volkswohlfahrt | National Socialist People's Welfare
OKH	Oberkommando des Heeres | Army High Command
OKW	Oberkommando der Wehrmacht | Armed Forces Supreme Command
SA	Sturmabteilung | Stormtroopers or Brown Shirts
SPD	Sozialdemokratische Partei Deutschlands | Social Democratic Party of Germany
SS	Schutzstaffel | Protection Squadron

ACKNOWLEDGMENTS

The editor thanks all copyright holders for permission to publish translations of the documents included in the present volume. He also thanks the archivists, most of all Professor Hartmut Weber, president of *Bundesarchiv*, and the librarians in the many institutions in which he pursued research relative to the entries in this volume for their dedicated help in locating many of the works referenced in the notes, and equally Susan Pelland, his copy editor, for applying stringent standards, and Eliza Wood for her help in the preparation of the index. The editor is grateful to the Landesstiftung Baden-Württemberg and to Horst von Oppenfeld for financial support.

BEHIND VALKYRIE

INTRODUCTION

One of the most difficult tasks for students of history is to see historical events and persons as their contemporaries saw them. Students must attempt to know and understand what those of another time knew and understood. They must attempt to know as fully as possible the historical situation and state of information. If their own experiences are not sufficiently similar to those of the persons they study, they must dissect the experiences into components with which they can identify. For example, in order to approximate the experiences of a soldier in the trenches in the First World War, students may imagine themselves being in rain and mud for days without an ability to get dry or change clothes; they may add shell shock, loss of comrades, fear of death. In order to comprehend what the persons they study were doing, they must understand the context, and they must understand what their subjects thought they were doing. Every selection in this book demands this effort. The next most difficult task is to learn what the actors in fact did and what effects their actions had.

Students' need for original sources in order to accurately grasp past events and persons motivates the first principle behind this book. The value of whole documents, where only fragments or none were available in print before, motivates the second.

The documents in this book provide an immediate approach to the most disturbing epoch in twentieth-century German history – the twelve years of Adolf Hitler's and his National Socialist German Workers' Party's rule.

In the police-state conditions in which the German people lived during Hitler's rule, opposition was repressed or crushed by the secret state police or Gestapo (Geheime Staatspolizei), which, through a vast network of informers, reached into virtually every household. People who carried on conversations critical of the regime, even if they only referred to a shortage of certain goods, tended to cover their telephones with pillows, as it was rumoured that the Gestapo could listen in. During the war, harsh penalties, in some cases death sentences, were imposed by Special Courts (Sondergerichte) for tuning in to neutral or enemy radio stations, this act being considered treasonous. When a neighbour suddenly disappeared, and someone had seen two men in leather coats take him away at 5:00 a.m., the rumour of it struck fear into people. The existence of concentration camps was officially acknowledged, but former inmates were forbidden to talk about their experiences, enhancing the sense of the sinister. At the same time, through guards and their families, as well as former inmates, a great deal of information about beatings and killings did leak out and deepened the atmosphere of terror. The sense of ubiquitous surveillance was exaggerated, but uncertainty prevented easy communication. Opponents of the regime had little opportunity to inform themselves of events inside and outside Germany, or to discuss them and form opinions in the way one is accustomed to do in a free society.

From the first days of his reign, Hitler abrogated individual liberties and put in place the policing and judicial machinery of terror. On 17 February 1933, Hermann Göring, as Interior Minister of Prussia, which amounted to about two-thirds of Germany, decreed: "Communist terrorist acts and attacks must be met with all severity and, when necessary, with ruthless use of weapons. I shall cover for police officers who use firearms in the discharge of these duties regardless of the consequences of the use of firearms. Those who display weakness, however, will be subject to disciplinary action." This "shooting decree" was published verbatim on the front page of the National Socialist Party daily newspaper, *Völkischer Beobachter*, on 21 February.[1] A decree of 28 February 1933 suspended the Constitution articles that had guaranteed personal liberties. Special Courts were charged with the prosecution of "insidious" acts, including the statement of known facts that the government would have considered secret if they had not already been public knowledge. The Special Courts could pass sentence without hearing witnesses; appeals were not allowed.

Helmuth James von Moltke, who had opposed Hitler from the very beginning and who was hanged on 23 January 1945 for that opposition, wrote to a friend in England through a friend in neutral Sweden in March 1943:

Can you imagine what it is like if you
a) cannot use the telephone;
b) cannot use the post;
c) cannot send a messenger because you probably have no one to send, and if you have, you cannot give him a written message as the police sometimes search people in trains, trams, etc., for documents;

d) cannot even speak with those with whom you are completely d'accord, because the secret police have methods of questioning where they first break the will but leave the intelligence awake, thereby inducing the victim to speak out all he knows; therefore you must limit information to those who absolutely need it;

e) cannot even rely on rumour or a whispering campaign to spread information, as there is so effective a ban on communications of all kinds that a whispering campaign started in Munich may never reach Augsburg.[2]

Such conditions govern the origins and the preservation of the surviving documents of the Resistance. Some of the surviving "statements of fundamental tenets" were notes taken down in haste with a view to future consultation and discussion in order to later produce a more well-founded program or constitutional draft. In some cases, multiple authors were involved, and their contributions cannot be identified.

The thinking that prevails in democracies today has evolved since the Second World War. Democracy is now the dominant ideology, but it was not then, and its march forward has taken decades. During the years since 1945, international agreements, framed by the United Nations and the European Union, have produced increasingly binding canons concerning international and national behaviour of governments. The resisters whose selected testimonies are reproduced in this volume were fighters for these very principles of freedom, justice, and human rights. But they were not free of the influences of their time, and occasionally their expressions of fundamental principles reflect this.

While the resisters gave their lives to restore law and decency, their great trauma was the ease with which Hitler and his cohorts had been able to take over and destroy, in 1933, the first democratic German republic, after it had survived against great odds for fourteen years. The resisters were adamant that this must not happen again. They discerned causes of Hitler's rise in the ills of industrial mass society; a mechanistic, proportional electoral system; and a proliferation of political parties and selfish professional politicians during the "Weimar" years (1919–33). Socialists and conservatives alike looked with skepticism upon plans for the reintroduction of political parties; indeed, for a substantial transition period they did not want to allow them at all.[3]

The selections in this volume focus on what was "behind" Valkyrie, the movement that crystallized in 1938, at the time of the leadership crisis that was triggered by the Blomberg Scandal[4] and Hitler's veritable coup d'état in assuming direct command of the Armed Forces (Wehrmacht) by combining his offices of Chancellor and President with that of War Minister. At that time Hitler attempted to unleash war against Czechoslovakia through the Sudeten Crisis. Disaffection with Hitler had evolved at a high level of army command by 1941/42, occasioned by the murders of killing squads (Einsatzgruppen) in Poland and Russia, by the mistreatment of millions of Soviet prisoners of war, and also by mismanagement of the military campaigns. The most serious attempts to bring down the regime occurred in 1943 and 1944. The military wing of the conspiracy was led by Brigadier Henning von Tresckow and Colonel Claus Schenk Graf von Stauffenberg. The instrument for seizing executive control at home was a set of orders for the mobilization of the Home Army under the code-name "Valkyrie" ("Walküre") in case of an emergency such as an enemy invasion by airborne forces or a revolt among the millions of foreign, forced labourers in Germany. The plotters intended to use these orders to take control of all government, communication, and utility installations. The events are described in the editor's previous books, especially in *The History of the German Resistance 1933–1945* and *Stauffenberg. A Family History, 1905–1944*.[5]

Behind "Valkyrie," there were the earlier oppositional activities of civilians – socialist and conservative politicians, trades-union leaders, clergy, civil servants, professionals. The military plotters considered constitutional preparations by the civil conspirators so indispensable that, at the insistence of General Ludwig Beck, they made their own role as the conspiracy's military arm conditional upon the pre-existence of a prepared structure of laws and administrators.[6] These civil preparations for internal renewal and for a settlement to end hostilities, and the motivations of those who drafted and worked on them, are represented in this volume.

There were many other resistance activities unrelated to those leading to the insurrection of 20 July 1944. They have been researched and described less fully than those of the 20 July 1944 conspiracy, in part because access to sources has been difficult. The Communist underground was active throughout the years of Hitler's rule, with great sacrifice of lives.[7] The "Red Orchestra" group carried on similar subversive work.[8] A number of clergymen, equally unrelated to "Operation Valkyrie," deserve to be remembered for the stand they took against the killing ("euthanasia") of the feeble and the mentally ill, and against the murder of the Jews. A Social Democrat (Otto Wels) and two clergymen (Julius von Jan and August Graf von Galen), although unrelated to the central theme, are included for their unique value in representing views and links in the development of the Resistance. A number of military men, again independent of the conspiracy to overthrow Hitler, protested against mass executions in Poland in 1939 and 1940. These voices, the opposition of the Scholl Group of students (Hans and Sophie Scholl and their friends), and numerous individual resisters shall be given their due in English translations in a further volume.

Some of the resisters in this book were professionals (lawyers or clergymen) doing military service (Moltke, Bonhoeffer). They worked out constitutional drafts (Hassell, Popitz, Moltke) or established foreign contacts during the war (Goerdeler, Trott). Political categorization would be misleading and uninformative. They were all revolutionaries in their efforts to overthrow the dictatorship. They were not conservatives in the sense of aiming at the preservation or restoration of some status quo – the monarchy (although some favoured a new monarchy), the pre-1933 republic, much less the post-1933 dictatorship. What was "conservative" in many of the resisters, be they politically left-leaning or tending to authoritarian government, was a commitment to fundamental human values. Moltke, Trott, and others of his friends in the "Kreisau Circle" were socialists in their political outlook; their "Kreisau Circle" included trades-union leaders.

Critics may have expected the inclusion of one or another document that is not in this volume, or will note that one or another group or current of resistance is unrepresented. The editor hopes they will understand that the two principles – acquainting students with an important aspect of German history in the twentieth century and the inclusion of complete documents rather than fragments – as well as the need to keep the volume to a size that would not prohibit its marketing imposed limitations. No specific justifications will be offered because they could impinge upon the worth of testimony that was not included. If the limitations of this edition lead others to produce a different selection, this would only enhance the purpose of the present edition, namely, the dissemination of information about the essence and motivations of Hitler's German enemies and their commitment to their convictions.

The documents printed in this volume have been carefully selected, authentic sources and their locations established, their accurate transcription and translation ascertained, the comprehension of their contents enhanced by commentary and annotation. They were chosen and translated from a larger number of surviving drafts, notes, and letters. They are grouped in subject categories: Internal Policy, with the sub-categories of Persecution of the Churches, Persecution of the Jews, and Euthanasia; Foreign Policy; Military Resistance.

Some documents have been destroyed or lost whose general contents are known. Notes critical of Hitler's policy that then-Captain Claus Schenk

Count Stauffenberg kept during the crisis over Czechoslovakia in 1938 are a case in point.[9] Stauffenberg's wife gave the notes to friends for safekeeping; after the 20 July 1944 insurrection, the secret state police came to search some of Stauffenberg's friends' houses, and although they did not find the notes, the friends who had them considered that they had had a close call and burned the notes as soon as the police left.[10]

Forty-three documents included here are translated from German documents; twenty-two are reproduced from their English originals or in translations prepared in the British Foreign Office. With the exception of nos. 5, 10, 14, 15, 18, and 22, all are taken from archival or otherwise closely contemporary sources. In a few cases, detailed in the source notes, the original documents were either no longer extant or inaccessible. In the case of the selections from the Hassell diaries, the family was not willing to give unrestricted access to the originals.

Previously published selections from extant German Resistance documents reproduced only fragments of longer documents and did not apply stringent editorial principles. The selections in the earlier publications are not, or not adequately, supported by background, context, and source references. The German Federal Government in 1952 published a then-valuable collection of documents: it consists mostly of excerpts, and the English translation that appeared in 1960 contains numerous errors. Walter Lipgens, in his 1985 collection in English of Resistance plans for a European federation, followed scholarly editorial principles; his collection, however, also consists largely of fragments and none of the documents in the present volume appear at all or as more than a fragment in Lipgens' edition. Gerhard Ringshausen and Rüdiger von Voss published, in German only, a collection of programmatic documents from the entire political spectrum of the Resistance. Martyn Housden published document excerpts that are mainly concerned with attitudes toward persecution and mass murder.[11] The reader may rest assured that there is little or no duplication between the present volume and previously published selections in either conception or contents. The combined characteristics of the present work ensure that it is new in all respects: selection, source accuracy, translation, background, commentary, and annotation.

With the exception of the excerpt from Goerdeler's long memorandum "The Aim" (Das Ziel), and the excerpts from Hassell's diaries, the editor has reproduced full translations of the chosen documents. This results in a limitation of the numbers of documents, but it avoids the frustrations of a more numerous collection of fragments.

Most of the documents reproduced in this volume are introduced briefly; in a few cases a more extensive introduction seemed appropriate. The editor endeavoured to refrain from comment and interpretation as much as seemed justifiable in view of the goal: to offer students an opportunity to read primary sources, to experience the immediacy of historical research, and to develop their own research, interpretations, and analyses for a fuller understanding of the documents.

These documents present challenges to new students of the subject and seasoned scholars alike. In many cases, knowledge is still incomplete; archival and published materials offer scope for original research. Where further research would be impracticable for most students, as when explanatory and corollary materials are available only in German, the editor provided more information. Published primary and secondary sources are listed in a bibliography at the end of the volume, intended to serve students in starting their own research and to establish the historical context in which the document in question came into being.

Note on printing style and spelling, grammar, syntax:

McGill-Queen's University Press has certain conventions for the reproduction of documents: Numberings such as "1.," "2.," etc., are rendered as "1," "2," etc.; commas, full stops, semi-colons, and colons following quotations have been placed inside the final quotation marks. Italics, rather than underlining, has been used to indicate emphasis. Otherwise, the original spelling, grammar, syntax, and punctuation are preserved, whether archaic or not. Cases of incorrect English spelling have been corrected in the text with the original version provided in the notes.

NOTES

1 *Völkischer Beobachter*, Munich ed. (21 Feb. 1933): 1.
2 Helmuth James von Moltke, *Letters to Freya 1939–1945*, 284.
3 Peter Hoffmann, *Stauffenberg. A Family History, 1905–1944*, 20–209.
4 War Minister Field Marshal Werner von Blomberg.
5 Hoffmann, *The History of the German Resistance 1933–1945; Stauffenberg; German Resistance to Hitler; Hitler's Personal Security,* revised and expanded edition (New York: Da Capo Press 2000).
6 Hoffmann, *The History*, 349.

7　See especially Detlef Peukert, *Die KPD im Widerstand. Verfolgung und Untergrundarbeit an Rhein und Ruhr, 1933 bis 1945* (Wuppertal: Peter Hammer Verlag 1980); Allan Merson, *Communist Resistance in Nazi Germany* (London: Lawrence & Wishart 1985); Eric D. Weitz, *Creating German Communism, 1890–1990. From Popular Protests to Socialist State* (Princeton, New Jersey: Princeton University Press 1997); Hermann Weber and Andreas Herbst, *Deutsche Kommunisten. Biographisches Handbuch 1918 bis 1945* (Berlin: Karl Dietz Verlag 2004).

8　See Anne Nelson, *Red Orchestra* (New York: Random House 2009).

9　Document no. 26 of the spring of 1939 reveals Stauffenberg's fundamental position.

10　Hoffmann, *Stauffenberg*, 104.

11　Hans Royce, *20. Juli 1944*, 3rd newly expanded edition supplemented by Erich Zimmermann and Hans-Adolf Jacobsen (Bonn: Berto-Verlag 1961); Erich Zimmermann and Hans-Adolf Jacobsen, eds., *Germans against Hitler. July 20, 1944*; Walter Lipgens, ed., *Documents on the History of European Integration* (Berlin: de Gruyter 1985); Walter Lipgens, ed., *Europa-Föderationspläne der Widerstandsbewegungen 1940–1945. Eine Dokumentation* (Munich: R. Oldenbourg 1968); Martyn Housden, *Resistance and Conformity in the Third Reich* (London: Routledge 1997); Gerhard Ringshausen and Rüdiger von Voss, eds., *Die Ordnung des Staates und die Freiheit des Menschen. Deutschlandpläne im Widerstand und Exil* (Bonn: Bouvier Verlag 2000); some historiographic works also contain documents, selected according to their relevance to the historian's subject, as does Gerhard Ritter, *Carl Goerdeler und die deutsche Widerstandsbewegung*; Gerhard Ritter, *The German Resistance. Carl Goerdeler's Struggle against Tyranny* (Salem, New Hampshire: Ayer Company 1992, reprinted from the edition New York: Praeger 1958); Ger van Roon, *German Resistance to Hitler. Count von Moltke and the Kreisau Circle*; Hoffmann, *Widerstand, Staatsstreich, Attentat. Der Kampf der Opposition gegen Hitler*, 4th rev. edition (Munich: R. Piper & Co. 1985); idem, *The History of the German Resistance*; idem, *Stauffenberg*; Theodor Steltzer, *Von deutscher Politik. Dokumente, Aufsätze und Vorträge*. Some biographic sketches may be found in the incomplete work of Wolfgang Benz and Walter H. Pehle, eds., *Encyclopedia of German Resistance to the Nazi Movement*.

INTERNAL POLICY

1

Dietrich Bonhoeffer's Attack upon Hitler's Leader Concept, January–February 1933

The Reformation had made the monarchs of Lutheran and Reformed territories bishops of their territorial churches. The Lutheran hierarchies had been part of the government, and this had influenced their national and political attitudes. Many sympathized with the National Socialists' extreme nationalism and racism, especially since the National Socialist German Workers' Party (NSDAP) had increased its support in national elections from 2.4 percent in 1928 to 18.6 percent in 1930. A large group of Lutheran ministers formed a pro-National-Socialist association, called German Christians, which dominated synods in 1933 and managed to gain temporary control of a number of parishes and even regional churches. Approximately 6,000 Lutheran ministers opposing the German Christians, about a third of the total number, at first formed the Pastors' Emergency League in 1933 and then a secession group called the Confessing Church in 1934. Among the leaders were Martin Niemöller and Dietrich Bonhoeffer.

From 1931, Dietrich Bonhoeffer was a lecturer in theology in the University of Berlin and college chaplain (Studentenpfarrer) at the Technical College (Technische Universität) in Berlin-Charlottenburg. On 1 February 1933, only two days after Hitler's appointment as chancellor, college chaplain Bonhoeffer spoke over the radio about "The Younger Generation's Changed View of the Concept of the Führer," warning the listeners against a leader becoming an idol.[1] He had sent an advance excerpt to a radio-listeners' magazine, which printed it under the date of 27 January 1933, announcing the broadcast for Wednesday, 1 February.[2] While he spoke, however, Bonhoeffer was removed from the air. It was early in Hitler's dictatorship, and the print media were not yet totally censored, so Bonhoeffer was able to have the text of his address printed, only slightly shortened, a few weeks later, on 26 February 1933, in a respected regional newspaper with broad national circulation, the *Kreuz Zeitung* (circulation 13,600).[3] He also gave his lecture at the Charlottenburg Technical College and at the College for Political Science (Hochschule für Politik) on 23 February and at the beginning of March 1933, respectively.[4]

The style of German intellectual discourse in the 1920s and 1930s was often verbose, tortuous, and obscure. In contrast with his otherwise uncompromising criticism of the idolization of the leader (Führer), Bonhoeffer used terms that seemed to accept the outward political reality as God-given.

Three Types of Leader in the Young Generation
by Students' Pastor Lic. Dr Bonhoeffer-Berlin[5]

Three brothers, the eldest of whom was born in 1900, the second in 1905, the third in 1910, who are now thirty-three, twenty-eight, and twenty-three years old, today represent the difference between three generations. But they all belong to what has come to be termed "the young generation."

There are the eldest, who lived through the period of his intellectual maturation during the war; the second, who lived through it under the impression of the years after the collapse; the third, who lived through it in the years of a yet unnamed epoch – let us say since 1926.

The fast pace of historical events has accelerated the rapidity of the succession of the generations almost ten times. Today a period of three to five years separates the generations.

We must speak of a generational change where, on the one hand, the youngest cohort of the generation of the *same age* has reference to an experience of its own for its entire intellectual attitude and thereby perceives itself, in contrast with the older ones, as an independent group founded upon a specific unity of experience, and where, on the other hand, among the older ones, their own process of *clarification* of the contents of their own experience and of their intellectual attitude has set in.

The great difficulties of the current intellectual debate with and within the young generation have their cause in this same inner disunity. Still, something *comprehensive may be said* about the young generation as a whole.

WORLD OUT OF JOINT

It has matured in a historic environment in which the *thus far* firmly founded world of the Occident went out of joint, in war, postwar, crisis. So its allotted inner task could be none other than the attempt to not let itself be pulled into a full collapse, but rather to find some kind of footing that would enable it to continue its existence.

It reached for this footing under a threefold set of impressions:

Firstly, the experience of the collapse revealed the triumph of things over the human being, of the machine over its inventor; *secondly*, the powerlessness of the entire political world view and religious ideology up to that time was proven; *thirdly*, however, the millions of those who had fallen in the World War, the revolutionary masses of the postwar era, the army of millions of unemployed in the crisis were bound to give the young person a persuasive impression of the meaninglessness and complete isolation of the individual and of the dull power of the masses.

MASSES AND INANIMATE MATTER

It appeared as if the masses and inanimate matter were destined to emerge as victors from this collapse. The young person was unable to find in either the stability that would have been capable of sustaining his life in this chaos.

Out of this distress grew the passionate cry for a new authority, for a bond, for community.

With the postwar youth movement, the *leader concept*, in its new form, was propagated throughout Germany for the first time. Naturally there have always been leaders. Where there is community, there is leadership. But we are concerned here only with the particular form that the leader concept has assumed in the young generation, and one thing is characteristic here: whereas leadership formerly found its expression in the teacher, the statesman, the father, that is, in the preordained *orders* and *offices*, the leader has now become an *autonomous* figure.

The leader is severed completely from the office; he is essentially merely leader. The leader, as conceived in the youth movement, emerged from within a small group; he was not a superior, but chosen by the group. He was the good, the noble character, who was thus to be elevated and trusted by the group. The group is the mother's womb of the leader. It gives him everything, including his authority. All the authority, all the honour, all the glory of the group are transferred to him. Leadership is not an office that is independent of the leader.

The group expects from the leader who thus emerges from the group that he embody its ideal in the flesh. This inherently impossible duty is facilitated for the leader by the fact that the group that produced him sees him already bathed in the light of its ideals. It sees him, not for what he is but for what he is meant to be. It is essential for the *image* of the leader that the group does not see the face of the one who is leading the way, but only sees his back as the figure of the one who is preceding them; his humanness is veiled in his figure as leader.

When the youth movement members who belonged to the war and postwar generations had to enter vocations and professions, they were at the same time replaced by the *third* generation, today the youngest one. Originally endowed with a stronger sense of reality and more goal-oriented than their elder brothers, they saw the lack of prospects and meaning in their own futures and in that of their compatriots as due quite essentially to political distress. Thus, the goal of this new youth was considerably more concrete and more sharply defined to begin with than that of the older group; and the lack of authority in political thought and action was now much more strongly perceived as the ultimate cause of all calamities.

In the face of the far-reaching dissolution of form and order, the call for political authority here too was bound to be the call for the political leader; and in this call – that is the great and characteristic thing – suddenly and broadly the generational differences among the young dwindled. Even the "father-and-son problem," which had been at the centre of the youth movement, faded wholly into the background; one no longer insists on the antithesis but on the common obligation.

The figure of the political leader was divested of its intimacy; comradeship took the place of friendship; *obedience* took the place of devotion. The individualistic remnants of the youth movement have been overcome. An enormous distance is put between the leader and the follower, but – and this is now the crucial thing – he is leader only as the one chosen by the followers, the one grown out of them; he receives his *authority* solely from his *followers*, from below, from the people.[6] The national spirit – so one thinks – brings forth, from its metaphysical depths, the leader and elevates him to utter loftiness.

Precisely this concept, however, meets with wide and decided protest among the young generation. In the wholly unanimous call for political authority, a most profound polarity reveals itself in the particular definition of this authority. At bottom, it consists of the question: *authority of the leader* or *authority of the office*? And with this we face the most burning question of our time.

The leader has authority from below; the office has authority from above; the authority of the leader depends on his person; the authority of the office is suprapersonal; authority from below is self-justification of the nation; authority of office is the acknowledgment of the given limit; authority from below is borrowed authority; authority of office is original authority.

WHAT IS IT ABOUT AUTHORITY?

The following is to be said about this dispute. In the concept of *"authority"* there is contained, according to its origin, the concept of *authorship*. Authority is more primary than he for whom it is authority. Therefore I can acknowledge authority only as authority *ordained to me*.

The authority that I concede to another over me is fundamentally merely my own authority. Therefore the former is genuine and limited authority; the latter is false authority and in danger of becoming limitless authority. Therefore I am bound within the former authority; in the latter I merely again liberate myself; I assert myself.

There is a crucial *difference* between the authority of the father, the teacher, the judge, the statesman, on the one hand, and the authority of the leader on the other. The former have authority by virtue of and solely in their office; the leader has authority by virtue of his person. The authority of the former can be infringed upon, violated, but it remains in existence; the authority of the leader is thoroughly at stake at every moment; it is in the gift of his followers.

I choose the leader for myself; I cannot choose father and teacher; I submit to the authority of the leader; I am subordinated to the authority of the father and teacher.

The father, the teacher, the statesman are, essentially, not leaders, but administrators of their offices. Whoever expects something else does not see the reality, is a fantast.

RESPONSIBILITY OF THE LEADER

Reference, however, has no doubt been made now, through the leader concept, to a necessity that is historical and that is present also in a certain youthful sense of life, and there remains only the question of the place that is legitimately due to the "leader" – in the incisive sense of the word – in the structure of the authorities. The human being, and particularly the young person, will have a need to give a leader authority over himself as long as he does not himself feel mature enough, strong enough, responsible enough to achieve the entitlement placed in this authority. The leader will have to be responsibly conscious of this clear limitation of his authority. If he perceives his function differently than it is thus objectively grounded, if he does not again and again give the follower clear information about the limitation of his task and about the latter's very own responsibility, if he allows himself to be carried away by the follower and desires to represent his idol – and the follower will always hope for this of him – then the image of the leader passes over into that of the seducer.

The genuine leader must be able to disappoint at any time. That has to be part of his responsibility and objectivity. He must lead the followers away from his person to the acknowledgment of the genuine authority of the *orders* and of the *office*. The leader must lead the follower into responsibility toward the orders of life, toward father, teacher, judge, *state*. He must radically deny himself the temptation of becoming the false god, i.e., the *ultimate* authority of the follower.

He must confine himself to his assignment with complete level-headedness. He serves the order of the state, the community, and his service can be incomparably valuable, indeed, it can be indispensable. In this service to the other authority, however, the leader directs attention to that ultimate authority itself, before which the state and the community are also merely penultimate authorities. Only the leader who himself has his place in the service of the penultimate *and* the ultimate authority finds loyalty.

NOTES

1 Dietrich Bonhoeffer, "Wandlungen des Führerbegriffs in der jungen Generation," *Dietrich Bonhoeffer, Werke, Band 12* (1997), 240-2; Dietrich Bonhoeffer, *Works, Vol. 12*, 266-8; for full text, see *Werke, 12*, 242-60, *Works, 12*, 268-82, 240-2; Eberhard Bethge, *Dietrich Bonhoeffer. A Biography,* 259-64; *Works, 12*, 240, note 1: *Der Rundfunk Hörer* 10, no. 5 (Friday, 27 January 1933): 4, announced the broadcast: "Lic. Dietrich Bonhoeffer, Student Chaplain at the Technical College Charlottenburg, who will be speaking on 'Changes in the Concept of the Leader among the Young Generation' on Wednesday (1 February 1933) in the Berliner Funkstunde at 5:45 p.m., sends us the following remarks upon this topic." A manuscript and a typescript of the radio lecture are in Bonhoeffer's papers (NL A 36, 1a and NL A 36, 1b). The typescript of the article in *Kreuz Zeitung* of 26 February 1933 is also in NL A 36, 4 (1); the version printed in *Kreuz Zeitung* is not identical, however, with the script printed in *Werke, 12*, 242-60, and *Works, 12*, 268-82. Bonhoeffer also gave his lecture at the Technical College Charlottenburg (Technische Hochschule Charlottenburg) on 23 February 1933, and, at the request of Theodor Heuss, at the College of Political Science (Hochschule für Politik) at the beginning of March 1933.
2 *Works, 12*, 266.
3 *Sperlings Zeitschriften-u. Zeitungs-Adreßbuch. Handbuch der deutschen Presse. 58. Ausgabe 1933.* Verlag des Börsenvereins der Deutschen Buchhändler zu Leipzig, o.J. The editors of *Works* do not mention the publication in *Kreuz Zeitung.*
4 The version in *Works, 12*, 268-82 is Bonhoeffer's expanded version.
5 Source: Dietrich Bonhoeffer, "Wandlungen des Führerbegriffs in der jungen Generation," *Kreuz Zeitung* (26 February 1933); this varies somewhat from the script published in *Werke, 12*, 242-60 and *Works, 12*, 268-82. Emphasis in print is rendered by italics. See also Eberhard Bethge, *Dietrich Bonhoeffer. A Biography.*
6 "Volk" is here translated as "people," meaning the general public, "the ordinary people"; "Volksgeist" is more accurately translated as "national spirit."

2

Otto Wels against
Passage of the Enabling Act,
23 March 1933

Immediately after Hitler's appointment as Chancellor on 30 January 1933, the National Socialist government began to consolidate its hold on political power in Germany. Through a series of decrees, they suspended most civil liberties and began immediately to place their political enemies in jails and prison camps. In an atmosphere of national euphoria and SA terror, they held Reichstag elections on 5 March. The National Socialists received the most votes but not a majority. Hitler was resolved never to relinquish power and moved to make himself dictator by passing an Enabling Law. This law would allow him to issue decrees and laws without the scrutiny or approval of the Reichstag. The only parliamentary opponents to such legislation were the Social Democratic Party and the Communists. The elected Communist Members of the Reichstag were not allowed to take their seats after the election, and most of them were in prison by mid-March 1933.

Otto Wels (15 September 1873–16 September 1939), leader of the Social Democratic Party, rose in the Reichstag on 23 March 1933 to speak against the National Socialist government's Enabling Bill. The bill was passed and Otto Wels, constantly in danger of imprisonment, finally went into exile in Prague on 1 May 1933. In 1938 he went to Paris where he remained until his death.

Reichstag Meeting, 23 March 1933

The day's meeting is resumed at 6:12 p.m. after a three-hour break during the afternoon.[1]

Speaker Göring:[2] The meeting is re-opened. We begin with the discussion of the government's policy statement in connection with the consideration of the motion by Dr Frick,[3] Dr Oberfohren[4] and others (no. 6 of printed motions[5]). Deputy Wels has the floor.

Wels (SPD), Deputy: Ladies and Gentlemen! We Social Democrats all the more emphatically agree to the foreign policy demand for German equal rights that the Reich Chancellor has put forward, as we have always fought for it as a matter of principle.

("Very true!" from the Social Democrats.)

In this connection I may rather permit myself the personal remark that I, as the first German before an international forum, at the Berne Conference on 3 February of the year 1919, opposed the untruth of Germany's guilt for the outbreak of the world war.

("Very true!" from the Social Democrats.)

Never has any principle of our party had the potential for hindering us or hindered us from representing the just demands of the German nation to the other nations of the world.

("Bravo!" from the Social Democrats.)

The Reich Chancellor, on the day before yesterday in Potsdam, also uttered a sentence that we subscribe to. It reads: "Out of the folly of the theory of eternal victors and vanquished came the madness of the reparations and, in consequence, the catastrophe of the world economy." This sentence is valid for foreign policy; it is no less valid for domestic policy.

("Very true!" from the Social Democrats.)

Here, too, the theory of eternal victors and vanquished is folly, as the Reich Chancellor has said. The Reich Chancellor's expression also reminds us, however, of another, which was uttered on 23 July 1919 in the National Assembly. Here it was said: "We are defenceless, but defenceless is not honour-less."

(Lively agreement from the Social Democrats.)

Certainly, the enemy want to dishonour us, of that there is no doubt. But that this attempt at slander one day will redound upon the originator himself, since it is not our honour that is destroyed in this world tragedy; that is our belief until our last breath.

("Very true!" from the Social Democrats. Interjection from the National Socialists: "Who said that?")

This is in a policy statement which a Social-Democratic-led government issued in the name of the German nation before the entire world, then, four hours before the armistice expired, in order to prevent the further advance of enemies. That declaration forms a valuable complement to the statement of the Reich Chancellor. No blessings come from a forced peace,

("Very true!" from the Social Democrats)
especially not at home.

(Renewed approbation from the Social Democrats.)

A real national community cannot be founded on it. Its first precondition is equal rights. The government may protect itself against coarse polemical excesses; it may prevent calls for violent acts, and violent acts themselves, with rigour. That may be done if it is done on all sides equally and impartially, and if one refrains from treating defeated opponents as though they were outlaws.

("Very true!" from the Social Democrats.)
Freedom and life they can take away from us, but not our honour.

(Lively applause from the Social Democrats.)

After the persecutions which the Social Democratic Party has experienced in recent times, nobody will fairly be able to demand or expect it to vote for the Enabling Act that has been introduced here. The elections of 5 March have produced a majority[6] for the government parties and have thereby given them the possibility to govern strictly according to the wording and meaning of the constitution. Where this possibility exists, the duty to do so exists.

("Very right!" from the Social Democrats.)

Criticism is beneficial and necessary. Never before, since the birth of the German Reichstag, has the control of public affairs by the elected representatives of the people been excluded to such an extent as is now happening,

("Very true!" from the Social Democrats)
and as shall happen even more through the new Enabling Law. Such an omnipotence of the government must have all the more serious consequences, as the press also lacks any freedom of conduct.

Ladies and gentlemen! The conditions that today prevail in Germany are frequently described in garish colours. As always in such cases, exaggerations are not lacking. Insofar as my party is concerned, I hereby declare: we have neither asked Paris for intervention, nor have we smuggled millions to Prague, nor have we sent abroad exaggerated news.

("Very true!" from the Social Democrats.)

It would be easier to refute such exaggerations if a form of domestic reporting were possible that separated the true from the false.

(Lively agreement from the Social Democrats.)

It would be even better if we could, in good conscience, testify that the full rule of law had been restored for all.

(Renewed lively agreement from the Social Democrats.)

That, gentlemen, rests with you. The gentlemen of the National Socialist Party call the movement that they have unleashed a national revolution, not a national-socialist one. The relationship between their revolution and socialism has until now confined itself to the attempt to destroy the social-democratic movement that for more than two generations has been the champion of socialist ideas

(Laughter from the National Socialists)

and will remain so. If the gentlemen of the National Socialist Party wanted to perform socialist deeds, they would need no Enabling Law.

("Very true!" from the Social Democrats.)

Overwhelming majority support for you in this House would be a certainty. Every proposal from you put forward in the interests of the workers, the farmers, the employees, the civil servants, or the middle class could be expected to pass, if not unanimously, then with a powerful majority.

(Lively agreement from the Social Democrats. Laughter from the National Socialists.)

Nevertheless you want, first of all, to eliminate the Reichstag in order to continue your revolution. But destruction of what exists is not yet a revolution. The nation expects positive achievements. It expects thoroughgoing measures against the terrible economic misery that prevails not only in Germany, but in all the world. We Social Democrats have borne co-responsibility at the most difficult times and have had stones cast upon us for it.

("Very true!" from the Social Democrats. Laughter from the National Socialists.)

Our achievements for the reconstruction of state and economy, for the liberation of the occupied territories, will stand the test of history.

(Agreement from the Social Democrats.)

We have put in place equal rights for all and social labour legislation. We have helped to establish a Germany in which not only princes and barons, but men from the working class have access to positions of leadership in the state.

(Renewed agreement from the Social Democrats.)

You cannot retreat from this without abandoning your own leader.

(Applause and clapping from the Social Democrats.)

Futile will be the attempt to turn back the wheels of history. We Social Democrats know that one cannot remove facts of power politics through mere legal appeals. We see the power-political fact of your present rule. But the people's sense of justice is a political power, too, and we shall not cease to appeal to this sense of justice. The constitution of Weimar is not a socialist constitution. But we stand by the principles of a state ruled by law, by equal rights, by social justice, all of which have been established in it. We German Social Democrats, in this historical hour, solemnly avow the principles of humanity and justice, of freedom and socialism.

(Lively agreement from the Social Democrats.)

No Enabling Law will give you the power to destroy ideas that are eternal and indestructible. You yourselves have avowed socialism. The Socialist Law[7] did not destroy Social Democracy. German Social Democracy can also draw new strength from new persecutions.

We greet the persecuted and the distressed. We greet our friends in the Reich. Their steadfastness and loyalty deserve admiration. Their courage of their conviction, their unbroken confidence –

(Laughter from the National Socialists. "Bravo!" from the Social Democrats)

guarantee a brighter future.

(Repeated lively applause from the Social Democrats. Laughter from the National Socialists.)

NOTES

1 Source: *Verhandlungen des Reichstags. VIII. Wahlperiode 1933.* Band 457 (Berlin: Reichsdruckerei 1934), 32–4. Cf. Adolph, H.J.L. *Otto Wels und die Politik der deutschen Sozialdemokratie 1894–1939* (Berlin: de Gruyter 1971).

2 Reichstag Deputy Hermann Göring became leader of the largest Reichstag party faction (NSDAP) after the elections of July 1932; when the Reichstag was convened on 30 August 1932, Göring was elected Reichstag Speaker.

3 Wilhelm Frick, Chairman of the Reichstag caucus of the Deutsche Nationalsozialistische Arbeiterpartei (NSDAP) and Reich Minister of the Interior in Hitler's cabinet.

4 Ernst Oberfohren, Chairman of the Reichstag caucus of the Deutschnationale Volkspartei (DNVP), the coalition partner of NSDAP.

5 Enabling Bill.

6 The National Socialist German Workers' Party received 288 seats for 43.9 percent of the popular vote; the German National Peoples' Party received 52 seats for 8.0

percent. Together, the "government parties" gained 51.9 percent of the vote and a slim majority of the seats: 340 of the total 647 seats. See Eberhard Kolb, *The Weimar Republic* (London: Unwin Hyman 1988), 194–5, for comprehensive election statistics.

7 Law against socialist activities and agitation of 1878, known as Sozialistenge-setz.

3

Law for the Restoration of Ordered Conditions in the State Judiciary System (Provisional Basic Constitutional Law), 1938–1940

Johannes Popitz, Minister of Finance of Prussia, and the lawyer Carl Lang-behn together drafted the 'Law' in consultation with other conspirators, including former Ambassador Ulrich von Hassell, General Ludwig Beck ("holder of executive power" in the Law), Undersecretary of State Erwin Planck, and Professor Jens Jessen.[1] Langbehn's wife destroyed Langbehn's copy after her husband had been arrested on 22 September 1943.[2]

The first German edition of Hassell's diaries in 1946 contains, in addition to the document, a brief comment by Popitz's daughter, Cornelia Schulz-Popitz.[3] The note reveals that Popitz had hidden the final formulation of his draft, the surviving one on which the translation below is based, in his library after the arrest of Langbehn in September 1943.[4] Popitz's daughter further explained that the drafting of the document had been in progress since 1938, in consultation mainly with Jessen, Hassell, Planck, and Beck.[5]

The document printed below was first published as one of several ap-pendices in the first German edition of Hassell's diaries.[6] Most of the diar-ies were kept in Switzerland during the war; parts for the last years were buried in Hassell's garden in Ebenhausen, near Munich.[7] The first edition of the diaries and appendices was prepared by Hassell's widow, Ilse von Hassell née von Tirpitz, who died in 1982.

The version of the document that appeared in the first German edition of Hassell's diaries is reprinted in the new German edition. The editors of the new German edition say that their text of the document is identi-cal with the typewritten copy in the German Federal Archives and that it follows the first (Swiss) edition of the diaries.[8] Only the second part of this statement is correct. The first publication in 1946 had rather serious gaps. These can be explained as attempts by the editor, Ilse von Hassell, to avoid the sort of negative criticism that tended to find affinities to National Socialism and now-discredited German nationalism in the mentalities of enemies of the regime as well as in those of its supporters. Despite their statement to the contrary, the editors of the new German edition of Hassell's diaries did not correct these manipulations.

An example follows:

In his draft, in Article 1/10, Popitz wrote: "The military forces are not only *the power instrument*[9] of the Reich, which is indispensable in view of Germany's geographical position, but also an educational institution for the intellectual-moral rebirth of the nation."

The 1946 edition of the diaries and the 1988 edition have this version: "The military forces are not only *the safeguard of the peace*[10] of the Reich, which is indispensable in view of Germany's geographical position, but also an educational institution for the intellectual-moral rebirth of the nation."

The translation of the "Law" printed below is based on a typewritten copy from Johannes Popitz's papers in the German Federal Archives in Koblenz.[11] It represents the full text of the document and it corrects the faulty transcription in the editions of Hassell's diaries.

Law for the Restoration of Ordered Conditions in the State and Judiciary System (Provisional Basic Constitutional Law[12])

The previous leadership of state has brought about the conditions of an absence of a constitution and of lawlessness. The foundations of the social life of the German people, already shaken since the end of the world war, contrary to oath and duty, have been completely destroyed. Even the most basic laws of humanity have been disregarded. In order to remedy this distress and to restore to the German nation an order appropriate to its nature and its history, I, as a holder of executive power, and with the consent of the men who have agreed to form a government, enact the following basic law. It shall be binding upon government and nation, until a definitive constitution can be promulgated for the German Reich, with the collaboration of all strata of the nation.

The following principles are to be realized in the conduct of all Germans toward each other and in the measures of the government and its authorities:

1   In all aspects of life the rules of propriety and of common decency shall be the supreme law of action.

2   The inviolability of the law, the independence of the judicial administration, the securing of personal liberty, of the family and of property are to be restored.

3   Christianity and Christian ethics form, as they have done for centuries, an irreplaceable foundation of German life. Undisturbed religious observance is to be guaranteed. Recognized Christian religious associations will be corporations under public law [Körperschaft des öffentlichen Rechts].

4   The defence of the German nation and its Reich against influences from abroad and internal subversion[13] from within is the duty of every German. Every German must act in such a way that the common good is not diminished and the honour of Germany is not violated.

5   All of the nation's classes share in the material and intellectual resources according to their contribution. The community must bear the responsibility for a humane standard of living for all who fulfill their duties to nation and state. This includes social security for the aged, aid in illness and unemployment, as well as the provision of dwellings that make healthy family life possible.

6   In the economy, the responsibility of independent entrepreneurs is to be restored. It behooves the state to guide the entire German economy in order to guarantee the maintenance of the nation and the increase of the prosperity of social classes.

7   In agriculture, the most important source of strength of the nation, a distribution of property is to be aimed at that guarantees the greatest possible yield of food necessary for the national economy. The migration from rural areas is to be countered generally by raising rural living conditions, particularly by fair remuneration for the contributions of the rural population, and by improving domestic living conditions.

8   Schools and educational institutions of all levels are called upon to impart the foundations of knowledge, physical fitness, character, and morals to the new generation of the civil service, of

the clergy, and of the sciences, art, and the economy. They serve the development of a truly German culture. Instruction will take place, as a matter of principle, in public institutions of the state or its regional bodies. Religious instruction is an indispensable means of education in the schools devoted to a general education.

9 Research, teaching, and the arts are only limited in their activities in so far as external and internal security and due respect for the intellectual and moral riches of the nation require.

10 The German military forces are based on the universal draft; men with the character and the intellectual and moral qualities of the great soldiers of German history are called upon to lead them. The military forces are not only the power instrument of the Reich, indispensable in view of Germany's geographical position, but also an educational institution for the intellectual-moral rebirth of the nation.

11 In accordance with historical development, the state requires, in the exercise of its authority, a civil service trained for its tasks. Its position of trust in the nation is to be re-established. Only whoever is ready to place one's full capacity for work in the service of the state and nation and to devote oneself to one's tasks with true patriotism, selflessness, and loyalty can be a civil servant; in exchange, the state guarantees him employment for life and assures the acknowledgment of genuine merit. Civil servants shall not be appointed for tasks that are not distinguishable from those in general economic endeavours.

ARTICLE 2

1 There is only one executive authority in the Reich territory: that of the Reich.

2 The inequality of present lands in terms of size, economic, and financial strength, as well as the incompatibility of the administrative structure in various regions of the Reich, makes a reorganization of the Reich imperative. Prussia will consummate its mission to form the Reich by relinquishing the union of its provinces as one land.

3 The Reich shall be divided into lands [Länder] that are both administrative districts of the Reich and regional bodies with home rule. The structure will be based on the appendix [to this document].

4   To the lands, under the supervision of the Reich, will be transferred tasks to be discharged in home rule and autonomous responsibility that designate them [the lands] for active co-operation in the cultivation of the economy and culture in the parts of the Reich entrusted to them. They shall here be guardians of the valuable tradition of the German nations and the former German territories. A balancing of finances and burdens of the entire Reich territory will ensure the development of a home rule capable of the fulfillment of assigned tasks in all parts of the Reich.

5   Every land as an administrative district shall have as its head a governor; he shall also act as a deputy of the Reich government in exercising the supervision of the state over a land as a regional body. The land chief minister [Landeshauptmann] is to be the highest home-rule authority of a land. The governor and the land chief minister will each have at their side an advisory land council for their respective areas of responsibility. There will be in place in every land a Chamber of Agriculture, a Chamber of Commerce, and a Chamber of Labour.[14] Every land shall form a military district headed by the military district commander; a military district can also comprise several lands.

6   Lands shall be divided into prefectures that are administrative districts of the Reich, and these divided into land and municipal districts that are both administrative districts and regional bodies with home rule.

7   The Reich government will determine by ordinance the time at which restructuring shall be considered complete; alternatively, this determination may be made for parts of the Reich. Until then, the existing divisions and jurisdictions remain in place. The management of the budget of the hitherto existing lands, particularly concerning payments from those lands to the regional bodies integrated in them, shall be administered for Prussia directly by the Reich Minister of Finance and the other appropriate Reich ministers, and, for the remaining lands, by agencies entrusted with this by the Reich government. The Reich shall be the legal successor of the hitherto existing lands. It shall transfer appropriate shares of the assets of those lands to the newly formed lands. Analogous arrangements will apply to the Prussian provinces and to the hitherto existing Reich regions [Reichsgaue].

8   Regulations in clauses one to seven will apply in the same sense to the three Reich cities.[15]

ARTICLE 3

1 Administration will be exercised either directly by state authorities or by authorities of the regional bodies. It is to be conducted
in close contact with and responsive to the people. Administrative affairs are to be delegated, under the direction of the central
Reich authorities, largely to the authorities at the state, district,
and county level.

2 In order to assure administrative unity, there will be, alongside
the command headquarters of the Armed Forces, the general administrative authorities and the law courts, and special national
authorities solely for the administration of taxes and customs, the
railways, and the postal service.

3 Administrative acts that impinge upon personal freedom or limit
the control of property, insofar as regular courts do not have
jurisdiction, will be subject to scrutiny by independent administrative courts.

ARTICLE 4

1 The authority of the state shall be exercised in the name of the
Reich by the Head of State and by the Reich government.

2 The Head of State and the Reich government shall be assisted by
a state council.

ARTICLE 5

1 The Head of State will be the guardian of the principles upon
which the recovered order of Germany is founded.

2 The Head of State shall be the regent of the German Reich. He
shall be responsible to God and the German name, and, as the
patron of all works of peace and the foremost servant of the state,
he shall be equally close to Germans of every national group. In
the hour of danger, he will lead the nation, in arms, as supreme
warlord.[16]

ARTICLE 6

1 The Reich government shall consist of the Reich Chancellor, as
chairman, and the Reich ministers.

2 Reich ministers shall be:
    1) the Reich Minister and Minister of Foreign Affairs,
    2) the Reich Minister and Minister of War,
    3) the Reich Minister and Minister of the Interior,
    4) the Reich Minister and Minister of Finance,
    5) the Reich Minister and Minister of Justice,
    6) the Reich Minister and Minister of Agriculture,
    7) the Reich Minister and Minister of Economy and Labour,
    8) the Reich Minister and Minister of Education,
    9) the Reich Minister and Minister of Transport.
3 Upon the recommendation of the Reich Chancellor, the Head of State can appoint additional Reich ministers for certain portfolios and Reich ministers without portfolio.
4 The Reich Chancellor shall issue the order of business of the Reich government with the consent of the Reich government.

ARTICLE 7

The prerogatives of the Head of State shall be:
1 the international representation of the Reich;
2 the supreme command of the Armed Forces;
3 the appointment and dismissal of the Reich Chancellor and, upon his recommendation, of the other ministers; before dismissing the Reich Chancellor, the Head of State shall deliberate with the Reich government, which is convened under his chairmanship for this purpose;
4 the appointment and dismissal of officers and Reich civil servants; the appointment of officers and Reich civil servants may be delegated, by an ordinance issued by the Head of State, with the consent of the Reich Chancellor, to the appropriate Reich ministers or other armed forces or administrative authorities;
5 the right of clemency;
6 the bestowal of titles, orders, and decorations.

ARTICLE 8

The Head of State shall require the counter-signature of the Reich Chancellor or of the Reich minister with the respective portfolio for all ordinances and decrees to have legal force. Counter-signature is not required for the exercise of the supreme command over the Armed Forces, in so far as it is a question of command matters; this does not include the appointment and dismissal of officers, which is subject to the counter-signature of the Reich Minister for War.

ARTICLE 9

1   The Reich government will issue laws with the consent of the Head of State, who will sign and promulgate them. The Reich government has to hear the Privy Council [Staatsrat] before issuing laws, unless their issuing does not permit delay.

2[17]   The Head of State shall decide upon war and peace with the consent of the Reich government. The same applies to the conclusion of alliances and treaties, unless their contents require the form of a law.

3[18]   The budget is to be established by law before the beginning of every fiscal year. The raising of loans and credits also requires a law. The annual account will be approved by the Head of State upon the recommendation of the Reich government, after a previous examination of fiscal management by the state-court-of-audit and after consultation with the Privy Council [Staatsrat].

ARTICLE 10

1   A Privy Council [Staatsrat] will be formed. The Privy Council shall be composed of men who, based on their achievements, their qualifications, and their character, are worthy of the trust of the nation. The Reich ministers and the governors shall be ex officio members of the Privy Council. Other members shall be appointed for a duration of five years, by the Head of State, upon the recommendation of the Reich government. Unless the Head of State is in the chair of the state council, the Reich Chancellor or a minister appointed by him shall be in the chair.

2   The Privy Council shall represent the nation as a whole, until consolidation of the general living conditions of the German nation permits the formation of popular representation on a wide basis.

3   The powers of the Privy Council follow from Article 9; beyond that, the Privy Council shall be consulted before important administrative measures are taken.

ARTICLE 11

1   The Reich ministers, members of the land governments, state secretaries, Reich governors and district governors, the chairmen
of the supreme Reich agencies, the Chief of German Police, the
chiefs of the regular police, and the security police who are in
office before this law takes effect will be relieved of their offices.
The same applies for the Reich Protector for Bohemia and Moravia, the Governor General of Poland, and the Reich commissars
in the occupied territories. The Reich Defence Council, as well as
the offices of the Reich defence commissars, of the supreme police
leaders, and of the plenipotentiaries for the Four Year Plan, will
be abolished.

2   The purging of unsuitable persons from the civil service will be
carried out by appropriate application of the Reich law of 7 April
1933 (*RGBl.* I, 175). A dismissal from the service shall take place
only if a civil servant's conduct in office heretofore has demonstrated his lack of qualification or if he has abused his office. Previous membership in the Party is not a reason for removal from
office. Dismissed civil servants will receive a pension, in accordance with the regulations of the Reich Civil Service Law, provided that the dismissal does not occur in the course of disciplinary proceedings.

ARTICLE 12

Acts of reprisal against office-holders of the previous form of government must not take place. Guilty persons will be sentenced in criminal proceedings or in disciplinary proceedings of the service.

ARTICLE 13

1   The Party and its subdivisions will be dissolved. Their office holders are to abstain immediately from all activity. Uniforms and in-
signia of the Party and of its subdivisions may no longer be worn.

2   The property of the party and of its subdivisions shall fall to the
state; in suitable cases, it may be relinquished to the regional
bodies. Buildings owned by the Party or its subdivisions are to
be used for redressing the housing shortage of the population, if
they are suitable for this purpose.

3 The formation of new political associations is inadmissible.

ARTICLE 14

1 The Secret State Police [Geheime Staatspolizei, Gestapo] will be dissolved. Insofar as the powers it has exercised cannot be dispensed with for the securing of public order, these powers will be exercised by the authorities of the general administration, in accordance with the laws.

2 Concentration camps will be abolished. Their inmates are to be released. Special regulations will be issued concerning the time of the release and concerning the reintegration of inmates into the general economy.

ARTICLE 15

1 The laws and the decrees issued on the basis of the laws shall remain in place and be observed until their repeal or change. This applies with the following provisions:

1) In so far as the laws contain references to the National Socialist worldview, they are to be administered according to the principles established in Article 1.

2) Authorizations of the Reich government or of individual Reich ministers in laws to generally supplement or amend them [the laws], can no longer be exercised.

3) Insofar as powers were transferred to the Führer or Reich Chancellor in laws and ordinances, these powers belong to the Head of State or the Reich government.

4) Regulations concerning the sterilisation or castration of persons are not to be administered until the definitive regulation on the subject.

5) § 1 para. 2; § 3 para. 1, sentence 4 and para. 2; § 4 para. 1; § 7 para. 4; and § 71 of the Reich Civil Service Law are repealed.

6)[19] Insofar as the laws and ordinances for Jews and persons of mixed descent[20] contain special regulations, the following will apply until definitive settlement:

a) Regulations which disadvantage persons of mixed descent[21] shall be repealed; this applies also for the regulation of § 25 of the Reich Civil Service Law and for § 15 of the Defence Law.

b) Regulations and measures disadvantaging Jews shall be suspended.

2 The Reich government will forthwith assure that, beyond the directives of para. 1, German law in all its parts will be brought into conformity with the principles of Article 1.

ARTICLE 16

1 The profound disruption of public life makes it necessary, until further notice, to impose a state of emergency and to assign executive authority to the armed forces. It is expected of every German that he will contribute, through his behaviour, to the restoration of security and order and that he thereby makes possible the early lifting of the state of emergency.

2 During the state of emergency, the provisions of the law on the state of emergency will be in force and come into force at the same time as this law.

Directives for the Administration of the Law for the State of Siege[22]

§ 1

1 During the State of Siege, the military district commander is authorized to issue directives to all authorities in his district. Insofar as circumstances permit, he shall consult with the chief of the authority in question before issuing a directive.

2 The military district commander shall appoint as his advisor a senior official of the general and internal administration. As long as a person is not designated for this position by the central authority (Reich Minister for War, who secures the agreement of the Reich Minister of the Interior), he himself shall select him. The previous most senior chief of the general and internal administration of his district (Reich governor, provincial governor,[23] ministers of the interior in the lands other than Prussia and Bavaria) will generally not be considered for this (cf. § 2), but rather, depending on who is suitable and politically reliable, the deputy of the above-mentioned senior chief (district governor[24] attached to a Reich governor or provincial governor[25]) or the district governor or deputy district governor in a [land] government. The appointed advisor is responsible for the entire district of the

military district commander, regardless of his previous area of responsibility. The Reich Minister for War must be notified of the appointment at once.

3   The relationship of the military district commander to the judicial authorities shall follow from the Law on the State of Siege.

4   The powers of the previous Reich defence commissioners shall pass immediately to the military district commander.

5   Insofar as it is required, the military district commander will appoint a liaison officer to every administrative agency of his district or he will commission a trusted representative (officer or civil servant) with the direction of the administrative agency; the latter shall be applicable primarily in the case of presidents of police.

§ 2

1   Gauleiter are to be forbidden the exercise of their authority, even if they are also Reich governors, provincial governors,[26] or land ministers; they are to be prohibited from setting foot in their offices. In general, it will be necessary either to detain them in their homes or to take them into protective custody. The Reich governors, provincial governors, and, in non-Prussian lands, land ministers who are not also Gauleiter, will be dealt with in an analogous manner, if their character does not assure their loyalty. Other civil servants (district governors, presidents of police, land councillors, mayors) could be considered in like manner case-to-case.

2   Kreisleiter are to be treated like the Gauleiter.

§ 3

1   Higher ss and police leaders are to be taken into protective custody at once; their offices are to be closed.

2   Inspectors of the security police are to be prohibited from exercising their duties. The same applies for heads of secret-state-police offices.

§ 4

Heads of the propaganda offices are to be relieved of their posts. If necessary, it is to be assured, through the imposition of protective custody, that they abstain from all activity. In the meantime, it will be expedient to subordinate their offices to the care of the superior authorities of the general and internal administration.

§ 5

Acts of retaliation by the population against office-holders of the Party or against civil servants of the previous regime shall be suppressed. Endangered persons are to be taken into protective custody.

§ 6

The radio stations in the district are to be occupied at once.

§ 7

The utilities installations in the district (electricity, gas, and water works) are to be secured.

§ 8

It is not advisable to close down the postal, telegraph, and telephone facilities generally. A general prohibition against using the rail system is equally inadvisable. Through suitable measures (delegation of reliable men-of-confidence into the offices), postal, telegraph, and telephone communications of persons from whom disturbances are to be expected must be supervised; specifically, for such persons a postal and telephone communications ban can be imposed.

§ 9

1 The Party and its subdivisions shall be forbidden to wear badges and uniforms.
2 The motor cars and motorcycles, as well as the motor fuel, of the Party agencies and subdivisions, are to be seized.
3 Office-holders of the Party and members of its subdivisions are to be compelled at once to hand in their weapons and their marching boots.
4 Draft exemptions for office holders are to be repealed.

§ 10

The offices of the SS are to be occupied; its heads are to be taken into protective custody if necessary.

§ 11

The agencies of the NSV[27] are to be ordered to continue in their duties for the time being. They are to be placed under the supervision of the mayor or land council.

§ 12

1 In order to avoid an interruption in the distribution of ration cards, etc., persons who have been administering this service or have participated voluntarily are to continue to perform their activities. They are to be conscripted if necessary.

2 The same applies for the branches of the air (civil) defence.

§ 13

1 Persons who are in security imprisonment for political reasons are to be released forthwith, unless special circumstances dictate otherwise. If necessary, they are to be turned over to the public prosecutor's office.

2 Concentration camps are to be occupied; their guards are to be disarmed. Discharges are to be carried out with caution and limited, for the time being, to cases in which the detention unquestionably violates justice and fairness. Humane treatment of prisoners is to be ensured under all circumstances. The released are to be provided with money for travel and subsistence.

§ 14

1 Assemblies and demonstrations are to be prevented, strikes suppressed, and persons who incite them taken into protective custody and prosecuted.

2 Prisoners of war and foreign workers are to remain at their workplaces for the time being.

§ 15

1 Insofar as the district of the military district command borders on a foreign country or an occupied territory, it is to be assured that the borders remain closed, that fugitives do not go abroad, and that nobody from abroad crosses over the border into Germany. Exceptions are admissible only with the consent of the central authority (Reich Minister for War).

2 Insofar as officials of the frontier guard (border police) appear to be unreliable, they are to be replaced by others, possibly officers. It may be advisable to transfer their powers completely or in part to the customs authorities of the Reich fiscal administration.

§ 16

Regardless of strict procedures that circumstances may require, all measures must be taken in such a way that the population will become aware of the contrast with the arbitrary methods of the previous rulers. Persons who are taken into protective custody are to be treated humanely; they are to be released if the purpose of protective custody is achieved.

NOTES

1 Ulrich von Hassell, *Vom andern Deutschland. Aus den nachgelassenen Tagebüchern 1938–1944*, 385; Irmgard Langbehn (Langbehn's widow) to Ricarda Huch, 18 Sept. 1946, Gerhard Ritter, Papers, Bundesarchiv, Koblenz, NL 166/000155/1 and NL 166/00156; Hans Mommsen, "Gesellschaftsbild und Verfassungspläne des deutschen Widerstandes," 129. For background and sources, see also document no. 14.

2 Irmgard Langbehn (Langbehn's widow) to Ricarda Huch, 18 Sept. 1946, in papers of Gerhard Ritter.

3 Hassell, *Vom andern Deutschland*, 385.

4 On Langbehn, see Allen Welsh Dulles, *Germany's Underground*, 147–62; see also Klemens von Klemperer, *German Resistance against Hitler*, 21–2, 36, 168, 223–4, 284, 393, 325–7.

5 See at document no. 5.

6 See introductory note on Hassell at no. 5; Hassell, *Vom andern Deutschland*, 385–92.

7 Hassell, *Die Hassell-Tagebücher 1938–1944*, 27–8, 41–5; for biographic sketch of Hassell, see doc. no. 15.

8 Hassell, *Die Hassell-Tagebücher*, 454.

9 Machtinstrument.

10 Friedenssicherung.

11 "Gesetz über die Wiederherstellung geordneter Verhältnisse im Staats- und Rechtsleben. (Vorläufiges Staatsgrundgesetz)."

12 Source: Typed copy in Popitz's Papers in Bundesarchiv, Koblenz, N 1262 Popitz/79. The printed versions in all editions of Hassell, *Die Hassell-Tagebücher,* 454–61, have errors and a few significant gaps (indicated below in the notes). The German term "Staatsgrundgesetz" may be translated "Constitutional Basic Law" or "State Basic Law." See also Gregor Schöllgen, *A Conservative against Hitler.*

13 The German term "Zersetzung" can be translated as "sedition" or "decomposition." The National Socialists preferred this latter meaning, with its biochemical suggestion, and made frequent use of it. Cf. Cornelia Schmitz-Berning, *Vokabular des Nationalsozialismus* (Berlin: Walter de Gruyter 1998), 698–706.

14　The typewritten copy in the Bundesarchiv, Koblenz, N 1262 Popitz/79 has "Wirtschafts- und Arbeitskammer" (chamber of commerce and labour), with a handwritten insertion (in Popitz's hand) "Landwirtschaftskammer und," which apparently was meant to be inserted before "Wirtschafts- und." In the margin there is a handwritten note by Cornelia Popitz: "Korrektur Vatis: Landwirtschaftskammer und [ebenso? eine?]." The editors of Hassell, *Die Hassell-Tagebücher*, neither record nor comment on these handwritten notations – further evidence that they did not consult the copy in Bundesarchiv, Koblenz.

15　"Reichsstadt": literally, "Reich City," with home rule analogous to that of the Länder.

16　The words "and in the hour of danger he leads the nation in arms as supreme warlord" (und führt in der Stunde der Gefahr als oberster Kriegsherr das Volk in Waffen) are omitted from Hassell, *Vom andern Deutschland*, 389, and Hassell, *Die Hassell-Tagebücher*, 458.

17　The two sentences of this point 2 are omitted from Hassell, *Vom andern Deutschland*, 390, and Hassell, *Die Hassell-Tagebücher*, 459.

18　In Hassell, *Vom andern Deutschland*, 390, and Hassell, *Die Hassell-Tagebücher*, 459, this is point 2. Article 9 there has no point 3.

19　In Hassell, *Vom andern Deutschland*, 392, and Hassell, *Die Hassell-Tagebücher*, 461, point 6 reads without the sub-points a) and b) in the copy in Bundesarchiv, Koblenz: "Insofar as the laws and ordinances for Jews contain special regulations, these regulations will be suspended until the definitive settlement. This applies also for the regulation of § 25 of the Reich Civil Service Law and for § 15 of the Defence Law." (Soweit die Gesetze und Verordnungen für Juden besonderes bestimmen, werden diese Bestimmungen bis zur endgültigen Regelung ausgesetzt. Dies gilt auch von der Bestimmung des § 25 des Reichsbeamtengesetzes und des § 15 des Wehrgesetzes.)

20　Mischlinge.

21　Mischlinge.

22　Nachlass Johannes Popitz, Bundesarchiv, Koblenz, N1262 Popitz/94, printed in Hassell, *Vom andern Deutschland*, 393–6, with minor typing errors and unimportant ellipses (e.g. "Die Kraftwagen sowie Betriebsstoffe ..." instead of "Die Kraftwagen und Krafträder sowie die Betriebsstoffe ..."); Hassell, *Die Hassell-Tagebücher*, 462–5, has the same and some additional errors, all of which indicate that the printed version has not been collated with the copy in Popitz's papers, contrary to the editors' claim.

23　Oberpräsident.

24　Regierungspräsident.

25　Oberpräsident.

26　Oberpräsidenten.

27　Nationalsozialistische Volkswohlfahrt – National Socialist People's Welfare.

4

Helmuth von Moltke's Constitutional Concepts for the Reconstruction of Germany, October 1940

Helmuth James von Moltke (1907–23 January 1945), trained in international law, served as a war administration counsellor[1] in the German Armed Forces Supreme Command[2] from 1939 until his arrest on 19 January 1944. In his war service post, he was active in numerous, often successful, efforts to save hostages from execution by German military authorities and to prevent the deportation and murder of Jews.[3]

In 1934 he travelled to South Africa, the home of his mother's family. If he was to have employment in National Socialist Germany as a lawyer, he had to prove his non-Jewish descent and had to acquire certain documentation. On the way back, he and his wife spent several weeks in England and confronted the question, much like Dietrich Bonhoeffer,[4] whether or not to return to Germany at all. He decided that his commitment to Germany and Europe and to his paternal family meant that he must return. He had no illusions about what to expect in the future.[5]

As an opponent of Hitler and National Socialism from their beginnings, convinced that Hitler would make war and that Hitler's war would end in senseless death and destruction and in Germany's defeat, he sought ways to prepare Germany for the time after Hitler's regime fell. In the 1930s he developed contacts, and this activity became increasingly focused in 1938 in the face of a looming war over the Sudetenland. From January 1940 onward, he gathered a group of friends and like-minded persons who worked to lay the political, social, and philosophical foundations for a post-Hitler Germany. On some occasions, they met at Moltke's Kreisau estate in Silesia, hence "Kreisau Circle," to discuss post-Hitler political and social reorganization.[6]

The members of this group produced a number of drafts. From October 1940 to December 1943, Moltke and other members of the Kreisau Group drafted at least twenty further memoranda about the changing situation, Germany's position at the end of the war when she would be defeated, agrarian and economic concepts, church and state, foreign policy, and the punishment of violators of law and justice. References to the rejection of the "racial concept" as "absurd," found in the longer version of April 1941, are absent from the later memoranda. The 9 August 1943 final draft for the New Order, however, without a heading except "Draft of 9 August 1943," reproduced in this volume (p. 77), declares: "The right to work and property, regardless of race, nationality, and religious affiliation is protected by public authority." The draft presumes the continued existence of a Greater Germany, albeit within a united Europe and with reduced sovereignty. The writers stressed Christianity as the future social basis that would overcome divisions of class, religion, and political persuasions. The ramifications of the group's activities were explored by Ger van Roon and others. For example, Pius XI's 1931 social encyclical *Quadragesimo Anno*[7] had an influence on the text agreed upon at the Second Kreisau Conference on 18 October 1942 and on Moltke's 9 August 1943 drafts.

Moltke's activities were thus not limited to planning and to efforts to prevent atrocities through the influence he had in his official position. In July and December 1943, Moltke twice travelled to Istanbul in efforts to solicit commitments of support from Germany's enemies for an internal alternative regime.[8] These travels relate to the similar efforts of, among others, Adam von Trott, a member of the Kreisau group.[9] In the summer and autumn of 1943, Moltke, who had no confidence in "the generals'" alleged or hoped-for intentions to overthrow their Führer, took an active role in the conspiracy to remove Hitler when "the colonels" – Tresckow, Stauffenberg – seized the initiative.[10] The documents in section 7 reflect Moltke's involvement in the preparations for a coup that seemed imminent in August 1943.[11]

The documents survived, firstly, because Freya von Moltke had kept them in her care, hiding them in her beehives from the Gestapo. The Russian soldiers and the Poles who came in search of women and for purposes of looting were interested in more material valuables and did not look for letters and constitutional drafts. Secondly, in September 1945 the British Prime Minister, Ernest Bevin, asked Field Marshal Bernard Montgomery, then British Sector commander in Berlin, to ask the Russian and Polish authorities to allow English emissaries to bring Freya and her two children from Kreisau to Berlin. Permission was granted, and in October a British major came with two soldiers, a large car, and a small truck, and took them to Berlin. Freya von Moltke was able to take with her the papers and other belongings she still had.[12]

The document below presents Moltke's fundamental constitutional ideas of October 1940.

On the Foundations of Political Science[13]

I

In an attempt to picture the state that is to be created, one must start at the beginning. All that appeared certain and firmly established has, in these days, become doubtful.

First of all, one must obtain clarity about the substance of the state, from which the state derives its life, and about the way in which the state differs from a large, organized band of people. Once one has clearly perceived this substance, then this substance can be realized under any form of the state. Therefore the question of the organization of the state can be posed only when one is clear about the substance; hence organization will not be dealt with here. I do not consider the organization irrelevant, but rather, very meaningful; however, I believe that its substance must be established first.

II

The substance of the state can be comprehended in three relationships: in the relationship between state and individual, in the relationship between state and economy, and in the relationship between state and religious faith. In addition, there is foreign policy, which deals with the relations between a state whose substance and form are established and other states and their citizens. Only the substance of the state shall be discussed here, that is to say, the three relationships.

The substance of the state manifests itself entirely in the three relationships. Every activity of the state concerns one of these three relationships. If we examine in our minds the presently existing agencies of the state and imagine which additional agencies would have to be created, we find – with the exception of foreign affairs and military matters, which are effective towards the outside – no tasks that do not belong to one or more of these three relationships. Civil and penal laws, in their original meanings, belong to the sphere of relations between state and individual; other parts of the law belong to the sphere of relations between state and economy; education belongs to the relations between state and religious faith, and between state and individual.

At the same time, these three relationships, however, comprise the entire substance of the state. It is not possible to leave out one or another. If the relationship between state and religious faith were missing, education would be inconceivable. The economy and the glorification or suppression of the individual could increase immeasurably, since there would be no standard whatever for their censure. The idea that there is no relationship between state and economy is absurd.

Finally, these three relationships also exist independently alongside each other. Each of these three relationships has its own independent meaning; the substance of the state, which results from its relationship to the individual, cannot be deduced from the relationship between state and religious faith or state and economy; the relationship of the state to religious faith cannot be replaced by the relationship to the individual. These relationships exist in a status of tension and, to a certain degree, of antagonism, so that they require a constant balancing. The practical solution of each separate task alone will have to be regularly assessed from the viewpoint of several of these relationships.

III

I believe it is possible to summarize the relationship between the state and the individual in a single sentence, as follows:

It is the purpose of the state to provide individuals with that freedom that will enable them to perceive the natural order[14] and to contribute to its fulfillment.

This thesis places only a formulated puzzle in the place of an unformulated one, and therefore requires further thoroughgoing clarification. This formulation of the puzzle, however, does constitute progress.

1   To provide freedom to the individual is a fundamental task of the state. This requires keeping the individual free from oppression by others, and giving him the opportunity to acquire economic commodities through his own activity, which can let him become

master over nature and thereby take from him reason for hate and fear. This part of the thesis is obvious and therefore needs no further discussion: the unfree person is an animal or a machine.

2   In order to provide the individual with the freedom that another person does not want to grant him, the state must use power[15] and thereby reduce the freedom of the other. This use of power therefore appears to contradict the task of the state to also provide freedom to the other. This apparent contradiction is eliminated by the second part of the thesis, through which the natural order is introduced as a limitation of freedom.

3   Before I discuss further the question of knowing the natural order, I want to insert an interjection about the relationship between freedom, law, and power. Insofar as the law[16] (in the true sense of the word) limits my freedom, it does not reduce my freedom, but it limits my arbitrariness to the sphere of freedom. I recognize as legitimate the power that is used in order to forcibly limit my arbitrariness. I recognize as legitimate, in this sense, however, only those measures that limit me that do not arise from the arbitrariness of other people who, overstepping the bounds of their own freedom, strive to limit mine. This is true especially of the arbitrariness of the legislator. Law, in the true sense of the word, therefore cannot come from the arbitrariness of individuals but must result from the nature of things or, as I called it above, the natural order. The use of power without such law is arbitrariness; law without the support of power is worthless against illegal arbitrariness. Hence I come to the conclusion that the use of power for the purpose of enforcing the natural order is legitimate and is not a restriction of freedom, but merely of arbitrariness.

4   The natural order cannot be defined; it can be perceived, and individual characteristics can be described. Thus, the physical and spiritual inviolability of the person, reverence for all other people, for their spiritual and physical existence, and reverence for animate and inanimate nature, are part of the natural order. This includes the recognition that one's degree of freedom must be varied according to the position of the person within his realm of responsibility: a child, for his own protection, must have less freedom than an adult. Without doubt, all these things are correct without it being necessary to prove them.[17]

The level of perception[18] and the ability to act according to perception differs in all individuals. Since application of power must replace lack of perception, the level of perception on the part of the statesman is of pivotal importance. This question will have its place in the discussion of the relationship between state and faith.

5   Freedom of the individual[19] is a part of the natural order; it is not above this but within it and is therefore created and limited by the natural order; any system without freedom of the individual is not viewed by us as natural order. This order is called "natural" because it flows from the nature of things and carries its sanction within itself: every breach of the natural order is balanced again by nature in a slow and painful process.[20] The legitimate application of power, which, again, wants to remove disturbance of the natural order by human means, is not a part of the natural order, but is positioned outside it and serves only to relieve nature of the sanctioning function and to preserve the natural order, through a particular human sanction, without the intervention of the natural sanction being needed.

6   It follows from this that the use of power would be superfluous if all individuals completely recognized the natural order and put it into effect. Because the use of power has limitations, since its outcome is always in doubt and absorbs resources, it is desirable to provide all individuals with recognition of the natural order. The higher the recognition of the natural order by all individuals, the smaller is the amount of power required for the upholding of this natural order and, consequently also, of the freedom of the individual. The lesser the amount of force, the easier it is for the individual to recognize the natural order, for it emerges all the more clearly and indisputably. The uses of power and perception by individuals are therefore in the following correlation: higher understanding enables reduction of the use of power; reduced use of power increases understanding. In this connection, the sequence of the two sentences is also important because their repositioning signifies the attempt to find the natural order through the method of the renunciation of all order. Power can only be replaced by an already existing understanding. If the state relinquishes power before the necessary understanding is in place, then the empty space created by the renunciation will be filled with the use of force by individuals or a group using power against the state. Seen in the practice of statecraft, the right path is between[21] the two poles of excessive and insufficient use of power.

7   To increase recognition of the natural order is a task of youth education as well as of adult education. The furthering of recognition of the natural order is, moreover, one of the tasks of state organization. This must give the individual the opportunity to prove his recognition of the natural order by participating in its realization.[22] Recognition without the possibility of exercising it is unproductive and uncontrollable. Active participation in the establishment of order conveys recognition. This is the meaning of the last part of the thesis put forward above, namely, that it is one of the tasks of the state to enable the individual to contribute to the realization of the natural order.

IV

The relationship between state and economy I summarize as follows:

A   The state is the unlimited master of the economy; whether economic freedom or economic controls shall be chosen as the means for the attainment of economic goals is not a question of principle, but one of expediency.

B   It is the task of the state, through the distribution of the economic product,
   a) to enable all individuals to obtain essential foodstuffs;
   b) to prevent individuals from obtaining an unjust part of a surplus of the means of life, and to prevent individuals, many or all, from abusing economic possibilities for mere diversion or to form conditions of economic domination;
   c) to advance the non-economic purposes of the state, for example, youth and adult education, the creation of viable administrative units, and the widest possible distribution of the population of the whole territory;
   d) to provide the means for all higher purposes without allowing the economy to influence the substance of these purposes.

C   It is the task of the state to ensure that independence from nature, achieved through economic activity, will not be purchased at the expense of an increased purely economic dependency upon other people.

1   What belongs within the sphere of the state is not free, but bound. The economy was transferred in the last hundred years from the sphere of the individual into that of the state; therefore restraint has taken the place of the original freedom of the economy. Today the statesman decides, according to considerations of expediency,

which part of economic activity he will leave to economic freedom and which part not. It is futile to establish a general guideline for which activities must be free and which may be free, or to distinguish levels of economic freedom or restraint. Every new situation requires new decisions.

2   More important are the principles that must be observed in the distribution of economic output. First it is necessary that everyone receive the goods he needs to live. Whether the state sees to this through wage rates, old-age and sickness insurance, or through taxes and direct provision of these goods is fundamentally immaterial and is to be decided with consideration of the aimed-for economic purposes and of the tasks of the state in relation to the individual. In this field, full responsibility today falls on the state.

In the distribution of surplus goods for the sustenance of life, the state has the task to restrict: it must prevent the misuse of these goods. Thereby it also achieves the positive goal of the just distribution of these provisions for living.

The advancement of the non-economic purposes of the state with economic means is of decisive importance. In the furtherance of these purposes and in the solution of the problems this poses, the individual statesman must prove himself. With correct planning, such tasks can be performed in part without a distribution process becoming discernible, for example, promoting a healthy distribution of population through a suitable choice of locations.

All means for higher purposes must be drawn from the economy neutrally. Free from explicit or implicit demands or expectations of any kind, these means must be at the disposal of individuals or groups who have proved themselves. This applies to all research, especially in the sphere of the humanities and in institutions for the cultivation of the humanities.

3   The economy also has meaning for the individual in that it gives him the opportunity to prove himself in a visible and tangible way. The state must give each individual the possibility of proving himself in this sphere; success must be connected with consequences for the shaping of the life of the individual. Many can only be educated to recognize the natural order if they have the opportunity to prove themselves in the economic sphere, and if the fruits of their success remain in their possession. It is difficult

for one who has become a victim of the unnatural order to recognize the natural order while one is not even allowed to prove oneself; it is also difficult if one derives advantages from an unnatural order. It follows that it is the task of the state to so manage the economy that the individual will be provided with an appropriate development of his abilities and the possibility of employment in the economic process.

4   Through the use of its sovereign prerogatives over the economy, the state must prevent from coming into being relationships of purely economic domination by some people over others. This is not aimed against the necessary relationships of dominance and dependence that result from the work process as such; nor is it aimed against the conditions that flow from the direction of the economy by the state. These two relationships of domination are functional; they arise from the relations of those concerned with each other; they do not transgress the sphere of necessary relationships, and a responsibility corresponds to the relationship of domination and dependence. That dependence that the state must prevent is purely economic dependence, in which the dominant part bears no responsibility but, at the most, employs economic values.

V

I sum up the relationship between state and religious faith in the following theses:

A   There is no theological doctrine of the state, only one of the human being in the state; hence there is no Christian state.[23]

B   In formulating a basic doctrine of the state, we proceed from principles of ethics that are binding for the individual, that are a humanistic ethic and independent of the content of the revelation of a Christian religion or of another one.[24]

C   The state, however, is amoral, because it is abstract.[25]

D   In order to fulfill the meaning of the state, the statesman must feel committed to ethical precepts, from whatever source he may derive them; he must be able to recognize the order arising from the nature of things and to act according to this recognition. Most human beings will be equal to this task only through [religious] faith. The creation and education of the right statesman will therefore mean, in its result, the education of the Christian statesman.

E It is part of the task of the state to promote the recognition of the natural order in all individuals; this requires of these individuals [religious] faith, since it is given only to a few to recognize this order without, and outside of, revelation.

1 In Christian revelation, the state does not occur. In the Old Testament only the Jewish state occurs, organized as a theocracy. This doctrine, which is barely a part of Old Testament revelation, has become for us completely devoid of content. Christian revelation deals with the individual, not with the state. No state can claim to be a Christian state. Therefore one also cannot derive from Christian revelation the content and meaning[26] or organization of the state.

2 The same is true for moral teaching. The state is abstract and is thereby outside the sphere of moral teaching. Any attempt to make moral reproaches to the state because of its actions or to forbid it one or another manner of action on moral grounds must fail; allegedly violated moral laws do not exist for the state; therefore such reproaches also will not accomplish anything.

3 It follows from these two basic theses that there are only acts of individuals, which are under the imperative of their faith and their ethics. Even as there is no moral guilt of the state, there is no particular moral justification of the actions of the state. If one removes the state from a possible moral justification of its actions, the ethical responsibility of the individual emerges focused. There are only actions of individuals as agents of the state; for these actions, they are fully responsible; they cannot exculpate themselves with the argument that what they did had been required for reasons of state ethics: the state cannot give an individual cover for his actions. This fact must be understood quite clearly so that no one will attempt to hide behind the state.

4 A fundamental doctrine for the state can be formulated only on the basis of an ethical concept. Precisely because the state is amoral, and the individual acting for the state is fully responsible to himself alone, the fundamental doctrine of the state must proceed from the basis of the ethical precepts that obligate the individuals who act in its behalf; otherwise, the individual comes continuously into conflict with his duties as a civil servant and as an ethically responsible person.

5 The ethical principles from which we proceed are humanistic. There exists a moral doctrine that is binding for all humans in the

orbit of occidental culture, and that is independent of the revelation substance of the Christian religion, even if, for the Christian, it has found its clearest formulation in Christian moral doctrine. Therefore it is possible to formulate a fundamental theory of the state that is binding for all and recognizable by all, without requiring the revelation of Christianity or another religion.

This first part of the foundation of the theses demonstrates to what extent [religious] faith and the state are separate. [Religious] faith is of importance at the moment in which the individual, be it as a statesman, be it as a citizen, enters into a relationship with the state.

6   Statesmen are they who are charged with fulfilling the purpose[27] of the state. They lead an amoral machine whose operation derives its meaning[28] from them. If one wants to avoid catastrophe, one must make high ethical demands on the group of statesmen responsible. They must recognize the natural order and act in accordance with this recognition. Precisely because the machine of state is amoral and needs not produce any restraints from within, the demands upon the group of statesmen are tremendously large. To meet these demands requires great strength, which is given to only a very few people as a result of mere perception. This energy can, as a rule, flow only from revelation, i.e. from [religious] faith. Therefore the right statesman is, as a rule, the Christian statesman. In his actions as an agent of the state, he will use the Christian faith as the font from which he draws the strength to comply with the precepts of morality.

7   The state needs a living and effective [religious] faith for the fulfillment of its task of promoting the recognition of the natural order. All human passions are so many obstacles in the recognition of the natural order.

A state that wants to promote this recognition through reason alone or through arguments of enlightened self-interest will never thrive for long: the understanding[29] of its citizens will be slight. This understanding, which always can be achieved only approximately, is promoted mainly through [religious] faith; [religious] faith is also here the most important source of strength for providing the individual with understanding and for motivating him to act in accordance with his understanding. What was said above about the statesman applies here accordingly.

8 Finally, [religious] faith is an essential factor in criticism[30] of the state and of the actions of its agencies. A broad spectrum of religious people will judge the statesman according to the ethical precepts that they draw from their [religious] faith, and consciousness of any criticism[31] will be conducive to keeping the statesman on the right path. Any statesman can corrupt a faithless mass, but not a stratum of faithful people.

They who act as agents of the state on instructions or guidelines stand between the statesman and the citizen. Depending on how responsible these agents are, the theses about the significance of [religious] faith for the statesman or for the citizen are more applicable to them.

9 I now sum up the significance of [religious] faith for the state as follows: the state needs [religious] faith for the formation of the right statesman, for the education of the citizen to recognition of the natural order, and for conservation of true criticism[32] of the actions of the agents of the state.

Berlin, 20 October 1940

NOTES

1 Kriegsverwaltungsrat.
2 Oberkommando der Wehrmacht.
3 Ger van Roon, *Helmuth James Graf von Moltke. Völkerrecht im Dienste der Menschen*, passim.
4 See document no. 10.
5 Roon, *Neuordnung im Widerstand. Der Kreisauer Kreis innerhalb der deutschen Widerstandsbewegung*, 66–7; Roon, *German Resistance to Hitler. Count von Moltke and the Kreisau Circle*, 26–7.
6 See Roon, *Neuordnung*, 211–61; Roon, *German Resistance*, 101–66; Peter Hoffmann, *History of the German Resistance*, 49–53.
7 Pius XI, *Qudragesimo Anno ... Acta apostolicae sedis* 23 (1931), 177–228; D.J. O'Brien and T.A. Shannon, eds, *Catholic Social Thought. The Documentary Heritage* (New York: Maryknoll 1992), 42–79.
8 Roon, *Neuordnung*, 317–22; Roon, *German Resistance*, 195–200; Hoffmann, *History*, 225–7.
9 Cf. documents in no. 23; Roon, *Neuordnung*, 312–22; Roon, *German Resistance*, 191–200; Hoffmann, *History*, 228–34; Klemens von Klemperer, *German Resistance against Hitler. The Search for Allies Abroad, 1938–1945*, 327–40.

10   See Hoffmann, *Stauffenberg. A Family History, 1905–1944*, 186, 190–224; Hoffmann, "Oberst i.G. Henning von Tresckow und die Staatsstreichpläne im Jahr 1943," 331–64.

11   Document no. 7.

12   Freya von Moltke, *Memories of Kreisau and the German Resistance (Erinnerungen an Kreisau)* (Lincoln and London: University of Nebraska Press 2003), 76–82, gives a detailed and vivid account of life under Russian occupation and of how the Poles began to evict and replace the Germans in Silesia.

13   Source: Typed copy, headed "Ueber die Grundlagen der Staatslehre," with MS notations by Helmuth James von Moltke in Moltke, Papers, Bundesarchiv, Koblenz N 1750 Bd. 1; printed in Roon, *Neuordnung*, 498–507, and Roon, *German Resistance*, 310–17 (the present translation varies from Roon's English version). See also Günter Brakelmann, *Helmuth James von Moltke 1907–1945. Eine Biographie*, 149–53.

14   Moltke's MS marginal note: "right order."

15   Moltke's word "Macht" is translated as "power," or, occasionally, "authority"; it does not literally mean "force" but implies it.

16   "Recht" in this context has the meaning of "justice" as well as "law."

17   Moltke's MS marginal note: "Minimal rights indispensable."

18   Moltke uses the word "Erkenntnis"; it is translated "perception" or, depending on context and nuance, as the nearly synonymous "recognition" or "understanding."

19   Moltke's MS insertion "des Einzelnen" = "of the individual."

20   Moltke's MS marginal note: "kein Gegensatz zu oben oder Freiheit gemindert" = "no contradiction to the above or freedom diminished"; Roon, *Neuordnung*, 500, notes only the words "Kein Gegensatz zu oben"; the reading of the words "oder Freiheit gemindert" is uncertain.

21   Crossed out by hand: "bureaucratism and anarchy as."

22   Moltke's MS marginal note: "Realization of recognition is important!"

23   Moltke's MS marginal note, difficult to decipher, is not recorded in Roon, *Neuordnung*, 501: "A Es gibt nur eine Lehre [?]f. d. Verhalten des Menschen, nicht d. Verhalten des Staates, es kann daher auch [?] keinen christlichen Staat geben, sondern nur christliche Menschen im Staat" = "There is only a doctrine for the behaviour of humans, not for the behaviour of the state; therefore there cannot be a Christian state but only Christian persons in the state."

24   Moltke's MS marginal note, not in Roon, *Neuordnung*, 501: "B Um den Sinn des Staates zu erfüllen, muss jeder Einzelne vor allen der Staatsmann [sich] verpflichtet fühlen, die Ord[nun]g in der Natur der Dinge zu erkennen u[nd] nach dieser Erkenntnis zu h[an]deln." = "In order to fulfill the meaning of the state, every individual and most of all the statesman must feel obliged to recognize the order in the nature of things and to act according to this recognition."

25   Moltke's MS marginal note, not in Roon, *Neuordnung*, 501: "C Die Macht zur [?] Erfüllung [?] der natürlichen Ord[nun]g ist dem Menschen durch den Staat [?] gegeben" = "the power to fulfill the natural order is given to the human being through the state."

26 "Sinn" may mean "purpose" or "meaning."
27 See note 24.
28 See note 24.
29 Here "Erkenntnis" seems best translated as "understanding."
30 "Kritik" in the sense of "assessment," "judgment."
31 See note 30.
32 See note 30.

5

Programme for Post-Hitler Emergency Governance, January–February 1940

The "Programme" was first published as one of several appendices to the first German edition of Ulrich von Hassell's diaries.[1] Most of the diaries were kept in Switzerland during the war; the parts for the last years were buried in Hassell's garden in Ebenhausen near Munich.[2] The first edition of the diaries and appendices was prepared by Hassell's widow, Ilse von Hassell née von Tirpitz. In the typescript for the first German edition, Ilse von Hassell described the document, in her own handwriting, as "Programm, verfaßt von Ulrich v. Hassell, Januar/Februar 1940."[3] In the first printed edition in 1946, it is headed "Programm. Verfaßt von U.v. Hassell, nach Beratung mit Beck, Goerdeler und Popitz, Januar–Februar 1940 (geplant bei Regime-Änderung nach verhindertem Einmarsch in Belgien)." In the 1948 English edition, it is headed "Programme. Written by U. von Hassell after consultation with Beck, Goerdeler, and Popitz, January–February 1940 (planned in the event of a change of regime after action to prevent the invasion of Belgium)."[4] This description was accepted by scholars everywhere, and it remained unrevised for forty-two years.

The new German edition of Hassell's diary includes additions not published in the first print edition of the diary in 1946, although there are still ellipses in the new edition. The editors did not find, however, in Hassell's papers or elsewhere, originals of the three main appendices: the "Programme," the projected "Law for the Restoration of Ordered Conditions in the State and Judiciary System (Provisional Basic Constitutional Law)" and the "Directives for the Application of the Law on the State of Siege." Typed copies of the "Law for the Restoration of Ordered Conditions in the State and Judiciary System (Provisional Basic Constitutional Law)" and the "Directives for the Application of the Law on the State of Siege" were found in Popitz's papers and were identified by Cornelia Schulz-Popitz as her father's work.[5] They found nothing in Hassell's diary that said or suggested that he was the author of the "Programme." They found only that the typescript for the 1946 publication of the three documents was typed on the same typewriter as the typescript of the 1946 edition of the diary. Therefore an "original," most likely a contemporary (1940) one, existed from which the typescript was prepared for the printer. It is inconceivable that anyone could have composed the contents and language of the "Programme" after Germany had lost the war and had been occupied by Allied military forces. In the case of the diary, the original was written in Hassell's hand and it still survives. In the case of the "Programme," there is no evidence that the "original" was in Hassell's hand. The likelihood is that it never was. One of Hassell's sons, Johann Dietrich von Hassell, asserted that everything in Hassell's own hand was "sacred" to his mother, and he therefore believed that she would not have destroyed a manuscript of the "Programme" if she had possessed one.[6] When the new, 1988 edition of Hassell's diary was in preparation as a volume in a series, the editor of the volume, Friedrich Hiller von Gaertringen, and Hassell's son, Johann Dietrich von Hassell, opposed the inclusion of the "Programme" on the ground that Hassell's authorship could not be verified. Hans Mommsen, as one of the series' editors, insisted on its inclusion on the ground that it reflected the views of Hassell and the conservative opponents of Hitler with whom Hassell was in close contact.[7] Since no contemporary copy of the "Programme" appears to be extant, the translation below is based upon the published version.

Three points strongly suggest that Hassell participated in the composition of the "Programme," and that he supported several of the key points in it.

The first indication is Ilse von Hassell's identification of the document as composed by Hassell. The editors of the 1988 edition of Hassell's diary say that it was no longer possible to clarify whether Ilse von Hassell, who had died in 1982, "knew or only supposed" that Hassell was the author of the "Programme."[8]

The second indication consists of several references by Hassell in his diary to discussions about the character of a post-Hitler government, although the editors of the 1988 edition of Hassell's diary say that these references were not indications that a written "Programme," in which Hassell had "collaborated in any way," had been in preparation.[9] On 19 October 1939, Hassell talked with Johannes Popitz[10] about discussions they were having in preparation for the situation after Hitler was removed. In Popitz's view (not Hassell's), it was necessary at first to govern in an authoritarian manner.[11] Popitz, as the Reich Finance Ministry's parliamentary representative before 1933, had had so many negative experiences with party politics, in which the National Socialists had played a pernicious role, that he had come to despise the parliamentary system. He believed for a long time, so his Private Secretary[12] recalled soon after the Second World War, that it would be necessary to install an authoritarian government for a lengthy transition period during which the damage to political culture might be repaired; but gradually Popitz accepted that one must begin with democratization soon after the overthrow of the dictatorship. His wish to avoid a revival of the pre-1933 political parties was shared by many, including the trades-union leaders Wilhelm Leuschner, Jakob Kaiser, and Max Habermann, who attributed Hitler's rise to flaws in the Constitution of the Weimar Republic and its proportional electoral system.[13]

On 28 December 1939, Hassell again spoke with Popitz about "the practical procedures of a new government" and about judicial and church issues. Popitz emphasized the establishment of "true" national and social principles[14] and of Christian morality based on German tradition. Hassell pointed out the need to build the state upon local and corporate self-rule.[15]

The third indication of Hassell's participation consists of repetitions in Hassell's diary of points from the "Programme." On 19 March 1940, before the German invasions of Denmark, Norway, Luxembourg, Belgium, The Netherlands, and France, Hassell made some "points" to Generalleutnant Georg Thomas, Chief of Armed Forces Economics and Armaments Office: An offensive through neutral territory, with a result consistent with Germany's interests, was not thinkable. After a German offensive, there would be no chance for an acceptable peace.[16] The preconditions for striving for a permanent, "usable" peace were: First, Germany and its armed forces had to be intact so that the continuation of the war would be a heavy risk for the enemy.[17] Power in the state had to pass from the unclean hands holding it then into those of the army, in order to end the war.[18] Second, after 15 March 1939, when German troops had occupied Czechia, and after the atrocities committed in Poland, the regime had no standing as a negotiating partner. Change of regime was an internal German matter. Foreign demands to change the regime had to be rejected. But peace was possible only with a change of regime. There was no guarantee even then, but there were certain indications.[19]

Some historians have imputed authoritarian and undemocratic views to Hassell on the basis of the "Programme."[20]

The document has to be considered in its historical context. The "Pro-gramme" was designed as a statement of policy for the period during the change from the National Socialist dictatorship to a state based on self-rule and the rule of law.

Further, those who would overthrow Hitler needed to avoid making him a martyr of German "Greatness," and they needed to win immediate pol-itical and popular support. Several of the prepared pronouncements must be seen in this light. Thus the declaration that the new government would continue the war until there was an acceptable peace settlement must be considered in light of the following facts: To begin with, there was, at the time, no substantial level of combat, apart from air sorties and occa-sional reconnaissance operations on the ground. In addition, following the German attack against Poland, the countries of Britain, France, Australia, New Zealand, South Africa, and Canada had declared war on Germany in September 1939. It was not in Germany's power alone to end the war. Ger-many also had the military advantage while she was not attacking France and Britain. Furthermore, the conspirators who wanted to overthrow Hitler needed, immediately after their coup, to obtain popular and political support for their new regime. As well, the belief was widespread in Ger-many that the country once again was involved in a struggle for survival against a numerically superior enemy coalition. Hassell understood foreign relations better than most of the anti-Hitler conspirators. He understood that the British position, long characterized as appeasement, had changed fundamentally after Hitler's occupation of Czechia on 15 March 1939; that it would not readily become compromising again; and that the British gov-ernment had not informed German conspiracy emissaries, who contacted them through the Vatican, of what they planned for post-Hitler Germany. They had spoken vaguely of decentralization and a plebiscite in Austria, but not of Foreign Secretary Lord Halifax's views as he had expressed them in a note to Prime Minister Neville Chamberlain on 13 February 1940: "If we could get such an internal disruption of Germany, it would I imagine be what we want – and I should be inclined to feel that we could get the German creators of a South Germany to agree to an Austrian plebiscite and that we on our side could agree that the Sudetenland should be a matter for negotiation or perhaps dealt with by way of population transfer [...] This may of course all be worth nothing: but I hanker after a German revolu-tion."[21] Halifax here anticipated the expulsion of ethnic Germans from the Sudetenland. Germany would not have accepted such a measure unless she had been defeated, had surrendered unconditionally, and had been disarmed. Moreover, the historical context includes the contacts that the

German underground opposition established with the British government through the Vatican between October 1939 and March 1940.[22] Finally, the National Socialists had, through the democratic process, grown to become the largest political party, and Hitler's appointment as Chancellor had come about within constitutional processes; it had certainly violated the spirit of the Constitution, but the question was how to prevent someone determined to destroy the Constitution from again becoming Chancellor; the drafters of the "Programme" did not include any constitutional lawyers or parliamentarians; in any case, no constitution can succeed if those living with it do not want it to succeed.

"Programme" for initial measures following an overthrow[23]

1   The German government is determined to prosecute with all its capacity the war into which Europe has been disastrously plunged, until a peace is secured that will ensure the existence, independence, way of life, and security of the German Reich and nation and that will essentially restore the old borders of the Reich with Poland.

2   The German government, which is convinced that the entire German nation-in-arms supports this demand, on this basis strives for an early peace. Its members have therefore opposed a course of action of the previous German government that would have destroyed these prospects for peace through a violation of the neutrality of neighbouring states.

3   The German government leaves the judgment of the principles and accomplishments of National Socialism to history. It acknowledges the healthy and progressive ideas included in it. Unfortunately, in clear contradiction to them, the German government in office until now had long since begun to pursue a policy that was likely to kill the soul of the German nation and to undermine its economic prosperity.

4   An intolerable Party rule, in the form of Party bosses seeking their own benefit, was established and, like an iron net, spread itself over the entire nation.

   Every free expression of opinion, even on non-political topics, was branded a felony; all free intellectual activity was suppressed. An unheard-of measure of spying and defamation became the rule. The administration of justice, especially in criminal cases, became more and more subordinated to the viewpoint of the Party. The methods of the Gestapo violated the most elementary principles of morality and destroyed the human personality. Severe violations of justice and law, attacks upon life and limb, or upon the freedom of blameless people remained unpunished and were even encouraged from on high. Particularly of late, in connection with the war, the highest office in the state countenanced things that are unheard of in German history. The horrible atrocities committed with impunity against the Jews at the behest of the Party are part of that same chapter.

5 The organism of the state was on its way to becoming entirely hollowed out or destroyed by the Party organization. The once-unparalleled German civil service was divested of its most important functions and reduced to an ever lower status. The Party boss everywhere was given the real power and exploited it.

6 In the economic sphere, the government in office until now has, in recent years, pursued an evermore unscrupulous overexploitation of the energies of the nation and a reckless waste of money, most of all for every kind of palatial building, while insufficient funds have been spent on social projects, especially on the construction of homes and apartments. One could no longer call the financial management of the state ordered while tax burdens grew without limit.

7 In addition to all that, foreign policy, since the beginning of the year 1938, took on an increasingly adventurous character.

The people were led to believe that ignoring all principles and obligations was "Realpolitik." Through lack of political wisdom on the part of those involved, it came to war; this, after twenty years of laborious reconstruction, conjures up the immediate danger that the supreme European values will be destroyed to the benefit of Bolshevism. The [new] German government does not abandon the hope that Germany's opponents, too, will acknowledge the necessity now of reaching a peace settlement on the basis of the premises given above, and of giving the world the possibility of coming to a state of health and of satisfaction built upon the will of all nations, in good faith, with armaments reduced as much as possible, through the exchange of intellectual and economic resources, to form a community of nations. It is the absurdity of the treaties of Paris after the World War that is the deepest cause of all misfortune that has now come over the world.

Should Germany's opponents close their minds to this insight, the German government will, without hesitation, draw the consequences and prosecute the war to the utmost.

8   Until it is possible to rebuild normal constitutional life, the supreme authority in the German Reich will be in the hands of a regency that consists of the Reich Regent and two members. This regency will appoint the ministers.

9   In order to guide the life of the German nation out of the system in place until now into new and sounder paths, the regency decrees the following:

a) The NSDAP, with all its subdivisions, is dissolved. The Minister of the Interior will take the required measures; he can appoint commissars for this. He will propose to the regency which institutions of the Party, such as the NSV,[24] the Winter Relief Organization, and others should be incorporated. He will particularly examine the question whether or not the SA, the NSKK, the NSFK,[25] and others can be converted into other institutions. The SS will be dissolved. The extent to which it can be incorporated into one of the mentioned associations will be determined in good time. The War Minister will organize the transfer of individual arms-bearing SS and SA men into the Wehrmacht. The Minister of the Interior will bring about the reorganization of the police in a provisional manner and will make definitive proposals to the regency.

b) The Labour Service will be continued, but reorganized. The Minister for Labour will make the relevant recommendations to the regency.

c) The Labour Front is to be rebuilt. The Economics Minister, in consultation with the Minister for Labour, will take the prerequisite provisional measures and will make definitive proposals to the regency.

d) The organization of the economy will remain unchanged for the time being. It will be reorganized in the context of the reform of the state. The Economics Minister will provide for the necessary personnel changes.

e) The property and income of all Party organizations and of the Labour Front pass to the Reich. The Minister of Finance will make the prerequisite arrangements in consultation with the appropriate ministers and submit proposals on the use of the funds to the regency.

f) In order to prepare the structure of the state, the regency will appoint a constitutional council that shall formulate proposals under the chairmanship of the Minister of the Interior. These proposals must be guided by the principle that the German unitary state will be organized politically and economically, with special consideration for the historical tradition, and that a co-operation of the nation in the political life of the Reich and a control of the functioning of the state on the basis of local and corporate self-government will be guaranteed.

g) The Minister of Justice will issue the necessary provisional directives to restore the disrupted rule of law, which has been corrupted, to ensure a dispensation of justice by judges subject only to the law, and to effect the necessary personnel changes. He is to prepare the definitive structure of the justice system. All procedures that were used outside of law and justice against the individual are to be eradicated.

h) The Armed Forces is at once to be sworn in under the regency. The Reich Regent will be the supreme commander of the entire Armed Forces and will appoint the commanders-in-chief of the services.

i) The executive power in all states, except Prussia, the Prussian provinces, and the occupied territories, will pass to defence commanders appointed by the Reich Regent.

k) The Reich governors[26] are abolished. In Prussia the Reich Regent will have supreme executive authority.

l) In all spheres of state[27] activity, the civil service will be renewed so that, in principle, the regularly trained professional civil servant is to replace persons appointed under Party auspices. The regency determines which civil servants it will appoint and which ones the departmental ministers will appoint.

m) The regency will put in place a legislative council that has to examine the legislation since 30 January 1933 and recommend to the regency laws, ordinances, regulations, etc., for abolition. All regulations issued by the NSDAP or by one of its organizations as a public corporation are to be repealed, particularly the legislation concerning Jews.

n) The legislative council will put in place a committee that has to produce proposals for regulating relations between the state and the churches. The prerogative of the state will herein be the guiding principle.

o) The press will be subject, during the war, to censorship by the executive authority; for the time after the war, new regulations will follow on the basis of freedom of the press, within the limits of state security.

p) Science[28] and its teaching are to be free.[29]

q) The written word[30] will be subject to the supervision of the executive authority during the war. After the war, the protection of the state and nation against excesses of the written word will be assured through legislation.[31]

10 The regency knows that its task is infinitely difficult and little calculated to rapidly acquire popularity. It must liquidate a system that has imposed heavy burdens on the German nation for a long time to come. It will strive to carry out this liquidation without any sentiment of revenge and to gradually remove these burdens in a way that will demand the fewest conceivable material sacrifices. Nevertheless, these will be great enough. The regency is convinced that the German nation will make these sacrifices with determination and will find compensation in the fact that law and justice will again be honoured, as will be decency, ethical sensitivity, and true liberty.

NOTES

1 Ulrich von Hassell, *Vom andern Deutschland. Aus den nachgelassenen Tagebüchern 1938–1944*, 381–4; Hassell, *The von Hassell Diaries 1938–1944. The Story of the Forces against Hitler inside Germany, as Recorded by Ambassador Ulrich von Hassell, A Leader of the Movement* (1948 ed.), 333–7.

2 Hassell, *Die Hassell-Tagebücher 1938–1944. Aufzeichnungen vom Andern Deutschland*, 43; Hassell, *Vom andern Deutschland*, 5, 372–3; Hassell, *The von Hassell Diaries*, 6.

3 Johann Dietrich von Hassell (Hassell's son) to the editor, 23 Jan. 1996.

4 Hassell, *Vom andern Deutschland*, 381; Hassell, *Diaries*, 333.

5 Hassell, *Vom andern Deutschland*, 385; Hassell, *Die Hassell-Tagebücher*, 449–50; cf. Gerhard Schulz, "Über Johannes Popitz (1884–1945)," *Der Staat* 24 (1985): 485–511; Johanna Bödeker, "Johannes Popitz: Auf der Suche nach einer neuen Wirtschaftsordnung," *Der Staat* 24 (1985): 513–25.

6 Johann Dietrich von Hassell to the editor, 23 Jan. 1996.

7 See note 6.

8 Hassell, *Die Hassell-Tagebücher*, 449.

9 Ibid., 133, 449.

10 On Popitz, see document 14.

11 Hassell, *Die Hassell-Tagebücher*, 133.

12 Persönlicher Referent.

13 Dr H.v. zur Mühlen, "Betr. Popitz. Zusammenfassung der Besprechung mit Ministerialdiregent Ernst Burkart in Thedinghausen am 26.4.1948," Gerhard Ritter, Papers, Bundesarchiv, Koblenz, Nl 166/000156, 4; *Spiegelbild einer Verschwörung*, 205; Ger van Roon, *Neuordnung im Widerstand. Der Kreisauer Kreis innerhalb der deutschen Widerstandsbewegung*, 589.

14 Cf. below, point 3.

15 Hassell, *Die Hassell-Tagebücher*, 155.

16 Cf. below, point 2.

17 Cf. below, point 1.

18 Cf. below, point 4.

19 Hassell, *Die Hassell-Tagebücher*, 182.

20 Hans Mommsen, "Gesellschaftsbild und Verfassungspläne des deutschen Widerstandes," 127.

21 Peter W. Ludlow, "The Unwinding of Appeasement," 40.

22 See Peter Hoffmann, "The Question of Western Allied Co-operation with the German Anti-Nazi Conspiracy, 1938–1944," 446–51.

23 Source: Hassell, *Vom andern Deutschland* (1946), 381–4.

24 National Socialist People's Welfare.

25 SA = Sturmabteilung (storm troopers); NSKK = National Socialist Motoring Corps; NSFK = National Socialist Flying Corps.

26 Regional or state governors appointed as chief administrators for states or regions under the National Socialist legislation in 1933. Cf. "Zweites Gesetz zur Gleichschaltung der Länder mit dem Reich. Vom 7. April 1933" (Reichsstatthaltergesetz), *Reichsgesetzblatt Teil I. Jahrgang 1933* (Berlin: Reichsverlagsamt 1933), 173.

27 "State" here refers to government administration at the national, as well as at the individual, state level.

28 The German term here is "Wissenschaft," which includes the liberal arts as well as the natural sciences.

29 The slightly archaic legislative language here closely follows the strong turn of phrase in the German original: "Die Wissenschaft und ihre Lehre ist frei."

30 The German term "Schrifttum" most commonly means the printed published word but could include other forms of written expression.

31 Many European states, including the Federal Republic of Germany, have laws against holocaust denial, incitement to ethnic and racial hatred, and "National Socialist activities" (Austria); some laws (Belgium) provide penalties of imprisonment and withdrawal of citizenship rights. Art. 5 and 18 of the German Constitution prohibit the abuse of freedom of expression.

6

Co-ordination Meeting of
Anti-Hitler Plotters,
8 January 1943

On 8 January 1943, representatives of two major civilian resistance groups, members of the "Kreisau Circle" and the Beck-Goerdeler-Hassell-Popitz group, met at Peter Graf Yorck von Wartenburg's house at 50 Hortensien-strasse, in the Berlin suburb of Lichterfelde. They were, of the older generation, Generaloberst (ret.) Ludwig Beck; Ambassador (ret.) Ulrich von Hassell; the Prussian Minister of Finance, Professor Johannes Popitz; the former Mayor of Leipzig and candidate for Reich Chancellor, Dr Carl Goerdeler; Professor Jens Peter Jessen; and of the younger generation, War Administration Counsellor (Kriegsverwaltungsrat) Helmuth James Graf von Moltke; Senior Government Counsellor (Oberregierungsrat) Dr Peter Graf Yorck von Wartenburg; Legation Counsellor (Legationsrat) Dr Adam von Trott zu Solz; Lieutenant (Res.) Fritz-Dietlof Graf von der Schulenburg; Consistorial Councilor (Konsistorialrat) D. Eugen Gerstenmaier.[1]

Goerdeler had no residence in Berlin; Beck's or Popitz's house would have been the natural choice of venue in a hierarchic order, but both houses were under Gestapo observation, as was Hassell's; Graf Yorck's was not.[2]

The group led by Helmut James von Moltke had a socialist orientation; the one led by General Beck was conservative. Both groups had close ties with social-democratic politicians and trades-union leaders, high-ranking civil servants, and clergymen of both major churches.[3] The meeting was held at the time when German forces were losing the battle of Stalingrad, suffering their worst defeat of the war. In the developing coup-d'état conspiracy, the meeting of 8 January 1943 was an effort to provide the foundation and support for the military conspirators around Colonel Henning von Tresckow and General Friedrich Olbricht. There are indications that then-Major Claus Schenk Graf von Stauffenberg, although he was about to be posted as senior staff officer to a front-line panzer division, was at least marginally involved.[4] The meeting aimed to co-ordinate, and if possible to combine, forces for the destruction of the National Socialist regime.

The groups that met at Peter Graf Yorck's had been forming themselves in some ways before 1938 through professional contacts in various walks of life and family relations. All were, by that time, opponents of the regime; some, like Moltke and Trott, had been opponents from 1933. Beck had led a coup d'état attempt in July and August 1938;[5] Schulenburg was also involved in anti-National Socialist conspiratorial activities and in the September 1938 coup plans. Their opposition had intensified through the years, but also had their frustration and sense of impotence, because they lacked the means to remove the regime. This meeting was a remarkable attempt at consolidating the two potentially most potent conspiratorial groups with concepts of removing and replacing the existing regime. They had loose contacts with Colonel Henning von Tresckow's conspiratorial group in the military forces. Through the year 1943, these contacts grew more intense, as diary entries by Hassell and by Captain (Res.) Hermann Kaiser, in the Home Army Command staff, show. Ever mounting urgency increased with each war development: the defeat and loss of the entire German 6th Army at Stalingrad in January 1943, the overthrow of Mussolini in July, the fire-bombing of Hamburg and subsequent partial evacuation of Berlin in July and August.[6]

The documents below include excerpts from the observations of three participants.

Account by Helmuth James von Moltke[7]

In a letter dated Berlin, 9 January 1943, to his wife, Freya, Moltke summarized the meeting:

My evening lasted until 1:00 a.m. It was odd, because we didn't really reach a conflict until 11:00; instead every attempt to penetrate to fundamentals was deflected by the other side into facile civilities. At last there was a chance, and on the subject[8] of our night session at Kreisau in October. After a few sallies from our side, a really incredible statement emerged: flat, unimaginative, etc. I seized the opportunity and declared it made no sense to reply to that at 11:35, for at this point the real discussion was just beginning.[9] We would therefore not reply today. Then I shot off a poisoned arrow that I'd kept in my quiver for a long time, "Kerensky solution,"[10] that hit home quite firmly and visibly – and with that the affair ended dramatically, and luckily not flat. We then ate yellow pea soup and slices of bread. The others[11] were gone by 12:00, and Trott, Eugen,[12] Peter, and I then held a post-action review.

Account by Eugen Gerstenmaier[13]

Van Roon's account of the meeting of the Kreisauers with Goerdeler, Hassell, Popitz, and others, under the chairmanship of Beck on 8 January 1943, is insufficient, considering the significance of this gathering. Van Roon can indeed claim that this evening was sufficiently described by others, for example by Ulrich von Hassell. Moltke, moreover, did not utter the comment "Kerensky solution" to Goerdeler's statements, but he said – sitting beside me – half-audibly to himself: "Kerensky!" This subjectively and probably also objectively unjustified word was also caught by other participants of the discussion and did not have a good effect.

Account by Ulrich von Hassell[14]

Berlin, 22 January 1943
If the Josephs [Generals] had the ambition to delay their intervention until it was obvious that the corporal was leading us into the abyss, then this dream of theirs has fulfilled itself. The bad part of it is that our certain prognosis is also confirmed, that it would then be too late, and any new regime would be a liquidation commission. One probably cannot say with certainty that the war is lost, but surely that it cannot be won anymore, and that the prospect of still bringing the opposing side to an acceptable peace is preciously slight. The consequence is that, on the part of the Josephs, the insight that something must speedily be done has greatly increased, but so have the weakness of the home front and the fronts in the field.
[...]

In the inner circle, strong contentions, while leadership by Geibel [Beck] hitherto all-too-weak. For one, grave reservations from various sides against Pfaff [Goerdeler], at least as political leader, then also against Geißler [Popitz], who is reproached for earlier questionable attitude of subordination to Göring, as well as grave mistakes in financial policy, finally, all-too-long collaboration in the system. Adlerheim [Falkenhausen] is widely rejected because he had allegedly participated in the terrorist regime.

[...]

Rather interesting but basically not very satisfactory a great discussion of the "young" and the "old" at [Yorck von] W[artenburg]'s.[15] The "young," who, in contrast to the "old," acted ostensibly as a united bloc toward the outside, were led intellectually by the, to me, rather unattractive, Anglo-Saxon-pacifistic < >[16] Ch[ief of the] Gen[eral Staff Moltke[17]]. Again I liked Roggenmüller [Gerstenmaier] best, with whom Geissler and I had previously had a discussion. Geibel led very weakly and reservedly. Sharp, by Pfaff consciously but unsuccessfully, veiled dichotomy between himself and the young, primarily in the social sphere. Pf[aff] is really a kind of reactionary. The unity of the young, by the way, does not extend to Lehrberg [Schulenburg], who is more embracing of Realpolitik, although he is one of the "Sauls."

Recollection by Dr Clarita von Trott zu Solz, Adam von Trott zu Solz's widow[18]

According to most accounts, it was in January 1943 that the great discussion between the older and younger members of the Opposition took place at the Yorck's house. If I remember correctly, Adam tried on that occasion to bridge the many and serious differences, in order not to endanger the whole plot. He was convinced that once Hitler's regime was overthrown, the situation would enforce the replacement of men with out-dated ideas, and he was at the same time convinced that there would be no lack of capable younger people. Only if given genuine tasks would the latent capacities and talents of the younger generation be awakened, and so far they had not been given a chance to prove themselves. This he told me on our last day together in Stuttgart on 17 June 1944, when I was alarmed by a talk he had had about available future administrators for the Land Württemberg. I thought that if there were not even suitable men for the highest positions, what would happen with the many minor posts. But this did not seem to worry him at all.

Recollections by Hans Bernd Gisevius[19]

DR LATERNSER: Witness, in replying to a question of my colleague Dr Dix, you told the Tribunal that, after the defeat at Stalingrad, a military revolt was to be organized. You testified on this point that discussions had already taken place, that preparations had been made, and that the execution of the military revolt was prevented because the field marshals in the East had deserted the group of conspirators.

I ask you now to give us more details on this question, so that I can understand why you came to the conclusion that the field marshals had deserted the conspiracy group.

GISEVIUS: From the outbreak of the war, Generaloberst Beck tried to contact one field marshal after another. He wrote letters and he sent messengers to them. I particularly remember the correspondence with General Field Marshal Von Manstein, and I saw with my own eyes General Von Manstein's answer of the year 1942. To Beck's strictly military explanations that the war had been lost and why, Manstein could reply only: A war is not lost until one considers it as lost.

Beck said that, with an answer like that from a field marshal, strategic questions could certainly not be raised. Several months later, another attempt was made to win General Field Marshal Von Manstein. General Von Tresckow, also a victim of 20 July, went to the headquarters of Manstein. Oberstleutnant Count Von der Schulenburg also went to the headquarters of Manstein, but we did not succeed in winning Herr Von Manstein to our side.

At the time of Stalingrad, we contacted Field Marshal Von Kluge, and he, in his turn, contacted Manstein. This time discussions reached a point where Kluge definitely assured us that he would win over Field Marshal Von Manstein at a discussion definitely fixed to take place in the Führer's headquarters. Because of the importance of that day, a special telephone line was laid by the General of the Signal Corps, Fellgiebel, between the headquarters and General Olbricht at the OKW in Berlin. I myself was present when this telephone conversation took place. Even today I can still see the paper which said, in plain language, that Manstein, contrary to his previous assurances, had allowed himself to be persuaded by Hitler to remain in office. And even Kluge expressed himself as satisfied at the time with very small military strategic concessions. This was a bitter disappointment to us, and, therefore, I would like to repeat again what Beck said at that time: "We were deserted."

DR LATERNSER: What further preparations had been made in this special connection?

GISEVIUS: We had made definite agreements with Field Marshal Von Witzleben. Witzleben was the Commander-in-Chief in the West, and therefore he was very important for starting or protecting a revolt in the West. We had made further definite agreements with the Military Governor of Belgium, Generaloberst Von Falkenhausen. In addition, as on 20 July 1944, we had assembled a certain contingent of armoured troops in the vicinity of Berlin. Furthermore, those commanders of the troops who were to participate in the action had been assembled in the OKW.

DR LATERNSER: All this happened after Stalingrad?

GISEVIUS: At the time of the Stalingrad revolt.

DR LATERNSER: Please continue.

GISEVIUS: We had made all other political preparations that were necessary. It is difficult for me to tell here the entire story of the revolts against the Third Reich.

DR LATERNSER: Yes. What were the reasons why this intended military revolt was not carried through?

GISEVIUS: What was that?

DR LATERNSER: Witness, what were the reasons why this revolt, which was intended by the group of conspirators, was not carried through?

GISEVIUS: Contrary to all expectations, Field Marshal Paulus capitulated. This, as is known, was the first wholesale capitulation of generals, whereas we had expected that Paulus, with his generals, would issue, before his capitulation, a proclamation to the German people and to the East Front, in which the strategy of Hitler and the sacrifice of the Stalingrad army would be branded in suitable words. When this cue had been given, Kluge was to declare that in future he would take no further military orders from Hitler. We hoped with this plan to circumvent the problem of the military oath, which kept troubling us more and more; the field marshals, one after the other, were to refuse military obedience to Hitler, whereupon Beck was to take over the supreme military command in Berlin.

DR LATERNSER: Witness, you just mentioned the military oath. Do you know whether Blomberg and Generaloberst Beck opposed, or tried to oppose, the pledge the Armed Forces took to Hitler?

GISEVIUS: I know only that Beck, up to the last day of his life, considered the day he gave his pledge to Hitler as the blackest day of his existence, and he gave me an exact description of how completely taken unawares he had felt at the rendering of the oath. He told me that he had been summoned to a military roll call, and that suddenly it was announced that an oath of allegiance was to be given the new head of State, that unexpectedly a new form of oath was to be used. Beck could never rid himself of the awful thought that, at that time, he perhaps should not have given his oath. He told me that while he was on his way home, he said to a comrade, "This is the blackest day of my life."

NOTES

1 For background on Beck, see document no. 19; for Hassell, see document no. 15; for Popitz, see document no. 14; for Goerdeler, see documents nos. 16 and 22; Jessen (1895–30 Nov. 1944) held a chair for National Economics at the University of Berlin and was in war service as a Captain (Res.) with the Army Quartermaster-General's staff; Moltke (1907–23 Jan. 1945; see document no. 4), a lawyer specialized in international law, worked in the Armed Forces Supreme Command Counter-Intelligence Section; Yorck worked in the office of the Reichskommissar für die Preisbildung; see Ger van Roon, *German Resistance to Hitler. Count von Moltke and the Kreisau Circle*; Trott (see document no. 23) worked in the Foreign Office; Lieutenant (Res.) Schulenburg (1902–10 Aug. 1944) was Deputy President of Police in Berlin from 1937–39, Deputy Provincial President for Upper and Lower Silesia until 1940, then on war service as a Lieutenant (Res.) in the field, and in 1943 with Sonderstab of General Walter von Unruh; Gerstenmaier (1906–86), a Protestant theologian, worked in the Aussenamt der Evangelischen Kirche Deutschlands.

2 Information from Freya von Moltke, 4 June 2008; Ulrich von Hassell, *Die Hassell-Tagebücher 1938–1944. Aufzeichnungen vom Andern Deutschland*, 27, 42.

3 See Roon, *Neuordnung im Widerstand. Der Kreisauer Kreis innerhalb der deutschen Widerstandsbewegung*; Peter Hoffmann, *The History of the German Resistance 1933–1945*.

4 See Hoffmann, *The History*, 359–63; Hoffmann, *Claus Schenk Graf von Stauffenberg. Die Biographie*, 261–82; Hoffmann, "Oberst i.G. Henning von Tresckow und die Staatsstreichpläne im Jahr 1943," 331–64.

5 Cf. Hoffmann, "Ludwig Beck: Loyalty and Resistance," 332–50.

6 Hassell, *Die Hassell-Tagebücher*, passim; Hermann Kaiser, "Mut zum Bekenntnis." Die geheimen Tagebücher des Hauptmanns Hermann Kaiser 1941/1943. Herausgegeben und kommentiert von Peter M. Kaiser, unpublished, passim; Hoffmann, "Oberst i.G. Henning von Tresckow," passim.

7 Source: Moltke's letters to his wife, transcribed by Beate Ruhm von Oppen, in Papers of Freya von Moltke, Deutsches Literaturarchiv, Marbach a. N., 4–5; Helmuth James von Moltke, *Letters to Freya 1939–1945*, 270–1. The present translation follows the original. Cf. Michael Balfour and Julian Frisby, *Helmuth von Moltke. A Leader Against Hitler;* Ger van Roon, *German Resistance to Hitler. Count von Moltke and the Kreisau Circle.*

8 Economic and social policy.

9 Cf. Hassell's diary entry of 22 January 1943, which bears out this description and calls Goerdeler "really something of a reactionary" (*The Von Hassell Diaries* [Doubleday 1947 ed.], 283).

10 Allusion to Alexander Kerensky, who in 1917 became so moderate a provisional premier that the Bolsheviks overthrew his government before the year was out.

11 Among them: Schulenburg, the mediator between the two groups. The "elders" were led by Dr Carl Goerdeler (1884–1945), Mayor of Leipzig 1930–37 (when he resigned in protest against the removal of the statue of Felix Mendelssohn), Prices Commissioner 1934–35, and from 1938 on, active in economic life and in opposition to the regime; he soon became the civilian head of successive plots; he was executed 2 February 1945. Ludwig Beck was present, but very ill, and soon after, had a cancer operation. Ulrich von Hassell (1881–1944) had been German Ambassador in Italy until 1937 and, from then on, active in the opposition, as was Johannes Popitz (1884–1945), former Under-Secretary of State in the Reich Ministry of Finance, then Prussian Finance Minister, and a professor at the University of Berlin. Another participant was Jens Jessen (1895–1944), a professor of economics, an early National Socialist, then a strong opponent, who was executed November 1944.

12 Gerstenmaier.

13 Source: Eugen Gerstenmaier, "Der Kreisauer Kreis: Zu dem Buch Gerrit van Roons 'Neuordnung im Widerstand,'" 245; see also Gerstenmaier, *Streit und Friede hat seine Zeit*, 169.

14 Source: Hassell, *The Von Hassell Diaries*, 253–5; Hassell, *Die Hassell-Tagebücher*, 345–7.

15 The meeting of 8 January 1943. See Eugen Gerstenmaier to Wolf Ulrich von Hassell in Hassell, *Vom andern Deutschland*, 379–80; Gerstenmaier, *Streit und Friede*, 168–9; Moltke, *Letters to Freya*, 270–1.

16 Insertion by the editors of the diary, indicating loss of text through deletion by Hassell or possibly someone else after Hassell's death; Hassell, *Die Hassell-Tagebücher*, 43. Moltke was a great-great-nephew of the 19th-century Prussian Field Marshal Helmuth Graf von Moltke (1800–91, known in historiography as the

Elder Moltke; his nephew was General Helmuth von Moltke, 1846–1916, known as Moltke the Younger).

17 Insertions by the editors of the diary. "'Chief of the General Staff' either must have been intended as the 'code' for Helmuth James Graf von Moltke, a son of a great-nephew of the Elder Moltke, or it was part of the lost text that might have read 'great-nephew of.'"

18 Source: Clarita von Trott zu Solz, *Adam von Trott zu Solz. Eine erste Materialsammlung und Zusammenstellung*, 227; an English version of this, Clarita von Trott zu Solz, *Adam von Trott zu Solz. An Account*, 177, has "January 1942," an error.

19 Source: *Trial of the Major War Criminals before the Nuremberg Military Tribunal*, v. 12, 240–2; spellings and punctuation are here rendered as printed in the source.

7

The Kreisau Circle's Preparations for Hitler's Overthrow, August 1943[1]

However well-founded Moltke's skepticism toward "the generals" was – and in his years in Wehrmacht Supreme Command he had got to know them only too well – when there appeared to be a realistic chance of a revolt led by colonels who were doubtful about engaging with civil Resistance leaders, Moltke attempted to influence the course of events after the coup and to secure, if possible, the dominant influence for his and his "Kreisau" friends' ideas. The alternative would have been the ascendancy of the Goerdeler-Hassell-Popitz group, whom Moltke, leaning further to the left, had denounced in the January 1943 meeting, with a reference to "Kerenski."[2] On 4 August 1943 he wrote to his wife Freya:

In the field that interests me most there has been a major hitch: Uncle[3] has joined the club of Their Excellencies, under rather unpleasant circumstances, and this has so much encouraged the reactionaries that we'll probably skid into the Kerensky solution. In that case the hope for a sound and organic solution in our lifetime would be buried; and that unfortunately means a lot. But it has not yet happened, and perhaps it can still be prevented. Friedrich[4] is coming on Saturday, and then we'll see whether there is still an effective remedy for it. It is, however, a serious symptom of the immaturity of our people and of our situation. It seems that much more must be laid in rubble and ashes until the time is ripe. What a struggle it is to accept that conclusion.[5]

This consideration, too, is evidence of Moltke's intention to complete the three documents of August 1943, under great pressure of time, and of his will to secure for his group a decisively active role. Following the fire-bombing of Hamburg from 24 to 30 July – Air Marshal Arthur T. Harris' "Operation Gomorrha" – the general panic that ensued in Berlin added urgency to the coup preparations.[6] Moltke had already taken a trip to Turkey in July to establish a contact with Britain; in December, in Istanbul, he attempted to convey to the Western Allies an undertaking by the Resistance group that he now represented to enable the Allies to occupy France without German opposition; this could not be put into practice unless Hitler was first removed. Everything points to Moltke's active involvement in the preparations for the coup d'état and his determination for his group to have a decisive role in the shaping of the future.[7]

However, who could put Moltke's concepts in place as the foundation of the new order? In the nature of the overthrow of Hitler by military leaders, there would be a military dictatorship in the first post-coup-d'état days. On whom was Moltke expecting to rely? General Ludwig Beck? Would the colonels – Tresckow, Stauffenberg – seize control from the older generals? Frictions with Stauffenberg emerged in November 1943. Nevertheless, he went to Istanbul to try to offer to the Western Allied Powers a German surrender in the West. Again, only military men could follow through on such a commitment. On the civil side, Carl Goerdeler, Johannes Popitz, Ulrich von Hassell might prove problematical. There is scope for further research.

All the documents exist in typed copies, either top copies or, in some cases, carbon copies. They were usually typed by Moltke's secretary (from the private law firm in which he had worked in Berlin until 1939) Katharina Breslauer, whom he could trust entirely, sometimes by his wife Freya, and on occasion by himself.[8]

Draft of 9 August 1943[9]

BASIC PRINCIPLES OF THE RECONSTRUCTION

The government of the German Reich[10] sees in Christianity the foundation for the moral and religious renewal of our nation, for overcoming hatred and deception, and for the reconstruction of the European community of nations.

The starting point lies in the committed reflection of the human being about the divine order, which supports man's inward and outward existence. Only when one succeeds in making this order the standard for relations among individuals and nations can the disruption of our time be overcome and a genuine state of peace be created.

The internal new order of the Reich is the basis for implementing a just and lasting peace.

Amid the collapse of a power structure that has lost its [ethical] commitments and was based exclusively on the rule of technology, European mankind, most of all, faces this problem. The path to its solution lies open in the determined and energetic realization of the values of Christian life. The Reich government is therefore resolved to implement, with all the means at its disposal, the following requirements, which are indispensable both domestically and externally:

1 The law has been trampled upon and must be restored and brought to rule over all orders of human existence. Under the protection of scrupulous, independent, and fearless judges, it is the basis for the entire future formation of peace.

2 The freedom of [religious] faith and conscience is guaranteed. Existing laws and regulations that violate these principles are repealed at once.

3 Breaking the totalitarian coercion of conscience and recognition of the inviolable dignity of the human person [form] the basis of the aimed-for order of law and peace. Everyone participates with full responsibility in the various social, political, and international areas of life. The right to work and property, regardless of race, nationality, and religious affiliation is protected by public authority.

4 The basic unit of peaceful communal life is the family. It is protected by public authority, which shall ensure, besides education, the material requirements of life: food, clothing, housing, garden, and health.

5 Work must be so organized that it encourages the willingness to accept personal responsibility and does not allow this to atrophy. Besides the creation of material working conditions and continuing vocational education, this includes every person's effective co-responsibility in the workplace and, beyond that, in the general economic fabric to which his work contributes. Thereby he shall collaborate in the growth of a healthy and durable way of life in which the individual, his family, and communities can develop organically in balanced economic spheres. Economic authorities must guarantee these basic requirements.

6 The personal political responsibility of everyone requires one's co-determining participation in the newly-to-be-revived self-government of the small and transparent communities. Rooted and proven in these communities, one's participation in decisions in the state and in the international community must be ensured by elected representatives so that one will have imparted to one the vivid conviction of co-responsibility for political events overall.

7 Special responsibility and loyalty, which every individual owes to his national origin, his language, the intellectual and historical traditions of his nation, must be respected and protected. It must not, however, be misused to accumulate political power, degrade, persecute, or suppress foreign national traditions. The free and peaceful development of national culture is no longer to be reconciled with the maintenance of the absolute sovereignty of an individual state. Peace requires the creation of a polity encompassing the individual states. As soon as the free consent of all the nations involved is assured, and for the highest political authority of the international community, those supporting this polity must have the right to demand of every individual obedience, respect, and if need be, commitment of life and property.

REICH STRUCTURE

The Reich remains the highest leadership authority of the German nation. Its political constitution shall be sustained by genuine authority, co-operation, and co-responsibility of the people. It rests upon the natural divisions of the nation: family, municipality, and land. The Reich structure shall follow the principles of self-government. In it, freedom and personal responsibility are combined with the requirements of order and leadership.

This structure shall ensure the unity and concerted leadership of the Reich and make its integration into the common life of European nations possible.

The formation of the political will of the nation shall transact itself within a framework that remains transparent to the individual. Geographically, economically, and culturally cohesive lands are founded upon the natural divisions of municipalities and counties. In order to enable effective self-government, the lands shall contain approximately between three and five million inhabitants.

The distribution of responsibilities follows the principle that every entity is responsible for the independent performance of all tasks that it can carry out meaningfully itself.

Starting today, it is incumbent upon all public authorities to be guided in every action and public pronouncement by the ultimate goal of a legal constitutional condition of a certain character. At the same time, with the elimination of the turmoil and abuses resulting from the National Socialist war and collapse, [turmoil and abuses] that threaten the life and limb of the German nation, the constitutional Reich structure must be initiated as soon as possible and with all the human resources that are becoming available for this, according to the following principles:

I The Municipality

Municipal representative assemblies are to be elected by all eligible voters in secret, direct vote.

All who have completed their twenty-first year or have fought in the war have the right to vote; heads of family have an additional vote for every child not entitled to vote; all those may stand for election who have completed their twenty-seventh year and whose candidature is agreed upon by a number of voters determined according to the size of the municipality; persons belonging to an armed force may not stand for election.

II The County

Representative assemblies in the counties and in the cities outside the counties are to be elected according to principles corresponding to those for municipal representative bodies. The same applies to subdivisions of cities outside the counties. Voting districts that are too large to be transparent to the individual voter are to be subdivided.

III The Land

1 The legislature of the lands and the municipal assemblies of cities that are [administrative districts in their own right] outside the counties are to be elected by the representative assemblies of the counties and municipalities, and by the representatives of the political subdivisions of such municipalities, respectively. Every

male citizen of a land or municipality who has completed his twenty-seventh year may stand for election. Politically appointed civil servants and persons belonging to an armed force are not electable. Electoral regulations have to ensure that at least half of those elected do not belong to one of the electoral bodies.

The land legislature shall have the following responsibilities: deciding upon budget, taxes, and land laws; the right to question the land chief minister and the right to pass resolutions on all issues of general land policy and land administration; election of the land governor, upon nomination by the land council.

2　The land government shall consist of the land chief minister and of the requisite number of privy councillors. The land chief minister is to be elected by the land legislative assembly upon nomination by the land governor; privy councillors are to be appointed by the land governor upon nomination by the land chief minister. Members of the land government must have their hereditary domicile in their lands.

The land government is responsible for the government of the land and for the implementation of Reich business in the territory of the land.

3　The land council has the responsibilities to propose candidates to the land legislature for the election of the land governor, to address recommendations to the land legislature, and to exercise disciplinary jurisdiction over the members of the land government.

4　The land governor is to be elected by the land legislative assembly upon nomination by the land council for a term of twelve years and confirmed in office by the Reich governor.

The land governor shall be responsible for the supervision of the entire land administration and for the appointment of civil servants.

He shall bear the responsibility for the implementation of Reich policy in the land.

He shall preside over the land council.

IV The Reich

1　The national parliament [Reichstag] is to be elected by the land legislatures. Every male citizen of the Reich who has completed his twenty-seventh year may stand for election. Politically appointed civil servants and members of an armed force may not stand for election. For the time being, the electoral regulations ensure that at least half of those elected do not belong to one of the electoral bodies.

The national parliament [Reichstag] shall have the following responsibilities:

Enactment of the national budget, national taxes, and national laws.

The right to question the Reich chancellor and to pass resolutions on all issues of national policy.

Election of the Reich governor upon nomination by the Reich council.

2 The national government shall consist of the Reich chancellor and the departmental ministers. The Reich chancellor is to be appointed by the Reich governor with the approval of the national legislature; the ministers are appointed by the Reich governor upon nomination by the Reich chancellor.

The Reich governor can discharge the Reich chancellor; the discharge will become effective upon the appointment of a new Reich chancellor; the Reichstag has the right to request, with a qualified majority, the discharge of the Reich chancellor, provided that it proposes the appointment of a new Reich chancellor to the Reich governor at the same time.[11]

3 The Reich council shall consist of the land governors, of the speakers of the national parliament [Reichstag] and the Reich economic chamber, and of the Reich councillors appointed by the Reich governor, with the approval of the national government, for eight years.

The Reich council shall

propose candidates to the Reich national parliament [Reichstag] for the election of the Reich governor,

establish principles for the transfer of civil servants from one land to another and from land service to national service,

address recommendations to the national parliament [Reichstag],

exercise disciplinary jurisdiction over the national government and the land governors.

4 The Reich governor shall be elected, upon the nomination of the Reich council, by the national parliament [Reichstag] for twelve years.

The Reich governor shall have supreme command of the armed forces and the chair in the Reich council.

He shall represent the Reich externally with the countersignature of the Reich chancellor.

He shall promulgate Reich laws, and appoint and dismiss Reich ministers and civil servants.

CHURCH, CULTURE, EDUCATION

The Reich government welcomes the steadfast co-operation of both major Christian churches in the formation of public life.

The public discharge of the worship, pastoral, and educational functions of both Christian churches will not be obstructed and is placed under the protection of the Reich government. The propagation of religious literature will again be made possible. Christian ideas will have their proper place in the entire education system, as well as in films and on radio.

The statutory relationship between the German Reich and the German Evangelical Church,[12] as well as the Roman Catholic Church, will be newly defined according to these principles, in friendly agreement with the two churches. The agreements of the Concordat[13] remain untouched.

The future statutory position of other religious and ideological organizations will be determined in detail, following negotiations with them.

Parents shall have the right to educate their children according to the principles of the Christian faith and according to the demands of their own conscience. The state also has to contribute to overcoming the inner and outward disruption of the family. Sunday shall be free of obligatory events organized by the state.

Family, church, and school carry out the work of education together. The school shall provide the right of the child to an education appropriate to him. It shall awaken and strengthen his moral powers, and convey that measure of knowledge and qualification to him that corresponds to the required expectation of proficiency of his age level.

Character education forms a decent person of fundamentally religious bearing who is capable of setting, as the guidelines of his life, good morals and righteousness, truth and sincerity, neighbourly love, and faithfulness to his conscience. A person thus educated will have the maturity to make responsible decisions. Learning serves the moral formation of the personality and preparation for practical life.

Technical schools and post-secondary colleges, which build upon the elementary school or on its primary level, produce organically cohesive knowledge and skills in vibrant continuation of elementary school work and with increasing co-responsibility of the pupil.

The state school shall be a Christian school with[14] religious instruction as a compulsory subject for the members of the two religious faiths. Instruction is to be provided[15] under the authority of the churches, wherever possible by clergymen.

ECONOMY

1   All those participating in the economy have to fulfill the same minimum obligations. These minimal obligations include honesty and propriety in economic management, and the honouring of contract and work obligations in the framework of signed agreements.

The guarantee to labourers of their livelihood, for the sake of their dignity as human beings, is the responsibility of economic management. At the same time, all efforts are to be made to improve, as soon and as generally as possible, the minimal standard of living, which has been diminished by the serious economic damage caused by the war. The contributions necessary for this are to be provided by individuals, business,[16] the self-governing entities of the economy, the German Trades Union, and the state, with consideration also to giving security to the family, which depends upon the worker.

2   The Reich government considers, as the basis for economic reconstruction, an orderly, productive competition that transacts itself within the framework of state economic direction and is subject to permanent state supervision with regard to its methods.

Where existing commitments and interlocking conditions of the economy (monopolies, cartels, and corporations) exclude this productive competition, it is the task of economic direction to put the principles of orderly, productive competition into practice and to protect the interests of the collectivity.

The common interest of the economy in the basic industries requires, especially in these branches of industry, firm economic management by the state. The key industries of mining, the iron-

and metal-producing industries, and the basic chemical and energy industries will be transferred to public ownership. Publicly owned industries are to be managed and supervised according to generally valid economic principles.

The economic direction of the Reich will advance the economic policies of the lands through its influence on markets and basic industries, and provide for an economic process with as little friction as possible. The Reich government supports the development of businesses[17] into economic communities of human beings. In such communities – called shop trades unions – the participation of the workforce in the management of business and in business profits and debits, particularly in the value increment of the enterprise,[18] is to be agreed upon between the owner of the enterprise and the representatives of the workforce. This agreement is subject to approval by the economic self-governing body of the land.

3 The "German Trades Union" is a necessary means to implementing the economic program described above and the structure of the state therein presumed. It will find its fulfillment in pushing through this program and in transferring the tasks it has been responsible for to the agencies of the state and to economic self-government. Should tasks for which the "German Trades Union" has responsibility require its continued existence, then its structure is to be adapted to the structures of the state and the economy.

4 In the economic self-government structured into land organizations, the enterprises of industry, commerce, and trades are to be members in the chambers of industry. Agricultural enterprises are to be members in the chambers of agriculture.[19] The land chambers of trades and of agriculture shall be combined in the land chambers for economic affairs.[20]

The chambers of industry and of agriculture will be composed of equal numbers of management and labour representatives, who will be elected. The land chambers for economic affairs[21] will be formed by delegates of the chambers of industry and agriculture.

The chambers shall write their own statutes; these will be approved by the land governor. The presidents of the chambers and their deputies will be elected by the chambers and require confirmation by the land governor.

The chambers' responsibility is the self-government of the economy. They can be simultaneously charged by the respective economic land authorities (land economic agency, etc.) with responsibilities for Reich and land business. Their self-government tasks shall include, particularly, the supervision of vocational apprenticeship, which builds upon nine years of schooling and which is to be adjusted to the requirements of the economy as a whole and set generally for two years. Continuing vocational development is to be provided through appropriate specialized and physical institutions.

The Reich economic chamber, as the head of economic self-government, will be composed of delegates from the land chambers for economic affairs.

The economic administration is part of the overall administration of the state. The Reich economic ministry shall interact with the regional self-governing organizations of individual enterprises and with individual enterprises through the land economic agencies.

Draft of 9 August 43[22]

FIRST INSTRUCTION TO THE LAND GOVERNORS

The inward and outward distress of the German people can only be mitigated, and the energetic reformation of its lot can only be initiated on the basis of a clear and coherent conception of the German future. Such a firm view is all the more necessary since military and political developments may lead to the military occupation and separation of parts of the country, or even to the absence of a German Reich government or to its inability to issue binding orders.

It is a compelling necessity that, in such circumstances, responsible leaders in the various lands and parts of the country, even if they lack the opportunity for mutual consultation and contact, shall act in unity and in concert on fundamental matters, and in this way maintain and strengthen the internal cohesion of the German lands as a cultural nation.

The attached principles, which in view of the variety of possible developments are confined to the fundamentals, shall ensure that, in case of an unfavourable course of the war, the Germans shall present a united will to other nations.[23]

Liberty-minded German labourers and the Christian churches with them represent and lead those forces in the nation from whose midst reconstruction can be initiated. They alone, based upon their continually present spiritual traditions, in this moment guarantee the preservation of the substance of the German nation as a civilized nation, and its cohesion as a nation in a state can be rescued from its present peril. Supported by these strengths, we commission you with the high responsibility of assuming the office of land governor in the territory assigned to you and demarcated in the enclosed map, and of possessing yourself of the requisite means of exercising power. The military-district commanders shall be instructed to obey your directives.

The land governor shall be answerable to the Reich for the organization of the political, cultural, and economic resources of the land:

1   He shall attend to legal security, personal liberty, and a genuine co-responsibility of the entire land population, and thus promote the will to political expression in its natural development and help the particular character of the regions to come into their own in the aim of home rule.

    In order to offer to the constructive forces of the land opportunities for responsible co-operation, you will at once have to see to it that well-reputed and tried-and-proven persons in town and country shall be entrusted with these tasks.

2   The land governor, in close consultation with recognized cultural representatives of the land, shall pave the way to the re-creation of Christian education and thereby to a genuine renewal of spiritual and intellectual life. This requires, above all, an immediate co-operation of land and church, based upon mutual trust. To this end you are, without delay, to establish contact with representatives of the churches of your land.

3   In particular, the land governor shall put in place the responsible co-operation of workers in the administration and the economy. To this end you will, without delay, make contact with the representatives of the German Trades Union, which is to be recognized as the only legitimate representation of the workers. In Appendix 1,[24] these principles are set out in greater detail. The following guidelines are to be followed in their implementation:

1 You have an entirely free hand in appointing personnel to take all measures that you consider requisite to ensure an orderly administration and for the maintenance of peace and order. As a matter of principle, all who are, in any way, leading National Socialists are to be removed from important positions.

  After having chosen your closest co-workers, you are to fill key positions with unconditionally reliable persons. You also have the right to appoint personnel in Reich agencies and territorial entities in your land.

  Final appointments, according to civil service laws, can be completed only after your confirmation as land governor.

2 In the event that martial law (state of emergency) is declared, the military holder of executive power shall remain subject to your general political directives.

3 Regarding necessary arrests, the standard of personal culpability is to apply, particularly with reference to the regulations concerning defilers of the law (Appendix 2),[25] and culpability is[26] to be examined and passed sentence on as swiftly as possible, through the normal legal process.[27] Furthermore, all persons are to be arrested who are under suspicion that they could hinder the state in carrying out necessary measures.

  The liberation of those who have been deprived of their freedom illegally is to be initiated at once.

  You are enjoined to take all requisite measures without waiting for directives from superior authorities.

4 You are to carry out at once, in co-operation with the land governors of the neighbouring lands, the border adjustments that become necessary through the new land demarcations. Continuous contact with all neighbouring land governors is to be ensured as an urgent priority. For the time being, the existing territorial boundaries shall remain in place for the postal and railway administrations and for the Armed Forces.

II

1 All laws and ordinances that disadvantage individuals because they belong to a particular nation, race, or religion are not to be enforced; discriminating measures based upon them are to be

lifted immediately. Other existing laws and administrative ordinances, in principle, remain in force for the time being.

2 a) All measures that serve the maintenance of the fighting power of the German Armed Forces or orderly demobilization at a later time are to be carried out as Reich measures with precedence before all other material tasks; the actions necessary for this are to be forced through, regardless of any resistance.

b) Disruptions of the orderly continuation of the existing system of economic procurement and distribution must be avoided under all circumstances. Interventions in the flow of provisions and relaxations of the ration-card system are the greatest menace.

3 Besides maintaining the integrity of your land and of order and security in your land, your foremost task is to build up self-government according to the principles in Appendix 1.[28] In this endeavour, the economic interests and political forces in your land are to be integrated into the framework of this self-government as fully as possible, bureaucratic administration is to be reduced, and your own authority firmly consolidated from below.

4 You must do what is required so that the economy can carry out necessary restructuring measures, if possible without help from outside and while maintaining an adequate level of employment. For the creation of enduring conditions, the departure of non-resident labourers is to be encouraged. Immigration and residence restrictions for Germans are not permissible.

5 In order to cover necessary cash requirements, you are authorized to draw upon requisite monetary means, based upon Reich fiscal law.

Draft of 9 August 43[29]

SPECIAL DIRECTIVE

The Reich government will prevent with all available means the intrusion of enemy forces into Reich territory. In the event that an enemy occupation in your land cannot be halted, your foremost responsibility will be to maintain the interests of your land population and to protect the independent development of your economic and political structures against arbitrary interferences, treasonous subversion, and nationalist excesses.

To this end, the following Special Directive is issued:

1 The First Instructions to the Land Governors dated ... with Appendix[30] remain fully in place.
2 You will have to bring about the requisite balance between the requirements of the occupation and needs of the population through strictly businesslike co-operation with the enemy military authorities.
3 It is to be made clear to the occupation authority that you are prepared, in a correct manner, to co-operate in all tasks of land administration, especially for the maintenance of peace and order, but that you have no foreign policy authority, particularly that you can discuss or recognize neither a curtailment of your competence nor a change of the borders of your land. You have to consistently bear the consequences resulting from this declaration. You may retreat before physical force but not before its threat.
4 In issues arising through foreign occupation, the closest contact with the Reich government is to be maintained, and its respective directives are to be followed.

2nd Draft of 23.7.43[31]

INSTRUCTION FOR NEGOTIATIONS ABOUT THE PUNISHMENT OF DEFILERS OF THE LAW BY THE COMMUNITY OF NATIONS[32]

Under National Socialist rule, many violations of the law have been committed. In their character, extent, and intent, they are grave and abominable. Their punishment is an urgent commandment for the resurrection of the rule of law and thereby of internal and external peace. If the law is to be assisted to be victorious again, it can only happen through the method of law itself and not through measures determined by political ends or by passions.

The German nation is most interested in deserved punishment being imposed for desecration of the law. This is an utterly German concern. At the same time, the just demand for punishment by the international community is not to be denied.

After the war of 1914–18, the recovery of conditions of peace between nations, based on trust, was impaired by an insufficient consideration and treatment of "war criminals." At the time there arose in Germany grave internal conflicts that contributed to the origin of the new war. There must not be a misapprehension, however, that, after the World War of 1914–18, it was a problem of a different character. Nevertheless, with regard to the renewed demand for international punishment of "war criminals" for "systematic atrocities,"[33] a recollection of the terms of the Treaty of Versailles is of interest.

Article 227 arraigned the Emperor "for a supreme offence against international morality and the sanctity of treaties"[34] before a tribunal of five judges of the principal victorious powers. The foundations of the judgment were to be "the highest motives of international policy," with a view to "vindicating the solemn obligations of international undertakings and the validity of international morality." Punishment was left to the discretion of the tribunal.

According to Article 228, the Allied governments could bring before their military tribunals – with the German government under obligation to extradite them – persons accused of "having committed acts in violation of the laws and customs of war" for sentencing "to punishments laid down by law," regardless of any internal German punishment.

Article 229 established jurisdiction to the effect that [the accused] be brought, in cases of punishable offences against citizens of a victorious power, before its military courts; in cases of offences against members of various powers, before military courts to be composed of judges of these various countries.[35]

Therefore it was here a case of punishment, not by courts of the international community, but by organs of the victorious powers. In contrast with the failed solution of that time, which made the participation of German authorities practically impossible, a moral and dignified solution that grows out of the meaning of the law must now be sought. Only such a solution can become a cornerstone of peace rather than endangering it.

The demand for the extradition of defilers of the law for punishment by the courts of the individual victorious powers, or of all of them, conflicts with the natural dignity of the statesmen who acted personally and of the extraditing nation. An arrangement for acting with personal dignity, however, is a basic prerequisite for any successful shaping of the future of the international community.

Punishment by a universal international court and the placement of defilers of the law under its judicial authority does not injure law and dignity. Rather, it would be a contribution that could become the foundation and the touchstone of the future, common co-operation of the international community.

This universal court alone, [consisting of representatives] of all belligerents, regardless of which side, or even of all nations of the world, could have the necessary moral and legal authority to pronounce that measure of moral and legal condemnation that is due to desecrations of the law. A sham judgment by agencies not constituted according to law does not effect the restoration of law, but rather promotes the opposite.

Historically and practically, the obvious court to this end would be the Cour[36] in The Hague. Legal-political deliberations about entrusting it with criminal law tasks have occasionally pended, and fundamental reservations against it can have no effect in today's situation. Non-membership in the League of Nations is no obstacle to the Cour being seized [of a case in a non-member country] according to Article 35 of the Statute of the Cour. It would require a change of Article 4 of the Statute regarding the composition [of the Cour]. Benches of six judges (three [from] victorious powers, two neutrals, one [from the] defeated state) with the deciding vote of the president, according to Article 55 of the Statute, could seem to be expedient. The state with the injured interests would have the right to demand prosecution, according to Article 34 of the Statute. Defence counsels would have to be appointed by the state to whom the accused belongs; there is also the possibility of court-appointed counsel. The details of the procedure would have to be regulated by the rules of the Cour. By a material, criminal-code paragraph by which the Cour would have to judge, the same criteria for facts, set out with reasons in the attached law, would be proposed for the domestic condemnation of defilers of the law.[37]

The principle of *nulla poena sine lege* also would have to be binding for the Cour, in view of the emphasis it has received internationally in the last years vis-à-vis the actions of the German government. In the manner described in the attachment for internal German procedures, the Cour would have to determine the desecration of the law by declaration and find the penalty from the criminal law of the country to which the perpetrator belonged at the time and in accordance with that country's criminal law in force at the time. It can be left to the Cour, for actions in occupied territories, to demarcate competing criminal codes in these countries.[38]

Regarding the number of persons to be indicted, a practical experience from English history before 1689 might be of interest, which Macaulay (*History of England*, London, 1864, vol. I, chapter X, p. 312) expresses as follows: "The rule by which a prince ought after a rebellion to be guided in selecting rebels for punishment is perfectly obvious. The ringleaders, the men of rank, fortune, and education, whose power and whose artifices have led the multitude into error, are the proper objects of severity. The deluded population, when once the slaughter in the field of battle is over, can scarcely be treated too leniently."

The guarding of the accused to be placed under [the jurisdiction of] the Cour upon governmental request would have to be the task of the government of the Netherlands, based on special agreements. Punishment would be carried out by states determined by the Cour, excluding the injured state, with the Cour's authority of supervision and regulation.

If this attempt[39] succeeds to justly remove this obstacle[40] to peace that heavily weighs upon all concerned, it will be a further step toward the realization of the rule of law between nations, and from evil will spring good. If, however, the solution is applied purely politically, without a court that can be recognized as just, injustice will be answered with injustice, and force, which as a source of law must in fact be broken, will be newly confirmed in its function as ultimate arbiter.

2nd Draft of 23.7.43[41]

PUNISHMENT OF DEFILERS OF THE LAW[42]

To be punished as a defiler of the law[43] is he who breaks essential principles of divine or natural law, international law, or positive law that is overwhelmingly identical in the community of nations, in a manner that makes it clear that he culpably disregards the binding force of these legal axioms. A defiler of the law is he, too, who gives the order for a law-breaking act, who in responsible position enjoins it or issues general doctrines or directives of a law-breaking kind.

Complicity, being an accessory and instigation, is judged according to the general criminal code.

In the case of a desecration of the law under orders, the order is no reason for excluding a penalty unless it was a matter of immediate threat to the life and limb of the perpetrator, or another compulsion was present that, in view of the immediate circumstances, did not make following the order appear obviously immoral. Particularly, the order is no reason for excluding a penalty if the perpetrator, through his behaviour before, during, or after the deed has demonstrated that he approved of the order.

If desecrations of the law were perpetrated before the promulgation of this law,[44] the procedure is to be concluded with a judgment establishing that the accused is guilty of desecration of the law.

Whoever is sufficiently suspect of [having committed] desecration of the law can be proscribed by a publicly issued decision of the court, the public prosecutor's office, or the higher administrative authority. The proscribed person can be arrested by anyone.[45] He is to be handed over to the police, who are forthwith to present him to the competent court. All other protective regulations concerning provisional arrest and detention do not apply to the proscribed person. The proscription ends with the sentencing or acquittal of the proscribed person or by dropping the proceedings.

REASONING[46]

1 Under National Socialist rule, many violations of the law have been committed. In their character, extent, and intent they are grave and abominable. Their punishment is an urgent commandment for the resurrection of the rule of law and thereby of internal and external peace. If the law is to be assisted to be victorious again, it can only happen through the method of law itself and not through measures determined by political ends or by passions.

   Emanating from the law itself and equally from political expediency, an ethical, dignified solution must be found.

2 In fundamental [and] clear condemnation of crimes,[47] a special category of punishable offence, which is to be prosecuted in the normal penal law process, is created by the proposed criminal code paragraph, which imposes imprisonment or death upon the defiler of the law. In order to facilitate arrest, the possibility of proscribing defilers of the law is provided for.

   In addition to the proposed measures, material criminal code paragraphs are to be considered against persons who harbour the proscribed person, withhold him from arrest, or fail to denounce him.

3   The retroactive application of the new criminal code paragraph for desecration of the law contradicts the principle *nulla poena sine lege*. This concern does not affect the purely criminal-procedure regulation about proscription. The principle *nulla poena* [sic] has become common property of European criminal law since the eighteenth century. It has evolved historically in defence of absolutist arbitrariness. It does not correspond to a fundamental ethical imperative, regardless of which criminal-law method one starts from. It was unknown to the old criminal law, which was without firm penal prescriptions (before the Bamberg Criminal-Court Order and the C[onstitutio] C[riminalis] Caroli[48]), as it is still today in some Swiss cantons. It is also to be noted that the circles from which the perpetrators come deny the principle and have abolished it. The return to firm application of law and the reawakening of legal security and confidence in the law demand, however, to hold firm to the principle, therefore, to deny the criminal-code paragraph retroactivity. It follows from this that deeds committed before the issuing of this law cannot be punished on the basis of the new criminal-code paragraph. A penalty, therefore, can be imposed only insofar as the accused has also committed offences that were punishable according to the laws in place at the time of the offences. The principle of *nulla poena,* however, does not impede the purely declaratory determination by the court of the desecration of the law, even for retroactive cases. This application of the new criminal-code paragraph as *lex imperfecta* is a valuable support for the reawakening of awareness of the law and will be felt to be a kind of expiation. The majority of the defilers of the law of the Third Reich are so incriminated with common crimes, particularly because of complicity, that the maximum penalty for the desecration of the law can nevertheless be achieved.

4   Besides this criminal-law retribution, a separately-to-be-dealt-with restitution is required for persons who, through violence and arbitrariness, have been injured in life and limb, property, honour, and civil rights (concentration camps, unjust judgments, deprivations of citizenship, confiscations, demotion, and disenfranchisement of civil servants). Regulations will be issued that facilitate the prosecution of such proceedings against declared defilers of the law and generally heighten the liability of the defilers of the law with their property.

5   The impairment of civil and political rights through the designa-
tion [of a person] as a defiler of the law is also reserved for a special ruling.

NOTES

1   Cf. document no. 4; Helmuth James von Moltke, *Letters to Freya 1939–1945*, passim
and 332 (Moltke's letter of 10 August 1943 to his wife).
2   See document no. 6.
3   Wilhelm Leuschner, Social-Democrat and union leader; he was succeeded in the
"Kreisau Circle" by the Social-Democrat Julius Leber.
4   Carlo Mierendorff.
5   Source: Freya von Moltke's Papers, now in Deutsches Literaturarchiv, Marbach
a.N., no no.; cf. Moltke, *Letters to Freya*, 329.
6   Arthur T. Harris, *Despatch on War Operations 23rd February, 1942, to 8th May, 1945*
(London: Frank Cass 1995), 18–20 ("The Destruction of Hamburg"); Moltke, *Letters
to Freya*, 327 (2 August 1943); [Joseph Goebbels], *Die Tagebücher von Joseph Goebbels*,
Teil II, Band 9 (Munich, New Providence, London, Paris: K.G. Saur 1993), 156–224 (25
July–5 August 1943); *Völkischer Beobachter* (31 July–4 August 1943).
7   For context, see Peter Hoffmann, "Oberst i.G. Henning von Tresckow und die
Staatsstreichpläne im Jahr 1943," 331–64.
8   Information from Freya von Moltke, 25 July 2009; Moltke, *Letters to Freya*, 14,
329–33.
9   Source: Typed copy with Moltke's MS note "Entwurf v.9.8.43." In Moltke Papers, in
a folder entitled "Grundtexte"; the originals are in Bundesarchiv, Koblenz, N 1750
Bd. 1; printed in Ger van Roon, *Neuordnung im Widerstand. Der Kreisauer Kreis innerhalb der deutschen Widerstandsbewegung*, 561–7 and Roon, *German Resistance to
Hitler. Count von Moltke and the Kreisau Circle*, 347–54. Roon, *Neuordnung*, 561, and
Roon, *German Resistance*, 347, gave this document a heading, which is not found on
the original copy. The translations of this and of the following three documents in
Roon, *German Resistance,* are inaccurate.
10 "Reich" is either not translated, or rendered as "nation" or "national."
11 Article 67 of the German Constitution of 1949 (Grundgesetz, Basic Law) incorporates this "lesson" from the turbulent years leading up to 1933 as the "constructive
vote of no confidence": if parliament wishes to bring down a government by a vote
of no confidence, it can do so only by agreeing upon a successor to the incumbent
chancellor at the same time. The "qualified majority" demanded in Moltke's draft
means 50 percent +1 of the votes; common examples are a two-third or three-
quarter majority. The Grundgesetz only specifies "the majority of its Members" for
a vote of no confidence.

12 "Evangelische Kirche," in the European context, has the Reformation meaning of "based on the Gospel," as opposed to Papal decree; it designates usually the Lutheran church, but may also refer to the Zwinglian ("Reformed") and Calvinist (Presbyterian) churches, never to Baptist and similar "sects." "Protestant" is loosely used for the German "Evangelische Kirche" and for the Zwinglian and Calvinist churches, but strictly it means the churches in those states of the Holy Roman Empire of the German Nation that in 1529 protested against the re-instatement of the 1521 Edict of Worms.

13 A condordat is a treaty between the Vatican and a secular government.

14 "und" crossed out; "mit" written above it.

15 "erteilt" written over "ausgeübt."

16 The German "Betrieb" includes such English equivalents as "firm," "shop," "manufacture," "company," "corporation"; "enterprise" is also a possible equivalent, although it is the literal translation of "Unternehmen."

17 See note 15.

18 See note 15.

19 This sentence inserted in Moltke's hand.

20 "Landwirtschaftskammer" corrected in Moltke's hand to "Landeswirtschaftskammer."

21 See note 19.

22 Moltke's MS note "Entwurf v.9.8.43."; heading "Erste Weisung an die Landesverweser." Source: Typed copy with Moltke's MS emendations in Moltke, Papers, in a folder entitled "Grundtexte" in Bundesarchiv, Koblenz, N 1750 Bd. 1; printed in Roon, *Neuordnung*, 567–70, and Roon, *German Resistance*, 354–7.

23 Crossed out: "besonders den Feindmächten."

24 See the preceding document.

25 See at pp. 89–95, this book.

26 "Verschulden ist" inserted in Moltke's hand, "ist" at the end of the sentence crossed out.

27 "Rechtsschänder" = defilers of the law. For regulations concerning Defilers of the Law (Rechtsschänder), see Roon, *Neuordnung*, 556–60; Roon, *German Resistance*, 343–7.

28 See "Basic Principles of the Reconstruction," pp. 76–85.

29 Moltke's MS note "Entwurf vom 9.8.43."; the document is headed "Sonderweisung"; source: Typed copy with Moltke's MS emendations in Moltke Papers, in a folder entitled "Grundtexte" in Bundesarchiv, Koblenz, N 1750 Bd. 1; printed in Roon, *Neuordnung*, 570–1; not in Roon, *German Resistance*.

30 See "Basic Principles of the Reconstruction."

31 Source: Typed copy with Moltke's MS note "2ter Entwurf vom 23.7.43," Moltke, Papers; original in Bundesarchiv, Koblenz, N 1750 Bd. 1; printed with some variations in Roon, *Neuordnung*, 558–60, and Roon, *German Resistance*, 343–5, with additional variations from the original.

32 Source: "Instruktion für Verhandlungen über die Bestrafung von Rechtsschändern durch die Völkergemeinschaft," typescript, at top of p. 1, Moltke's MS note "2ter Entwurf vom 23.7.43" ("2nd draft of 23 July 43"), Bundesarchiv, Koblenz, N 1750 Bd. 1. Close reading suggests that this document had not reached the stage of a final draft. There are incomplete sentences and unclear grammar. The state of the draft is a sign of the urgency with which it was prepared, with the deadline of 10 August 1943 in the expectation that the coup d'état would take place on 13 August; cf. Moltke, *Letters to Freya*, 330–2; Roman Bleistein (Hrsg.), Dossier: "Kreisauer Kreis." Dokumente aus dem Widerstand gegen den Nationalsozialismus. Aus dem Nachlaß von Lothar König S.J. (Frankfurt a.M.: J. Knecht 1987), 340–1 (Peter Graf Yorck von Wartenburg an Lothar König S.J. 9. 8. 1943) and 315–35 (Erste Weisung an die Landesverweser; Sonderweisung; Grundsätze für die Neuordnung).

33 The document here uses the English term "systematic atrocities." The present translation, while attempting to be idiomatic, closely follows the original.

34 This and the following quotations from the Treaty of Versailles are those in the official English version; they correspond to the German ones Moltke used.

35 The German original here is grammatically garbled, although the meaning is clear.

36 Cour permanente de justice internationale.

37 See at pp. 92–5.

38 Meaning, between the criminal codes of Germany and those of the occupied territories.

39 Attempt: the proposals contained in the "Instructions."

40 Obstacle: the issue of punishing "defilers of the law."

41 Moltke's MS note "Zweiter Entwurf vom 23.7.43," Moltke, Papers; original in Bundesarchiv, Koblenz, N 1750 Bd. 1; printed with some variations in Roon, *Neuordnung*, 556–8, and Roon, *German Resistance*, 343–5, with additional variations from the original.

42 "Bestrafung von Rechtsschändern," top of p. 1, Moltke's MS note "2ter Entwurf vom 23.7.43" ("2nd draft of 23 July 43"), Bundesarchiv, Koblenz, N 1750 Bd. 1; Roon, *German Resistance*, 343, has the incorrect heading "The Punishment of War Criminals (Second Draft)."

43 "Rechtsschänder" and "Rechtsschändung" are used throughout in the German original. The terms are translated alternately "defiler of the law," "law breaker," or "desecration of the law," depending on the immediate context.

44 Referring to this document, "Punishment of Defilers of the Law."

45 This sentence is typed in the margin for insertion at this place.

46 "Begründung."

47 "Schandtat" also means "iniquity," "shameful action," or "infamous action."

48 The original has "C.C. Carolina."

8

Socialist Proclamation Drafted by
Carlo Mierendorff, 1943

Carlo Mierendorff was born in Grossenhein in Saxony on 24 March 1897. He grew up in Darmstadt and there became friends with Theodor Haubach, who became a socialist politician. Mierendorff and Haubach both volunteered for service at the outbreak of war in 1914. Mierendorff served at the front in the artillery and was decorated for bravery with the Iron Cross First Class by Emperor William II personally. After the war, he joined the Social Democratic Party (SPD), completed his university studies in Heidelberg in 1922, worked his way up in the party, and was elected as a member of the Reichstag in 1930. He was among the leading younger figures of the German Social Democratic Party who, before 1933, attempted to counter National Socialist propaganda by employing a language of symbols and enlarging the emotional appeal of socialist propaganda.

From 1933 to 1938 he was imprisoned in concentration camps. After his release he sought contact with other underground opponents of National Socialism and became attached to the Kreisau Group and Helmuth von Moltke. He was killed in an Allied air raid in Leipzig on 4 December 1943.

Berlin 14.6.43[1]

Today, Whit Monday 1943, the undersigned[2] have solemnly decided to confirm their joint activity as Socialist Action, by drawing up the following program of action.

Socialist Action is a non-partisan national movement to save Germany.

It is fighting for the liberation of the German nation from the Hitler dictatorship, for the restoration of the nation's honour, trampled underfoot by the crimes of Nazism, and for the nation's freedom in the socialist order.

The Action Committee is formed, as an expression of its solidarity and unity, by representatives of the Christian forces, of the socialist movement, the communist movement, and the liberal forces.

The struggle is being conducted under the banner of Socialist Action, the red flag with the symbol of freedom: the socialist ring combined with the cross as a sign of the unbreakable unity of the working people.

Socialist Action calls upon working people in town and country and upon our brave soldiers in this difficult hour to join in the battle, in the conviction that the rescue of the common fatherland from political, moral, and economic ruin is only possible through:

1 Restoration of law and justice;

2 Abolition of restraint of conscience and unconditional tolerance in issues of faith, race, and nationality;

3 Respect for the foundations of our culture, which is unthinkable without Christianity;

4 Socialist organization of the economy, in order to realize human dignity and political freedom and to guarantee the livelihood of employees and labourers in industry and agriculture, as well as the farmer on his land, this guarantee being the prerequisite for social justice and freedom;

5 Expropriation of key firms in heavy industry for the benefit of the German nation, as the foundation of the socialist organization of the economy, in order to make an end of the pernicious abuse of the political power of big capital;

6 Self-government in the economy, with equal rights of participation for the working people, as a fundamental element of the socialist order;

7 Protection of agriculture against the danger of becoming a puppet of capitalist interests;

8 Deconstruction of bureaucratic centralism and organic construction of the Reich out of the Länder;

9 Sincere co-operation with all nations, particularly in Europe with Great Britain and Soviet Russia.

Still the German nation has no opportunity to raise its voice. All the more loudly do the ruins and graves call to unity, to action! It is necessary to act before our homeland is destroyed entirely and the collapse is complete. Only the united front of all enemies of National Socialism can accomplish this deed.

Remembering the dead of the war and the martyrs of freedom who have been murdered by the power-madness of Fascism, and remembering the suffering of our soldiers, we pledge:

Never again shall the German nation stray into party strife!

Never again must the workers mangle each other in fraternal fighting!

Never again dictatorship and slavery!

A new Germany, in which the working nation organizes its own life in the spirit of true freedom, must emerge.

National Socialism and its lies must be exterminated root and branch, so that we can regain our self-respect, and the German name will once again become honourable in the world. The order of the hour is: Away with Hitler! Fight for justice and peace!

Burdensome years are before us. It almost exceeds human power to resurrect what Hitler's power-madness and the war have destroyed.

Nonetheless! Socialist Action is setting about the task with resolve. It calls upon all upright Germans for honest co-operation. We shall commit all our powers, all our ability, all our self-confidence; and thus we shall eventually prove before history that we are stronger than our fate, by mastering it.

NOTES

1 Source: Typed copy in Freya von Moltke's Papers; also in Bundesarchiv, Koblenz, N 1750 Bd. 1; cf. Kasimir Edschmid, ed., *In Memoriam Carlo Mierendorff. Literarische Schriften* (Darmstadt: Darmstädter Verlag 1947); Fritz Usinger, *Carlo Mierendorff. Eine Einführung in sein Werk und eine Auswahl*; Richard Albrecht, *Der militante Sozialdemokrat. Carlo Mierendorff 1897 bis 1943. Eine Biografie.*

2 There are no signatures on the copy. It was meant for publication in connection with the coup d'état, but Mierendorff was killed on 4 December 1943, and the contacts with the underground Communist leadership collapsed in June/July 1944 through the arrest of Adolf Reichwein, Julius Leber, Anton Saefkow, and Franz Jacob; Peter Hoffmann, *The History of the German Resistance, 1933–1945*, 362–4.

9

Confessing Church Memorandum to Reich Chancellor Hitler, July 1936

In the course of the struggle against National Socialism, the adherents of the Confessing Church, about one third of all German Lutheran ministers, in their Barmen Declaration of 31 May 1934, subscribed to the principle of "God's mighty claim upon our whole life," saying there were no "areas in which we would not need justification and sanctification through him."[1] A confession of faith, therefore, bears upon social and political life as much as upon the narrower concerns of religious doctrine. Many, if not most, churchmen failed to obey the injunctions of the Barmen Declaration. They became culpable by tolerating, whether with or without approval, atrocities inflicted upon Jews and other people – Poles, Russians, prisoners, Sinti and Roma, Jehovah's Witnesses, homosexuals, communists, political dissidents.[2] But among many gestures and actions of opposition by individual men of the Church, one by several Church leaders who risked liberty and life stands out.

On 4 June 1936, Hitler was sent a memorandum by the Provisional Board of the German Evangelical Church and the Council of the German Evangelical Church/Confessing Church.[3] The memorandum is dated 28 May 1936 and was signed by the members of the Provisional Board – Müller, Böhm, Forck, Fricke, and Albertz – and of the Council – Asmussen, Lücking, Middendorff, Niemöller, Thadden. Pastor Dr Wilhelm Jannasch, who had been forced into retirement and repeatedly arrested for continuing pastoral work illegally, prepared the final draft and personally delivered one copy to Heinrich Doehle, Department Head and Deputy Chief of the Reich Presidential Chancellery, on 4 June.[4] One other copy was held by Dr

Friedrich Weissler for the Provisional Board, and one was given to Pastor Birger Forell of the Swedish Legation in Berlin. There were many opportunities for copies to be made while the memorandum was on the desks of various bureaucrats in the Reich Chancellery and in the Reich Church Ministry.[5] Some weeks before 15 July 1936, the theologian Ernst Tillich borrowed D. Weissler's copy of the memorandum, read it, copied it in full, and, frustrated by the German government's silence about it, gave his copy to journalists. But it had reached at least one newspaper, *The New York Herald Tribune*, before that date from another source, Pastor Hermann Kötzschke.[6] *The New York Herald Tribune* published excerpts in English on 16 July and the entire memorandum in English on 28 July. On 23 July, a week before the Olympic Games opened in Berlin, the Swiss paper *Basler Nachrichten* published the memorandum with parts of the attachments, based on Kötzschke's copy. Notwithstanding publications in French, Dutch, Swedish, and Finnish papers, publicity abroad about the protest was subdued; perhaps the protest was pushed aside by the up-coming Summer Olympiad in Berlin.[7] Tillich and Weissler were arrested on 6 October 1936, Koch on 13 November, and placed in concentration camps. Weissler died from torture and other mistreatment in Sachsenhausen Concentration Camp on 19 February 1937. Koch was released in December 1938, Tillich a year later.[8]

The memorandum was apparently not shown to Hitler. The document did find its way into the files of Hitler's Personal Adjutancy Office, but there is no evidence that he was briefed on it.[9] It was passed on to the Ministry for Church Affairs as the appropriate agency for such matters. The memorandum, and the depth of feeling it reflected, may have had an influence upon Hitler's preference to keep a controlled peace, or truce, with the churches and to "deal with the churches" only after the war. Propaganda Minister Joseph Goebbels' diaries contain no reference to the memorandum, but numerous records of Hitler's preference.[10] Hitler no doubt coldly calculated that the churches were indispensable in helping maintain the morale of the troops during the war. The Protestant Church authorities, on their part, did not seek an open confrontation with the government. They were displeased and dismayed by the publication of the memorandum without prior consultation, and while they agreed in principle with the views set forth in the memorandum, they did not wish to publicize them "during the Olympiad." The Olympiad had "a retarding effect upon the church struggle."[11]

The Board and the Council of Brethren[12] of the Confessing Church, at a meeting in Kassel on 29 July 1936, drafted and sent to all parishes a message prepared by Generalsuperintendent of Kurmark, D. Dr Otto Dibelius.

The message had essentially the same contents as the memorandum. It was read on 23 August 1936 from about three quarters of the pulpits of the Confessing Church.[13] A million copies were distributed. But the memorandum had been handed to the Reich Presidential Chancellery without the knowledge of the bishops of the "intact" (not German Christian) land churches; that, and the publication of the memorandum abroad, led to a conflict between these churches and the Provisional Board of the German Evangelical Church. The Bishop of Württemberg, D. Theophil Wurm, among others, refused to distribute the message. He declared: "The Württemberg Church administration has not thought it proper to publicly read the message issued by the Provisional Board at this time and has advised its ministers to this effect; consequently a prohibition is superfluous."[14] He ordered that a Day of the Church[15] be held on 6 September and for that day prepared a statement of his own, generally supporting the contents of the memorandum.[16]

Bonhoeffer supported the memorandum: "Let the fellowship of Christ examine itself and see whether it has given any token of the love of Christ, which seeks to preserve, support, and protect life. Otherwise, however liturgically correct our services are, and however devout our prayer, however brave our testimony, they will profit us nothing, nay rather, they must testify against us that we have, as a Church, ceased to follow our Lord. God will not be separated from our brother: he wants no honour for himself so long as our brother is dishonoured."[17]

The Memorandum to Reich Chancellor Adolf Hitler[18]

The German Evangelical Church, represented by the clerical members of its Provisional Board and by the Council of the German Evangelical Church, respectfully greets the Führer and Reich Chancellor.

The German Evangelical Church is closely affiliated with the Führer and his advisors through the intercession it exercises quietly as well as publicly for nation, state, and government. Therefore we may take it upon ourselves to express, in the present document, the concerns and fears upon which they have meditated long and earnestly and that agitate many Christians in parishes,[19] councils of brethren, and church boards.

We hand over this document in obedience to God's charge to pronounce His Word and to bear witness to His Commandment without inhibition before everyone – even before the sovereigns and rulers of the nations. We trust that God will give us the wisdom to discharge our assigned task so clearly and unequivocally that thereby our concern for the Christian conscience and our love for the German nation equally will become unmistakably discernible.

We know, in any case, that in our expositions we are impelled only by the duty to help the suffering, confused, and imperiled members of the Evangelical Church with our word and our intercession, as our predecessors in office have done with their letter of 11 April 1935 (appendix 1), which sadly had no traceable effect. It is all-important to us that the Reich Government shall hear clearly and distinctly this voice speaking out of concern for the souls entrusted to the Church.

1 DANGER OF DE-CHRISTIANIZATION

The Provisional Board appreciates what it meant in 1933 and later on that those responsible for the National Socialist revolution were able emphatically to declare: "With our victory over Bolshevism, we have simultaneously defeated the enemy who also fought and threatened to destroy Christianity and the Christian churches."

But we experience that the struggle against the Christian Church is in effect and alive in the German nation as it never has been since 1918.

No power in the world, whatever its name, can either destroy or protect the Church of God against His will; *that* is *God's* business. But the Church has to look after the morally challenged consciences of its members.

Many baptised Christians are threatened with temporal and eternal disaster through the distress and confusion of today's religious struggle.[20] If even high places in the State and Party publicly assail the Christian faith (appendix 2), then members of the Church who already have become estranged to the Church and its message thereby will become ever more entangled in their unbelief; the waverers and uncertain ones will become completely uncertain and driven to apostasy. Indeed, there is grave danger that the Evangelical youth will let themselves be prevented from coming to Him, who is the only Saviour for German lads and girls as well. A church administration conscious of its responsibility must fend off such imperilment of the members of the Church. To such a defence belongs the clear question to the Führer whether the attempt to de-Christianize the German nation shall become the official policy of the Reich Government, through continued collaboration [in it] by responsible statesmen or simply through looking on and allowing [it] free rein.

II "POSITIVE CHRISTIANITY"

We trust that the Reich Government, in order to avoid escalations of the religious struggle in Germany, will hear the word of the Evangelical Church. When the NSDAP[21] declared in its platform that it stood upon the basis of a "Positive Christianity," the entire Church[-going] population could not but understand, and were meant to understand, that in the Third Reich the Christian faith, according to the Confessions and the preaching of the Church, was to be accorded freedom and protection, even assistance and support (appendix 3). Later, however, it came to pass that authoritative personages of State and Party arbitrarily interpreted the term "positive Christianity."

At one time the Reich Minister for National Enlightenment and Propaganda gave it out that positive Christianity was merely humanitarian performance (appendix 4), and he possibly combined with this interpretation an attack upon the Christian churches and their allegedly inadequate performance in the field of Christian charity, which the State itself, through its bans since 1933, had essentially restricted (appendix 4, no. 1[22]); at another time, Reich [Ideology] Instruction Director[23] Rosenberg proclaimed his mystique of the blood as positive Christianity (appendix 5, no. 1), and Party agencies, following his example, defamed Christianity based upon Confession and the belief in Revelation as negative (appendix 5, no. 2[24]). In the mouths of other representatives of the Reich Government, central concepts of the Christian faith (belief, love, eternity, prayer, resurrection), disguised as positive Christianity, were divested of their revelatory content and re-interpreted in purely worldly and psychological terms (appendix 4, nos. 4 and 5), even in utterances of Reich Church Minister Kerrl (appendix 4, no. 6). The harm done by such utterances is all the greater because the Church was never given the opportunity to refute, with equal reach, the misinterpretations of the Christian faith perpetrated by high quarters.

III DESTRUCTION OF THE CHURCH ORDER

The methods of the de-Christianization of the German nation will become comprehensible in their context if one remembers Reich

[Ideology] Instruction Director[25] Rosenberg's statement that, in the struggle for a German faith, one must "not spare the opposing side, but overcome it intellectually, make it atrophy organizationally and keep it politically impotent (*Mythos*, p. 636)." Action has been taken on this principle. Officially, any intervention in the internal structure and in the religious life of the Evangelical Church is denied (appendix 6[26]); but in fact, since the elections forced upon the Church in July 1933 until today, one interference after another has occurred (appendix 7[27]). The Evangelical public, whom the Führer had assured of the freedom of the Church just before the enforced elections (appendix 8[28]), could be only inadequately informed about the progress of the Church struggle. The so-called "Pacification Work," which had begun with the creation of the Reich Church Ministry and the installation of the church committees, has eliminated some abuses previously tolerated by the State and caused by State officials or Party members; but the Evangelical Christian who takes a closer look recognizes that, through this Pacification Work, the Church is kept in dependence upon the State in regard to its administration and finances, is robbed of its freedom of preaching and its order, and forced to tolerate the teaching of false doctrine. For him it must be a severe shock that the preamble of the law of 24 September 1935,[29] which introduced the "Pacification," gives an untrue description of the origin of the disturbances in the German Evangelical Church, and that it represents interferences of the State in the Church as non-interferences, nay, as services that the State renders to the Church.

This procedure by the State has laid a barely bearable burden upon the Evangelical parishioners who stand by the revealed Word of God and hold to the Confession of their fathers and who know, precisely because of that, what they, as Christians, owe their nation and its government.

IV DE-CONFESSIONALIZATION

A movement has begun under the watchwords "de-confessionalization" or "overcoming the confessional disunion" that is intended to make impossible the Church's work among the public. The Evangelical Church's own youth organizations have long since been taken away from it [the Church] by an agreement concluded between the Reich Youth Leader[30] and the Reich Bishop,[31] who had no authority to do this. But even the care for the Evangelical members of the

National Socialist youth organizations, the care which that agreement guaranteed to the Evangelical Church, is frequently being obstructed. Again and again, from the chief leaders of organized youth down to the lowest structures, the Evangelical youth's Church is made contemptuous and suspect, and the attempt is made to undermine the belief in Revelation entrusted to it [the Church] (appendix 9[32]).

While today's State officially holds to positive Christianity, its new organizations, such as the Year on the Land or the Labour Service, not only have next to no opportunities for pastoral care for their members; in them, even the contact of the pastor with his own young parishioners, be it through personal visit or merely through sending them Evangelical parish newspapers and literature, has been made largely impossible (appendix 10[33]). The fact, for example, that Evangelical members of a Labour Service camp were not permitted to attend divine service on Good Friday demonstrates how far, in some places, "de-Christianization" has been prosecuted (appendix 11). The regulations concerning the religious care of children in the Year on the Land program here speak a very clear language.

The de-confessionalization of the school is being deliberately promoted by the State (appendix 12). The abolition of the confessional schools is being pressed, in violation of the rights of the Church (appendix 13). The Party puts the consciences of the parents under the strongest pressure in this pursuit (appendix 14). Religious-teaching curricula, existing legally, are frequently disregarded. In many places already today, essential portions of Biblical instruction (the Old Testament) are expunged from religious teaching or unchristian materials (old-Germanic paganism) have become inserted in it (appendix 15). Divine service in school and school prayers are ever more neglected or transformed in aid of a de-Christianization, also, of the external forms of community life in school.

The training of the next generation of theologians in the universities is being entrusted ever more to professors and lecturers with proven credentials as teachers of false doctrine; particularly the destruction of theological faculties in Prussia provides a revealing picture here (appendix 16). In the area of examinations, the Ministry for Science, Education, and National Education has demanded the re-instatement in the examining boards of teachers of false doctrine (appendix 17).

The "de-confessionalization of *public* life" that evermore pushes back Christian influence and Christian participation in radio, the daily press, and public speaking is in reality de-Christianization (appendix 18).

V NATIONAL SOCIALIST WORLD VIEW[34]

Evangelical members of NS organizations are required to commit themselves unreservedly to the National Socialist world view (appendix 19[35]). This world view is frequently described and presented as a positive substitute for the Christianity that is to be overcome. When blood, ethnicity, race, and honour here receive the rank of eternal values, then the Evangelical Christian is forced by the First Commandment[36] to reject this valuation. When the Aryan human being is glorified, God's Word is witness to the sinfulness of all humans; when anti-Semitism, which binds him to *hatred* of Jews, is imposed upon the Christian in the framework of the National Socialist world view, then for him the Christian commandment to love one's fellow human stands opposed to it.

It is an especially grave conflict of conscience for our Evangelical parishioners when, according to their Christian duty as parents, they must combat the penetration of these anti-Christian thoughts in their children.

VI MORALITY AND JUSTICE

We see, with profound concern, that a morality essentially foreign to Christianity is invading our nation and threatens it with decomposition. We know well that the Führer has acknowledged, in his speech on 23 March 1933, the moral significance of the Christian Confessions for the life of the nation. But the power of the new moral thinking to date has been stronger than this statement. Widely, that is today viewed as good that is of utility to the nation (appendix 20). With the knowledge of Reich Office Director[37] Derichsweiler, it was possible to declare that the term "positive Christianity," in Article 24 of the Party Platform, was so used only in the manner in which one withholds the full truth from an ill person (appendix 21). Such behaviour places utilitarian considerations above the truthfulness demanded in God's Commandment. Disregard for the Divine Commandment to be truthful, a disregard that stems from the mentality of a morality of national utility, becomes especially clear to the Evangelical Christian in the manner in which, officially, the Church struggle is being described (see above), in the treatment of the Evangelical press and the practice of Evangelical gatherings, and in the perversion of the concept of what is voluntary into its opposite on the occasion of fund-collecting and solicitation for entry into organizations, etc. (appendix 22). In view of Christ's command in the Sermon on the Mount, the Evangelical Church welcomes with gratitude the fact that the number of oaths in courtrooms has dwindled to a fraction under the aegis of the new State. The more it must deplore as a victory of anti-Christian spirit the fact that the oath, as oath of allegiance and commitment, has undergone an alarming overuse and thereby a frightening depreciation. If every oath is a declaration or assertion given under the eyes of God, even when God's name is not expressly mentioned, the fact that many persons are caused to take oaths at short intervals must deprive the oath of its dignity and lead to the profanation and abuse of the name of God. Evangelical parents find it especially intolerable that commitments similar to oaths are taken from their children in their early years (appendix 23).

Already in the practice of pastoral care, cases are accumulating where persons declare that they did not feel bound by an oath, the refusal of which would have threatened their existence. The Evangelical Church would be more easily able to counteract in their members such a mentality that runs counter to Christian obligation if the Christian were permitted the understanding of an oath that he takes for granted, namely that no oath can cover actions contrary to God's Commandment. In fact it has come to pass that earnest Christians who were fully prepared to be obedient to authorities according to God's will were removed from their posts because they laid claim to that understanding for themselves (appendix 24). For many civil servants, an unconditionally truthful attitude is thereby made very difficult.

The weighting of the ballots in the last parliamentary [Reichstag] elections has placed many Christians in a severe conflict of conscience. It stems from placing above truthfulness whatever is useful to the nation. Evangelical Christians who, for the sake of truthfulness, confessed to their decisions [how to vote] have been ridiculed and abused (appendix 25).

Evangelical Christians are convinced, on the basis of Holy Scriptures, that God is the protector of justice and of those without rights; therefore, we regard it as turning away from Him if arbitrariness invades justice and if things happen "that are not right before the Lord." This includes not only many occurrences in the Church Struggle (appendix 26), but also what, in the final result, is denial of justice through the establishment and the behaviour of the Ecclesiastical Decree Office (appendix 27).[38] The Evangelical conscience that knows that it shares responsibility for the nation and the government is most severely burdened by the fact that, in Germany, which declares itself a state under the rule of law,[39] there are still concentration camps and that the actions of the Secret State Police[40] are exempt from any judicial review. Confessional-faithful Evangelical Christians, whose honour has been assailed often, have not and do not find the protection of their honour that is accorded to other citizens (appendix 26).

Evangelical Christianity sees in these matters, too, the danger that an anti-Christian spirit is coming to dominate in our moral-judicial thinking.

VII GOD'S REQUIREMENT

We have sought openly to justify the great concern, widespread in Evangelical circles, that authoritative forces in today's State are prosecuting a suppression of the Evangelical Church, a subversion[41] of its faith, an elimination of Evangelical morality, in short, a de-Christianization on the widest scale. We cannot allow references to contrasting utterances and facts to reassure us in this view of things that we have gained on the basis of careful observations. We beg the Reich Government to ask themselves whether in the long term our nation can benefit from the continued progression on the path hitherto taken. Already coercion of conscience, persecution of Evangelical conviction, mutual spying, and sounding-out are exercising a disastrous influence. Even a great cause, where it places itself in opposition to the revealed will of God, must in the end lead the nation to ruin. God's *Church* will exist, even if millions of Evangelical Christians lose their spiritual integrity.[42] But the German *nation* has no promise that the poison of an anti-Christian spirit shall not harm it, even if it comes to see, perhaps only after a long time, that it was robbed of its best legacy by those who took the Lord Christ away from it.

Our nation threatens to break the barriers set up by God: it wishes to make itself the measure of all things. That is human hubris, which rebels against God.

In this connection we must make known to the Führer and Reich Chancellor our concern that he often receives veneration in a form that is due only to God. Only a few years ago, the Führer himself disapproved of placing his picture on Evangelical altars. Today his judgment is taken ever more unrestrainedly as the standard not only for political decisions, but also for morality and justice in our nation, and he himself is being vested in the religious dignity of the national priest, even of the mediator between God and the nation (appendix 28).

What we have said to the Führer in this Memorandum we had to say under the responsibility of our office. The Church is in the hand of her Lord. But we ask for freedom for our nation to be allowed to go its way into the future under the sign of the Cross of Christ, so that the grandchildren will not one day curse the fathers for having built and left them a State on earth, but closed for them the Kingdom of God.

The clerical members of the Provisional Board of the German Evangelical Church, P. Müller, Dr Böhm, Pastor Forck, Lic.[43] Fricke Albertz

For the Council of the German Evangelical Church, Asmussen, P. Lücking, Pastor Middendorff, Pastor Niemöller, Dr von Thadden

NOTES

1 Kurt Dietrich Schmidt, ed., *Die Bekenntnisse und grundsätzlichen Äusserungen zur Kirchenfrage II: Das Jahr 1934* (Göttingen: Vandenhoeck & Ruprecht 1935), 87–98; Friedrich Keppler, ed., *Calwer Kirchenlexikon,* Erster Band (Stuttgart: Calwer Vereinsbuchhandlung 1937), 1073–5; Arthur C. Cochrane, *The Church's Confession under Hitler* (Philadelphia: The Westminster Press 1962) 206–7, 237–63.

2 Dietrich Bonhoeffer, *Ethik* (*Dietrich Bonhoeffer Werke,* vol. 6, 1992), 130; Dietrich Bonhoeffer, *Ethics* (London: William Clowes and Sons Ltd. 1955), 114; Dietrich Bonhoeffer, *Ethics* (*Dietrich Bonhoeffer Works,* vol. 6, 2005), 139; Cochrane, *The Church's Confession,* 206–7.

3 Vorläufige Leitung der Deutschen Evangelischen Kirche und Rat der Deutschen Evangelischen Kirche/Bekennende Kirche.

4 Martin Greschat, ed., *Zwischen Widerspruch und Widerstand. Texte zur Denkschrift der Bekennenden Kirche an Hitler (1936),* 100, 147.

5 Ibid., 148–9.

6 Bundesarchiv, Berlin-Lichterfelde, Persönliche Adjutantur des Führers und Reichskanzlers, NS 10/228 Bl. 24.

7   Ibid. A copy of Kötzschke's version, with appendices partially inserted, is in the files of the Reich Chancellery: Bundesarchiv, Berlin-Lichterfelde, Persönliche Adjutantur des Führers und Reichskanzlers, NS 10/228 Bl. 24–35.

8   Cochrane, *The Church's Confession*, 209–10; Eberhard Bethge, *Dietrich Bonhoeffer. Theologe, Christ, Zeitgenosse. Eine Biographie*, 602–9.

9   Kurt Dietrich Schmidt, ed., *Dokumente des Kirchenkampfes II. Die Zeit des Reichskirchenausschusses 1935–1937*, 695; Bundesarchiv, Berlin-Lichterfelde, Persönliche Adjutantur des Führers und Reichskanzlers, NS 10/228 Bl. 24.

10 Joseph Goebbels, *Die Tagebücher. Teil I*, Band 3/II (Munich: K.G. Saur 2001), 219, 375–9, 389; Band 4 (Munich: K.G. Saur 2000), 134; Band 5 (Munich: K.G. Saur 2000), 186, 382; Band 6 (1998), 205–6; Band 7 (1998), 158–60; Band 8 (1998), 324–7; Joseph Goebbels, *Die Tagebücher. Teil II. Diktate 1941–1945*, Band 1 (July–Sept. 1941) (Munich: K.G. Saur 1996), 232, 258, 504–5; Ian Kershaw, *Hitler. 1889–1936: Hubris* (London: Allen Lane The Penguin Press 1998), 575; Ian Kershaw, *Hitler. 1936–1945: Nemesis* (London: Allen Lane The Penguin Press 2000), 39–41. (Kershaw does not refer to the memorandum.)

11 Gerhard Schäfer, *Die Evangelische Landeskirche in Württemberg und der Nationalsozialismus. Eine Dokumentation zum Kirchenkampf*, Band 4 (Stuttgart: Calwer Verlag 1977), 853.

12 Brüderrat.

13 Greschat, *Zwischen Widerspruch*, 201–29; Cochrane, *The Church's Confession*, 209.

14 Gerhard Schäfer, *Die Evangelische Landeskirche*, Band 4, 852–3; Wurm to Reichskirchenministerium 22 August 1936, carbon copy, Landeskirchliches Archiv, Stuttgart, A 126/403.

15 Tag der Kirche.

16 Bishop Wurm's statement was published in *Beiblatt zum württembergischen Amtsblatt* 27 (28), and in *Allgemeine Evangelisch-Lutherische Kirchenzeitung* 69 (1936): col. 877 et seq.; Schäfer, *Die Evangelische Landeskirche*, vol. 4, 864–73; Greschat, *Zwischen Widerspruch*, 225–7.

17 Dietrich Bonhoeffer, *The Cost of Discipleship*, 2nd edition, trans. R.H. Fuller and Irmgard Booth (New York 1959), 117.

18 Source: The copy handed in to the Reich Presidential Chancellery, in Bundesarchiv, Berlin-Lichterfelde, Persönliche Adjutantur des Führers, NS-10/228 Bl. 24–36; its text is identical with that in Kurt Dietrich Schmidt, ed., *Die Bekenntnisse und grundsätzlichen Äusserungen zur Kirchenfrage II: Das Jahr 1934* (Göttingen: Vandenhoeck & Ruprecht 1935), 695–724, including all 28 appendices. The copy given to Pastor Birger Forell of the Swedish Legation in Berlin in June 1936 is also the version printed in *Dokumente des Kirchenkampfes II*. The Memorandum was published in short excerpts in English in *The Morning Post* (17 July 1936), 13, and "in full" in German in *Basler Nachrichten*, 2nd supplement to no. 200 (23 July 1936), based upon the copy Ernst Tillich had made overnight, presumably at some time between 4 June and 17 July 1936; it appeared in full in English in the *New York Herald Tribune* (28 July 1936). Cf. Wilhelm Niemöller, *Die Bekennende Kirche sagt Hitler die Wahrheit*

(Bielefeld: L. Bechauf 1954). The translation in Cochrane, *The Church's Confession*, 268–79, appears to be based on W. Niemöller's edition, with its variations from the original, and has additional errors. The secondary literature includes John S. Conway, *The Nazi Persecution of the Churches, 1933–45;* Ernst Christian Helmreich, *The German Churches under Hitler*; Peter Matheson, ed., *The Third Reich and the Christian Churches*; Klaus Scholder, *The Churches and the Third Reich,* 2 vols.

19 "Parish" is here the translation of "Gemeinde"; "Gemeinde," in the religious context, is more accurately translated as "parish" than as "community," which can mean "congregation," but then leaves out those not attending service at a given time, and which also means a municipality.

20 Translation of "Glaubenskampf," literally "combat of faith," distinct from "Kirchenkampf" or "church struggle."

21 Nationalsozialistische Deutsche Arbeiterpartei: National Socialist German Workers' Party.

22 Excerpt from the appendix: "Reich Minister Dr Goebbels on 2 March 1934 in Hamburg (*Chronik der Kirchenwirren*, 150): 'If the churches were animated by a true Christian spirit, they would never have left it to the State this winter to help the poor overcome hunger and cold […] I believe that Christ himself would discover in our activities more of his teachings than in this theological hairsplitting.'"

23 Reichsschulungsleiter.

24 Excerpt from appendix 5: "Letter from 11th SA Brigade of the NSDAP in Schwerin/Mecklbg to the Provisional Board of the German Evangelical Church, of 4 February 1936, no. 445/36: 'No positive Christian will be dismissed from the SA, but the negative Christians who through their adherence to mediaeval dogmas stand opposed to National Socialism cannot be members of the combat organization of a Movement that aims at realizing the divinely ordained order in their nation […] The negative Christian fights for the Church, to the detriment of the nation, for its dogmas and to uphold priests' lies, and with that, for the devil […] To be an SA man and to belong to the Confessing Front is a contradiction in itself […] If we as positive Christians do not think so badly of our fellow-humans, we nevertheless secure ourselves against the intrusion of vigilantes, spies, and elements of decomposition.'"

25 Reichsschulungsleiter.

26 Excerpt from appendix 6: "Reich Minister Kerrl, on 15 October 1935, before representatives of the press (*Junge Kirche*, 1021): 'If by now in the last two years' confusions [i.e. formation of the Pastors' Emergency League, the Confessing Church, the Church Struggle] have occurred within the Evangelical Church, they were caused, if at all, by individuals. Never by the Party as such, never by the State as such … [ellipsis in original].' Goebbels: 'If we preach the unity of the Protestant Church we do so because we consider it impossible at a time when the entire Reich unites that there continue to exist twenty-eight land churches. With this, we do not want to instigate any dogmas. We also do not meddle in the exegesis of the Gospels; we are not sensing within us any Reformational ambitions. […] In the exegesis of the Gospels one may place God's command higher than the command of human

agencies. In the interpretation of political expediency we regard ourselves as the instrument of God ... [ellipsis in original].' Adolf Hitler, in his Proclamation of the Führer, read on 11 September 1935, in Nürnberg (*Völkischer Beobachter* 12 September 1935): 'The Party did not formerly nor does it today intend in Germany to prosecute any struggle against Christianity. On the contrary, it has attempted to create a great Evangelical Reich Church through combining impossible Protestant land churches, without in the slightest degree meddling in confessional issues ... [ellipses in original].'"

27 "The main interferences by State and Party.

A.   Vis-à-vis the Church as a whole.

1   Installation of the State Commissar in Prussia on 24 June 1933, and of the State Commissars in Bremen, Hesse, Lippe, Mecklenburg, Saxony.

2   Order to hold general church elections by the Reich law of 15 July 1933 [*Reichsgesetzblatt Teil 1 Jahrgang 1933*. Herausgegeben vom Reichsministerium des Innern (Berlin: Reichsverlagsamt 1933, henceforth *RGBl.* 1 1933), 471; the elections were ordered to be held on 23 July 1933].

3   Radio speech by the Führer, on 22 July 1933, in favour of the German Christians [Deutsche Christen was the name of those in the Protestant churches in Germany who were adapting Christian doctrine to the National Socialist ideology].

4   Unpublished decree of the Reich Minister of the Interior of 6 and 7 November 1934, forbidding publications about Church affairs.

5   Installation of the State Finance Department by the Prussian law of 11 March 1935.

6   Establishment of the Decisions Agency ('Beschlußstelle in Rechtsangelegenheiten der Evangelischen Kirche.' 'Diese wird beim Reichsministerium des Innern gebildet.') by the Reich law of 26 June 1935 ('Gesetz über das Beschlussverfahren in Rechtsangelegenheiten der Evangelischen Kirche. Vom 26. Juni 1935,' *RGBl.* 1 1935 ([Reichsverlagsamt, Berlin 1935], 774).

7   The law of 24 September 1935 to secure the German Evangelical Church, and the implementation ordinances. 'Gesetz zur Sicherung der Deutschen Evangelischen Kirche. Vom 24. September 1935,' *RGBl.* 1 1935, 1178; this 'law' declared: 'Nach dem Willen des evangelischen Kirchenvolkes ist der Zusammenschluss der Landeskirchen in einer Deutschen Evangelischen Kirche vollzogen und in einer Verfassung verbrieft.' Es sei aber Kampf kirchlicher Gruppen untereinander und gegeneinander und die Reichsregierung sei tief besorgt, habe daher 'zur Sicherung des Bestandes der Deutschen Evangelischen Kirche' als Treuhänder der Kirche folgendes Gesetz erlassen mit diesem einzigen Paragraphen: 'Der Reichsminister für die krichlichen Angelegenheiten wird zur Wiederherstellung geordneter Zustände in der Deutschen Evangelischen Kirche und in den evangelischen Landeskirchen ermächtigt, Verordnungen mit rechtsverbindlicher Kraft zu erlassen. Die Verordnungen werden im Reichsgesetzblatt verkündet.'

B.   Vis-à-vis individual clergymen.

1   Arrest of the land bishops of Württemberg and Bavaria 1934.

2 Transportation of clergymen into concentration camps, particularly in Saxony and Nassau-Hesse.

3 Expulsion of clergymen from their parishes, some even from their home provinces, particularly in Prussia.

4 Arrest of over 500 pastors in Prussia on the occasion of the reading-from-the-pulpit ordered by the Old Prussian Synod, in March 1935, of the Proclamation against New Paganism.

5 Obstruction of Confessing-Church services, e.g. on 4 March 1934 in Dresden."

28 Telegram of the Reich Chancellor to the Reich President on 12 July 1933.

29 *RGBl.* l 1935, 1178.

30 Baldur von Schirach.

31 Ludwig Müller.

32 "[...] From a posting of HJ [Hitler Jugend = Hitler Youth] in Halle-Saale, Horde 17/216, at main entrance to the University clinics, end of 1935: 'Where are the enemies of our HJ? The religious fanatic who even today with longing, upward-turned gaze slides about on his knees, spends his time with visits to churches and prayers [...] We as Hitler Youths can only full of contempt or derision look upon the young people who today still are running to their ridiculous Evangelical or Catholic clubs in order to devote themselves to the most superfluous religious sentimentalities ... [ellipsis in original].' [...] Baldur von Schirach on 5 November 1934, on the occasion of a press course of the HJ press: '[...] Rosenberg's way also be the way German youth [...].' Superior-Region order 8/35 of Superior Region of BDM [Bund Deutscher Mädel = Federation of German Girls, the NSDAP female-youth organization], dated 5 December 1935: 'From this present date l forbid not only all girl-leaders but also all girls to assist in any form of confessional work (helper in Sunday schools etc.).'"

33 "Letter from Regional Governor in Breslau, of 22 October 1935, U 17/201: '... [ellipsis in original] In reply to your letter of 15 October to camp leader Schädel concerning the sending of religious literature l inform you of what the Reich and Prussian Minister for Science, Education, and National Education has emphasized in a decree, that sending religious literature to those serving the Year on the Land is forbidden.'"

34 German: Weltanschauung.

35 "Dr Ley in Passau on 22 July 1935 (*Deutsche Allgemeine Zeitung* vom ... [ellipsis in original] Nr. 337): 'The Party claims the totality of the soul of the German nation. It can and will not tolerate that another party or world view dominate in Germany. We just do believe that only through National Socialism can the German nation become eternal [...] And therefore we require every last German, whether Protestant or Catholic, that is the same to us ... [ellipsis in original]'"

36 Deuteronomy 5:11 = 5th Moses 5:17: "You shall not take the name of the Lord your God in vain." Deuteronomy 5:6–7: "I am the Lord your God, who brought you out of the land of Egypt, out of the house of bondage. You shall have no other gods before me."

37 Reichsamtsleiter.

38 The Ecclesiastical Decree Office was established by a Reich law of 24 June 1935; *RGBl.* I 1935, 774. It replaced judicial process in ecclesiastical disputes with a political-decision procedure. The Office had been in existence for a year, had seventy cases before it, and had not decided a single one of them.

39 Rechtsstaat.

40 Geheime Staatspolizei, Gestapo for short.

41 Translation here of "Zersetzung."

42 Translation of "Heil," also translatable as "health," or "salvation"; but it cannot be assumed that the signers of the Memorandum believed they knew the course of God's grace.

43 Clerical rank licentiate.

10

Dietrich Bonhoeffer's Decision against Emigration, June 1939

In June 1939, Dietrich Bonhoeffer accepted an invitation from Union Theological Seminary in New York. He was also invited, upon his arrival in New York in June 1939, to work with Christian German refugees in New York. Had he accepted this second invitation, it would have made impossible his return to Germany while the National Socialists were in power. When war became likely in the summer of 1939, Bonhoeffer decided to return to Germany rather than stay in exile in America. He stated his reasons in a letter to his friend Reinhold Niebuhr; in letters of 28 and 30 June 1939 to another friend, Paul Lehmann; and on 1 July 1939 to his parents.[1]

1

Paul Lehmann wrote to Reinhold Niebuhr on 31 July 1939[2] that Bonhoeffer had arrived in New York about the tenth of June, and that, before he had left Germany, he had pledged himself to return if war seemed imminent; after only a week in New York, he decided to return at once, reasoning "that one month of work before the hostilities would be of strategic importance for the confessional church." Lehmann's letter continues:

Now there are three other factors that play into this decision. The first is that Bonhoeffer had no definite job over here. The post that Leiper[3] offered him with the Refugee Committee could not be accepted without excluding himself permanently from Germany, which he was pledged not to do. On the other hand, if he had a definite teaching post, he would have regarded that as a prior obligation and not returned immediately. Occasional lectures seemed to him too dangerous in view of the imminence of war, which would certainly prohibit these opportunities to aliens. The second consideration was the discovery, during the short time that he was here, that he could not hope to make any contribution to the German future, if it were given him to survive, unless he suffered through this present time. This had not been quite so clear to him before his trip. But from the isolation of Coffin's[4] summer home he had looked across the seas and become convinced that voluntary exile was the path to permanent inactivity. Here was an additional ground for not endangering his return by accepting Leiper's offer. And of course, the third factor in his decision was the growing feeling that to remain here would have reduced itself to a violation of the gospel injunction that he that loseth his life shall save it.[5] On this point he could not bring his conscience to rest and in the face of the next few critical weeks, he simply had to return.

2

Hellmut Traub succeeded Bonhoeffer as a teacher at the underground Preachers' Seminary at Finkenwalde. When the Gestapo closed it, the seminary moved to a farm called Sigurdshof, near Schlawe in Pomerania. In his recollections, Traub writes of his satisfaction, in the early summer of 1939, that Bonhoeffer was safe in America, would survive the coming catastrophe, and would be there to rebuild the church after the war. The following quotation describes what followed:[6]

And then one day, after a short message that he was returning, Bonhoeffer stood before us. This was quite unexpected – indeed, there was always something extraordinary about him, even when the circumstances were quite ordinary. I was immediately up in arms, blurting out how could he come back after it had cost so much trouble to get him into safety – safety for us [sic], for our cause; here everything was lost anyway. He very calmly lit a cigarette. Then he said that he had made a mistake in going to America. He did not himself understand now why he had done it. His later messages from prison tell us that he never repented having returned from America. It is this fact – that he abandoned in all clarity many great possibilities for his own development in the free countries, that he returned to dismal slavery and a dark future, but also to his own reality – which gave to everything he told us then a strong and joyful firmness, such as only arises out of realized freedom. He knew he had taken a clear step, though the actualities before him were still quite unclear. He gave us two reasons for his return. First, simply his thought of the Confessing Church, which meant for him all the many young brethren, had not given him any rest. He could not stay away from them, he must not leave them. This meant – and this was the second reason – that he could not watch Germany's fate from outside and have no part in it. The idea of taking an active part in reconstruction later, after the war, was out of the question for him unless he shared in the affliction that was coming over Germany, unless he took a real part, and genuinely shared in its trials. Without this, any help, even in the best possible case, would only be help from outside. Only he could help, he said, who would bear what was coming and see it through. I objected, saying did he not realize that all was lost; that whatever happened, hardly one of us would survive? Yes, he saw that in precisely the same way; but for that reason – and this was Bonhoeffer's real answer – each of us had become quite clear about the fact that he was facing a decision: if he wanted Germany's victory he also wanted the end of its freedom and of Christianity in it. The possibility of freedom for Germany and of Christianity in Germany was only given in its defeat. A victory would destroy the real future. It impressed me greatly that to the goods of freedom and Christianity he added those of education and civilization. And then he named his second reason for coming back, the decisive one, speaking calmly, smoking his cigarette, as if he was not saying anything special: I know what I have chosen.

3

Willem Visser 'tHooft heard from Bonhoeffer the same statement about his view that he must wish Germany's defeat in the war. On an evening with Swiss friends in September 1941:[7] "One of us asked Bonhoeffer: 'What do you pray for in the present situation?' He answered without hesitation: 'Since you ask me, I must say that I pray for the defeat of my country, for I believe that this is the only way in which it can pay for the suffering that it has caused in the world.' That crystal clear answer characterized the man. Truth was to be served without reservation whatever the cost."

In a brief memoir entitled "An Act of Penitance," Visser 'tHooft quoted Bonhoeffer (1942): "'Only in defeat can we atone for the terrible crimes we have committed against Europe and the world.'"[8]

4

NIEBUHR'S QUOTATION FROM BONHOEFFER'S LETTER[9]

Sitting here in Dr Coffin's garden I have had the time to think and to pray about my situation and that of my nation and to have God's will for me clarified. I have come to the conclusion that I have made a mistake in coming to America. I must live through this difficult period of our national history with the Christian people of Germany. I will have no right to participate in the reconstruction of Christian life in Germany after the war if I do not share the trials of this time with my people. My brothers in the Confessional Synod wanted me to go. They may have been right in urging me to do so; but I was wrong in going. Such a decision each man must make for himself. Christians in Germany will face the terrible alternative of either willing the defeat of their nation in order that Christian civilization may survive, or willing the victory of their nation and thereby destroying our civilization. I know which of these alternatives I must choose; but I cannot make that choice in security.

NOTES

1 Source: Reinhold Niebuhr, "The Death of a Martyr." Niebuhr paraphrased the contents of the letter in an article on Bonhoeffer in 1945, indicating that the letter had been written in July 1939. Niebuhr introduced his paraphrase with these words: "He wrote somewhat to this effect." In the relevant source reference, the editors of Bonhoeffer's *Gesammelte Schriften* and of the new edition of Bonhoeffer's works in sixteen volumes, *Dietrich Bonhoeffer Werke*, reproduce the paraphrase as a quotation without identifying it as a paraphrase from memory, in fact saying that it was Niebuhr's quotation from the letter: "Original Brief bisher nicht gefunden. Dieses Stück von Niebuhr zitiert in 'The Death of a Martyr,' *Christianity and Crisis*, nr. 11,

vom 25 (Juni 1945), S. 6"; Bonhoeffer to Lehmann, 28 June 1939, *Dietrich Bonhoeffer Werke*, Fünfzehnter Band (Gütersloh: Chr. Kaiser Verlag 1998) 206, 208–10; Dietrich Bonhoeffer, *Gesammelte Schriften*, vol. 1, 320; Theodore S. Hamerow, *On the Road to the Wolf's Lair. German Resistance to Hitler* (Cambridge, Massachusetts: The Belknap Press of Harvard University Press 1997), 263–4 states: "The authenticity of this letter may be questioned, since the original has not been found. Perhaps it expresses therefore not what Bonhoeffer actually said but what he might have said or could have said or should have said." Not only is the absurdity of the charge of forgery against Eberhard Bethge, the editor of an early edition of Bonhoeffer's works, plain enough; in order to substantiate it, Hamerow would have had to show how Paul Lehmann had been conscripted into the alleged conspiracy to forge the letter, and how Hellmut Traub (of whom he does not seem to be aware) as well had become a part of it. By his outrageous charge, Hamerow demonstrates his failure to adequately research the events. Larry L. Rasmussen, *Dietrich Bonhoeffer. Reality and Resistance* (Nashville: Abingdon Press 1972), 60, note 132, confirms that the letter is not extant, that Niebuhr's recollection is not exact, and that the sense of the quotation is accurate. The literature on Dietrich Bonhoeffer is vast; the best work in one volume is Eberhard Bethge's biography: *Dietrich Bonhoeffer. A Biography.*

2 The letter was written in English; source: Dietrich Bonhoeffer, *Dietrich Bonhoeffer Works*, vol. 15, part 1, document no. 151 (publication scheduled 2011; I thank Victoria Barnett, General Editor, for permission to quote this).

3 Henry Smith Leiper, Ecumenical Secretary of the Federal Council of Churches.

4 Dr Henry Sloan Coffin, Professor of Practical Theology at and President of Union Theological Seminary in New York.

5 Matthew 10:39.

6 Source: Hellmut Traub, "Two Recollections," in Wolf-Dieter Zimmermann and Ronald Gregor Smith, eds., *I Knew Dietrich Bonhoeffer*, trans. from the German by Käthe Gregor Smith (New York: Harper & Row c. 1966), 156–61, esp. 159–60.

7 Source: W.A. Visser 'tHooft, *Memoirs* (London: SCM Press; Philadelphia: The Westminster Press 1973), 153.

8 Source: Visser 'tHooft, "An Act of Penitance," in Zimmermann and Smith, *I Knew Dietrich Bonhoeffer*, 194.

9 Source: Niebuhr, "The Death of a Martyr," 6–7.

11

Father Alfred Delp SJ's Motivations to Oppose Hitler

Father Alfred Delp (15 September 1907–2 February 1945) was born to a Catholic mother in Mannheim and baptised by a Catholic priest two days after his birth. He grew up in Hüttenfeld and Lampertheim, in Hesse, where Catholics were a working-class minority and where there were separate Catholic and Lutheran schools. Alfred, his two brothers, three sisters, and their mother, Maria née Bernauer, attended Catholic Church on Sundays. Alfred's father, Johann Adam Friedrich Delp, a merchant, was a descendant of Lutheran theologians and Church administrators in the Lutheran Duchy of Hesse. While Alfred's father served in the armed forces during the First World War, and until 1920 and afterwards, a Catholic priest – Johannes Unger – gave the children fatherly attention. Johann Delp had promised his wife that the children would be brought up as Catholics, but in 1915 he decided that they must attend the Lutheran primary school.

On 29 March 1921, Easter Monday, Alfred was confirmed in the Lutheran Confession. Once, during the time of catechetical instruction, Alfred was late and gave as a reason that he had been to see the Catholic priest (Johannes Unger). The Lutheran minister slapped him. Alfred was hurt and turned his back upon Lutheranism. He took Catholic catechetical instruction, received his first Holy Communion on 19 June 1921, and was confirmed in the Catholic Confession on 28 June 1921, by Bishop Ludwig Maria Hugo of Mainz. In retrospect, Alfred Delp described these events with the phrase "when I came to the Catholic Church." Although lexica refer to this as Delp's "conversion," it was nothing of the sort; it was a "reversion." The events reflect a difficult confessional and family situation – and Alfred's strength of character, pride, and even wilfulness.

From then on, his education was intensely Catholic. He rapidly learned Latin and Greek, as well as Hebrew and French, and was a brilliant pupil in the classical secondary school (Gymnasium) at Dieburg.[1] He graduated from the Gymnasium on 16 March 1926 with very good marks. Father Unger secured him a place in the Collegium Germanicum in Rome, but Alfred decided to enter the Jesuit Order (Societas Jesu).[2]

The 14 September 1930 national elections in Germany, in which the National Socialist German Workers' Party (NSDAP, "Nazi" Party) achieved its breakthrough, fell into the time of Delp's training in the Jesuit Order and of his studies in philosophy and theology. He wrote to his brother Ewald on 4 September: "On 14 September, do your voting duty well. If the Christian parties will not grow in these years, you can, in a few years, visit your brother in his banishment. If certain orientations receive the majority, we shall be the first to get knived."[3] In Munich, on 24 June 1937, the four hundredth anniversary of the ordination of Ignatius Loyola, Archbishop Michael Cardinal Faulhaber ordained Alfred Delp a priest at St Michael's Church.[4] Delp worked on the respected Catholic periodical *Stimmen der Zeit* until it was forced to cease publication in April 1941, and became rector of St Georg church in the Bogenhausen borough in Munich.

During the war, beginning in 1942, Delp participated in Helmuth James von Moltke's meetings at Moltke's Kreisau estate in Silesia and in Berlin to discuss and prepare principles upon which to base a post-Hitler renewal of German society.[5] Delp's activities and fate in the context of the conspiracy occurred, then, within the complex usually referred to as the Kreisau Circle.[6] As a Jesuit priest and pastor who opposed Hitler and National Socialism, Delp acted in ways contrary to those demanded by the regime in many other regards. In September 1941, after Nazi authorities had removed crucifixes from classrooms in schools in the Bogenhausen borough of Munich, Delp encouraged mothers and pupils to put up new ones and blessed these crucifixes. The Archbishop of Munich, Michael Cardinal von Faulhaber, did not support these protests and advised "caution."[7]

Delp preached a sermon against "euthanasia" on the day after All Saints, 1941.[8] Delp was engaged in helping Jews wherever he was able to, providing ration cards, money, shelter, hiding places, and scouting out escape routes. He was able to assist at least a dozen Jews directly, a small number compared to the Nazi mass murder, but he risked his life for such proscribed activities, which could have been punished by a Special Court[9] under the Insidiousness Law.[10]

A public statement condemning the persecution of the Jews and others no doubt would have brought posthumous honour to him or her who had made it, but it would most likely have been ineffectual in the prevailing circumstances.[11] The alternative was subversion of the government and an attempt to remove it. Dietrich Bonhoeffer, too, chose this course of action. In November 1941 Delp preached, on the occasion of the feast of St Elisabeth[12] and while trains carrying deported Jews from Germany were rolling eastward, about the expelled and abandoned, expressly deploring all destruction of life: "Woe to him from whom the creature has suffered! And woe to him by whom a human was destroyed, by whom an image of God was defiled, even if it was in its last agony and even if it was merely a reminiscence of humanity!"[13]

In the aftermath of 20 July 1944, around 700 of those more or less connected with the uprising were arrested, including most of the Kreisau Group, to which Delp belonged.[14] Delp was arrested on 28 July 1944, held without charge in Munich, and soon transferred to Berlin, where he was interrogated and tortured in the Prince-Albrecht-Strasse Gestapo prison.[15] He was not charged until December 1944, nor had he any opportunity to speak with an attorney until that time. He was "tried," together with Helmuth James von Moltke and others, in the People's Court,[16] and sentenced on 11 January 1945.[17] The prosecution failed to prove its charges of treason and participation in the 20 July 1944 conspiracy, but the president of the court, Dr Roland Freisler, sentenced Delp to death as a Jesuit and as a Christian and because Delp admitted that he had wanted to change National Socialist Germany back to a nation guided by Christian principles.[18]

The document that follows is a letter Delp wrote to his most trusted friends and a fellow Jesuit. It was written with shackled hands, two days after Delp had been sentenced to be hanged.[19] Together with others of the "Kreisau Circle," he was held in Tegel Prison, with his hands in irons most of the time, even during air raids; a guard allowed him occasional times without shackles so that he could celebrate mass secretly on Christmas and 6 January with his hands free.[20] He expected to be executed on the day he was sentenced or soon afterward, and wrote the letter as a last message. He was, in fact, hanged twenty days later, on 2 February 1945, and wrote at least thirty-six more letters.[21] The letters were smuggled out of Tegel Prison by Marianne Hapig and by chaplains, including Harald Poelchau, then taken to Munich by Dr Fritz Valjavec, a professor at the University of Berlin and a friend of Delp's; Valkjavec's teaching engagements involved weekly trips from Berlin to Munich so that he was able to serve as messenger.[22]

The letter translated below represents most fundamentally and powerfully Delp's reactions to the trial and sentence, to the theory and practice of Hitler's National Socialism, and to the prospect of his own violent death and its meaning. Delp's personal style and his character express themselves in the honesty and sincerity of his thoughts and also in the syntax, choice of words, irony and sarcasm, and a liking for alliterative pairs of words.[23] The handwriting of "Nach der Verurteilung" is even, controlled. Spaces between lines and slight changes in the heaviness of the ink show that the letter was written in stages, although within one day. There is no visible indication that Delp wrote the letter with shackled hands. He refers to the time "in the cellar" (of the Gestapo Headquarters on Prinz-Albrecht-Strasse or, perhaps, in the Lehrter Strasse Prison in Berlin) with fettered hands, as distinct from the time of writing. Nevertheless, the evidence cited above is conclusive that the letter was written with shackled hands. There is no underlining in ink by Delp, except the underlined title "Nach der Verurteilung" on the first (outside) page, and curved lines under the paginations. All other underlining is in pencil, presumably by P. Roman Bleistein sj, Delp's biographer and editor of his writings.

Father Alfred Delp's Letter of 13 January 1945 to his friends in the Jesuit Order

AFTER SENTENCING[24]

This is a peculiar life now. One gets so quickly again used to existing, and one must, now and then, forcibly recall to consciousness the death sentence. That is really the special thing about this death, that the will to live is unbroken, and every nerve is alive until the hostile force overwhelms everything. So that the ordinary signs and harbingers of death fail to appear here. One day the door will simply open and the good guard will say: "Pack up, the car is coming in half an hour." As we have so often heard and witnessed it.

Actually we had expected to be driven immediately to Plötzensee[25] on Thursday evening. We are apparently the first for whom grace periods are again observed. Or was this [delay] already due to the clemency pleas? I do not believe so: Frank also came back yesterday, although no plea had yet been filed for him.[26] That Frank would also be condemned, nobody would have thought. But there everything is subjectivity, not even official, but entirely personal subjectivity. The man[27] is clever, nervous, vain, and arrogant. He is play-acting, and the opposing player must be defeated. Where this already happens in the dialogue, as with Reisert,[28] who whined a bit much,[29] the superiority of the Gracious One[30] is manifest and effective.

I felt really quite uninvolved in the whole matter. It was like a bad Pullach disputation,[31] only the defendant constantly changed, and the permanent objicient[32] simultaneously decided who was right. The co-judges, the "people" at the People's Court, were ordinary, officious-looking, average faces who felt very solemn in their blue suits and very important next to the red robe of the Honourable Presiding Judge. Good, honest men,[33] who exercise the function of the people[34] to say yes.[35]

It is all there, nothing is missing: solemn entrance, large contingent of police, each of us has two men beside him; behind us[36] the "public": mostly Secret State Police,[37] etc. The faces of the cops[38] good-natured-familiar-ordinary. The "public," on average, is the type of the "one" Germany. The "other" Germany is not represented or is being condemned to death. Actually an overture was missing at the beginning and a finale at the end, or at least fanfares.

The trial itself was arranged cleverly and ingeniously. So ingeniously, that no one could get a hearing for anything that exculpated another or was of advantage to himself. Only that and exactly that was asked and admitted in testimony, which, according to the current hypothesis, sufficed for sentencing.

Our trial was arranged for Moltke's and my own destruction. All else was scenery and supernumeraries.[39] Whether Sperr was also going to fall remained open to the end in spite of the facts. When the proceedings opened with me, I sensed with the first question the intent to destroy me. The questions were nicely organized, prepared on a slip of paper. Woe, if the answers turned out differently than expected. Then it was Scholasticism and Jesuitism. At any rate, a Jesuit commits a crime with each breath he draws. And he can say and prove and do what he will: he is just a villain, and he will be believed on nothing, nothing at all. Gerstenmaier's situation[40] is factually much worse than mine: as a Protestant minister, of whom a usefulness[41] in the near future[42] is expected, as he himself told me, he is declared a "dim theoretician," and then everything is overlooked: Goerdeler, the 20th of July, Moltke, Kreisau, everything.[43] I am not saying anything against Gerstenmaier with this. He is a fine, deeply believing person whom I sincerely do not begrudge his life and who will yet do many good things. But thus the scenery[44] was put in place, and then that is "justice." O German people, in whose name at the end the sentence was pronounced!

The slanders levelled against the Church, the Order, church-historical traditions, etc., were terrible. I actually had to restrain myself in order not to burst out. But then that would have spoiled the atmosphere for everyone. This glorious opportunity for the Great Actor to declare the opponent a clever, outstanding, cunning person, and then to show himself so infinitely superior. It was all ready and done when he began. I strongly advise all of my confreres against going there. There one is not a human being, but an "object." And everything with an inflationary, wear-and-tear of legal forms and phrases. Shortly before this I read in Plato: This is the supreme injustice, one that transacts itself in the form of the law.

Our real offence and crime is our heresy against the dogma that NSDAP,[45] the Third Reich, the German People will live equally long. The three will die together. One will some day have to remind Herr Freisler how good it would have been if someone had carried out Moltke's post-war plans and defence plans. And how many of the men whom he had condemned were being missed.[46]

He who dares to doubt this NS[47] trinity, or rather triple unity, is a heretic, and the earlier heresy trials are child's play, compared to the cunning and lethal precision of these current ones.

With Moltke, too, everything would have gone better if he were not "religiously committed," if he had not been proven to have "re-Christianization intentions," if he had not had contacts with bishops and Jesuits. Oh, what fools we were to prepare ourselves for the proceedings in a businesslike manner. It was not at all about that. This is not a court of law, but a[48] function. An unambiguous echo and nothing else. How a man might wish to do this every day, I do not understand.

So, Thursday evening was the final session. Everything again in the same manner. Like handing out prizes in a small school that did not even have a proper room for the purpose. And afterward, Moltke and I thought we would go to Plötzensee.[49] But we are still in Tegel.

Even at the sentencing, I was inwardly as unconcerned as in the entire two days. I have had with me the Host[50] during these two days, and celebrated [Mass] before[51] the drive to the sentencing, and enjoyed as my last meal the Meal [Communion]. That is how I wanted to be prepared, but I am still in waiting.

Until now the Lord God has gloriously and sincerely helped me. I have not yet been frightened or broken down. The hour of the creature will surely strike. Sometimes a melancholy comes over me when I think of what I still wanted to do. For only now have I become a human being, inwardly free and much more genuine and truthful, more real than before. Only now has the eye the plastic vision for all dimensions and the wholesomeness for all perspectives. The diminishments and curtailments redress themselves. Yes, and then the people who remain behind.

Yes, and quite honestly said, I do not yet believe in the gallows. I do not know what that is. Perhaps it is a great favour and help of the fatherly God, who thus lets me endure the desert without having to die of thirst in it. During the entire proceedings, even when I realized that the "miracle" would not come, I was quite high above it and untouchable through all of the proceedings and prospects. Is this the miracle, or what is this? With respect to God, I am really in some predicament and must become clear about it.

All these bitter months of maturation and of misfortune stand under a quite peculiar law. From the first minute, I was inwardly certain it all would go well. God has confirmed me again and again in this certainty. I have in these last days doubted and thought about whether I had fallen victim to self-delusions, whether my will to live had sublimated itself in religious imaginations or what this was. But these many sensible elevations in the midst of misery, this certainty and imperviousness in all blows, this certain "obstinacy" that always lets me know, they will not succeed in destroying me; these consolations in prayer and in the sacrifice,[52] these hours of grace before the tabernacle, these prayed-for and again and again-given and granted signs: I do not know whether I may now put all that away. Shall I continue to hope? Does the Lord God want this sacrifice, which I do not want to refuse Him, or does He want to keep putting my faith and confidence to the test up to the utmost point of what is possible? When I was driven to the first interrogation in Berlin, the vision of the undetonated Ignatius-House bomb[53] swam into my consciousness, and I heard simply indisputably the words: it will not explode. Then I have waited for the fulfillment hour after hour, day after day, week after week. At first I believed in the elegant solution through cleverness and ability. But it was soon over with that.

And this is the second law under which these weeks stand: everything that I undertook to help myself has gone wrong. Yes, not only wrong, it was actually always for harm. So also now at the trial. The change of lawyer, which appeared so good at first, was not good.

When the man sensed the anti-Jesuit complex, he told me still during the trial: he was, in fact, also against Jesuitism. That someone sent Freisler the booklet[54] has only caused him to take me for clever and all the more dangerous. The things we had prepared for our defence were reinterpreted as new incriminations against us. The whole external course of events was failure and shipwreck and powerlessness upon powerlessness. And in between, the quite peculiar sort of our misfortune: that we remained in Tegel, that we are still alive today, although we had prepared ourselves for Thursday, etc.

What does the Lord God want with all of that? Is it education to full freedom and full devotion? Does he want the whole chalice to the last drop, and are these hours of waiting and of a peculiar Advent part of it? Or does he want the test of faith?

What shall I do now without becoming unfaithful? Shall I continue to hope in spite of hopelessness? Is it unfaithfulness if I desist? Shall I quite abandon myself and perform the farewells and quite focus upon the gallows? Is it cowardice or inertia not to do so and still to hope? Shall I simply remain on call and in readiness in the freedom [of God]? I do not yet rightly know the way, and I pray constantly for enlightenment and guidance. To this end, Urbi's accepted sacrifice, exactly seven months ago today? Oh, that one still must conduct trials in one's own heart! But they should be conducted with honesty, with the Holy Ghost presiding.

When I compare the quiet and detachment during the days of the trial and at sentencing with the fear that I sometimes had during the air raids in Munich, then much is quite different. But again the question: was this becoming-changed the purpose, the aim of this education, or is this inner elevation and help the miracle?

I do not know. Normally there is no more chance left. The atmosphere here is so spoiled for me that a plea for clemency also has no chance at all. Is it now foolishness to still hope, or illusion, or cowardice, or grace? I often sit there in front of the Lord and only look at Him inquiringly.

In any case, I must properly release myself inwardly and give myself up. It is the time for sowing, not for reaping. God sows; one day He will again reap. For one thing I will strive: at least to fall into the soil as a fruitful and healthy seed. And into the Lord God's hand. And to defend myself against the pain and the melancholy that sometimes want to assault me. If the Lord God wants this path – and all that can be seen points there – then I must go it voluntarily and without bitterness. Others shall one day live better and happier because we died.

I also ask the friends not to mourn, but to pray for me and to help me as long as I am in need of help. And afterwards, to rest assured that I was sacrificed, not slain. I had not thought that this could be my path. All my sails wanted to stand stiffly before the wind; my ship wanted a great putting-out to sea, the flags and pennants were to remain hoisted proud and high in all storms. But perhaps it would have been the wrong flags or the wrong direction, or the wrong freight for the ship and counterfeit booty. I do not know. I also do not want to comfort myself with a cheap belittling of earthly things and of life. Honestly and sincerely: I would like to go on living and now more than ever to go on working and to preach many new words and values that I have only now discovered. It has turned out differently. May God preserve me in the strength to measure up to Him and to what He directs and permits.

It remains for me to thank many people for their faithfulness and kindness and love. To the Order and the confreres, who gave me a beautiful and genuinely intellectual, existential space. And to the many genuine people whom I was allowed to meet. Those whom I mean know it. Alas, friends, that the hour never did strike and that the day never did dawn when we might openly and freely gather for word and work, toward which we were inwardly growing. Remain true to the quiet command that inwardly called us again and again. Hold this nation dear which has grown so deserted in its soul and so betrayed and so helpless. And in fact, so lonely and perplexed, despite all the marching and declamatory self-assurance. If, through a person, a little more love and kindness, a little more light and truth are in the world, then his life has had meaning.

And those, too, I will not forget to whom I must remain in debt. I remain in debt for a great deal to many. Those whom I have hurt, may they forgive me. I have done penance.[55] Those to whom I was untruthful or insincere, may they forgive me. I have done penance. Those to whom I was arrogant and proud and unkind, may they forgive me. I have done penance. Oh yes, in the cellar hours, in the hours of fettered hands of body and of spirit, much has been broken. There much was burned out that was not worthy and valuable enough.

So then, farewell. My crime is that I believed in Germany even beyond a possible hour of distress and night. That I did not believe in that simple and arrogant trinity of pride and violence. And that I did this as a Catholic Christian and as a Jesuit. These are the values for which I stand, here at the outermost edge, and must wait for the one who pushes me down:

– Germany beyond today as an eternal reality, always newly reforming itself

– Christianity and Church as the secret longing and the strengthening and healing power of this land and people

– the Order as the home of marked men whom others hate because they do not understand and know us in our free commitment or because, in[56] their own arrogant, pathetic bondage, they fear us as a reproach and question.

And so I will do in conclusion what I have so often done with my fettered hands, and what I shall do, always more gladly and more often, as long as I am allowed to breathe: bless. I will bless land and people, bless this dear German Reich in its distress and inner torment; bless the Church, that the springs in her will again flow purer and brighter; bless the Order, that it will remain true to itself, genuine and marked and free through selfless faithfulness to all that is genuine and to the entire mission; bless the human beings who believed and trusted me; bless the people whom I wronged; bless all who were good to me, often too good.

God protect you. Help my aged parents over the difficult days and, beyond that, keep them somewhat in your care. The Lord God's merciful protection to all.

I, however, will wait here honestly for the God the Lord's disposition and guidance. I shall trust in Him until I am taken away. And I shall strive to see that even this consequence and cue will not find me small and despondent.

NOTES

1 Roman Bleistein, *Alfred Delp. Geschichte eines Zeugen*, 17–25; Abiturzeugnis, in P. Alfred Delp sj, Papers.
2 Bleistein, *Alfred Delp*, 33–5.
3 Ibid., 48; the German "Richtungen" includes the meanings of "tendencies" and "movements."
4 Ibid., 122–3.
5 Ibid., 255.
6 Helmuth James von Moltke, *Letters to Freya 1939–1945*; Michael Balfour and Julian Frisby, *Helmuth von Moltke. A Leader Against Hitler*.

7   Bleistein, *Alfred Delp*, 202–3; Veröffentlichungen der Kommission für Zeitgeschichte, Reihe A: Quellen Band 34, *Akten deutscher Bischöfe über die Lage der Kirche 1933–1945*, V 1940–42 (Mainz: Matthias-Grünewald-Verlag 1983), 450, 530, 538.

8   Alfred Delp, *Gesammelte Schriften*, Band III (1983), 263–9.

9   Sondergericht.

10 Heimtückegesetz. Bleistein, *Alfred Delp*, 203–4. See also Guenter Lewy, "Pius XII, the Jews, and the German Catholic Church," *Commentary* 37, no. 2 (Feb 1964): 23–35; Michael Phayer, *The Catholic Church and the Holocaust, 1930–1965* (Bloomington: Indiana UP 2000), 114–16; Michael Phayer, "Questions about Catholic Resistance," 334–5; Martin Menke, "Thy Will Be Done: German Catholics and National Identity in the Twentieth Century," *The Catholic Historical Review* 91, no. 2 (2005): 300–20.

11 Peter Longerich, *"Davon haben wir nichts gewusst!" Die Deutschen und die Judenverfolgung 1933–1945* (Munich: Siedler Verlag 2006).

12 The feast day of St Elisabeth of Hungary in Germany is 19 November; Hermann Grotefend, *Taschenbuch der Zeitrechnung des deutschen Mittelalters und der Neuzeit*, 12th ed. (Hannover: Hahnsche Buchhandlung 1982), 50, 145; the feast day is 17 November in America, the day of St Elisabeth's death; in Canada it is celebrated on 19 November. In 1941, 19 November was a Wednesday, when Delp might have given an evening lecture; indications are, however, that he spoke on Sunday, 16 November; Delp, *Gesammelte Schriften*, III, 288; Sister Angela OSB to the editor, 12 April 2010.

13 Delp, *Gesammelte Schriften*, III, 292. An abridged English translation of the sermon was published in the Catholic magazine *America*: Lucia Simpson Shen (translator and editor), "A Martyr's Voice," *America* 152 (1985): 171–4.

14 Peter Hoffmann, *The History of the German Resistance*, 512 and 712, note 21.

15 Eugen Gerstenmaier, *Streit und Friede hat seine Zeit. Ein Lebensbericht*, 197.

16 Volksgerichtshof.

17 .Walter Wagner, *Der Volksgerichtshof im nationalsozialistischen Staat* (Stuttgart: Deutsche Verlags-Anstalt 1975), 933–42.

18 See Delp's letter at pp. 130–1.

19 Wagner, *Der Volksgerichtshof*, 773–82; Benedicta Maria Kempner, *Priester vor Hitlers Tribunalen*, 61–74. The German text was published in P. Bleistein's definitive edition, *Alfred Delp: Gesammelte Schriften*, vol. 4, 104–12, with the heading "An M.," otherwise without the names of those to whom it was addressed, dated "after 11 January 1945," beginning with the words "Nach der Verurteilung," without underlining and without an indication that it was Delp's own heading. It had previously appeared in P. Alfred Delp SJ, *Im Angesicht des Todes*, 223–33. The original manuscript of "Nach der Verurteilung" ("After Sentencing") is in P. Alfred Delp SJ, Papers, Arch. Prov. Germ. SJ, Munich, Abt. 47 Nr. 23,3. The editor examined the manuscript there on 29 July 2008. It is dated in pencil "14.I.45," with further pencil markings by, presumably, P. Roman Bleistein SJ, who edited and published (in many cases, including "Nach der Verurteilung," republished) P. Alfred Delp SJ's papers. In an introductory note in Delp, *Gesammelte Schriften*, IV, 19–20, P. Bleistein declares that "all texts were compared with the originals or their copies." Nevertheless, there are

a phrase and some words missing from P. Bleistein's edition of "Nach der Verurteilung"; some words were misread, punctuation was changed, and numerous abbreviations were spelled out without any indication of the fact; there are other in-
accuracies. Printed editions of Delp's "last letter" either give no date, or 14 January
1945, or other variants. The manuscript in Arch. Prov. Germ. SJ, Abt. 47 Nr. 23, 3 is
dated, in pencil, by another hand, probably by P. Roman Bleistein, "14.I.45." I am
most grateful to the Abbess of Kloster St Walburg, Bistum Eichstätt, for permitting
Sister M. Angela OSB to correspond and discuss with me issues of the translation
and dating of the letter. Delp's reference in his letter to "Urbi's accepted sacrifice,
exactly seven months ago today" establishes 13 January 1945 as the date of writing:
the death of Maria Urban ("Urbi"), director of the Soziale Frauenschule in Munich,
occurred in an air raid on 13 June 1944; Maria Urban had vowed to God to offer her
life if, thereby, Delp's life could be spared; see Bleistein, *Alfred Delp. Geschichte eines
Zeugen*, 201–2.

20 Gertrud Ehrle, *Licht über dem Abgrund. Aufzeichnungen und Erlebnisse christlicher
Frauen 1933–1945*, 197, 207; Marianne Hapig, *Tagebuch und Erinnerung*, 64, 77; Delp,
Gesammelte Schriften, IV, 74, 82, 90, 95, 115; Gerstenmaier, *Streit und Friede hat seine
Zeit*, 199, 206, 210.

21 Delp, *Gesammelte Schriften*, IV, 113–47; V, 180–4.

22 Ibid., II, 19, 32–3, 66, 76, 143–4. There are a several references to Valjavec in Delp's
prison letters; two of them – 22 December 1944, 24 January 1945 – and one from
Marianne Hapig to Delp of 26 January 1945, mention Valjavec's role as courier between Berlin and Munich; ibid., 66, 143–4; Bleistein, *Alfred Delp*, 299, 322, 457, 462.
For general information about Fritz Valjavec cf. Dietmar Müller, "Südostforschung
im Schatten des Dritten Reiches (1920–1960). Institutionen, Inhalte, Personen," Ta-
gungsbericht, in *H-Soz-u-Kult*, 19.12.2002, http://hsozkult.geschichte.hu-berlin.de/
tagungsberichte/id=148; Valjavec apparently also served as a "political advisor of
the SS" and participated as an interpreter in a deployment of Sonderkommando 10b
in the Bukovina.

23 Alliteration: "Fügung und Führung" = "disposition and guidance"; "Lösung und
Losung" = "consequence and cue" (see the last two sentences of the letter); "Lösung
und Losung" is here translated as "consequence and cue"; Delp may have taken
"Lösung" as short for and meaning "Erlösung" = "redemption"; the more prosaic
meaning of the resolution of his own fate is more plausible. Delp may or may not
have been acquainted with the word pair used in the editorial in *Zeitung für die ele-
gante Welt*, no. I (1 January 1835): 2: "Stillstand ist Tod, und Vorwärts! ist die Losung
und Lösung alles Lebens." It is very likely, however, that he had read Friedrich Gundolf, *Goethe*, 7th ed. (Berlin: Georg Bondi 1920) and on page 25 had come across
Gundolf's assertion that for Renaissance man Shakespeare's "to be or not to be"
was "the highest and most wholesome" "Faustian cue and consequence" ("'Der gute
Mensch in seinem dunklen Drange' ist ein relativ modernes und schwächeres Pro-
dukt als der Renaissancemensch, dessen oberste Aufgabe ist 'in Bereitschaft sein,'
dessen Problem nicht Streben, sondern 'Sein oder Nichtsein' lautet. Wie aber die

Welt damals war, ist jene faustische Losung und Lösung allerdings die höchste und heilsamste des geistigen Menschen gewesen." There is some likelihood that Delp was acquainted with a book by Arno Schmieder that had appeared in 1931 with the title *Lösung und Losung. Der Weg aus der Volksnot* (Leipzig: Adolf Klein Verlag 1931). The meaning here is not, of course, identical with that in Delp's letter where his own "distress" and his "way out of distress" were quite different; the context rather suggests a translation as "Solution and Watchword. The Way Out of National Distress." Schmieder advocated the superiority of humans of "the fifth dimension" over those of "the fourth dimension" and sought to locate the mythical Atlantis; while seeking to abolish the power of "the Church," he also wrote admiringly of the Jesuits. See also Delp on books he criticized, in *Gesammelte Schriften*, vol. 1, 111–88.

24 Source: Alfred Delp SJ's manuscript "Nach der Verurteilung" ("After Sentencing") in P. Alfred Delp SJ, Papers, Arch. Prov. Germ. SJ, Munich, Abt. 47 Nr. 23, 3. See also Alfred Delp, *Gesammelte Schriften*; id., *Im Angesicht des Todes*; id., *Advent of the Heart. Seasonal sermons and prison writings 1941–1944*; id., *The prison meditations of Father Alfred Delp*; Moltke, *Letters to Freya*; Günther Lewy, *The Catholic Church and Nazi Germany*.

25 Plötzensee Prison in Berlin was the location of many executions of convicted resistance members; P. Delp expected to be executed there on the evening after sentencing, "as it had been customary": Delp to one of the Mariannes on 12 January 1945, in Delp, *Gesammelte Schriften*, IV, 113.

26 Reinhold Frank, in the cell next to P. Delp's, was sentenced on 12 January 1945; Wagner, *Der Volksgerichtshof*, 917–19.

27 Freisler.

28 Franz Reisert, in Kreisau Group.

29 The words between this and the previous comma are in the manuscript (Arch. Prov. Germ. SJ, Abt. 47 Nr. 23, 3) but not in any of the published versions: "wie bei Reisert, der etwas viel gewinselt hat." Reisert was sentenced to five years in penitentiary and survived the war; Wagner, *Der Volksgerichtshof*, 933.

30 Two words after "Gnädigen" crossed out in original ink.

31 The College of Philosophy (Hochschule für Philosophie) in Pullach used to hold a learned public disputation annually.

32 The opponent in a disputation.

33 There is a typed transcript in the P. Alfred Delp SJ, Papers, by Luise Östreicher, that has "biedere SA-Männer"; the editors of the letter, beginning with Paul Bolkovac (*Im Angesicht des Todes*), and including P. Bleistein, probably used Luise Östreicher's transcript and also read "SA-men" ("SA"= Sturmabteilung; known as Stormtroopers or Brown Shirts) for some really indecipherable scribble; but the writing is unclear; it looks as if the beginning of a word was abandoned and partially crossed out; the sentence structure excludes reading "SA-men" since the "men" are the same as the co-judges in their blue suits, not "SA" or "SS"; Delp, *Gesammelte Schriften*, IV, 105.

34 Two words crossed out: "übernahmen" and, written above it, "ausübten," all in original ink.

35 The German editions have "Ja zu sagen ausüben."

36 One illegible word crossed out in original ink.

37 Geheime Staatspolizei, Gestapo.

38 Delp uses the Berlin colloquial "Schupos" for Schutzpolizei (regular police).

39 Delp wrote "Kulissen" and "Statisten" to describe the staging of the proceedings.

40 Gerstenmaier had actively supported Hitler's assassination and the coup d'état, had been present among the insurgents at Home Army Headquarters in Bendler-strasse, Berlin, on 20 July 1944, and was arrested there; Hoffmann, *The History of the German Resistance 1933–1945*, 371–2, 425–6, 492, 509.

41 Illegible word crossed out in original ink.

42 The German editors of Delp's works read "eine baldige Brauchbarkeit."

43 Dim theoretician: Moltke, *Letters to Freya,* 404, on 10 January 1945, wrote, describing his trial: "The submissions we all made in our defence – police knew, official business, Eugen didn't understand a thing, Delp always happened to be absent – must be struck off, as Freisler quite rightly struck them." Fabian von Schlabren-dorff, ed., *Eugen Gerstenmaier im Dritten Reich. Eine Dokumentation* (Stuttgart: Evangelisches Verlagswerk 1965), 35–6, published the following: Gerstenmaier's sister Hanna Schwarz testified on 13 April 1961 that the wife of Deputy Reich Press Chief Helmut Sündermann was her friend; that her friend knew Freisler; that she asked her friend to tell Freisler that her brother was "an honest and upright man who could not be suspected of anything bad"; and that Freisler had called Mrs Sünder-mann after the verdict and asked her whether she was satisfied with it; Mrs Elisa-beth Palmer-Gebhardt (divorced Mrs Sündermann) testified on 25 September 1961 that she had been approached by her friend Hanna Schwarz to intervene on behalf of Eugen Gerstenmaier; that she had invited Freisler (whom she did not know) and Mrs Freisler (she does not say whether or not she knew her) to dinner; that at the dinner she had put it to Freisler that she knew the Gerstenmaier family well and could not imagine any wrong-doing on the part of Dr Gerstenmaier, and that, even if there were any charges against Dr Gerstenmaier, surely for once one could put mercy before justice; and that Freisler had not replied but called her "afterward" and asked her whether she was satisfied with the sentence.

44 The original has "Kulissen," meaning the scenery on a stage or set.

45 Nationalsozialistische Deutsche Arbeiterpartei: National Socialist German Work-ers' Party.

46 Freisler was killed in an air raid on 3 February 1945.

47 National Socialist.

48 Original: "Funktion" crossed out in ink.

49 Plötzensee Prison, in the Berlin borough of Plötzensee, was where most of the con-spirators who were sentenced to death by the "People's Court" were hanged; Moltke was executed there on 23 January 1945.

50 Original: "Sanctissimum," "the Most Blessed Sacrament."

51 Original: "bei" is crossed out in ink and "vor" written above it.

52 Original: "Opfer," "the Sacrifice of the Mass."

53 The German editors (*Gesammelte Schriften*, vol. 4, 108) annotate: "During the air raids of 16 July 1944 a bomb smashed through the Ignatius House in Munich (Kaulbachstrasse 31a) down to the basement but did not explode there."

54 Man and History, *Gesammelte Schriften*, vol. 2, 349–429.

55 Original: The first word of the next sentence, "Denen," is crossed out.

56 Original: An illegible word following "in" is crossed out.

12

Dietrich Bonhoeffer:
The Church and the Jewish Question,
April 1933

Dietrich Bonhoeffer, then student chaplain[1] at the Charlottenburg Technical College,[2] wrote this essay, which he completed on 15 April 1933, in reaction to the government-ordered, nationwide anti-Jewish "boycott" of 1 April 1933, and the "Law for the Restoration of the Professional Civil Service" of 7 April 1933. He had his paper printed and published in the June 1933 issue of the Protestant monthly periodical "for politics and culture," *Der Vormarsch,* which he co-edited and which was forced to cease publication in September 1933. It was also published in the 1 July 1933 issue of the bi-monthly "for church and folkdom," the *Niederdeutsche Kirchenzeitung,* which turned itself into a "German-Christian"-affiliated periodical in July 1933.[3]

The "boycott" was planned for several days before it was announced in the NSDAP national newspaper, *Völkischer Beobachter,* on 29 March, as a reply to the "Jewish atrocity propaganda" against Germany; it was to take place only on Saturday, 1 April, beginning at 10:00 a.m., and to be directed explicitly against businesses owned or operated by Jews, Jewish physicians, and Jewish lawyers. The Party leadership ordered the SA and SS to post "guards" outside "Jewish" shops and to warn the public against entering the premises. Shops owned or operated by religious Jews were likely to be closed on Saturday (the Sabbath) or to close early on Saturday afternoon. The timing therefore enabled the government to limit the initial activities, but in many places the SA and SS had pressed ahead even before the announcement and had vandalized businesses and homes of Jews and mistreated their owners. Whether by plan or in response to the hostile and potentially damaging reaction abroad, the government called off the continuation of the boycott in the following week.[4]

The "Law for the Restoration of the Professional Civil Service" declared Jews retired and excluded from the civil service (excepting veterans, persons whose fathers or sons had fallen in the war, and civil servants who had been appointed before 2 August 1914). The terms of the law applied to all corporations under public law.[5] This included employees of the national railways, the postal services, the national bank, the public social service administration, municipal and provincial administrations, and the clergy of the established churches. In September 1933, the general synods of the Prussian and the national Lutheran Church adopted a Church law that applied the definitions of the 7 April law and the Church's definitions (issued in ordinances through the course of the year) so that baptized and "racial" Jews (descended from religious Jews) were excluded from the ministry. This was known as "the Aryan paragraph."[6]

Except for the pro-National-Socialist "German Christian" press, reactions to the "Aryan paragraph" and its ramifications in the Protestant (Lutheran, evangelisch) Sunday papers and other periodicals were predominantly negative.[7]

Bonhoeffer conceded in his essay "the unique fact in history that the Jew is subjected to special legislation by the state solely on account of the race to which he belongs," and that "without doubt our government is entitled to strike new paths" in dealing with "the Jewish Question." At that time, he subscribed to "conversion theology" and "mission" to the Jews, as this sentence in his essay illustrates: "And this homecoming [of the Jews to God] will take place in Israel's conversion to Christ."[8] He added that the History of Salvation was continuing, that God had not finished with His Own People. But he demanded action by the Church against persecution, and he continued to take positions on the persecution of the Jews.

At an ecumenical conference[9] in Sofia (15–20 September 1933), Bonhoeffer got a motion accepted to condemn the "Aryan clause" in the German Lutheran Church's adaptation of the "Law for the Restoration of the Professional Civil Service" of 7 April 1933 as a "denial of the teaching and the spirit of the Gospels." The Secretary-General of the World Federation of Churches, Henri Louis Henriod, noted in his diary: "20. Septembre. Une résolution sur minorités des races proposée par Atkinson, une modification du texte présentée par Bonhoeffer est acceptée." The resolution stated: "We especially deplore the fact that the State measures against the Jews in Germany have had such an effect on public opinion that in some circles the Jewish race is considered a race of inferior status. We protest against the resolution of the Prussian General Synod and other Synods which apply the Aryan paragraph of the State to the Church, putting serious disabilities upon ministers and church officers who by chance of birth are non-Aryan, which we believe to be a denial of the explicit teaching and spirit of the Gospel of Jesus Christ."[10] Bonhoeffer's position was comprehensive, concerning all Jews, not merely Christians with Jewish background or ancestry; but most of his fellow pastors did not support his position.

In July 1933, he was asked to be pastor for a German community in London; he had to decide in September and, still uncertain, accepted. He wrote to Karl Barth that he had always wanted to be a pastor, and:[11]

At the same time I also received an offer of a pastorate in east Berlin[12] and was certain of the vote there. Then came the Aryan paragraph in the Prussian church,[13] and I knew that I could not accept that pastorate for which I had been longing, particularly in that part of the city, if I was unwilling to give up my unconditional opposition to *this* church. It would have meant the loss of credibility before the congregation from the outset. It would have meant abandoning my solidarity with the Jewish Christian pastors – my closest friend is one of them and is currently without a future, so he is now coming to join me in England.[14]

So the alternatives were lecturer *or* pastor, and in any case, not as pastor in the Prussian church. I cannot give you a full account of my motives for and against, even though I am still dealing with them and perhaps shall never put them fully behind me. I hope I have not gone away out of pique at the situation of our church and in particular at the position taken by our group. In any case, it probably would not have taken long until I was forced to a formal parting of the ways with my friends – but really, I think all that spoke much more against London than in its favour. If it is at all desirable, after such a decision, to find well-defined reasons for it, I think one of the strongest was that I no longer felt inwardly equal to the questions and demands that I was facing. I felt that, in some way I don't understand, I found myself in radical opposition to all my friends;[15] I was becoming increasingly isolated with my views of the matter, even though I was and remain personally close to these people. All this frightened me and shook my confidence, so that I began to fear that dogmatism might be leading me astray – since there seemed no particular reason why my own view in these matters should be any better, any more right, than the views of many really good and able pastors whom I sincerely respect. And so I thought it was about time to go into the wilderness for a spell, and simply work as a pastor, as unobtrusively as possible.

In frustration about the half-hearted or half-approving reaction of his fellow pastors in the Confessing Church to the "Aryan paragraph," Bonhoeffer accepted a position as pastor of two German communities in London in 1934; returned to Germany after a year and a half; headed an illegal seminary for Confessing Church pastors, which was closed down in 1937; and was forbidden to preach or speak publicly.[16]

There are, in Bonhoeffer's writings after the essay printed below, no other fundamental references to relations between Christians and Jews until his *Ethics,* which he wrote in 1940 and 1941, where he referred to the Jews as brothers. In a section of his *Ethics* that he wrote in the last months of 1940 and the first months of 1941 at Ettal,[17] Bonhoeffer confessed the Church's guilt and failures: "The Church confesses that it has witnessed the arbitrary use of brutal force, the suffering in body and soul of countless innocent people, that it has witnessed oppression, hatred, and murder, without raising its voice for the victims and without finding ways of rushing to help them. It has become guilty of the lives of the weakest and most defenceless brothers and sisters of Jesus Christ."[18]

The Church and the Jewish Question[19]

Luther, 1546: "We would still show them the Christian doctrine and pray for them to convert and accept the Lord whom they should by rights have honoured before we did." ... "When they convert, leave their usury, and accept Christ, we will gladly regard them as our brothers."[20]

Luther, 1523: "If the apostles, who also were Jews, had dealt with us Gentiles [Heyden] as we Gentiles deal with the Jews, there would never have been Christians among the Gentiles. Since they dealt with us Gentiles in such brotherly fashion, we in our turn ought to treat the Jews in a brotherly manner in order that we might convert some of them. For even we ourselves are not yet quite ascended, not to speak of climbed over [the mountain].[21] But as we are pressing them only by force ... what good could we work among them? Again, when we forbid them to labour and practice among us and to have other human fellowship with us, thereby driving them into usury, how should that better them?"[22]

The fact, unique in history, that the Jew is subjected to special laws by the state, regardless of the religion to which he adheres, solely on the basis of his race, presents the theologian with two new problems, which must be dealt with separately.[23] How does the church judge this action by the state, and what duty arises from it for the church? What are the consequences for the church's position on baptized Jews in the communities? Both these questions can only be answered on the basis of a right concept of the church.

I[24]

There is no doubt that the church of the Reformation is not enjoined to interfere directly in specific political actions of the state. The church has neither to praise nor to censure the laws of the state. Instead, it has to affirm the state as God's order of preservation [Erhaltungsordnung][25] in the godless world; it has to recognize and understand the state's creation of order – whether good or bad, from a humanitarian perspective – as grounded in God's will for preservation in the midst of the world's chaotic godlessness. This judgment by the church on what the state does stands quite apart from any moralizing and is to be distinguished from every sort of humanitarianism, because of the radical separation between the place of the gospel and the place of the law. The actions of the state[26] remain free from interference[27] by the church. This is not a schoolmaster-like or peevish objection[28] on the part of the church. History is not made by the church but by the state. But it is certainly only the church, which bears witness to God's entering into history, that knows what history is and therefore what the state is. And precisely out of this knowledge the church alone bears witness to God's *breaking into* history through Christ and lets the state go on making history. Without doubt one of the historical problems that must be dealt with by our state is the Jewish question, and without doubt the state is entitled to strike new paths in doing so. It remains for the humanitarian associations and individual Christian men[29] who see themselves called to do so, to make the state aware of the moral aspect of the measures it takes in this regard, that is, should the occasion arise, to accuse the state of offences against morality. Every strong state needs such associations and such individual personages and will foster them with a certain amount of reserved encouragement. Insight into the finer art of state-craft will tell the state how to make use of this advice in a relative sense. In the same way, however, a church that is regarded essentially as a cultural function of the state will interfere in the work of the state with advice[30] of this kind, and all the more wherever the state incorporates the church more substantially, that is, by relegating essentially moral and educational duties to it.

But the true church of Christ, which lives by the gospel alone and knows the nature of state actions, will never interfere in the functioning of the state in this way, by criticizing its history-making actions from the standpoint of any sort of, say, humanitarian ideal. The church knows about the essential necessity for the use of force in this world, and it knows about the "moral" injustice that is necessarily involved in the use of force in certain concrete state actions. The church cannot primarily take *direct* political action, since it does not presume to know how things should go historically. Even on the Jewish question today, the church cannot contradict[31] the state *directly* and demand that it take any particular different course of action. But that does not mean that the church stands aside, indifferent[32] to what political action is taken. Instead, it can and must, precisely because it does not moralize about individual cases, keep asking the government whether its actions can be justified as *legitimate state* actions, that is, actions that create law and order, not lack of rights and disorder.[33] It will be called upon to put this question as strongly as possible wherever the state seems endangered precisely in its *character as the state*,[34] that is, in its function of creating law and order by force. The church will have to put this question with the utmost clarity today in the matter of the Jewish question. This does not mean interfering in the state's responsibility for its actions; on the contrary, it is thrusting the entire burden of responsibility upon the state itself for the actions proper to it. Thus the church spares the state any moralizing reproach, referring it instead to the function ordained to it by the One who sustains the world. As long as the state acts in such a way as to create law and order – even if it means new laws and new order – the church of the Creator, Reconciler, and Redeemer cannot oppose it through direct political action. Of course it cannot prevent individual Christians, who know that they are called to do so in certain cases, from accusing the state of "inhumanity"; but as church it will only ask whether or not the state is creating law and order. In doing so the church will, of course, see the state as limited in two ways. Either *too little* order and law[35] or *too much* order and law[36] compels the church to speak. There is too little [law and order[37]] wherever a group of people is deprived of its rights; although in concrete cases it always will be extraordinarily difficult to distinguish actual deprivation of rights from a formally permitted minimum of rights. Even under serfdom a minimum of law and order was preserved, and yet if serfdom were reintroduced now it would represent deprivation of rights. It is remarkable that Christian churches tolerated serfdom for eighteen hundred years, and only in an era when the Christian substance of the church could at least be called into question were new rights created, with the help of the churches (but not significantly or even solely due to their help).[38] Nevertheless, for the church today, a step backward in this direction would be the expression of a lawless state. From this it follows[39] that the concept of rights is subject to historical transformations, which, however, has the effect of affirming the state's proper right to make history. It is not the church but rather the state that makes and changes laws. The inverse of too little order and law is too much order and law.[40] This means[41] that the state so expands its use of force that it robs the Christian message[42] and the Christian faith (not the free conscience – that would be the humanitarian version, which is illusory, since all state life forces the so-called "free conscience") of its own right – a grotesque situation, since the state only receives from this [Christian] message and this [Christian] faith its proper right, so that it dethrones itself. The church must repudiate such an encroachment by the state, precisely because of its better knowledge about the state and the limits of its actions. The state that endangers the Christian message[43] negates itself. There are thus three possibilities for church action vis-à-vis the state: *first* (as we have said), questioning the state as to the legitimate state character of its actions, that is, making the state responsible [for what it does]. *Second*, service to the victims of the state's actions. The church has an unconditional obligation toward the victims of any societal order, even if they do not belong to the Christian community. "Let us do good to all men."[44] In both these ways of conduct the church, in its own free way, serves the free state, and in times when the laws are changing, the church may under no circumstances evade either of these duties. The *third* possibility is not just to bind up the wounds of the victims beneath the wheel, but to seize the wheel itself.[45] Such an action would be direct[46] political action of the church. This is only possible and called for if the church sees the state to be failing in its function of creating order and law,[47] that is, if the church perceives the state, without any scruples, creating either too much or too little order and law. It must see in either eventuality a threat to the existence of the state and with that to its own existence as well. There would be too little in the deprivation of rights of any group of state-subjects; there would be too much where the state were to intervene in the nature of the church and its message, such as in the compulsory exclusion of baptized Jews from our Christian communities, or in a ban on missions to the Jews. In such a case, the church would find itself in *statu confessionis*,[48] and the state would find itself in the act of self-negation. A state that incorporates a church that it has violated has lost its most loyal servant. But even this third kind of action by a church, which in a given case leads it into conflict with the existing state, is only the paradoxical expression of its ultimate recognition of the state, for the church itself is aware that it is here called upon to protect the state from itself and to preserve it. For the church today, the Jewish question poses the first two possibilities as challenges of the hour, which it has a duty to meet. The necessity for immediate political action by the church must, however, be decided by an "evangelical council" as and when the occasion arises and hence cannot be casuistically construed beforehand.[49]

The state measures against Judaism,[50] however, have for the church a quite particular context. Never in the church of Christ has the thought become lost that the "chosen people," who nailed the Redeemer of the world onto the cross, must endure the curse of its action in a long history of suffering. "The Jews are the most miserable people on earth, are plagued everywhere, and scattered about the countries, having no certain resting place[51] where they could with confidence stay and must always fear expulsion" (Luther, *Table Talk*).[52] But the history of suffering of this people that God loves and punishes[53] stands under the sign of[54] the final homecoming of the people Israel to its God. And this homecoming takes place[55] in Israel's conversion to Christ. "When the hour comes when this people humbles itself and, repentant, lets go of the sins of its fathers, to which it has been clinging with terrible obstinacy to this day, and begs for the blood of the Crucified One to come down to reconcile them, the world will be astonished at the wonders God performs![56] that he performs upon this people![57] And the scoffing Philistines will be like filth in the street and the dried hay on the roofs. Then he will gather this people together out of all nations and bring it back to Canaan. O Israel, who is your equal? Blessed is the nation whose God is the *Lord*!" (S. [sic] Menken, 1795).[58] The conversion of Israel is to be the end of its people's time of sufferings. From this viewpoint, the Christian church trembles at the sight of the people Israel's history, as God's own free, terrible way with his people. It knows that no state in the world can be finished with[59] this enigmatic people, because God has not yet finished with it. Every new attempt to "solve" the "Jewish question" comes to grief because of the meaning of this people for salvation history; and yet such attempts have to be made again and again. This knowledge of the church of the curse that weighs upon this people takes it far beyond any sort of cheap moralizing; instead, it knows itself as the church that is unfaithful to its Lord over and over again, and that it shares in the humiliation that it sees in this outcast people, and full of hope it views those Israelites who have come home, who have come to faith in the true God in Christ, and it knows it has a bond with them as brothers.[60] With that, we have arrived at the second question.

II[61]

The church cannot allow the state to prescribe for it the way it treats its members. The baptized Jew is a member of our church. For the church, the Jewish question therefore poses itself differently than to the state.[62]

From the point of view of Christ's church, Judaism is never a racial concept, but a religious one. It means not the biologically dubious entity of the Jewish race, but the "people Israel." The "people" Israel, however, is constituted by God's law; thus one can *become* a Jew by accepting the law. But one cannot become a racial Jew. At the time of the great Jewish missions to the Gentile world, there were various levels of belonging to Judaism (Schürer III 1909, 150 et seq.).[63] Equally, the concept of Jewish Christianity is determined religiously and not racially. The Jewish-Christian mission also extended to Gentile regions (Paul's opponents in the Letter to the Galatians).[64] There were Gentile-Jewish Christians and Jewish-Gentile Christians.

From the point of view of Christ's church, therefore, Jewish Christians are not people of the Jewish race who have been baptized Christians, but a *Jewish Christian,* in the church's sense, is he who sees his belonging to the people of God, to the church of Christ, as *determined* by the observance of a divine law. Gentile Christians, on the other hand, know no other prerequisite for their belonging to the people of God, to the church of Christ, than God's call through his Word in Christ.[65]

This difference alone in the understanding of the appearance of Christ, of the gospel, led to the first schism in the church of Christ into Gentile Christianity and Jewish Christianity (council of the apostles).[66] This schism was understood by some as an intolerable heresy, by some as an endurable schism.

An analogous occurrence in our time would exist where a church group within the church of the Reformation made church membership dependent on observance of a divine law, for example racial uniformity of the members of a community. Then the Jewish-Christian type is reality where this requirement is made, regardless of whether its [the community's] members actually belong to the Jewish race or not. Then there is the further possibility that the Jewish Christians of the modern type *withdraw* from the Gentile-Christian community and establish their own church community bound by laws. It would be, however, ecclesiastically impossible then to exclude persons in the community who are racially Jewish on the grounds that they spoil the claim to be Jewish Christian through the law. For that would mean claiming to make the Gentile-Christian community Jewish Christian, a claim that the community would rightfully have to refuse.

To exclude racial Jews from our ethnically German church would mean to make the latter into one of the Jewish-Christian type. Such exclusion is therefore an ecclesiastical impossibility.

From the presence of communities of ethnically foreign origin in Germany alone, that is, French, English, etc., it may be concluded that there would be no ecclesiastical obstacle to Christians of Jewish origin coming together voluntarily to form their own community (as happened with the Jewish-Christian Alliance in London in 1925).[67] But in no case is the compulsory expulsion permissible of Gentile-Christian Jews who already belong to the Gentile-Christian community of German descent, quite apart from the difficulty of proving that these Jews are not Germans (cf. Stöcker's thesis that the Jew became a German through baptism).[68] Such compulsory expulsion would always mean a genuine church schism, even if it had a purely corporate organizational character, precisely because it would make racial uniformity a church law to be fulfilled as a precondition for membership in the church. The church community *doing the excluding* would thus constitute itself as *Jewish Christian*.[69]

The question here is not at all about whether our church members of German descent can today[70] continue to bear church community with the Jews. Rather, it is the duty of Christian preaching[71] to say: here, where Jew and German[72] together stand under God's Word, is church; here it will be proven whether or not church is still church. No one who feels unable to continue in church fellowship with Christians of Jewish origin can be prevented from leaving this church fellowship. But it must be made clear to him, with ultimate seriousness, that he abandons the place where the church of Christ stands, and that he brings into existence the Jewish-Christian idea of a religion of laws, that is, he is lapsing into a modern Jewish Christianity.[73] It still remains an open question whether or not such a separation can be seen as an endurable schism. Besides, one must have an extraordinarily biased view not to notice that any other behaviour than the just mentioned one on the part of our church toward baptized Jews would meet with an extensive lack of understanding among our church people.

(Manuscript completed on 15 April 1933)

"There is no other rule or test for who is a member of the people of God or the church of Christ ... than this: where there is a little band of those who accept the word of this Lord, teach it purely and confess it against those who persecute it, and for that reason suffer what is their due."[74]

NOTES

1 Studentenpfarrer.
2 Technische Hochschule Charlottenburg.
3 Dietrich Bonhoeffer, "Die Kirche vor der Judenfrage"; see also *Leipzig* 3, Heft 9 (1933), front-page (now sub-titled "Unabhängige Monatsschrift für reformatorisches Christentum"); *Niederdeutsche Kirchenzeitung*. Evangelisch-lutherisches Halbmonatsblatt für Kirche und Volkstum in Niederdeutschland. Herausgegeben von der Niederdeutschen evangelisch-lutherischen Konferenz. Vorsitzender Synodalpräsident D. Dr Schöffel Hauptpastor an St Michaelis-Hamburg. Schriftleiter P. Karl Hasselmann und P. Theodor Rohrdantz in Verbindung mit P. Vietig-Stockels-

dorf (Eutin) [usw.]. Druck und Verlag: Eberhardtsche Hof- und Ratsbuchdruckerei, Wismar, published twice a month. The editor, Karl Hasselmann, published on page 233 (the year's issues are consecutively paginated), opening the issue of 3. Jahrgang 1. Juli 1933 Nummer 13, a statement headed "Der Zugriff des Staates" ("The Intervention of the State"); this intervention, he wrote, was necessary, because the church could not or would not act, was increasingly disunited, incapable of reconstructing its constitution out of its faith, and thus it was the only way for the church. On the second page (234) there begins "Die Kirche vor der Judenfrage. Von Lic. Dietrich Bonhoeffer.*" The * directs the reader to this footnote: "By permission of the editor taken from the Lutheran monthly *Der Vormarsch*, Heft 6 (1933). The next issue of *NKZ* will carry an article on the same matter by Lic. Herntrich-Kiel." From July 1933 the publication of *Niederdeutsche Kirchenzeitung* had become "impossible," and the periodical was replaced as at 15 August 1933 by *Kirche und Volkstum in Niedersachsen. Halbmonatsschrift.* The print runs of *Der Vormarsch, Leipzig,* and *Niederdeutsche Kirchenzeitung* could not be determined. Gerhard E. Stoll, *Die evangelische Zeitschriftenpresse im Jahre 1933*, Witten 1963, does not provide the numbers. Note in *Dietrich Bonhoeffer Works*, vol. 12, 361 (abbreviations spelt out): From *Der Vormarsch* 3, no. 6 (June 1933): 171–6 (the quotations from Luther at the beginning and end may have been inserted by the editor of *Der Vormarsch*); Larry L. Rasmussen comments that they are not in the three drafts written by Bonhoeffer. Previously published in Bonhoeffer, *Gesammelte Schriften,* 2, 44–53. See also the *Niederdeutsche Kirchenzeitung* 3, no. 13 (1 July 1933); reprint without the closing quote from Luther. The published manuscript has not been preserved. The carbon copy found in the Bonhoeffer Papers, Staatsbibliothek, Berlin, A 37, 3a (without the quotes from Luther at the beginning and end of the published version), with handwritten additions and corrections (cf. also the Bonhoeffer Papers, A 37, 3b: carbon copy without these), is apparently an earlier, shorter version, but does include Bonhoeffer's preliminary versions without significant changes, as follows: for Part I and the first paragraph of Part II, a handwritten manuscript (Bonhoeffer Papers, A 37, 2), which is a response to the beginning of discrimination against the Jewish population, the "Law for Restoration of the Professional Civil Service," which includes the so-called Aryan paragraph, of 7 April 1933 (*RGBl.* I, 175); for Part II, a carbon copy with six theses (Bonhoeffer Papers, A 37, 1, with handwritten corrections and a longer handwritten addition at the end), which Bonhoeffer had already prepared for discussion in the Berlin pastors' group (cf. Bethge, *Dietrich Bonhoeffer. A Biography,* rev. ed. 2000, 273) in late March/early April 1933. For details on the composition, content, and controversies in interpretation of this essay, see Marikje Smid, *Deutscher Protestantismus und Judentum 1932/33* (Munich: Chr. Kaiser 2000), 419–85. The editors of *Dietrich Bonhoeffer Werke, Volume 12,* call the reader's attention both to the differences between Bonhoeffer's drafts of this essay and the published version, as well as to some significant corrections made here to previous English translations. At present it is impossible to determine the editorial history of the published essay, particularly whether the changes were suggested by Bonhoeffer or someone else; given the extensive attention this essay receives, however, this would be a worthwhile research project. Regarding the differences, cf. ed. notes 9, 12, 14, 18, 22, 24, 25, and 27. The editors of volume 12 accepted several suggestions regarding the translation from the editor of *Behind Valkyrie*, who thanks the editors of *Dietrich Bonhoeffer Works* for permission to use their translation of "Die Kirche vor der Judenfrage," with modifications as indicated in the notes.

4 Boycott threat in *Völkischer Beobachter*, Munich edition (27 March 1933); boycott announcement in *Völkischer Beobachter*, Munich ed., no. 88 (Wednesday, 29 March 1933), had on the front page the banner headline "Aufruf der Parteileitung der N.S.D.A:P. Samstag, Schlag 10 Uhr, wird das Judentum wissen, wem des den Kampf angesagt hat!" Yitzhak Arad, et al., eds., *Documents on the Holocaust. Selected Sources on the Destruction of the Jews in Germany and Austria, Poland and the Soviet Union*, 36; Avraham Barkai, *Vom Boykott zur "Entjudung." Der wirtschaftliche Existenzkampf der Juden im Dritten Reich 1933–1943*, 23–35; Avraham Barkai, *From Boycott to Annihilation. The Economic Struggle of German Jews, 1933–1943*, 17–25.

5 Körperschaften des öffentlichen Rechts sowie diesen gleichgestellte Einrichtungen und Unternehmungen.

6 "Gesetz zur Wiederherstellung des Berufsbeamtentums. Vom 7. April 1933," *Reichsgesetzblatt. Teil I. Jahrgang 1933*. Herausgegeben vom Reichsministerium des Innern (*RGBl.* I 1933) (Berlin: Reichsverlagsamt 1933), 175–7; "Erste Verordnung zur Durchführung des Gesetzes zur Wiederherstellung des Berufsbeamtentums. Vom 11. April 1933," *RGBl.* I 1933, 195: "Zu § 3 2. (1) Als nicht arisch [sic] gilt, wer von nicht arischen [sic], insbesondere jüdischen Eltern oder Großeltern abstammt. Es genügt, wenn ein Elternteil oder ein Großelternteil nicht arisch [sic] ist. Dies ist insbesondere dann anzunehmen, wenn ein Elternteil oder ein Großelternteil der jüdischen Religion angehört hat. (2) [...] (3) Ist die arische Abstammung zweifelhaft, so ist ein Gutachten des beim Reichsministerium des Innern bestellten Sachverständigen für Rasseforschung einzuholen." "Dritte Verordnung zur Durchführung des Gesetzes zur Wiederherstellung des Berufsbeamtentums. Vom 6. Mai 1933," *RGBl.* I 1933, 245–56, with many definitions, including notaries, teachers, but not clergymen. "Gesetz über die Verfassung der Deutschen Evangelischen Kirche. Vom 14. Juli 1933," *RGBl.* I 1933, 471 and Verfassung, 472–8 ("Artikel 1 Der Deutschen Evangelischen Kirche ist am 11. Juli 1933 eine Verfassung gegeben, [sic] die nebst der Einführungsverordnung von Reichs wegen anerkannt und in der Anlage veröffentlicht wird. Artikel 2. (1) Die Deutsche Evangelische Kirche ist Körperschaft des öffentlichen Rechts des Reichs.") In "Verfassung der Deutschen Evangelischen Kirche" steht Abschnitt V, Artikel 10: "Die deutschen evangelischen Kirchengesetze werden von der Nationalsynode im Zusammenwirken mit dem Geistlichen Ministerium oder von diesem allein beschlossen, durch den Reichsbischof ausgefertigt und im Gesetzblatt der Deutschen Evangelischen Kirche verkündet." *Die Evangelische Kirche in Deutschland und die Judenfrage. Ausgewählte Dokumente aus den Jahren des Kirchenkampfes 1933 bis 1943*. Bearbeitet und herausgegeben auf Veranlassung des Flüchtlingsdienstes des Ökumenischen Rats der Kirchen, Oikumene, Genf, 1945, 35–46, esp. 35: "Gesetz über die Rechtsverhältnisse der Geistlichen und Kirchenbeamten" "wurde von der Generalsynode der Evangelischen Kirche der altpreußischen Union sowie von den Landes-

synoden einzelner anderer deutscher Landeskirchen angenommen, der Deutschen Evangelischen Nationalsynode vorgelegt und für die ganze deutsche Evangelische Kirche ebenfalls beschlossen"; "§1.(1.) Als Geistlicher oder Beamter der allgemeinen kirchlichen Verwaltung darf nur berufen werden, wer die für seine Laufbahn vorgeschriebene Vorbildung besitzt und rückhaltlos für den nationalen Staat und die Deutsche Evangelische Kirche eintritt. (2.) Wer nicht arischer Abstammung oder mit einer Person nicht arischer [sic] Abstammung verheiratet ist, darf nicht als Geistlicher oder Beamter der allgemeinen kirchlichen Verwaltung berufen werden. Geistliche oder Beamte arischer Abstammung, die mit einer Person nichtarischer [sic] Abstammung die Ehe eingehen, sind zu entlassen. Wer als Person nichtarischer [sic] Abstammung zu gelten hat, bestimmt sich nach den Vorschriften der Reichsgesetze." "§3. [...] (2.) Geistliche oder Beamte, die nichtarischer [sic] Abstammung oder mit einer Person nichtarischer [sic] Abstammung verheiratet sind, sind in den Ruhestand zu versetzen." Eberhard Bethge, *Dietrich Bonhoeffer. Theologe, Christ, Zeitgenosse. Eine Biographie*, 321–6 (on DB's paper), 357–78 ("Arierparagraph"; "Kirchengesetz betreffend die Rechtsverhältnisse der Geistlichen und Kirchenbeamten" imposed at the "Brown Synod," the Altpreußische Generalsynode on 5–6 September 1933 in the Berlin Herrenhaus).

7 Gerhard E. Stoll, *Die evangelische Zeitschriftenpresse im Jahre 1933*, 218; Ino Arndt, Die Judenfrage im Licht der evangelischen Sonntagsblätter von 1918–1933, collected the anti-Semitic, anti-Jewish voices in the Protestant press.

8 Heinz Eduard Tödt, "Judendiskriminierung 1933 – der Ernstfall für Bonhoeffers *Ethik*," in Wolfgang Huber and Ilse Tödt, eds., *Ethik im Ernstfall. Dietrich Bonhoeffer's Stellung zu den Juden und ihre Aktualität* (Munich: Chr. Kaiser Verlag 1982), 172–3, tries to give the two sentences, by linking them to Bonhoeffer's Menken-quotation in the same text ("Blessed is the people whose God is the *Lord*!"), a different sense: that Israel's coming home to God did not mean their integration into the Christian Church, which would involve their conversion; the evidence Tödt cites does not change Bonhoeffer's statement: "And this homecoming |355| will take place in Israel's conversion to Christ."

9 Weltbundtagung.

10 Bethge, *Dietrich Bonhoeffer. Theologe, Christ, Zeitgenosse*, 369 cites mimeographed minutes.

11 Source: Dietrich Bonhoeffer, *Works, Volume 13. London 1933–1935* (Minneapolis: Fortress Press 2007), 21–4.

12 The Lazarus Church; see Bonhoeffer, *Werke. Dreizehnter Band. London 1933–1935* (Gütersloh: Chr.Kaiser Verlag 1994), 12, n. 8.

13 The Prussian General Synod adopted the "Aryan Clause" for the Church on 5 September 1933.

14 Franz Hildebrand; Bonhoeffer, *Werke, Volume 13*, 13, n. 10.

15 Bonhoeffer, *Werke, Volume 13*, 13, n. 11: In September, in Berlin, Bonhoeffer and Hildebrandt had demanded the schism from the heretical church because of the Church's "Aryan paragraph," which excluded Christian "Jews" from the ministry, and had found no understanding or support.

16 Bethge, *Dietrich Bonhoeffer. Theologe, Christ, Zeitgenosse*, 379–480, 481–662.

17 Ibid., 789, 807; Bethge, *Dietrich Bonhoeffer. A Biography*, 471.

18 Bonhoeffer, *Ethik, Werke, Sechster Band*, 130; Bonhoeffer, *Ethics, Works, Volume 6*, 139. (This translation slightly alters the original German, e.g. by adding "sisters" to "brothers.")

19 Source: The text of the translation here follows the translation and annotations in Bonhoeffer, *Berlin 1932–1933* (Bonhoeffer, *Works, Volume 12*), 361–70; when the present text occasionally modifies it, as with a comma or semicolon, a restored "however" for "aber," or by using "community" for "Gemeinde" instead of "congregation" ("community" meaning adherents whether present in a congregation in a locality at a given time or simply belonging to a community all of whose or some of whose members may congregate in a given locality at a given time), or when the present version restores Bonhoeffer's word order to maintain meaning, character, and idiosyncrasies of Bonhoeffer's style, a note will indicate it.

20 Martin Luther, "Eine Vermahnung wider die Juden" (1546), *D. Martin Luthers Werke. Kritische Gesamtausgabe*, 51. Band (Weimar: Hermann Böhlaus Nachfolger 1914), 195, 25–7. Larry L. Rasmussen: This essay was not translated in the English *Luther's Works* edition; ellipses are those of the editors of Bonhoeffer, *Works*.

21 Luther, "That Jesus was born a Jew," *Luther's Works*, vol. 54: "Table Talk," ed. and trans. Theodore C. Tappert (Philadelphia, PA: Fortress Press 1967), 45, 200–1.

22 Ibid., 229; ellipses are those of the editors of *Works*.

23 Passage from Bonhoeffer, *Werke, Volume 12*, 352–3. German text: "Sowohl ein *Zuwenig* an Ordnung und Recht als auch ein *Zuviel* an Ordnung und Recht zwingt die Kirche zum Reden. Ein Zuwenig ist jedesmal dort vorhanden, wo eine Gruppe von Menschen rechtlos wird, wobei es in concreto jeweils ausserordentlich schwierig sein wird, wirkliche Rechtlosigkeit von einem wenigstens formaliter zugebilligten Minimum von Recht zu unterscheiden. Auch in der Leibeigenschaft war ein Minimum von Recht und Ordnung gewahrt und doch würde eine Wiedereinführung der Leibeigenschaft Rechtlosigkeit bedeuten. Es ist immerhin beachtlich, dass christliche Kirchen achtzehnhundert Jahre lang die Leibeigenschaft ertragen haben und erst in einer Zeit, bei der die christliche Substanz der Kirche mindestens in Frage gezogen werden könnte, mit Hilfe der Kirchen (aber doch nicht wesentlich oder gar allein durch sie) neues Recht geschaffen wurde. Dennoch |353| wäre ein Rückschritt in dieser Richtung heute für die Kirche der Ausdruck eines rechtlosen Staates."

24 Note by Larry L. Rasmussen: In the carbon copy (Bonhoeffer Papers, 37, 3a), there is a handwritten note here: "Ahasver peregrinus" ("wandering Ahasuerus"). According to a legend dating back to the early seventeenth century, the shoemaker Ahasuerus was condemned to wander eternally because he had driven Jesus away from the wall of his house when Jesus, exhausted by carrying the cross, leaned against it. This legend rendered Ahasuerus as a symbolic figure for the fate of the Jewish people, homeless after the crucifixion (cf. Else Liefmann, "Die Legende vom Antichrist und die Sage von Ahasver: Ihre Bedeutung für den Antisemitismus," *Judaica* 3 (1947), 122–56). As Liefmann's essay on this legend suggests, the "wandering

Jew" story became a central motif in the anti-Jewish teachings that converged with anti-Semitism.

25 Larry L. Rasmussen: Bonhoeffer here uses "order of preservation" in explicit contrast to "order of creation." As in *Creation and Fall*, given as lectures in the winter semester of 1932–33, he is countering natural theology and its misuse, which was to bolster the Nazi platform of "blood and soil." "Orders of creation" was used by conservative Lutheran theologians and German Christians in a natural theology that yielded autonomous orders, such as the state and family, apart from the revelation of God in Jesus Christ. Paul Althaus, for example, published a pamphlet, *Theologie der Ordnungen*, that argued that the German nation, or Volk, belonged to God's ordering of creation. "Orders of preservation," in contrast, removes the ordering of the world understood apart from Jesus Christ and locates it in the activity of God to preserve the world from chaos, in anticipation of its end, its redemption in Jesus Christ. God's ordering is thus understood eschatologically, not from its past or present "in nature." For an extensive discussion of the use of "orders of creation" at this time, see Robert P. Ericksen, *Theologians under Hitler* (New Haven, Connecticut: Yale University Press 1985), 98–104. See also the Editor's Introduction to Bonhoeffer, *Works, Volume 3*, 11–12, for Bonhoeffer's explicit choice of "order of preservation" as the alternative.

26 In the handwritten version (Bonhoeffer Papers, A 37, 2), this is followed by "in all circumstances."

27 Eingriff.

28 Einrede.

29 The carbon copy (Bonhoeffer Papers, A 37, 3a) has "people," corrected by hand to read "men."

30 Einreden.

31 Ins Wort fallen.

32 Teilnahmslos.

33 Note by Larry L. Rasmussen: Here and in the following passages there is a significant difference from previous translations of this essay that alter the meaning of what Bonhoeffer writes. The German word "Recht" can be translated as "justice," "law," or "rights," depending on the context. But the standard translation of "rechtlos" and "Rechtlosigkeit" is "without rights" or "deprivation of rights." Only with regard to a state (einem rechtlosen Staat) would "rechtlos" be translated as "lawless" or a "lack of law and order" – the implication being that this is a state without justice. This nuance is crucial to following Bonhoeffer's argument throughout this essay, for he is arguing that a state that deprives citizens of their rights (as was the case in the era of serfdom, which he subsequently gives as an illustration) is "lawless" in its very essence because it is exercising its God-given authority in an illegitimate manner, and hence (as he argues in the paragraphs that follow) the church may be called upon to challenge the legitimacy of that state. The German editor of this volume, Ernst-Albert Scharffenorth, concurs that this is the correct translation.

34 Staatlichkeit.

35 The translators of the English edition here reversed Bonhoeffer's order of words "Ordnung und Recht."

36 The translators of the English edition here reversed Bonhoeffer's order of words "Ordnung und Recht."

37 Insertion by the translators of the English edition.

38 The translators of the English edition reversed Bonhoeffer's word order "aber doch nicht wesentlich oder gar allein durch sie." As the mention of serfdom shows, Bonhoeffer was referring here, in the first place, to the liberation of German peasants from their masters toward the end of the eighteenth century. Churches did not participate actively in this change in the German states, whereas the abolition of slavery in the United States can be traced (in part) to criticism by Quakers and Methodists, among others. Cf. Bonhoeffer's memorandum on the "Social Gospel," *Works, Volume 12*, 236–43.

39 The translators of the English edition translate Bonhoeffer's "daraus folgt" as "from this we may conclude."

40 The translators of the English edition here reversed Bonhoeffer's order of words "Ordnung und Recht."

41 The translators of the English edition here have "this would mean," where Bonhoeffer wrote "es besagt," literally "it means"; Bonhoeffer's statement is not conditional, but indicative, a statement of fact.

42 Verkündigung.

43 Verkündigung.

44 Galatians 6:10.

45 Note by Larry L. Rasmussen: This is the famous phrase "dem Rad selbst in die Speichen zu fallen," often translated as "to fall within the spokes of the wheel." That, however, is not the common image used in English to convey the meaning, namely, to bring the apparatus of the unjust and illegitimate state to a halt. "To seize the wheel itself" is the English phrase; for this reason, we use that translation here.

46 Note by Larry L. Rasmussen: This is the reading in the manuscript (Bonhoeffer Papers, A 37, 2, 9); the published version in the *Niederdeutsche Kirchenzeitung* and *Gesammelte Schriften*, 2, 48 has "mittelbar" meaning "indirect." This error was pointed out by Ernst Feil in 1971 (*Die Theologie Dietrich Bonhoeffers. Hermeneutik, Christologie und Weltverständnis* [Munich: Chr. Kaiser Verlag; Mainz: Matthias-Grünewald-Verlag 1971], 264, ed. note 105); the English translation of Feil, *The Theology of Dietrich Bonhoeffer* (Minneapolis: Fortress Press 1985) is abridged by Feil and does not include this same footnote, but it does note the correction in endnote 37, 223–34. The correction first appeared in Huber and Tödt, *Ethik*, 245–50.

47 The translators of the English edition here reversed Bonhoeffer's order of words "Ordnung und Recht."

48 Note by Larry L. Rasmussen: In "statu confessionis" refers to a state of confessional protest in which such matters as church membership and rules are no longer mat-

ters of convenience and doctrinal indifference (adiaphora). Rather, they are matters in which the very "truth of the gospel and Christian freedom are at stake." The key passage in the Lutheran confessions that stands behind Bonhoeffer's reference is the following: "We believe, teach, and confess that in a time of persecution, when an unequivocal confession of the faith is demanded of us, we dare not yield to the opponents in such indifferent matters … For in such a situation it is no longer indifferent matters that are at stake. The truth of the gospel and Christian freedom are at stake. The confirmation of open idolatry, as well as the protection of the weak in faith from offence, is at stake. In such matters we can make no concessions but must offer an unequivocal confession and suffer whatever God sends and permits the enemies of His Word to inflict on us." Formula of Concord, Epitome, Article X/6, 516. Ellipses in Bonhoeffer, *Works, Volume 12*, 366, n. 14.

49 Note by Larry L. Rasmussen: The paragraph that follows appeared only in the published version. It is not in any of Bonhoeffer's three drafts of the essay.

50 Das Judentum.

51 The remainder of this quotation is not included in Bonhoeffer, *Works, Volume 12*, 367.

52 Cf. Martin Luther, *Werke. Kritische Gesamtausgabe. Tischreden. 3. Band* (Weimar: Hermann Böhlaus Nachfolger 1914), 36, 16–19; ellipsis in printed German version in Bonhoeffer, *Werke, Volume 12*, 354; not in "Table Talk," *Luther's Works*, vol. 54.

53 Bonhoeffer, *Works, Volume 12*, 367, translates "dieses von Gott geliebten und gestraften Volkes" in the past tense: "this people that God loved and punished"; the form Bonhoeffer used, however, has the meaning of love and punishment not only as being in the past, but as continuing.

54 Bonhoeffer, *Works, Volume 12*, 367, translates "steht unter dem Zeichen" as "will end in."

55 Bonhoeffer, *Works, Volume 12*, 367, translates "Heimkehr geschieht" as "homecoming will take place." While the German present tense implies a future event, it also expresses a definitive incontrovertible finality.

56 Bonhoeffer, *Works, Volume 12*, 367, translates "der Wunder, die Gott thut" (present) as "the wonders God has wrought" (past).

57 Bonhoeffer, *Works, Volume 12*, 367, translates "thut" (present) as "has wrought" (past).

58 Gottfried Menken, "Über Glück und Unglück der Gottlosen," in his *Schriften*, vol. 7 (Bremen: J.G. Heyse 1858), 97.

59 Bonhoeffer, *Works, Volume 12*, 367, translates "fertig werden" as "deal with," and "fertig ist" as "is […] finished"; the translation here follows the original more closely.

60 Bonhoeffer, *Works, Volume 12*, 367, adds "and sisters"; the German version has only "Brüdern."

61 The carbon copy (Bonhoeffer Papers, A 37, 3a) here has a handwritten addition: "Modernes Judenchristentum," "Modern Jewish Christianity."

62 Note by Larry L. Rasmussen: This paragraph is in the published version in *Niederdeutsche Kirchenzeitung* 237 but not in Bonhoeffer's drafts of this section. Both

drafts begin with "From the point of view of Christ's church, Judaism is never a racial concept." The drafts also differ in that each paragraph is numbered.

63 Emil Schürer, *Geschichte des jüdischen Volkes im Zeitalter Jesu Christi*, Dritter Band (Leipzig: J.C. Hinrichs'sche Buchhandlung 1909), 150–88, esp. 172 et seq.

64 See Galatians 1–4, esp. 4:8–11 and 21–31.

65 A "Jewish Christian" is, then, a Christian of Jewish descent in a spiritual and cultural sense, and a "Gentile Christian" (Heidenchrist) a Christian of heathen, in any case non-Jewish descent. None of this has anything to do with race.

66 Cf. Acts 15:1–29 and Galatians 2:1–10.

67 The phrase in parentheses was added only in the published version. According to Otto von Harling, "Judenmission," in *Die Religion in Geschichte und Gegenwart. Handwörterbuch für Theologie und Religionswissenschaft,* 2nd ed., vol. 3 (Tübingen: J.C.B. Mohr [Paul Siebeck] 1929), 468–9, the "international Jewish Christian Alliance in London, 1925" was founded to "bring Jewish Christians together in Jewish Christian congregations without removing them from the context of the Jewish people."

68 Note by Larry L. Rasmussen: This reference expanded in the carbon copy (Bonhoeffer Papers, 37, 3a) in Bonhoeffer's handwriting. On Stoecker's thesis, see Walter Frank, *Hofprediger Adolf Stoecker und die christlichsoziale Bewegung* (Berlin: Reimar Hobbing 1928), 102: "Even though he also reproached the Jews with being a nation within a nation, Stoecker as a Christian clergyman could not give up the standpoint that 'being reborn in the Spirit overcomes racial distinctions.'" Stoecker was among the most prominent Lutheran anti-Semites of the late nineteenth century and his writings were cited extensively in the Third Reich.

69 Note by Larry L. Rasmussen: This marks the conclusion of Bonhoeffer's first draft (Bonhoeffer Papers, A 37, 1b). The second draft of this section includes the final paragraph that follows in Bonhoeffer's handwriting (Bonhoeffer Papers, A 37, 1a) and additional handwritten comments in the margins.

70 "Today" (in the German original "heute") refers to the anti-Semitic National Socialist regime in power from 30 January 1933 and at the time of writing, April 1933; Bonhoeffer, *Works, Volume 12*, 370 leaves out "today."

71 Verkündigung.

72 Bonhoeffer's expression is "wo Jude und Deutscher zusammen unter dem Wort Gottes stehen, ist Kirche."

73 "that is ... Christianity" was added in the published version; it is not in Bonhoeffer's drafts.

74 Ellipsis in Bonhoeffer, *Werke*, Zwölfter *Band*, 358. Luther on Psalm 110:3; from Luther's sermon of 10 May 1535, on Psalm 110, *Werke. Kritische Gesamtausgabe* 41: 145, 31–4). Note by Larry L. Rasmussen: This concluding quotation appeared only in the published version, i.e., in *Der Vormarsch*. It is not in Bonhoeffer's drafts in Bonhoeffer Papers.

13

Pastor Julius von Jan's Protest against the 9 November 1938 Pogrom, 16 November 1938

With the appointment of Adolf Hitler as Chancellor on 30 January 1933, discrimination and persecution of German Jews began in the form of mob action, and through government directives, legislation, decrees, and ordinances. National Socialist German Workers Party (NSDAP) and storm trooper (SA) thugs committed outrages that were tolerated or encouraged by Party leaders. On 1 April 1933, Jewish businesses were vandalized, and Jews were pilloried in an officially declared nation-wide "boycott."[1] This "boycott" had been proclaimed on 29 March as a response to voices abroad calling for an embargo against German businesses because of the treatment of Jews in Germany. It attempted also to appease Party radicals who wanted a root-and-branch removal from Germany of all that was Jewish there and then. The "boycott" was scheduled for a Saturday when many Jewish merchants, professionals, and craftsmen kept their businesses closed to observe the Sabbath. The "boycott" was suspended on 2 April.[2] There followed, however, on 7 April, a Law for the Restoration of the Professional Civil Service that ordered the retirement of most Jewish civil servants, with exceptions for veterans and some other categories. Numerous laws, decrees, and regulations followed. The Nürnberg Laws of 1935 deprived German Jews of many of their rights as citizens. Expropriation of the property of Jews was in progress; some synagogues were closed or destroyed. In 1937 and 1938, measures against Jews were intensified. In Nuremburg the main synagogue was destroyed on 10 August 1938.[3]

In 1933, fearless clergymen admonished their congregations that a Christian had one leader: Jesus. Dietrich Bonhoeffer's warning against false leaders appeared in the nationally-circulating *Kreuz Zeitung* on 26 February

1933.[4] A regional bishop, Prälat D. Dr Konrad Hoffmann in Ulm on Danube, declared on 7 May 1933 that "the Prince of this world" – a biblical pseudonym for Satan – had killed Jesus, with the implied admonition to differentiate between the leaders of this world and the true leader, Jesus.[5] After the murder of dissident SA leaders in June and July 1934, most clergymen who deprecated the Party's policies and doctrine became more cautious.

Catholic clergymen sought protection in the Concordat, the treaty the German government and the Vatican concluded in July 1933, in which the government agreed to respect the rights and privileges of the Catholic Church.

On the Protestant side, the government attempted to replace the twenty-eight provincial churches by a unitary national Protestant Church headed by a National-Socialist Reich Bishop, and to modify church doctrine along the lines of the "German Christian" movement.[6] The "German Christians" abandoned much of traditional Protestant theology. They declared the nation, the racially pure "Volk," the highest guiding principle and authority (really in place of God); they emphasized the importance of race and blood in the church and strove to remove all Jewish elements from Christianity. They were theologically heretical and illegitimate. Protestant dissidents formed a secession called the Confessing Church; about a third of all pastors joined it. The Provisional Church Government of the Confessing Church[7] was established on 22 November 1934, and first chaired by Hanover Lutheran Land Bishop Marahrens. It represented the Confessing Church and the three "intact" land churches of Württemberg, Bavaria, and Hanover (Lutheran). The Confessing Church opposed the application of the "Aryan paragraph," which denied Germans of Jewish ancestry access to positions in the civil service and the church. The Confessing Church viewed itself as the only legitimate Protestant church in Germany, based on its adherence to theological orthodoxy as established by the Reformation confessions. Though outlawed, it trained and ordained clergy in the various land churches. On 4 June 1936, the leaders of the Confessing Church sent Hitler a memorandum about the conflicts between Lutheran Christianity and National Socialism; the memorandum explicitly condemned racial hatred. Two of Dietrich Bonhoeffer's students published the memorandum abroad; it appeared in the *Basler Nachrichten* and *The New York Herald Tribune* on 23 and 28 July 1936, respectively, a few days before the Olympic Games opened in Berlin.[8]

On 7 November 1938, a destitute seventeen-year-old Jew of Polish origin, Herschel Grynszpan, shot a German Embassy counsellor in Paris. The next day, the German propaganda machine threatened retaliation against the Jews. On 9 November, *The Times* anticipated a violent response against the

Jews in Germany,[9] and on that day and the next, synagogues in most cities and towns in Germany were burned or demolished, Jewish businesses devastated, scores of Jews mistreated and killed. The perpetrators were mostly SA troopers. Police forces and fire brigades had orders not to intervene.

As it happened, the annual Repentance Day in the Lutheran Church fell on the Sunday after the pogrom. The text on which to base the day's sermons was always chosen by one of the land churches and in 1938 the Lutheran Church in Hannover, in its turn, chose Jeremiah 22:29. A few clergymen in their sermons referred to the SA outrages. The most outspoken was Pastor Julius von Jan, in the humble south German community of Oberlenningen, near Kirchheim/Teck.

Jan had been born as the fourth child (of seven) to Albert von Jan. He grew up in Gerhausen, near Blaubeuren, served as a volunteer in the artillery in the First World War, rose to the rank of senior non-commissioned officer and officer candidate, was wounded and spent two years in English captivity, studied theology, and served as parish pastor in several communities. After his 16 November 1938 sermon in Oberlenningen, he was beaten by SA thugs, and the judiciary authorities took him into discovery custody.[10] He was tried in the Stuttgart Special Court,[11] found guilty of offences against the Pulpit Paragraph[12] and the Insidiousness Law,[13] and sentenced to sixteen months imprisonment, of which he served five months.

The church authorities protested against the harsh treatment of Jan and pressed criminal charges for various criminal acts committed against him and some other pastors, acts which included shootings, breaking and entering, causing bodily harm, and kidnapping. The Bishop of Württemberg, D. Theophil Wurm, wrote to the state prosecutor on 19 October 1939, four weeks before Jan's trial, that Jan's criticisms had been occasioned by the "tumultuous proceedings of 9/10 November 1938, for which, in their official statements, the authorities of the state had taken no responsibility" and which, according to a statement of the Minister for Church Affairs, Hanns Kerrl, to Bishop D. Theophil Wurm on 17 August 1939, had been "deprecated by the Führer"; Wurm asked how one could be punished for holding the same view as the Führer. He described Jan as a "respectable and competent pastor." But he also said that it would have been preferable that Jan had avoided the statements in his sermon that were criticized. Internally, the church authorities agreed that Jan had erred in engaging in a polemic that conflated religious with political argumentation.

After a series of letters written on behalf of von Jan by Wurm to Reich Interior Minister Frick, Reich Justice Minister Gürtner, and the Presiding Justice of the Stuttgart Special Court, Cuhorst, and after a plea for clemency had all failed,[14] Pastor von Jan began serving his sentence on 3 January 1940 in the detention centre in Landsberg/Lech. After various other pleas for clemency, he was released early, on 28 May 1940, but placed on probation until 31 May 1943. Immediately thereafter, he was drafted into the army, with loss of rank, and sent to the eastern front. After an illness, he served with logistic units in Hungary and Austria. After a few days as a prisoner-of-war in American custody, he was released on 15 May 1945.

Jan returned to his parish in Oberlenningen, almost seven years after his fateful sermon on the Day of Repentance in 1938. In 1949 he was transferred to Stuttgart-Zuffenhausen, and after a kidney embolism and heart attack in 1958, he retired to Korntal, where he died on 21 September 1964.[15]

Pastor Julius von Jan's Repentance Day Sermon[16]

Jer. 22, 29.
Dear Congregation!

The Prophet calls: O land, land! Hear the word of the Lord!

If we merely hear this one little sentence, we do not yet understand what difficult struggles and distresses have brought Jeremiah to this exclamation. He stands amid a nation in which the Lord, during an extended history, has revealed himself as a father and deliverer, as a leader and helper full of power and grace and glory. But this nation of Israel and, first of all, its kings and princes have trampled the law of God with their feet. Jeremiah has fought an unyielding battle in the name of God and justice against all these wrongs. For nearly thirty years he has preached the Lord's word to the nation. He contradicts the lying sermons of those who, with national enthusiasm, proclaim Hail and Victory. But he is not heard. More and more alone becomes the faithful man of God. Then comes the great hour when God calls his Prophet: "Go down to the house of the king himself and speak this word":

Hear the word of the Lord, O King of Judah, who sits on the throne of David, you, and your servants, and your people who enter these gates. Thus says the Lord: Do justice and righteousness, and deliver from the hand of the oppressor him who has been robbed. And do no wrong or violence to the alien, the fatherless, and the widow, nor shed innocent blood in this place. For if you will indeed obey this word, then there shall enter the gates of this house kings who sit on the throne of David, riding in chariots and on horses, they, and their servants, and their people. But if you will not heed these words, I swear by myself, says the Lord, that this house shall become a desolation. For thus says the Lord concerning the house of the king of Judah: You are as Gelead to me, as the summit of Lebanon, yet surely I will make you a desert, and uninhabited city. I will prepare destroyers against you, each with his weapons; and they shall cut down your choicest cedars, and cast them into the fire. And many nations will pass by this city, and every man will say to his neighbour, "Why has the Lord dealt thus with this great city?" And they will answer, "Because they forsook the covenant of the Lord their God, and worshipped other gods and served them. (Jer. 22:2–9.)

The king hardened himself against God's word and was suddenly led off by the enemy into captivity; his successor persecuted the prophet and died after a brief reign; and the third king was at the helm only three months; then he fell into the hands of the Babylonians! All this our chapter tells us.[17] In a short time, the reigns of three recalcitrant kings of Jerusalem were over. In deep sorrow of this, Jeremiah shouted into his nation: O land, land, hear the word of the Lord!

Why do you become unfaithful to the faithful God? Why do you no longer honour his commandments? Do you not see how your kings fared because of it? O land, dear homeland, hear the word of the Lord! In these days, a questioning is pervading our nation: Where in Germany is the prophet who will be sent into the king's house in order to speak the word of the Lord? Where is the man who calls out in the name of God and justice, as Jeremiah has called out: Uphold law and justice, save the robbed from the evildoer's hand! Oppress not the strangers, orphans and widows, and violate none, and shed not innocent blood.

God has sent us such men! They are today either in concentration camps or forced into silence. Those, however, who come into the princes' houses and are able still to perform sacred rites there are lying preachers like the national enthusiasts in Jeremiah's time and can only cry Hail and Victory, but not preach the word of the Lord. The men of the Provisional Church Government, about whom the newspapers reported in the last week, have, in the order of divine service, clearly pronounced the commandment of the Lord and have bowed themselves before God for church and nation because of the appalling disregard of the divine commandments by our nation.[18] Everyone knows how they have been pilloried for that as enemies of the nation and have been placed on unsalaried status – and it is distressing that our bishops have not recognized it as their duty to place themselves on the side of those who have spoken the word of the Lord.

If the one *must* remain silent and the other does not *want* to speak, then today we have every reason indeed to hold a Day of Repentance, *a day of mourning* over our and the nation's sins.

A crime has occurred in Paris. The murderer will receive his just penalty because he has violated divine law.

We mourn with our nation for the victim of this criminal act. But who would have thought that the consequence of this one crime in Paris could be so many crimes among us in Germany? Here we have received our deserts for the great apostasy from God and Christ, for organized anti-Christianity. The passions are unleashed, the commandments of God dishonoured, houses of God that were sacred to others have been burned down with impunity, the property of strangers has been robbed or destroyed, men who have loyally served our German nation and have conscientiously done their duty have been thrown into concentration camps merely because they belong to another race! Even if the injustice is not conceded from on high, sound popular sentiment feels it keenly, even where one dares not speak about it.

And we, as Christians, see how this injustice incriminates our nation before God and must draw his punishments upon Germany. For it is written: "Do not be deceived; God is not mocked, for whatever man sows, that he will also reap!"[19] Yes, it is a horrible seed of hatred that has now been sown again. What a horrible harvest will grow from it, if God does not grant to our nation and to us his grace for the purpose of sincere repentance.

When we speak thus of God's judgments, we know well that many silently think: How can one speak even today of God's penalties upon Germany, where things are so visibly looking up and where, in this year, ten million Germans have been united with the Reich?[20] There, indeed, one sees God's blessing upon our nation! Yes, an astonishing patience and grace of God is at work over us. But just for this reason the words apply: O land, land, hear the word of the Lord!

Now finally hear! Do you not know that God's grace guides you to penance? In our chapter, God instructed the prophet to say: As I live, says the Lord, though Coniah, the king of Judah, were the signet ring on my right hand, yet I would tear you off and give you into the hand of those who seek your life! How can a human and a nation be elevated by God to the highest honours – if he closes his heart before the word of the Lord, he will suddenly be plunged into the depths. Outward fortune, outward successes only too easily lead us humans into hubris that debases the entire divine blessing and therefore ends in a deep fall. Therefore the Day of Penance is for us a day of mourning over our and our nation's sins, which we confess before God, and *a day of prayer*: Lord, give us and our nation a new hearing of your word, a new honouring of your commandments! And begin with us. We so gladly go our own ways. We do so much and take so little time for the stillness in which we would be allowed to hear the word of the Lord, be it in divine service or in the little chamber. Therefore many a day goes by without our letting God be our Lord, because on the morning we were not with him to receive our orders. A Christian who does not every morning seek this stillness to hear endangers himself and does harm to the business of his Lord. For without the word of the Lord, we are surrendered to all demoniac forces and to all the seductive voices of the netherworld. When I ask, from time to time, in the youth group, where -we are in the daily readings of Scripture, one or two in a dozen can answer. The others went into their day without the word of God. How might it be with us grown-ups? Here certainly lies a great guilt of us Christians. Were we more faithful in hearing our Lord's order of the day, even the churchless people would more often hear a testimony of the Lord and would be saved from many an evil step. Therefore O land, land, land, hear the word of the Lord!

Yet in conclusion we do not want to forget that for us Christians the word of the Lord is even plainer and more valuable than for a Jeremiah. For it is fulfilled in Christ our Lord, who has said: "Repent, for the kingdom of heaven is at hand."[21] Through him, the Day of Repentance becomes for us *a day of thanks*. The world is so fond of mocking repentance because it has no notion that true repentance becomes the gate to the happiest life, and not only in the beyond, but even here on earth. I may remind you of the story of the prodigal son, of his repenting return home, and the rich life that now began for him at home through the kindness of his father. Whoever has returned home to his Lord through this gate of repentance knows how close at hand the kingdom of heaven has thereby, in fact, become. And if today we stood with our nation in repentance before God, then this confession of guilt, of which one believed it was not permitted to speak, this would be for me, at least today, like throwing off a great burden. God be praised! It has been spoken out before God and in the name of God. Now the world may do with us what it will. We stand in the hands of our Lord. God is faithful! But you, O land, land, land, hear the word of the Lord! Amen.

On 2 December 1938, the High Consistory, in the district court in Stuttgart, pressed the following written charges of breach of the public peace against the perpetrators of the attack on Julius von Jan.[22]

On 16 November 1938, Pastor Julius von Jan preached a sermon in Oberlenningen for which he will have to answer in the course of legal proceedings, which are already underway, as well as before his ecclesiastical supervisory authority.

On 25 November, there occurred in Oberlenningen tumultuous events that presumably are to be dealt with under the criminal code regarding breach of the public peace. At the parsonage in Oberlenningen, in the morning of Friday, 25 November, four posters were affixed (printed on red background): "Jew lackey." A specimen of these posters is enclosed. The posters in question are the same as those that, last Sunday, 27 November 1938, had been hung onto the persons of two citizens of Ludwigsburg, and the same as posted on the Lutheran deanery[23] in Ludwigsburg (see details below).

A rumour is circulating in Nürtingen that on 25 November the Nürtingen SA and Hitler Youth, in civilian clothes, were alerted without reason and given leaflets with the following contents: "The Confessing rabble-rouser von Jan in Oberlenningen has uttered, in his sermon on 16 November 1938 concerning the settling of accounts of the German nation with the Jewish world crime, as follows: Meritorious compatriots[24] (Jews) had been robbed of their most sacred possessions and these had been burned. What the government had done to the Jews would yet be avenged. May God give Hitler the necessary reverence so that the crimes will cease. Regaining the ten million compatriots in Austria and the Sudetenland was only an external success; internally, vengeance would not fail to come to pass."

These leaflets were also distributed in Oberlenningen on 25 November 1938 on the occasion of the tumultuous events described below. That Pastor von Jan has not made these statements emerges from the text of the sermon, which has since become known.

On the evening of 25 November between 8:00 and 9:00, numerous automobiles (cars and trucks), license III K, occupied by men in civilian clothes, entered Oberlenningen from the direction of Nürtingen-Kirchheim. The unloaded crew assembled in front of the gymnasium in Oberlenningen where, as it is recounted in Oberlenningen, Hitler Youth regimental commander Riegraf of Nürtingen spoke to the crowd, estimated at 300 to 500 persons. From the gymnasium, the crowd moved to the Lutheran parsonage. There the doorbell was rung and Pastor von Jan was asked for. The domestic servant answered that Pastor von Jan was not there, that he was in Schopfloch. After a short time, the doorbell was rung again at the parsonage, but this time the finger was kept on the doorbell. Again, the pastor was asked for. The answer, that he was in Schopfloch, found no credence. Thereupon the door of the parsonage was broken down. A considerable number of men penetrated into the house and searched for the pastor from attic to cellar.

Therefore, criminal charges are laid. The spokesman of those who penetrated into the house was Walker, MD, of Neckartenzlingen, formerly leader of the local branch of the NSDAP, currently SA Doctor. Dr Walker asked about the whereabouts of the pastor; he was recognized by a female resident of the house. Pastor von Jan was, in fact, in Schopfloch on this evening, where he had to hold a Bible course from 8:00 to 9:00 p.m. His wife had accompanied him.

From Oberlenningen, a passenger car with the license III K 10016 (from Nürtingen) drove to the parsonage in Schopfloch. One of the passengers rang the bell at the parsonage. Pastor Mildenberger of Schopfloch was asked about Pastor von Jan, whom one wished to speak to. When both pastors, Mildenberger and von Jan, stepped out of the house, Pastor von Jan was forced, after a short exchange of words, to enter the car, in which two other passengers assumed a menacing attitude. Even upon inquiry, no names, orders, or destination were indicated by the occupants of the car. Pastor von Jan was taken in the car to the front of the parsonage in Oberlenningen. Opposite the parsonage, across the street, there is a shed that is covered with a flat, tiled roof at about the height of a man. Pastor von Jan was tossed onto this roof, accompanied by the howling and verbal abuse of those present. In the process, he was beaten and pushed. It is also reported that on this occasion his pants' pocket was reached into and that his wallet with twenty-two RM stolen. Pastor von Jan was unable to fend off this physical abuse, even if he had wanted to. After a considerable time, Pastor von Jan was pulled down from the shed roof and taken to Oberlenningen Town Hall, accompanied by the mob with continuous howling, verbal abuse, shouting, and manhandling.

Doubtless at the instigation of the Schopfloch parsonage, several police officers from Kirchheim then arrived in a car. This car drove up to the Town Hall entrance, but had to be moved away again, upon the tumultuous demands of the mob, to permit an opportunity to form a gauntlet for von Jan's transfer to the car. This was done and the terrorists contemplated whether to beat or to spit on von Jan. They shouted at a policeman who tried to restore the public peace in front of the town hall that if it did not suit the munchkin, he would be hauled out too. The country constable who also tried to restore the public peace was told that he was an even greater scoundrel than the pastor. When Pastor von Jan was led into the police car, one of the breakers of the public peace[25] walked backwards, ahead of the pastor, and shone a flashlight into his face. Pastor von Jan's face shows a badly bruised spot below his eye and also cuts on his head. Whether there are other injuries we do not know. We are laying criminal charges based on sections 185, 223, 232 paragraph 3, 196, and 200 of the Criminal Code.[26]

Pastor von Jan was taken to the district court[27] jail in Kirchheim, and the participants of the attack in Oberlenningen drove back in the direction of Nürtingen in the automobiles in which they had come.

It hardly needs to be mentioned that universal outrage over these incidents prevails in the Oberlenningen parish and throughout the whole church district. Pastor von Jan joined the army as a seventeen-year-old volunteer on 7 August 1914, served at the front with a brief interval (as officer candidate) from 5 February 1915 to 8 April 1917, and was a prisoner-of-war in England from 9 April 1917 to 25 October 1919.

It was suggested above that these events in Oberlenningen must have an organizational connection with proceedings that took place in Ludwigsburg on 27 November of this year. A poster (printed on red background), "Jew-lackey," was affixed at the Lutheran deanery on the market place in Ludwigsburg. The name of the dean of Ludwigsburg was added in handwriting: "Dörrfuss." Shortly before the beginning of the main Sunday church service, a procession of demonstrators led two residents of Ludwigsburg, with the same red placard tied to their persons, through the streets past the deanery. In front of the deanery, there was chanting: "Dörrfuss, Jew lackey, shame!" In the market place, there was a rally in progress while the bells were ringing to summon the worshippers to church. As Dean Dörrfuss had to pass the demonstrators on the way to his sermon, he was pointed at and shouted at: "There goes the Jew lackey." A reason for this abusive demonstration is not known. We shall press criminal charges concerning this in a separate communication. The police, informed by telephone, declared themselves unable to remove the placard from the dean's office, although the prevention of another criminal act might be presumed not beyond their authority.

In order to complete this picture, the breach of the peace[28] perpetrated in Böckingen-Heilbronn on the night of 10–11 November (not, to be clear, 9–10 November) must be mentioned here, too. Criminal charges have been laid concerning this with the Chief Attorney Chief State Prosecutor[29] at the land court in Heilbronn. Towards 2:30 a.m. that night, there appeared in front of Parsonage I, in Böckingen, about twelve men in civilian clothes; they surrounded the house at the corners and opened fire with revolvers in order to prevent the observation of the proceedings. A neighbour who wanted to open a window had to take cover because immediately he heard a bullet whistle past his head. During this gunfire attack, the window panes of the parsonage were smashed with paving stones. The bedstead of the wife of the minister was hit. The beds were strewn with broken glass. There are three revolver bullet holes in the ceiling of the children's room. Live ammunition, as well as blanks, were used, as is to be concluded from the empty shells that were found. Following this attack, the windows at the parish association hall in Böckingen were smashed too, and additional assaults were perpetrated in the city. When the minister summoned the police in Heilbronn by telephone, the response was that they had their hands full with the Jews and had no time.
p.p. Schauffler.

On Sunday, 4 December 1938, Regional Bishop[30] D. Dr Konrad Hoffmann of Ulm conducted the church service in Oberlenningen. Before the sermon, he addressed the congregation to say that he came under instructions from the Land Bishop to demonstrate how the church leadership felt with them in view of what had happened to their pastor, and continued that God had wanted to fulfill these words from the Bible: "The men sought to do me evil, but God thought to do me well." (1 Moses 5:20) During the sermon and the concluding prayer, Hoffmann prayed for "all those who are pressed hard and in need of aid," and especially for "your pastor in his imprisonment," and for Pastor Martin Niemöller.[31] During a meeting of the Oberlenningen church council that followed, he communicated to the church council a statement by the High Consistory. Several points were discussed. One of the council members, named Leuthold, mentioned that he had earnestly warned Pastor von Jan in the past against sharply critical statements, whereupon Jan had asked him whether, as a Christian, he could call injustice justice; thereupon, Leuthold said he had not been able to say anything more. On his way back to Ulm, Prälat Hoffmann visited Pastor von Jan in prison in Kirchheim. Jan was in good spirits, and quietly brave.[32]

Statement of the High Consistory, Communicated by Prelate Hoffmann to the Parish Council in Oberlenningen on 4 December 1938

With pain and outrage, the Church Government has taken notice of the undignified proceedings that took place here in the community on Friday, 25 November at the parsonage and also in front of the parsonage in Schopfloch. The High Consistory[33] has learned with satisfaction that the community of Oberlenningen did not take part in these tumults and that it is, on the contrary, in agreement with the Church Government in the condemnation of what happened here. The High Consistory Church Council has brought charges[34] with the Chief Prosecutor for the crimes of aggravated breach of the peace, theft, breach of domestic peace, bodily assault and harm, and insult, and, insofar as required, has pressed criminal charges.[35]

Pastor von Jan, who is being accused of illicit utterances in his sermon on Repentance Day, 16 November, will have to answer to the state judge and also to his ecclesiastical supervisory authority. Distorted statements about this Repentance Day sermon have also been spread and broadcast in leaflets. But the verbatim text of the sermon is in the hands of the state judge and has become known in the meantime also to the church government.

In view of the criminal proceedings pending because of this Repentence Day sermon, and with regard to the subsequent official ecclesiastical review of the matter, this is not the place to take a position in detail concerning the sermon of Pastor von Jan. It is the specific obligation of the Lutheran Church on Land Repentance Day, through the proclamation of God's word, to sharpen consciences. Even if the Repentance Day sermon of Pastor von Jan is to be subject to criticism, it is credible that he intended to give witness for the purpose of sharpening consciences. The members of the Church Council [of Oberlenningen] and the parishioners are requested to think of and intercede before God for the pastor and his family, who are being severely tested by the events.

On 28 November 1938, the district court[36] of Kirchheim issued a warrant for the arrest of Pastor von Jan. The case against Pastor von Jan eventually came under the jurisdiction of the Special Court for the Superior Land Court District of Stuttgart. The Special Court in Stuttgart rejected an appeal against the arrest warrant of the same day, on 12 December 1938. Pastor von Jan was imprisoned in Kirchheim/Teck, then in Stuttgart. On 27 March 1939, upon a further appeal against Pastor von Jan's detention, the arrest warrant was rescinded, but immediately upon his release by the court, he was placed in custody by the Secret State Police in Stuttgart. Finally, on 13 April 1939, Pastor von Jan was released but simultaneously expelled from the territory of Württemberg-Hohenzollern. He and his family found accommodation in a Bavarian church home near Hersbruck, and he was commissioned for pastoral work in the Lutheran diaspora region of Passau. On 23 May 1939, the district attorney[37] at the Special Court of the Superior Land court district of Stuttgart indicted Pastor von Jan.[38] On 15 November 1939, the Special Court sat to hear Pastor von Jan's case. The verdict follows:

Copy[39]

SPECIAL COURT FOR THE SUPERIOR COURT DISTRICT
STUTTGART IN STUTTGART

SM Nr. 102/1939
SG Nr. 1103/1938[40]
In the name of the German People!

Verdict

In the criminal case against the Lutheran Pastor Julius von Jan, born on 17 April 1897 in Schweindorf, district of Aalen, married, previously resident in Oberlenningen, district of Kirchheim/Teck, now in Ortenburg via Vilshofen (Lower Bavaria), because of offences against the Insidiousness Law and other matters, the Special Court for the Land Superior Court District[41] of Stuttgart has reached the following verdict in its session of 15 November 1939, after oral proceedings, in which Senate President Cuhorst participated as chair, Land Court Counsellor Payer as recorder, Land Court Counsellor Dr Azesdorfer as assessor, Prosecuting Attorney Wendling as counsel for the prosecution, and non-permanent Justice Inspector Schlumberger as registrar:

The defendant is sentenced to one year and four months in prison for an offence under section 2, paragraph 1 of the Insidiousness Law, concomitantly with an offence according to section 130a of the Criminal Code. The four months of pre-trial detention are included in the calculation of the sentence. The accused has to bear the costs of the proceedings.

Reasons

I The defendant, who is descended from a Württemberg parsonage, passed the Land Examination and attended the Lutheran Theological Seminaries of Maulbronn and Blaubeuren. At the outbreak of war, at the age of seventeen, he enlisted as a volunteer in Artillery Regiment 49 in Ulm. From February 1915 to April 1917, he served at the western front. He proved himself as a brave soldier, was promoted to senior non-commissioned officer, and was decorated with the Iron Cross II, the Württemberg Silver Military Medal of Merit, and the Front Soldier Cross of Honour. On 9 April 1917, lightly wounded, he fell into English war captivity, from which he returned home only in November 1919. After the war, he studied Lutheran theology in the Seminary in Tübingen. Upon the completion of his study and multiple temporary appointments, he received his first permanent pastoral position in Herrentierbach. Later he was pastor in Brettach. On 11 September 1935, he came to Oberlenningen as local pastor. He is married and the father of a four-year-old boy. He has no prior criminal record.

The defendant has been a member of the National Socialist People's Welfare Organization[42] since 1933. In the same year, he took on an SA sponsorship and for a long time has spent five RM per month for the outfitting of an SA man. Moreover, he once took in an SA man for ten days' rest.

On account of the incidents that form the subject of these criminal proceedings, the accused was taken into protective custody in connection with a demonstration conducted against him on 25 November 1938. Until 13 April 1939, he has been in protective and investigative pre-trial custody. Subsequently, he has been forbidden to reside in Württemberg. Since then, he has sojourned in the Lutheran retreat centre in Engelthal, district Hersbruck. Lately he has been administering the parsonage in Ortenburg (Bavaria).

II The defendant, a fanatical adherent of the "Confessing Church," has repeatedly given cause for criticism in the political regard. In the Württemberg church struggle, he was one of the pastors who, in October 1934, publicly read the declaration of the Land Bishop from the pulpit,[43] although this had been forbidden. The proceedings initiated against him at that time were suspended by a decision of 23 September 1935. Further frictions with the Party authorities in Brettach resulted from the fact that the accused believed it necessary, time and again, to intercede publicly for his fellow pastor Niemöller. After his transfer to Oberlenningen, difficulties arose in increasing measure because the accused could not refrain from dragging politics into the pulpit and from taking a position against State and Party in a veiled manner. Various attempts to stop his political expectorations in his sermons, which were undertaken with good intentions not only by the local Party group leader[44] and his deputy, but also by parish Church Council member Keller, by the manufacturer Scheufelen, and the parish nurse Herrmann, could not bring the defendant to a change of heart. He did not even desist from his political-sermon reflections when Keller vigorously took exception to them in an open discussion in the parish Church Council and refused to continue attending services under such circumstances because Keller feared incidents and did not want to come forward as a witness against his pastor. The defendant left unheeded even the earnest warnings of the Land Councillor[45] to avoid political and religious-political statements from the pulpit and elsewhere. There followed such warnings in the spring of 1937, ultimately on the express orders of the Secret State Police head office in Stuttgart, and in September 1938 because of an article by the defendant about the "Hindenburg" Zeppelin catastrophe that he had published in the May issue of his parish newspaper.[46] In the article about the air ship disaster, the defendant stated, among other things: "But the disaster is also a warning for the German nation to bow in humility before the Lord God and not to make itself into the Lord God. Therefore we reject the politicized German Christian Church,[47] which teaches: We believe first in the German nation and its Führer, and after that also, as long as the two are compatible, in the Word of God in the Holy Scriptures. Whoever knows and loves Christ the Lord cannot serve two masters,[48] and most certainly not when the first rank is held by the German nation and the second by the Father of Jesus Christ."

III The incidents which parish Church Councillor Keller had feared came to pass on 25 November 1938 occasioned by the sermon that the defendant had given in the church in Oberlenningen on Repentance Day, 16 November 1938. There occurred against the defendant a demonstration that made it necessary to place him in protective custody.

The High Consistory Church Council had prescribed the lesson for the sermon on Repentance Day: Jeremiah 22:29: "O land, land, land hear the word of the Lord!" On the basis of this text, and using other verses from the chapter, the defendant gave a sermon that, according to the submitted manuscript and the credible admissions of the defendant, who claims to have essentially kept to his notes, contained among others the following statements:

He [Jeremiah] contradicts the lying sermons of those who with national enthusiasm proclaim, Hail and Victory.
[...[49]] In these days, a questioning is pervading our nation: Where in Germany is the prophet who will be sent into the king's house in order to speak the word of the Lord? Where is the man who calls out in the name of God and justice as Jeremiah has called out: Uphold law and justice, save the

robbed from the evildoer's hand! Oppress not the strangers, orphans, and widows, and violate none, and shed not innocent blood! God has sent us such men. They are today either in concentration camps or forced into silence. Those, however, who come into the princes' houses and are able still to perform sacred rites there are lying preachers like the national enthusiasts in Jeremiah's time and can only cry Hail and Victory, but not preach the word of the Lord. The men of the Provisional Church Government, about whom the newspapers reported in the last week, have in the order of divine service clearly pronounced the commandment of the Lord, and have bowed themselves before God for church and nation because of the appalling disregard of the divine commandments by our nation.[50] Everyone knows how they have been pilloried for that as enemies of the nation and have been placed on unsalaried status – and it is distressing that our bishops have not recognized it as their duty to place themselves on the side of those who have spoken the word of the Lord.

If the one *must* remain silent and the other does not *want* to speak, then today we have every reason indeed to hold a Day of Repentance, *a day of mourning* over our and the nation's sins. A crime has occurred in Paris. The murderer will receive his just penalty because he has violated divine law. We mourn with our nation for the victim of this criminal act. But who would have thought that the consequence of this one crime in Paris could be so many crimes among us in Germany? Here we have received our deserts for the great apostasy from God and Christ, for organized anti-Christianity. The passions are unleashed, the commandments of God dishonoured, houses of God that were sacred to others have been burned down with impunity, the property of strangers has been robbed and destroyed; men who have loyally served our German nation and have conscientiously done their duty have been thrown into concentration camps merely because they belong to another race! Even if the injustice is not conceded from on high, sound popular sentiment feels it keenly, even where one dares not speak about it. And we, as Christians, see how this injustice incriminates our nation before God and must draw his punishments upon Germany. For it is written: "Do not be deceived; God is not mocked, for whatever a man sows, that he will also reap."[51] Yes, it is a horrible seed of hatred that has now been sown again. What a horrible harvest will grow from it, if God does not grant to our nation and to us his grace for the purpose of sincere repentance.

When we speak thus of God's judgments, we know well that many silently think: How can one speak even today of God's penalties upon Germany, where things are so visibly looking up and where, in this year, ten million Germans have been united with the Reich? There, indeed, does one see God's blessing upon our nation! Yes, an astonishing patience and grace of God is at work over us. But just for this reason the words apply: "O land, land, hear the Word of the Lord!"[52]

During this sermon, the accused at least twice used the expression "poor Germany!" as was established on the basis of the emphatic, apparently credible evidence by the witness Dietrich and contrary to the denials of the defendant. The defendant concluded his disquisitions with the words: "God be praised! It has been spoken out before God and in the name of God! Now the world may do with us what it will. We stand in the hands of our Lord. God is faithful. But you, O land, land, hear the word of the Lord."[53]

Almost every Sunday after the conclusion of the sermon, the defendant read an "Intercession List" of pastors incarcerated, forbidden to speak, and expelled from their land. Finally, he concluded his closing prayer with the imploration that God might grant even the Führer and all the authorities the spirit of repentance and of obedience to God's Word.

IV Concerning these facts, the defendant stated the following in the main hearing:

He had made the statements in his sermon knowingly, especially with a view to the demonstrations and excesses that had been perpetrated against the Jews throughout Germany on 9 November 1938. Based on verse 3, "Do justice and righteousness, and deliver from the hand of the oppressor he who has been robbed. / And do no wrong of violence to the alien, the fatherless, and the widow, nor shed innocent blood in this place,"[54] he found himself compelled to take a position on these incidents. It was his view that injustice had been done to the Jews in Germany, who were, after all, innocent of the murder of Embassy Counsellor vom Rath in Paris. He had in mind, in the first instance, the baptized Jew Dr Bär, in Böhringen, who was well known in Oberlenningen since his wife was a daughter of the late Pastor Rheinwald of Oberlenningen, and whose incarceration and removal to the concentration camp had also produced bad blood in his village. That was what this sentence had referred to: "Men who have loyally served our German nation and have conscientiously done their duty were thrown into concentration camps simply because they belonged to another race." For him, as a Christian, the destruction of the synagogues and the causing of other damages, as well as the incarceration of the Jews, had been crimes against the commandments of God and thereby unjust. As a pastor, he had taken it to be his duty to go before God with these sins and crimes and to implore him for mercy for the nation. He had not, in that, intended to act in an inciting or provocative manner against State, Government, and Party; rather he had merely, out of obedience to God and the church, wanted to point to things that had to be rectified before God. The excessive raging of feelings against the Jews had only been possible, in his view, because the German nation had become ever more removed from the Word of God and had been removed even more from it through ideological indoctrination. In this sense, he had spoken of "organized anti-Christianity," described the actions against the Jews as a "horrible seed of hatred," and expressed the fear that a "horrible harvest" would grow from it. It was his view that one could feel even now how hated we were in the world abroad and how much these occurrences had contributed to the intensification of enmity against the Reich and had perhaps even led to war.

With the "lying preachers" who, like the national enthusiasts in Jeremiah's time, only cried hail and victory but did not preach the Word of the Lord, he had meant the Reich Bishop Müller and his adherents. The utterance about the men emulating Jeremiah, who were today either in concentration camps or forced into silence, had been a reference to Pastor Niemöller, who was in protective custody, and to the reprimanded men of the Provisional Church Government.

V In the assessment of these facts of the case, the Special Court became convinced that the defendant was guilty of an offence against section 2, paragraph 1 of the Insidiousness Law,[55] concomitant with an offence according to section 130a of the Penal Code. The defendant prepared his sermon carefully. As he has himself admitted, he committed it to writing in full and learned it by heart. As he has himself admitted, he prepared it in clear knowledge of its contents. He acted, however, also in full knowledge of the effect that it had to have upon the hearers, and taking the risk of thereby coming into conflict with the laws of the state. This emerges clearly and distinctly from his closing words, in which he stated: "Praise be God! It has been spoken out before God and in the name of God! Now the world may do with us what it will."

1 The defendant did not confine himself to ecclesiastical-religious affairs, as he has tried to show, but rather, as he had done repeatedly, he drew political matters into the sphere of his considerations. Apart from his attacks against the Reich Bishop, whom he described as a "lying preacher," and against the South German bishops, including his own Land Bishop, whom he accused from the pulpit of neglect of duty because they had distanced themselves from the course of action of the Provisional Church Government, the defendant in his sermon mainly treated the measures implemented against Jews living in Germany and occasioned by the murder of Embassy Counsellor vom Rath in Paris by the Jew Grünspan. Apparently without any understanding of the need for drastic measures against the foreign Jewish race, he was not content to deplore possible excesses on the occasion of the demonstration of 9 November 1938; rather, he took a stand in a provocative and inciting way in his disquisitions against the Führer's and generally the Reich Government's Jewish and racial policy. Not only did he, from his pulpit, speak up for the Jews in the person of Dr Bär, whom he called a loyal servant of the German nation, he also declared it an injustice and in contradiction to wholesome popular sentiment that the government took the Jews in Germany into protective custody as a countermeasure against the murder in Paris, although the defendant must have known that the Third Reich is locked in the fiercest battle with World Jewry,

who consider fair any means to damage the German Reich. He described the actions against Jews quite generally as a horrible seed of hatred and, in an unmistakable allusion to the war, he went so far as to prophesy a horrible harvest for "poor Germany." Moreover, he held the Party responsible for this ill fortune, which in his view the German nation had to expect, and accused it of promoting organized anti-Christianity in its ideological indoctrination. When he spoke further of the National Socialist enthusiasts who cried only victory and hail,[56] he not only meant to refer to the Reich Bishop and brother clergymen who had turned away from the Confessing Church, but he also thereby pointed his attacks indirectly against the National Socialist movement and its culture. The defendant did not, as a German pastor, shy away from diminishing and disparaging the joining of Austria and the Sudetenland to the German Reich in its significance for the German nation, and depicted the position as if these successes were also only temporary and could not prevent the downfall of the German nation. When he finally said that men like Jeremiah should stand up and tell the personages in authority that they must act lawfully and with justice, then this attack went against the Führer and the Reich Government, who were thereby accused, at the very least, of tolerating injustices, if not of acting unjustly themselves. The same accusation lay in pointing to the protective custody of Niemöller, of which the accused allegedly knew that it was being continued upon the highest orders.[57] He thereby stated that Niemöller was being illegally detained only because he had spoken the truth, and that, for the same reason, the members of the Provisional Church Government had been reprimanded unjustly.

2 With such statements, which necessarily had to have the effect mentioned above, the defendant, in front of his parishioners, has subjected measures of the Führer, the Reich Government, and the Party, in discussion that in no manner belonged in the pulpit, to a hateful criticism in a veiled and inciting manner. With his exaggerated and generalized portrayal of the events of 9 November 1938, and with his other statements, he has created in every unbiased hearer the appearance that law and justice no more existed in Germany, as if arbitrari-

ness and violence had free reign, as if the truth were forcibly suppressed in Germany, and as if the Party's main concern were directed upon the suppression of Christianity. If the accused did not name the responsible personages, he knew nevertheless that it had been made clear to every hearer that such conditions were tolerated and approved by the leading authorities in Government and Party, even if they had not deliberately brought them into being. The fact that thereby the leading men in Germany, among them the Führer, were most seriously insulted requires as little additional substantiation as the further finding that the statements of the defendant from the pulpit were liable, especially also in view of the dark prophesies he had pronounced, to undermine the nation's confidence in the political leadership. In this regard, the defendant had to be convicted of an offence under section 2, paragraph 1 of the Insidiousness Law. The Reich Minister of Justice has ordered criminal prosecution.

3   The utterances of the defendant, however, also constitute a violation of section 130a of the Penal Code. As already demonstrated, the defendant has, as a clergyman, in his sermon, to a large extent made things that concern governmental measures the topic of preaching and discussions. That has occurred in a manner endangering the public peace. The accusations of arbitrariness and violent tyranny as well as organized anti-Christianity that he made against State and Party, and the conclusions he drew from them, were so grave that they are bound to represent a danger to the public peace. For the National Socialists among his hearers, they represented a slap in the face. His words were bound to be particularly provocative for them. But they were also otherwise likely to put persons in opposition to the state and to incite action against governmental measures and orders. The defendant knew this since he had been warned repeatedly about his political attacks in his sermons. He is therefore guilty of an offence under section 130a of the Penal Code, compared with section 73 of the Penal Code, concomitantly with an offence under section 2, paragraph 1 of the Insidiousness Law.

VI   The statements of the defendant constitute a dangerous incitement. At a time when the German nation is locked in fierce battle with its foes in order to battle for its freedom and its vital rights, it would have been the duty of the defendant to stand for freedom and unity. Instead of that, he made statements from the pulpit that could only be destined to create unrest and confusion and to deepen existing divisions. All warnings from the private and official side were not able to keep him from doing this. All of those things had to be taken into consideration against him in the establishment of the sentence. The lack of contrition that he displayed in the main hearing had to be taken into consideration as particularly aggravating. He declared that he did not have to ask what he might to do as a citizen; for him the sole criterion was what he must do according to God's Word (as he interpreted it). He was thus evidently not willing to respect state law in fighting for the interests of his church. Therefore he represents a particular danger for the State. For the purpose of deterrence alone, he therefore had to be punished severely. He could claim as a mitigating factor that he had no previous criminal record, and that he had fought as a brave man in the war. In weighing these grounds, the Court deemed sentence of imprisonment for one year and four months to be an appropriate expiation. The four months of investigative and protective custody served are deducted from the sentence according to section 60 of the Penal Code.

VII The decision on costs is based on section 465 of the Code of Criminal Procedure.[58]

Cuhorst. Payer. Azesdorfer.

NOTES

1 See document no. 12.
2 Raul Hilberg, *The Destruction of the European Jews*, revised and definitive ed. (New York, London: Holmes & Meier 1985), 34; boycott threat in *Völkischer Beobachter*, Munich edition (27 March 1933); boycott announcement in *Völkischer Beobachter*, Munich ed., no. 88 (Wednesday, 29 March 1933), had on the front page the banner headline "Aufruf der Parteileitung der N.S.D.A.P. Samstag, Schlag 10 Uhr, wird das Judentum wissen, wem es den Kampf angesagt hat!" Yitzhak Arad, et al., eds., *Documents on the Holocaust*, 36. Avraham Barkai, *Vom Boykott zur "Entjudung." Der wirtschaftliche Existenzkampf der Juden im Dritten Reich 1933-1943*, 23-35; Avraham Barkai, *From Boycott to Annihilation. The Economic Struggle of German Jews, 1933-1943*, 13-25.

3 http://www.ashkenazhouse.org/synagogue-main.htm; Saskia Rohde, "Die Zerstörung der Synagogen unter dem Nationalsozialismus," in Arno Herzig, Ina Susanne
Lorenz, Saskia Rohde, *Verdrängung und Vernichtung der Juden unter dem Nationalsozialismus* (Hamburg: H. Christians 1992), 156–7.

4 See document no. 1.

5 Papers of D. Dr Konrad Hoffmann, in the editor's possession.

6 Deutsche Christen (DC).

7 Vorläufige Kirchenleitung der Bekenntniskirche.

8 See document no. 9.

9 Leader in *Völkischer Beobachter* (8 November 1938); Joseph Goebbels, *Die Tagebücher*,
Teil I, Band 6: see entries for 7–10 Nov. 1938.

10 Untersuchungshaft.

11 Sondergericht. A decree of 21 March 1933 had established special courts with unlimited jurisdiction to hand down unlimited prison sentences or the death penalty without hearing evidence and without the possibility of appeal; "Verordnung
der Reichsregierung über die Bildung von Sondergerichten. Vom 21. März 1933,"
Reichsgesetzblatt Teil I 1933 (Berlin: Reichsverlagsamt 1933), 136–8; "Verordnung
der Reichsregierung über die Zuständigkeit der Sondergerichte. Vom 6. Mai 1933,"
Reichsgesetzblatt Teil I 1933, 259; "Verordnung des Reichspräsidenten zur Abwehr
heimtückischer Angriffe gegen die Regierung der nationalen Erhebung. Vom 21.
März 1933," *Reichsgesetzblatt Teil I 1933*, 135. A further law expanded judicial authority and also established a "People's Court" (Volksgerichtshof) for cases of treason,
whose judgments also could not be appealed against; "Gesetz zur Änderung von
Vorschriften des Strafrechts und des Strafverfahrens. Vom 24. April 1934," *Reichsgesetzblatt Teil I 1934* (Berlin: Reichsverlagsamt 1934), 345–8.

12 Reference to the so-called Maulkorberlaß (muzzling decree) of Reich Bishop Müller,
dated 4 January 1934, asking clergy "to desist from the unlawful and unconstitu-
tional demands and to take no steps that must be disastrous for our evangelical
church and for our German fatherland equally"; in Gerhard Schäfer, *Die Evangelische Landeskirche in Württemberg und der Nationalsozialismus. Eine Dokumentation
zum Kirchenkampf*, vol. 2, 1020–1.

13 The Insidiousness Law (Law against Insidious Attacks against the State and
Party and for the Protection of the Party Uniform – "Gesetz gegen heimtückische Angriffe auf Staat und Partei und zum Schutz der Parteiuniformen. Vom
20. Dezember 1934)," *Reichsgesetzblatt I 1934*, 1269–71, replaced the Insidiousness
Decree of 21 March 1933 ("Verordnung des Reichspräsidenten zur Abwehr heimtückischer Angriffe gegen die Regierung der nationalen Erhebung. Vom 21. März
1933," *Reichsgesetzblatt Teil I 1933*, 135); the Insidiousness Law made the utterance
of untrue statements a criminal offence with a maximum sentence of death if the
statements were designed to stir up the German populace or create difficulties for
the Reich abroad.

14 See Schäfer, *Evangelische Landeskirche*, vol. 6, 139–59.

15 Landeskirchliches Archiv Stuttgart, A 227 Personalakte Julius von Jan.

16 Source: Carbon copy in Landeskirchliches Archiv, Stuttgart, A 227 Personalakte Julius von Jan; the copy, presumably the top copy, that was part of the evidence in Jan's trial is assumed to have been destroyed by aerial bombing in 1944; Staatsarchiv Ludwigsburg to the editor 25 July 2008; the sermon is printed only in an abridged variant version in Gerhard Schäfer, *Vom Wort zur Antwort. Dialog zwischen Kirche und Welt in 5 Jahrhunderten* (Stuttgart: Konrad Theiss Verlag 1991), 151–3. Cf. also John Conway, *The Nazi Persecution of the Churches, 1933–1945*; Ernst Christian Helmreich, *The German Churches under Hitler. Background, Struggle, and Epilogue*; Klaus Scholder, *The Churches and the Third Reich.*

17 This was the Babylonian exile of the leading classes, under King Nebukadnezar II in 597 (1st exile; the 2nd is dated 587 and 582).

18 See the "Order of Prayer of the Vorläufige Kirchenleitung" in Schäfer, *Die Evangelische Landeskirche*, vol. 5, 1119–22; cf., 318–19.

19 Galatians 6:7.

20 Reference to Anschluss of Austria and annexation of Sudetenland in March and October 1938.

21 Matthew 4:17.

22 Source: Landeskirchliches Archiv, Stuttgart, A 227 Personalakte Julius von Jan; Schäfer, *Die Evangelische Landeskirche*, vol. 6, 120–4. For an account of the attack on Pastor Mörike of Kirchheim, see Schäfer, *Die Evangelische Landeskirche*, vol. 5, 936–53.

23 Evangelisches Dekanatamt.

24 Volksgenossen.

25 Landfriedensbrecher.

26 These charges included breach of the public peace, theft, unlawful entry, bodily assault, and defamation.

27 Amtsgericht.

28 Landfriedensbruch.

29 Oberstaatsanwalt.

30 Prälat.

31 Pastor Martin Niemöller, a submarine captain in the First World War, became a pastor after the war, and in 1933 the founder of the Pastors' Emergency League and one of the Leaders of the Confessing Church; he was dismissed as a pastor in November 1933 but continued to work until his arrest on 1 July 1937; cf. Eberhard Röhm and Jörg Thierfelder, eds., *Evangelische Kirche zwischen Kreuz und Hakenkreuz* (Stuttgart: Calwer Verlag 1990), 154, 156; Leonore Siegele-Wenschkewitz, "Auseinandersetzungen mit einem Stereotyp: Die Judenfrage im Leben Martin Niemöllers" in Ursula Büttner, ed., *Die Deutschen und die Judenverfolgung im "Dritten Reich"* (Hamburg: Christians 1992), 303–4; cf. James Bentley, *Martin Niemöller, 1892–1984* (New York: Free Press 1984).

32 Prälat of Ulm [D. Dr Konrad] Hoffmann to Ev. Oberkirchenrat, Stuttgart, 5 Dec. 1938, Landeskirchliches Archiv, Personnel File of Pastor Julius von Jan.

33 Oberkirchenrat.

34 Strafanzeige.

35 Here the German term is Strafantrag = to lay criminal charges, as opposed to Strafanzeige = to bring a charge (against).

36 Amtsgericht.

37 Oberstaatsanwalt.

38 Indictment in Schäfer, *Die Evangelische Landeskirche*, vol. 6, 126–31.

39 Source: Landeskirchliches Archiv, Stuttgart, A 227 Personalakte Julius von Jan; Schäfer, *Die Evangelische Landeskirche*, vol. 6, 124–8, 131–9.

40 MS notes "B. 9.1.40 Umlauf i. Coll W[urm]."

41 Oberlandesgerichtsbezirk.

42 Nationalsozialistische Volkswohlfahrt, NSV.

43 Bishop Wurm's statement was published in *Beiblatt zum württembergischen Amtsblatt,* vol. 27 (28), and in *Allgemeine Evangelisch-Lutherische Kirchenzeitung*, vol. 69 (1936): col. 877 et seq.; Schäfer, *Die Evangelische Landeskirche*, vol. 4, 864–73; Martin Greschat, *Zwischen Widerspruch und Widerstand. Texte zur Denkschrift der Bekennenden Kirche an Hitler (1936)*, 225–7.

44 Ortsgruppenleiter.

45 Landrat.

46 Gemeindeblatt.

47 Indictment against Jan, 23 May 1939, Landeskirchliches Archiv, Stuttgart, A 227 Personalakte Julius von Jan.

48 Matthew 6:24.

49 Ellipsis in the quotation from Jan's sermon.

50 See the "Order of Prayer of the Vorläufige Kirchenleitung" in Schäfer, *Landeskirche*, vol. 5, 1119–22; cf. 318–19.

51 Galatians 6:7.

52 Jeremiah 22:29.

53 Jeremiah 22:9.

54 Jeremiah 22:3.

55 *Reichsgesetzblatt Teil I 1933*, 135; "Gesetz gegen heimtückische Angriffe auf Staat und Partei und zum Schutz der Parteiuniformen. Vom 20. Dezember 1934," *Reichsgesetzblatt Teil I 1933*, 1269–71. The Insidiousness Decree of 1933 and the Insidiousness Law of 1934 declared saying anything factually untrue a criminal offense with a maximum penalty of death if the statement was potentially damaging to state interests or government prestige or designed to incite the public.

56 Note the change in terminology, from von Jan's "national enthusiasts" (Schwärmer), who cried only "hail and victory" (Heil und Sieg), to "National Socialist enthusiasts" (Schwärmer), who could cry only "victory and hail" (Sieg und Heil).

57 Highest orders must here mean Hitler's orders.

58 Strafprozessordnung.

14

Johannes Popitz, Prussian Minister of Finance, Protest against the 9 November 1938 Pogrom

Johannes Popitz (1884–2 February 1945) was a jurist; from 1919, he worked in the Reich Ministry of Finance; from 1925 to 1929, he served as State Secretary in this Ministry; from 1932 to 1933, as Reich Minister without Portfolio; from April 1933 to 20 July 1944, he was Prussian Minister of Finance.

Popitz's position on discrimination and persecution of the Jews was differentiated. From 1933–35 he was concerned mainly with the rule of law and orderly procedures, and with ending the extralegal, unregulated, and unpredictable hooliganism of SA troopers and individual Party functionaries. He did not question, to use the phrase in the note of 18 October 1938 that the American Ambassador conveyed to the Foreign Office in Berlin, "Germany's entire right to take measures of internal effect with regard to the political opinions, the religious beliefs, and the racial organization of its citizens."[1]

In March 1933, Popitz sent a draft for the "Law for the Restoration of the Professional Civil Service" to Vice Chancellor Franz von Papen. A different version was promulgated on 7 April 1933. The law was intended to justify the numerous patronage replacements of civil servants with friends and supporters of the new regime. Apparently Popitz agreed that the government should have the ability, if it wished, to remove Communists and Jews from the civil service. When a meeting of ministers, including Popitz and chaired by the Prussian Ministerpresident Hermann Göring, met on 5 May 1933 to discuss details of the law's implementation, the protocol declared unanimous agreement with the proposals, in particular with Popitz's suggestion that civil servants could be retired with full pension rights but without being given reasons, so that neither political nor "racial" motives would be given and any defamation avoided.[2] Again, in discussions preceding and preparing for the Nürnberg racial laws, on 20 August 1935, Popitz said he wished "that the government set a clear limit – it did not matter where – for the treatment of the Jews, but then firmly see to it that the limit be respected."[3]

After his arrest for having participated in the conspiracy to overthrow the regime, the Secret State Police (Geheime Staatspolizei/Gestapo) quoted Popitz as having agreed that the Jews should be removed from positions in the state and in the economy, but having recommended a somewhat more gradual method, especially because of foreign-policy considerations.[4] The vulgar language in the German Gestapo report shows that it contained the style of the interrogator, which could only have become Popitz's through torture. His alleged expression of "approval of the National Socialist state in every way" is incorrect, and Popitz contradicted it in testimony at his trial in the "People's Court" on 3 October 1944, when he said that "the manner and speed of the solution of the Jewish Question" had caused his "inner detachment from National Socialism."[5] He disagreed with the manner of the "solution of the Jewish Question," namely, mass murder.

Popitz was hanged on 2 February 1945, on the same day as Carl Goerdeler. Both appear to have been spared, on Himmler's orders, until long after their trials because of their foreign contacts, which Himmler had thought might prove useful to him.[6]

Ulrich von Hassell's Account of Johannes Popitz's Protest against the 9 November 1938 Pogrom[7]

After the pogrom, Popitz actually tendered his resignation to Göring, who had promised to pass on the request to Hitler. He, P[opitz], had felt that he, at least, must take this action, since those responsible – Gürtner,[8] [Schwerin-]Krosigk,[9] Neurath[10] – as Reich Cabinet ministers, once again had failed ignominiously. Neurath was simply lazy and indolent: when P[opitz] had wanted to talk with him about the matter, he had let him know through some secretary that he could not arrange it just now. This is indeed just like N[eurath]. P[opitz] said he had talked the matter over with Göring in the most candid manner and had clearly referred to Göring's future position and pointed out the impossibility of Göring taking part in such things. G[öring] had been profoundly upset and apparently entirely convinced. But he had it not in him for the ultimate consequence because he was completely dependent upon Hitler and in fear of Himmler and Heydrich. Nevertheless, G[öring] had spoken to the latter quite roughly and said that now he, too, would burn something, namely, his honorary uniforms the SA and SS had given him. (Equally he gave the Gauleiters a dressing down so that the whole building had reverberated.[11] Ilse G[öring][12] told me yesterday, which is interesting enough, that the decent Gauleiters afterwards unreservedly acknowledged the justice of such language.)

I asked P[opitz] about Himmler's attitude in the Jewish matter; it seemed to me obscure. P[opitz] confirmed this: H[immler] had created a shrewd alibi for himself by writing or wiring Hitler to the effect that he could not carry out the orders. Since he received no reply, he did carry them out. Now he can say that he had done what he could. It follows from this that quite strict orders had been issued by Hitler himself; the provincial governors had mimeographed, detailed instructions for the destructions (I[lse] G[öring]). P[opitz] has told Göring that those responsible must be punished. Answer: "My dear Popitz, do you wish to punish the Führer?"

NOTES

1 AA PA R 99366 and document no. 16. On Popitz cf. Gerhard Schulz, "Über Johannes Popitz (1884-1945)," *Der Staat* 24 (1985): 485-511; Johanna Bödeker, "Johannes Popitz: Auf der Suche nach einer neuen Wirtschaftsordnung," *Der Staat* 24 (1985): 513-25.

2 Hans Mommsen, *Beamtentum im Dritten Reich*, 39-42; Popitz to Ministerialdirektor im Preussischen Staatsministerium Dr Friedrich Walter Landfried, 23 March 1933, Geheimes Staatsarchiv, Berlin, HA Rep. 90, Nr. 469; Protokoll über die Chefbesprechung am 5. Mai 1933 of Ministerpresident Göring (in the chair), Staatsminister Kerrl, Professor Dr Popitz, Rust, Staatssekretäre Körner (d. St M.), Dr Wiskott (Landw.), Grauert (Min. d. Inn.), Ministerialdirektor Dr Schellen (Min. d. Inn.), Ministerialrat Bergbohm als Protokollführer, Leiter der Pressestelle des St M. Oberregierungsrat Sommerfeldt, Geheimes Staatsarchiv, Berlin, HA Rep. 90a, B III 2 b Nr. 6 Bd 182 Bl., 130-5.

3 Otto Dov Kulka, "Die Nürnberger Rassengesetze und die deutsche Bevölkerung im Lichte geheimer NS-Lage- und Stimmungsberichte," *Vierteljahrshefte für Zeitgeschichte* 32 (1984): 617.

4 *Spiegelbild einer Verschwörung*, 448-9: "Ich bejahe in jeder Weise den nationalsozialistischen Staat und sehe in ihm die geschichtliche Notwendigkeit gegenüber

dem Internationalismus und der Verjudung der Systemzeit und gegenüber den unerträglichen Krisen der parlamentarischen Parteien, das deutsche Volk in seinen gesamten nationalen Grenzen zu einen und es so zu regieren, wie es nach seiner geographischen Lage allein regiert werden kann. [...] In der Judenfrage war ich als recht eingehender Kenner der Zustände in der Systemzeit durchaus der Auffassung, daß die Juden aus dem Staats- und Wirtschaftsleben verschwinden müßten. In der Methode habe ich mehrfach ein etwas allmählicheres Vorgehen empfohlen, insbesondere aus Rücksichten der äußeren Politik."

5 A.W. Dulles, Papers, Princeton University, IV g 10 b 57/44 gRs, 4. Okt. 1944.

6 Gerhard Ritter, *Carl Goerdeler und die deutsche Widerstandsbewegung*, 411–45.

7 Source: Ulrich von Hassell, *Die Hassell-Tagebücher 1938–1944*, 70: Hassell lunched with Popitz on 17 December 1938 and recorded the conversation in his diary.

8 Franz Gürtner, Reich Justice Minister.

9 Lutz Count Schwerin von Krosigk, Reich Finance Minister.

10 Constantin Freiherr von Neurath, Reich Foreign Minister.

11 According to the editors of Hassell, *Die Hassell-Tagebücher*, the Gauleiter meeting took place on 24 November 1938, but they do not cite supporting evidence; Goebbels mentions it in Joseph Goebbels, *Die Tagebücher*, 201 (25 Nov. 1938); minutes of the conference on 12 November 1938, see in Herbert Michaelis und Ernst Schraepler, *Ursachen und Folgen. Vom deutschen Zusammenbruch 1918 und 1945 bis zur staatlichen Neuordnung in der Gegenwart*, vol. 12 (Berlin: Dokumenten-Verlag Dr Herbert Wendler & Co. 1967), 588–602.

12 Ilse Göring, a cousin of Hermann Göring and the widow of Göring's brother Karl, who had fallen in the First World War, had been an acquaintance of Hassell since 1913. Hassell cultivated this connection after 1933 as a source of inside information on Göring.

15

Ulrich von Hassell on the 9 November 1938 Pogrom

Ulrich von Hassell (1881–1944) was born in Anklam in Pomerania into a Hanoverian family with a tradition of military service.[1] His mother, Margarete von Stosch, was a niece of the Prussian Chief of the Admiralty, Alfred von Stosch. His father was a Hanoverian army officer, who had fought against Prussia in 1866 and then served in the Prussian army. During the last two years of the First World War, Hassell's father was active in the German Fatherland Party,[2] led by Grand Admiral Alfred von Tirpitz, who resigned as Secretary of the Navy[3] in 1916, and Wolfgang Kapp, the director-general of the East Prussian Agrarian Credit Bank. After studying law, Hassell served for a year in the 2nd Guards Regiment, worked in the Prussian justice system, and, in 1909, entered the Foreign Service. In 1911 he married Tirpitz's daughter, Ilse. While he was posted to Genoa, war broke out. He joined the Army in August 1914 and was shot in the chest in the Battle of the Marne on 8 September 1914; the bullet lodged in his heart and was never removed. He worked again in the civil service until 1919 and became active in the conservative German National People's Party (Deutschnationale Volkspartei, DNVP). Hassell unsuccessfully sought to tone down the anti-Jewish plank in the DNVP's platform. He argued in favour of conservative and socialist co-operation, provided that the old administrative machinery, the non-partisan professional civil service, and the institutions of local self-government were preserved. He also argued in favour of general suffrage in an organic form based upon self-government, and for a strong executive in government. This was Hassell's position in 1918, at a time when neither the House of Commons, nor the Chambre des

Députés, nor the Congress were elected by general suffrage. Later, in 1933, the ignominious collapse of the Weimar Republic, when it turned itself over to a gang of murderers, caused Hassell and many others in the Resistance to Hitler to be wary, not of the principle of popular sovereignty and democracy but of aspects of its exercise, of an unprotected form of democracy. Hassell, Claus and Berthold Stauffenberg, and Helmuth James von Moltke, as well as Socialists such as Carlo Mierendorff, Adolf Reichwein, Hermann Maass, Wilhelm Leuschner, Jakob Kaiser, and Max Habermann, deprecated any simple restoration of the Weimar multi-party system. In 1919 Hassell was posted to Rome as an Embassy Counsellor; in 1921, to Barcelona as a Consul-General; in 1926, to Copenhagen and in 1930, to Belgrade as Minister; and from 1932 to 17 February 1938, as Ambassador to Rome.

For his opposition to a policy he believed was leading to war, Hassell was recalled as part of the great changing of posts on the occasion of the removal of the War Minister, Fieldmarshal Werner von Blomberg, and the Commander-in-Chief of the Army for similar opposition to Hitler's policies. Hassell did not receive another posting; he was retired from the Foreign Service on 10 February 1943. During the years 1938–1944, he served on the board of the Central European Economic Conference (Mitteleuropäischer Wirtschaftstag) and in the Institute for Economic Research in Berlin.[4] From 1938, he worked actively for the overthrow of the Hitler dictatorship, in association with Carl Goerdeler,[5] Ludwig Beck,[6] and Johannes Popitz.[7] He was to become Foreign Minister in the Cabinet of the future government to be headed by Goerdeler. Hassell also attempted to mediate between the resistance circle round Goerdeler and the Kreisau Circle in planning for the future economic and social organization of Germany after the National Socialist regime was overthrown.

Hassell was arrested on 28 July; he was sentenced to death and hanged on 8 September 1944.[8]

Hassell kept a diary until his arrest in July 1944. From time to time, portions of the handwritten entries were smuggled to Switzerland for safekeeping. The parts written in the last few years were buried in Hassell's garden in Ebenhausen, near Munich.[9] The first edition of the diaries and appendices was prepared by Hassell's widow, Ilse von Hassell, née von Tirpitz.

Hassell's sources of information were usually excellent. He was acquainted and in frequent contact with ambassadors, ministers, secretaries of state, field marshals, and generals. He was a respected personage of considerable prestige at home and abroad as an experienced and wise diplomat, but also well-connected through his family relations to Stosch and Tirpitz and through his acquaintance, dating from 1914, with Hermann Göring and Göring's sister Olga Rigele. After his dismissal in 1938, he maintained his contacts with Olga Rigele and others, such as Secretary of State Ernst Freiherr von Weizsäcker, Reich Minister of Finance Lutz Graf Schwerin von Krosigk, Reich Bank President and Reich Economics Minister Hjalmar Schacht, and Prussian Minister of Finance Johannes Popitz.[10]

In the diary, he commented on all significant contemporary events and expressed his reactions and thoughts, particularly on human-rights violations and crimes. Hassell's daughter Fey noted in her diary on 18 September 1935 how appalled her father was by the Nürnberg Laws. He condemned the laws as signifying "for our country the end of its culture." After the November 1938 pogrom, she wrote that he had said "that it is the end of all civilization in Germany."[11] Throughout the published diaries, he refers to the persecution of the Jews more than forty times.

Ulrich von Hassell's Reactions to the 9 November 1938 Pogrom[12]

Ebenhausen, 25 November 1938
I write under the impression, which weighs heavily, of the vile persecution of the Jews following the murder of vom Rath.[13] Never since the World War have we lost so much credit in the world as this time, and that shortly after the greatest foreign-policy successes. But my chief concern is not the effect abroad, such as any foreign-policy backlash, in any case not for the moment. The weakness and dissipation of the so-called great democracies are too enormous for that. Proof: the conclusion of the German-French anti-war agreement at the very moment of the wildest, world-wide indignation against Germany and, simultaneously, with the British ministerial visit in Paris. The really serious concern relates to our internal life, which is being gripped more and more completely and firmly by a system capable of such things. Goebbels may seldom have won so little credence for an assertion (although at home there are indeed people who fell for it) as when he said that a spontaneous popular anger had perpetrated the violent acts and had been stopped after a few hours. At the same time, he laid himself open to the convincing reply that – if such things could happen unhindered – the authority of the state must be in a bad way. There is, in fact, no doubt that it was an officially organ-

ized anti-Jewish riot, unleashed at the same hour of the night in all of Germany – an unequivocal disgrace! Naive Party functionaries have freely admitted that. One of them, speaking to Hans Dieter,[14] cited his stressful activity in the pogrom as an excuse for poor preparations for military billeting. A mayor near here complained to the Pastor Weber, as early as Wednesday, the 9th, that he had orders to take action against a decent Jew, and added that, on the 10th, all the synagogues in Germany would burn. They were not ashamed to mobilize school classes (in Feldafing they even armed them with bricks); in a Swabian village, Leyen[15] said, the Catholic teacher had let himself be cajoled, but the Lutheran one had refused.

There is probably nothing more bitter in life than to be forced to acknowledge the justice of attacks made by foreigners on one's own nation. As a matter of fact, abroad they are making a proper distinction between the people themselves and the group that is responsible for this thing. But it is undeniable that the lowest instincts have been aroused; the effect, especially among the young, must have been repulsive in some cases. There is some consolation in the fact that this time the indignation has taken hold not only of the overwhelming majority of the educated class but of quite broad sections of the people. It seems to me that, in the upper hierarchy, one senses darkly how bad a turn one has done to the cause of National Socialism. Low-keyed back-pedaling is to be observed, and the *Schwarze Korps*,[16] in blind rage, lashes out against the grumblers, falsely claiming they were once again only the cursed educated class.

All decent persons were ashamed most of all to read names such as Gürtner[17] and Schwerin-Krosigk[18] among those who decided on penalties against the Jews. These persons probably no longer notice how they are disgracing themselves and how they are serving as fig leaves.

We lived through the worst days while in Switzerland, with Willes,[19] in an atmosphere that is as different from this swinishness as water from fire.

Berlin, 20 December 1938[20]
The days in Berlin – in icy cold – are marked by gloomy feelings, personally,[21] objectively by the shameful events in November, which heavily weigh on all decent and thoughtful people. There is hardly anything else that people talk about. Our rulers are apparently fully aware of the devastating effect of this vulgar and stupid action. In camera caritatis, it is being condemned by the majority of those

who are responsible; more or less openly they blame each other, and shamefacedly attempt to make minor amends. This does not change a whit in the matter. On the contrary, one has the impression that the paroxysm is spreading dynamically into all fields, domestic and foreign, and one must anticipate the new year as a dark fate. Perhaps the worst of it is that Göring, who condemned the pogrom most sharply and most openly before all Cabinet ministers and Gauleiters, could not bring himself to refuse his co-operation and, with Brauchitsch in tow, to call a fundamental halt. That would have been a very favourable psychological moment for an initiative that at once would have made him the declared leader of all good forces in Germany. Apparently it is true that he said something like this being the last filthy business to which he had lent his name. But this is reminiscent of the lieutenant in the café who, upon receiving a box on the ear, cried: "Sir, one more such slap and I shall challenge you to a duel!" (Or of the Anglo-French policy in response to Hitler's "offence blow"). G[öring] is, after all, more "façade" than "wall"; he melts before Hitler and fears Himmler[22] and Heydrich.[23] In any case, a great chance has been missed.

NOTES

1   See the biographic sketch by Gregor Schöllgen, *A Conservative Against Hitler. Ulrich von Hassell: Diplomat in Imperial Germany, the Weimar Republic and the Third Reich, 1881–1944.*
2   Vaterlandspartei.
3   Staatssekretär im Reichs Marine Amt.
4   Ulrich von Hassell, *Die Hassell-Tagebücher 1938–1944. Aufzeichnungen vom Andern Deutschland*, 19.
5   On Goerdeler, see document no. 16.
6   On Beck, see document no. 19.
7   On Popitz, see document no. 14.
8   Schöllgen, *A Conservative against Hitler*, 119–21.
9   Hassell, *Die Hassell-Tagebücher*, 43; Hassell, *Vom andern Deutschland. Aus den nachgelassenen Tagebüchern 1938–1944*, 5, 372–3; Hassell, *The Von Hassell Diaries 1938–1944. The Story of the Forces against Hitler inside Germany, as Recorded by Ambassador Ulrich von Hassell, A Leader of the Movement*, 6.
10 Hassell, *Die Hassell-Tagebücher*, 473–4 (note 43), and passim.
11 Fey von Hassell, *Niemals sich beugen*, 2nd ed. (Munich: Piper 1991), 32; Fey von Hassell, *A Mother's War*, 16, 35.

12 Source: Hassell, *Die Hassell-Tagebücher*, 62–7.

13 Ernst vom Rath, Legation Secretary in the German Embassy at Paris, was shot on 7 November 1938 by a seventeen-year-old Jewish Pole, Herschel Grynszpan. See Helmut Heiber, "Der Fall Grünspan," *Vierteljahrshefte für Zeitgeschichte* 5 (1957): 134–72; Michael R. Marrus, "The Strange Story of Herschel Grynszpan," in Michael R. Marrus, ed., *The Nazi Holocaust. Historical Articles on the Destruction of European Jews* (Westport, Connecticut: Meckler 1989), 597–607; Fritz Wiedemann, *Der Mann, der Feldherr werden wollte* (Velbert und Kettwig: blick + bild Verlag für politische Bildung 1964), 189–92. See also Hans-Jürgen Döscher, *"Reichskristallnacht." Die November-Pogrome 1938* (Frankfurt/M.: Ullstein 1988).

14 One of Hassell's sons.

15 Erwein Otto Prince von der Leyen (1894–1970).

16 SS paper *Schwarzes Korps*.

17 Franz Gürtner, 1881–1941, Reich Minister of Justice, 2 June 1932–29 Jan. 1941.

18 Johann Ludwig (Lutz) Schwerin von Krosigk (1887–1977); Reich Minister of Finance, 2 June 1932–May 1945.

19 Ulrich Wille, Swiss Lieutenant-General (Oberstkorpskommandant).

20 The English edition, Hassell, *The Von Hassell Diaries*, 25, has ellipses, compared with Hassell, *Die Hassell-Tagebücher*, 67.

21 Hassell's elder son was ill.

22 Heinrich Himmler, 1900–23 May 1945, Reich Leader of SS; 17 June 1936–30 April 1945, Chief of German Police; 24 Aug. 1943–30 April 1945, Reich Minister of the Interior.

23 Reinhard Heydrich, 7 March 1904–4 June 1942, SS General; 1934–42, Chief of Secret State Police; 1936–42, Head of Reich Main Security Office; 27 Sept. 1941–4 June 1942, Deputy Protector of Bohemia and Moravia.

16

Carl Goerdeler's Plan to Protect the World's Jews, 1941/1942

I

Carl Friedrich Goerdeler was Mayor of Leipzig until his resignation in 1936 and departure from office in 1937. Subsequently, he worked as a consultant for the Robert Bosch GmbH in Stuttgart, residing in Berlin. The founder of the company, Robert Bosch, opposed National Socialism and saved many Jews.[1] Goerdeler's employment was a cover for his attempts to prevent and later to halt the war and the crimes and outrages committed by the National Socialist dictatorship.

In a passage (printed below) on the status of the Jews in a memorandum written in 1941/42, Goerdeler began by demanding "a new order of the position of the Jews" in the entire world, "because everywhere there are movements in progress that, without an organic order in place, cannot be halted, and that, without such order, will lead only to injustices, atrocities." The solution, in Goerdeler's view, was a Jewish state, and citizenship of that state for the Jews in the entire world. Once this state was established through international agreement, "there will result the following natural settlement[2] for German conditions: The Jew is a citizen of his Jewish state; like every other foreign citizen in Germany, he has the right to carry on a trade[3] within the laws that apply to everyone else."

Under the German citizenship law of 1913, persons who acquired another citizenship lost their German citizenship, unless they met certain conditions, including residence in Germany and the authorities' permission to hold dual citizenship.[4] Goerdeler's plan, however, after a few words of comparison with Englishmen or Frenchmen living in Germany, and the resulting irrelevance of the Nürnberg Racial Laws, suddenly adds this: "No rule without exception! Jews are German citizens" who or whose ancestors served as German soldiers during the World War, who or whose ancestors were German citizens in 1871, or who met two other, minor criteria. Goerdeler exempted German Jews from the rule of the German citizenship law in the four categories he listed.

Goerdeler's memorandum "The Aim" ("Das Ziel") is a ninety-nine-page typed document.[5] It sets out what policies must guide Germany and other Great Powers, and what constitutional and legal changes needed to be made. The section headed "II The Foreign Policy Aim," consists of a series of comments and proposals on international issues such as free trade; the Far East, where Japan was engaged upon a campaign to conquer Indochina, Thailand, Netherlands East Indies, and the Philippines in what it called the "Greater East Asia Co-Prosperity Sphere"; Africa and colonies; Hitler's appalling foreign-policy bungles and bullying; conditions for peace and European co-operation. Point 11 contains proposals for "a new order of the position of the Jews" in the entire world. The next part is headed "III Internal Policy." The "position of the Jews in the entire world" was primarily an international issue, not primarily a German internal one, and thus was placed in the foreign-policy part of the memorandum.[6]

The time of the memorandum's composition has been established as after June 1941 and before the end of January 1942, its completion as in the months of December 1941 and January 1942.[7]

In 1941, while the German attack upon the Soviet Union and the simultaneous mass-killing operations against Jews were in progress, and when Colonel Henning von Tresckow, Senior Staff Officer (Operations) in Army Group Centre High Command, took the initiative, sending his special-missions officer, Fabian von Schlabrendorff, to Ulrich von Hassell to see if there were "useful crystallization points at home" and assuring Hassell that in the Army Group High Command they were "ready for anything,"[8] Goerdeler wrote his memorandum "The Aim." Its meaning depends in part on the intended readership.

Neither Goerdeler's biographer, Gerhard Ritter, nor the recent editors of a large body of Goerdeler's political writings say to whom Goerdeler addressed his memorandum. They (except Hans Mommsen) also appear to have missed Hassell's references to his discussions about the same issues Goerdeler was working on with Hassell, Beck, the Prussian Finance Minister Johannes Popitz, Professor Jens Peter Jessen, the lawyer Helmuth James von Moltke of the Foreign-Countries division of Armed Forces Supreme

Command, Peter Graf Yorck von Wartenburg of the Reich Prices Commissioner's office, Adam von Trott of the Foreign Office, and Karl Ludwig Freiherr von und zu Guttenberg of the Armed Forces Supreme Command Foreign Countries Counter-Intelligence office.[9]

Memoranda that mention "inhuman crimes" of the regime or stipulate, like "The Aim," that a state of siege become effective "immediately" for all of Germany,[10] were meant for those planning and supporting the overthrow of Hitler's dictatorship. General Ludwig Beck ranked foremost among them.

At the end of October 1941, Goerdeler, Hassell, Popitz, and Jessen discussed "the whole situation" in case Hitler's regime came to an end.[11] The "whole situation" included the failure of the German offensive before Moscow and the lack of winter clothing and equipment for over two million German soldiers. It included the "intolerable conditions" developing in the occupied territories, as deportations of Jews from occupied France had begun in July 1941; the shooting of Jewish men, women, and children in their tens of thousands by the Einsatzgruppen in the East; and the murder of Jews with gas in killing centres in Poland and in Auschwitz (annexed to Germany). As well, about 6,000 German Jews from Breslau, Munich, Frankfurt/Main, Vienna, and Berlin were deported to Kowno and Riga and shot upon their arrival.[12] Hassell recorded the "revulsion of all decent human beings at the shameless measures in the East against Jews and prisoners, and in Berlin and other large cities against harmless, respected Jews." The measures included the shocking insidiousness and cynicism of the "Eleventh Decree to the Reich Citizenship Law" of 25 November 1941.[13] As German Jews were beginning to be deported to the mass-murder camps and ghettos in Poland and the Baltic states, this decree declared that Jews who took their permanent residence beyond the German frontiers lost their German citizenship:[14] "The habitual residence abroad is a given if a Jew resides abroad in circumstances that indicate that he is not merely temporarily residing there." Further, the property of Jews who lost their German citizenship on the basis of this decree became Reich property, and this applied also to Jews without citizenship, who were stateless[15] if they had or took their habitual residence abroad; such property, the decree said, was to be used "for purposes connected with the solution of the Jewish Question." At the beginning of 1942, Goerdeler also recorded his outrage at the deportations of Leipzig Jews on 19 and 27 January 1942. While expressing sympathy and commiseration, he predicted that the German nation would experience horrific retribution.[16]

On 1 November 1941, Hassell noted: "Numerous conversations with Geissler [Popitz]; repeatedly together with him and Nordmann [Jessen], once each with Forster [Beck, Halder?] and Pfaff [Goerdeler]. Four of us (Geissler, Nordmann, Pfaff, and I) once talked over the whole situation 'in case of the case.' Pfaff [Goerdeler] was relatively agreeable but evidently held something back, so that one had the impression that he would possibly go his own separate route."[17] On 21 December, Hassell noted that "during the last weeks" he had "numerous conversations about the basic issues of a system change, very often with Geissler [Popitz], repeatedly together with him, Pfaff [Goerdeler], Geibel [Beck], once also with Otto [Planck], and once with Nordmann [Jessen]. A principal difficulty always resides in the sanguine, viewing-things-in-a-desired-light, and in some respects really 'reactionary' Pfaff [Goerdeler], who has otherwise brilliant qualities."[18] At that time, Hassell also established contacts with Trott, Yorck, Moltke, Guttenberg, and Fritz Dietlof Graf von der Schulenburg and sought to bring about "a kind of trait d'union to the Younger Ones." These rejected Goerdeler, who for his part "assumes an almost entirely negative position", toward their ideas.[19] It was a time of feverish discussions, planning, and search for a solution.

Goerdeler showed or read the first part of his memorandum to the Social-Democrat trades-union leader Wilhelm Leuschner after New Year's 1942. And Goerdeler discussed his memorandum, in the days before 15 January 1942, with Popitz, Beck, Hassell, Colonel Hans Oster of Armed Forces Supreme Command Foreign Countries Counter-Intelligence office, and Oster's co-worker Hans von Dohnanyi.[20] Goerdeler and Beck were proposing to start the overthrow of Hitler with a separate armistice in the West, but General Alexander von Falkenhausen, the Military Governor for Belgium and Northern France, and Commander-in-Chief West Field Marshal Erwin von Witzleben considered this utopian.[21] On 28 March 1942, Hassell noted intensive conversations at Jessen's with Beck and Goerdeler, and recorded: "Few prospects. Geibel constituted as centre."[22]

To understand Goerdeler, who thought and wrote as a lawyer and as a dyed-in-the-wool Prussian civil servant, it is useful to note that the League of Nations Covenant did not provide an option for intervention in domestic matters in a foreign state in order, for example, to protect a minority. The Covenant's article 15, in essence, declared that members of the League of Nations or the League of Nations Council would not intervene in "a matter which by international law is solely within the domestic jurisdiction" of a party or member.[23]

From 30 January 1933, the day of Adolf Hitler's appointment as Chancellor, the German government continually increased and intensified the discrimination and persecution of Jews in Germany, a process of which the pogrom of 9 November 1938 was an intermediate culmination.

In April 1933, when SA thugs were maltreating Jews in Leipzig, Goerdeler, as Mayor of Leipzig, went in full formal dress to a Jewish quarter of his city to protect Jews and Jewish businesses, and he used the city police to free Jews who had been detained and beaten by storm troopers. From 1933–35, he protected the right of Jewish physicians to practice under public health insurance plans.[24] In 1936, when the monument to Felix Mendelssohn-Bartholdy in front of the Leipzig Gewandhaus concert hall was removed, contrary to Goerdeler's, the Mayor's, directives, Goerdeler resigned. The National Socialists regarded Mendelssohn-Bartholdy, although baptized, as a Jew.[25]

During the time of relentlessly intensifying persecution against Jews, Goerdeler, in August, November, and December 1938 and in March 1939, repeatedly met with a representative of the British government and urged Britain to press the German government to discontinue its practices against the Jews; he made appeals on behalf of the 10,000 Jews of Polish origin whom the National Socialists tried to deport to Poland and whom Poland refused to accept; and he urged Britain to break diplomatic relations with Germany.[26] He committed, on behalf of German and non-German Jews, what German law defined as "treason against the country,"[27] which carried the death penalty.[28]

In June 1939, with war imminent, Goerdeler travelled in Libya, Egypt, Palestine, Syria, and Turkey. In his report on Palestine, he argued that Palestine could absorb a large Jewish immigration because the Jewish settlers were competent, industrious, and successful: "For the solution of the Jewish Question in the world, this would only be an advantage." Since the Arabs always opposed whatever the Jews were doing in Palestine, Goerdeler acknowledged the difficulties facing the British mandate authorities. No doubt he was aware of the 17 May 1939 British White Paper that limited Jewish immigration to Palestine to approximately 75,000 for the next five years.[29] In any event, he predicted: "The last word about the development in Palestine will be spoken through further European events." He favoured the formation of a Jewish state in Palestine and predicted that "the English difficulties" with getting Jews and Arabs to co-operate would decrease if Germany came into a "conflict" (war) with the Western powers.[30]

After German mass killings of Jews, priests, and university professors in Poland in 1939 and 1940, and when the mass killings of Jews had begun in Russia in 1941, Goerdeler, in his memorandum, sought comprehensive measures not only for the Jews "in the entire world," but for international relations and national renewal.

The Nürnberg Racial Laws explicitly did not change the Reich and State Citizenship Law of 1913.[31] The term "Reichsbürger" had no meaning in law except that it now reserved the right to vote and to stand for election to public office to non-Jewish citizens.

The Nürnberg "Law for the Protection of German Blood"[32] equally became moot in Goerdeler's memorandum: he left it to individual Jews and non-Jews whether or not they decided to marry a partner in another category.

In Goerdeler's proposal, those whom he declared Germans in his four defined categories of "exceptions" were not affected by the Reichsbürgergesetz at all: Farther down in his memorandum, Goerdeler declared that every citizen from the age of twenty-four had the right to vote.[33] This included all Germans, and therefore the Jews whom he had declared Germans.

Goerdeler's drafting was hurried and not very careful. In his proposal in "The Aim," he removed restrictions, but not in a systematic manner. Goerdeler asserted the right of citizens of a Jewish state to follow a trade[34] and that "the restrictions upon Jews in access to food supplies, housing and telephone service, in their cultural activities, health care,[35] adoption of names[36] are to be abolished." What he was declaring abolished were the most serious discriminating measures in the Nürnberg Racial Laws and their implementation decrees.[37] The implementation decrees *were* the laws.

Goerdeler's proposal for a Jewish state and its citizenship for all Jews was utopian in the strictest sense of the word, but also in other respects. How likely was it that Jewish citizens of states that did not allow dual citizenship would give up their German citizenship? Would Jewish citizens of states that did allow dual citizenship accept Jewish citizenship if they did not intend to reside in the Jewish state?

The draft was not the result of a parliamentary introduction, committee report, and plenary debate. The memorandum was noticeably written in desperate haste, understandable in the pressures of the time and considering formidable rivalry, of which Goerdeler was aware, from the left led by Moltke.[38] Goerdeler's aim to protect Jews, and especially German Jews, is nevertheless evident not merely in his deprecation of the Nürnberg Laws (for Jews with Jewish-State citizenship the laws would be "completely disposed of"), but also in his declaring abolished, without differentiating between German and non-German Jews, the restrictions against Jews, which he enumerated and which were contained in the decrees implementing the Nürnberg Racial Laws.

II

Did Goerdeler's categories of Jews who were to be considered German citizens include the majority of German Jews? Would Goerdeler's categories restore German citizenship to Jews who had lost it through the acquisition of another citizenship? Would Goerdeler's categories restore German citizenship to Jews whose German citizenship had been lost through revocation of naturalization or withdrawal of citizenship under the National-Socialist regime? Goerdeler was uncompromising; he did not address these complicating legal issues.[39] But his singling out the German Jews for his "exception," contradicting his own determination of the "natural settlement for German conditions" ("the Jew is a citizen of his Jewish state"), underscores Goerdeler's desperation in trying to protect, especially, German Jews: The regime was killing Jews by the tens of thousands in Poland and in the Soviet Union already, and now the deportation and extermination of the German Jews had begun.

No one could have known precisely how many German Jews were likely to be affected by what Goerdeler proposed. But the 1871–1933 census results provided a reasonably accurate notion of the numbers involved.

Concerning Goerdeler's category a: Anti-Semitic agitation during the First World War resulted in statistics that showed there were in Germany, as at 1 August 1914, a "population of 550,000 Jewish German citizens." About 100,000, or 18 percent of the total German Jewish population, served in the Army, Navy, and Colonial Forces (Schutztruppe) during the First World War, about 80,000 of them (80 percent) at the front; 12,000 of them fell.[40]

These figures show that 88,000 Jewish males, regardless of whether they came from old German-Jewish stock (German at or before 1 July 1871), were guaranteed German citizenship, based on the German citizenship law of 1913. Their majority may be presumed to have been in the population of 550,000 reichsdeutsche Juden and included an unknown proportion of immigrants or descendants of immigrants because military service gave them the automatic right to German citizenship.[41] If 60,000 of the veterans of the First World War married and had an average of one child, the number would reach 208,000, already the majority of the German-Jewish population in Germany in 1933.

Concerning Goerdeler's category b: The overall numbers of German Jews declined by close to 111,000 from 1871 (512,158[42]) to 1933 (400,935[43]).

Restrictive German immigration and naturalization policies exclude any massive population exchange as a possible consideration.[44] Since immigration and naturalization policies were severely restrictive, and since residency requirements were ten years, expanded to twenty in 1931,[45] the overlap between emigration and immigration/naturalization also must be considered negligible.

The census results distinguished: total population present on census day; German citizens and foreigners; German population according to their religious affiliations – Protestant, Catholic, sub-groups, and "Israelites." The same distinctions were made *within* the group of foreigners in census results in 1910 and afterward. While the censuses before 1939 counted only religious Jews (400,935 German Jews and 98,747 foreign Jews in 1933),[46] the 1939 census also counted persons defined as Jews under the Nürnberg Racial Laws.

All of this means that the overwhelming majority of German Jews fell into Goerdeler's categories a and b.[47]

Concerning Goerdeler's category c: A minimum of 16,929 Jews were baptized in a Protestant denomination from 1881–1932. Newborn babies who were baptized were usually not registered as baptized Jews, so that Goerdeler's category c would contain a greater number.[48] Goerdeler's categories c and d answered the National Socialists' persecution of "racial" Jews. The categories were likely substantial because of the growing numbers of baptisms, intermarriages, and the 75 percent of children of mixed marriages being raised as Christians.[49]

The number of German Jews who would not have been protected in Goerdeler's categories c and d against losing their German citizenship would be exceedingly small; they would still be protected against the murderers by their Jewish citizenship.

The statistical evidence proves that the vast majority of German Jews would have qualified for Goerdeler's categories a and b, while the numbers in categories c and d, uncertain due to lack of conclusive evidence, still would have further increased the total "exceptions."

Memorandum[50]

A new order of the position of the Jews seems required in the entire world because everywhere there are movements in progress that, without an organic order in place, cannot be halted, and that, without such order, will lead only to injustices, atrocities,[51] and, if to nothing else, to an unsatisfactory disorder. It is a commonplace that the Jewish nation[52] belongs to another race. Opinion is divided in the Jewish nation on whether or not it ought to seek independence in the form of a state. The Zionists have always been demanding and preparing for their own state. Until 1933, they had not played a significant role. Yet the world will come to rest only if the Jewish nation receives a truly practicable opportunity to found their own state and to maintain it. Such a territory, with conditions quite worth living in, can be found either in parts of Canada or South America. Once this question has been resolved through the powers' concerted action, there will result the following natural settlement[53] for German conditions: The Jew is a citizen of his Jewish state; like every other foreign citizen in Germany, he has the right to carry on a trade[54] within the laws that apply to everyone else. But he is excluded, as is every Englishman, Frenchman, etc., from becoming a public official, electing people's representatives, or being elected. On the other hand, he enjoys exactly the same rights as every other foreigner who lives in Germany and who has or has not property. As far as the so-called Nürnberg racial laws are concerned, they will be entirely disposed of through this settlement. The question of racial mixing must always be left to the wholesome sense of the people. A marriage between a Jew and a non-Jewish woman forces her to assume the nationality of the husband, just as if she intended to become a Frenchwoman or an Englishwoman. Conversely, the same legal consequence occurs, but only if the marriage was concluded before the Nürnberg Laws;[55] otherwise, only the grandchildren will receive German citizenship. No rule without exception! Jews are German citizens

a) who served in the war as German soldiers, and their direct descendants;
b) who, or whose direct ancestors possessed German citizenship on 1 July 1871;
c) who, and whose direct descendants, possessed German citizenship on 1 August 1914 and belonged to Christian religious denominations;[56]
d) who are descendants of a mixed marriage that was concluded before 1 February 1933, if they belong to a Christian religious denomination.

In past years, undoubtedly an injustice has been bred through expropriation, destruction, etc., of Jewish property and life in Germany; this we cannot answer for before our consciences and before history. Here the possibilities for a new settlement can be examined and resolved only when the whole dimension of the events[57] has been determined. It will then emerge that we, with a view to our standing in the world and to our own conscience, must on our own initiative take the path to healing. Besides the pursuit of this aim, those immediate measures must be taken that are necessary for reasons of foreign policy to detoxify public opinion, indispensable for the restoration of German self-esteem, and required out of a clear sense of justice of which we are fully conscious:

a) restrictions upon Jews in access to food supplies, housing, and telephone service, in their cultural activities, health care, adoption of names[58] are to be abolished;

b) the ghettos in the occupied territories are to be arranged humanely; the relevant indigenous authorities will decide upon their further destiny with the approval of the military governors since, for example, the Poles have a different attitude toward the question than the Dutch.

NOTES

1   Joachim Scholtyseck, *Robert Bosch und der liberale Widerstand gegen Hitler 1933 bis 1945*, 265–82.

2   Goerdeler's term is "Regelung."

3   Goerdeler's term is "Recht der gewerblichen Betätigung"; Reich law included in the term "Gewerbe" such occupations as those of physicians, pharmacists, advocates, lawyers; see "Gewerbeordnung für den Norddeutschen Bund. Vom 21. Juni 1869," *Bundesgesetzblatt 1869* (Berlin: Redigirt im Büreau des Bundeskanzlers, gedruckt in der Königlichen Geheimen Ober-Hofbuchdruckerei [R.v.Decker] 1869), 245–82; ordinances regulated details for some occupations.

4   "Reichs- und Staatsangehörigkeitsgesetz. Vom 22 Juli 1913," (*RuStAG*) *Reichs-Gesetzblatt* (henceforth cited *RGBl.*) 1913 (Berlin: Herausgegeben im Reichsamte des Innern. Zu beziehen durch alle Postanstalten, n.d.), 583–93.

5   The memorandum was published in 1965 by Wilhelm Ritter von Schramm, *Beck and Goerdeler. Gemeinschaftsdokumente für den Frieden 1941–1944* (Munich: Gotthold Müller Verlag 1965), 81–166, based on a typed copy that is in the German Federal Archives (Goerdeler, Bundesarchiv, Koblenz, N 1113/53). The most recent publication of the text of "Das Ziel" was edited by Sabine Gillmann and Hans Mommsen in *Politische Schriften und Briefe Carl Friedrich Goerdelers*, 873–4; they say that their edition was based on another version than Schramm's; that Schramm had made

"stylistic and text-forming changes" (stilistische und textgestalterische Korrekturen) that he did not indicate and that raise "source-critical concerns" (Gillmann/Mommsen, p. lxxix) in his edition; and that the text from which they were printing was in private hands. According to information from the Bundesarchiv, Hans Mommsen in 2004 turned over to the Bundesarchiv this and other documents from which Gillmann/Mommsen had produced their edition. The editor of the present collection asked for a copy of this version of the text; the Bundesarchiv was able to locate this version on 14 September 2010.

6 Fritz Kieffer, "Auszug aus dem Entwurf vom Dezember 2005: Carl Friedrich Goerdelers Vorschlag zur Gründung eines jüdischen Staates," 476–7.

7 Kieffer, "Goerdelers Vorschlag," 475–6, cites Hermann Graml, "Die aussenpolitischen Vorstellungen des deutschen Widerstandes," in Walter Schmitthenner und Hans Buchheim, eds., *Der deutsche Widerstand gegen Hitler*, 43 and note 85; Mommsen, "Gesellschaftsbild und Verfassungspläne des deutschen Widerstandes," 133 and note 109; Gillmann and Mommsen in *Politische Schriften*, Band 1 (continuous pagination through Band 2), 873.

8 Ulrich von Hassell, *Die Hassell-Tagebücher 1938–1944. Aufzeichnungen vom Andern Deutschland*, 278.

9 Gerhard Ritter, *Carl Goerdeler und die deutsche Widerstandsbewegung*, 1st edition, 1954, 280; Gillmann/Mommsen, *Politische Schriften*, lxxxiv, 863; cf. Hassell, *Vom Andern Deutschland. Aus den nachgelassenen Tagebüchern 1938–1944*, 243–9; Mommsen, "Gesellschaftsbild und Verfassungspläne des deutschen Widerstandes," 269–70, note 109.

10 Gillmann/Mommsen, *Politische Schriften*, 897.

11 Hassell, *Die Hassell-Tagebücher*, 279–80; Ritter, *Carl Goerdeler*, missed Hassell's references to discussions with Goerdeler.

12 Peter Longerich, *Politik der Vernichtung. Eine Gesamtdarstellung der nationalsozialistischen Judenverfolgung* (Munich: Piper 1998), 434–44, 452–8, 464; Christopher R. Browning, *The Origins of the Final Solution. The Evolution of Nazi Jewish Policy, September 1939–March 1942* (Lincoln and Jerusalem: University of Nebraska Press and Yad Vashem 2004), 304–5.

13 "Elfte Verordnung zum Reichsbürgergesetz. Vom 25. November 1941," *RGBl. 1941 I*, 722–4.

14 Staatsangehörigkeit.

15 Staatenlos.

16 H[elmut] Kr[ausnick], ed., "Goerdeler und die Deportation der Leipziger Juden," 338–9.

17 Hassell, *Die Hassell-Tagebücher*, 279–80.

18 Ibid., 288–9.

19 Ibid., 289–91.

20 Mommsen, "Gesellschaftsbild," 269–70, note 109, errs in his reading of Hassell's note about a "document" that Goerdeler had composed as referring to "Das Ziel"; the "document" in question was a (much shorter) proclamation for the time of the

coup d'état; Hassell, *Die Hassell-Tagebücher*, 293–4; Detlef Graf von Schwerin, *"Dann sind's die besten Köpfe, die man henkt." Die junge Generation im deutschen Widerstand* (Munich: Piper 1991), 231–2; Ludwig Beck, *Studien*, 227–58.

21 Hassell, *Die Hassell-Tagebücher*, 297.

22 Ibid., 307; Hassell used "Geibel" as code for Beck.

23 "If there should arise between Members of the League any dispute likely to lead to a rupture" that is not submitted to arbitration by a court agreed to by the parties to the dispute, the Members agree that they will submit the matter to the League of Nations Council. "If the dispute between the parties is claimed by one of them, and is found by the Council to arise out of a matter which by international law is solely within the domestic jurisdiction of that party, the Council shall so report, and shall make no recommendation as to its settlement." *The Covenant of the League of Nations with a Commentary thereon. Presented to Parliament by Command of His Majesty, June 1919* (London: His Majesty's Stationery Office 1919), 6–7.

24 Peter Hoffmann, "The German Resistance to Hitler and the Jews: The Case of Carl Goerdeler," 278–9. In this and other articles, I have cited evidence against branding Goerdeler a conservative anti-Semite. See Hoffmann, "The German Resistance and the Holocaust" in John J. Michalczyk, ed., *Confront! Resistance in Nazi Germany* (New York: Peter Lang 2004), 105–26; Hoffmann, "The German Resistance to Hitler and the Jews" in David Bankier, ed., *Probing the Depths of German Antisemitism. German Society and the Persecution of the Jews, 1933–1941* (Jerusalem, New York-Oxford: Yad Vashem, Leo Baeck Institute, Berghahn Books 2000), 463–77; Hoffmann, "The Persecution of the Jews as a Motive for Resistance Against National Socialism" in Andrew Chandler, ed., *The Moral Imperative. New Essays on the Ethics of Resistance in National Socialist Germany, 1933–1945* (Boulder, Colorado: Westview Press 1998), 73–104; Hoffmann, "The German Resistance, the Jews, and Daniel Goldhagen," 73–88. Now I am profoundly indebted to Fritz Kieffer for his analysis of Goerdeler's proposals on behalf of the Jews. Kieffer accepts Mommsen's and Gillmann's dating of the memorandum for the end of 1941 and beginning of 1942; this bears upon its meaning, and Kieffer examines the context and the juridical aspects of the passage in Goerdeler's memorandum dealing with the position of the Jews in the world. Forthcoming: Peter Hoffmann, *Carl Goerdeler and the Jewish Question, 1933–1942* (Cambridge: Cambridge University Press, 2011).

25 Hoffmann, "The German Resistance to Hitler and the Jews," 280–1.

26 A.P. Young, *The 'X' Documents*, 45–9, 59, 139, 154–62, 177; Hoffmann, *German Resistance to Hitler*, 281–2.

27 Landesverrat.

28 "Gesetz gegen heimtückische Angriffe auf Staat und Partei und zum Schutz der Parteiuniformen. Vom 20. Dezember 1934," *RGBl. Teil I Jahrgang 1934* (Berlin: Reichsverlagsamt 1934), 1269–71; "Gesetz zur Änderung von Vorschriften des Strafrechts und des Strafverfahrens. Vom 24. April 1934," *RGBl. I 1934*, 341–8 (death penalty for high treason against the Reich President, Reich Chancellor, or "Constitution," and for relations with a foreign government for such a purpose); *Strafgesetzbuch mit Ne-*

bengesetzen und Erläuterungen. Vierunddreißigste Auflage (Berlin: Walter de Gruyter 1938), §§ 88–93a, 210–26 (§ 89: "Wer es unternimmt, ein Staatsgeheimnis zu verraten, wird mit dem Tode bestraft." § 88: Staatsgeheimnisse = Tatsachen oder Nachrichten darüber, "deren Geheimhaltung vor einer ausländischen Regierung für das Wohl des Reichs, insbesondere im Interesse der Landesverteidigung, erforderlich ist." "Verrat im Sinne der Vorschriften dieses Abschnitts begeht, wer mit dem Vorsatz, das Wohl des Reichs zu gefährden, das Staatsgeheimnis an einen anderen gelangen läßt, insbesondere an eine ausländische Regierung oder an jemand, der für eine ausländische Regierung tätig ist, oder öffentlich mitteilt."

29 "Palestine: statement of policy. Presented by the secretary of state for the colonies to Parliament by command of His Majesty, May 1939," *Accounts and papers: [12] state papers. Session 8 November 1938–23 November 1939*, vol. 27 [London: 1939]).

30 Marianne Meyer-Krahmer, *Carl Goerdeler und sein Weg in den Widerstand. Eine Reise in die Welt meines Vaters*, 127–8; Ritter, *Carl Goerdeler*, 211; Gillmann/Mommsen, *Politische Schriften*, 627–34; cf. Joachim Scholtyseck, *Robert Bosch und der liberale Widerstand gegen Hitler 1933 bis 1945*, 260–1. Remarkably little has been published about Goerdeler's trip to Palestine. Ines Reich, *Carl Friedrich Goerdeler. Ein Oberbürgermeister gegen den NS-Staat*, 270–1, only records a reference to Palestine in Goerdeler's account of his 1937 journey to the USA. Dipper (Christof Dipper, "Der Deutsche Widerstand und die Juden," *Geschichte und Gesellschaft* 9 [1983]: 365; Christof Dipper, "The German Resistance and the Jews," *Yad Vashem Studies* 16 [1984]): 51–93), whose research was tenuous, and who criticized that Goerdeler had suggested the foundation of the Jewish state in parts of Canada or South America, thought it proper to say "also gerade nicht in Palästina"; Christof Dipper, "Der 20. Juli und die 'Judenfrage,'" *Die Zeit* 27 (8. Juli 1994): 20.

31 *RuStAG* § 3.

32 "Gesetz zum Schutze des deutschen Blutes und der deutschen Ehre. Vom 15. September 1935," *RGBl. 1935 I*, 1146–7.

33 Gillmann/Mommsen, *Politische Schriften*, 931.

34 Recht der gewerblichen Betätigung includes trades, commercial, and professional occupations; in the cases of physicians and lawyers, practitioners had to meet the same standards as other Germans or other foreigners.

35 "Vierte Verordnung zum Reichsbürgergesetz. Vom 25. Juli 1938," *RGBl. 1938 I*, 969–70; "Verordnung über die Teilnahme von Juden an der kassenärztlichen Versorgung. Vom 6. Oktober 1938," *RGBl. 1938 I*, 1391. See also Hoffmann, *Carl Goerdeler and the Jewish Question, 1933–1942*.

36 "Gesetz über die Änderung von Familiennamen und Vornamen. Vom 5. Januar 1938," *RGBl. 1938 I*, 9–10; "Zweite Verordnung zur Durchführung des Gesetzes über die Änderung von Familiennamen und Vornamen. Vom 17. August 1938," *RGBl. 1938 I*, 1044.

37 "Reichsbürgergesetz. Vom 15. September 1935," *RGBl. 1935 I*, 1146; "Gesetz zum Schutze des deutschen Blutes und der deutschen Ehre. Vom 15. September 1935," *RGBl. 1935 I*, 1146–7; "Erste Verordnung zum Reichsbürgergesetz. Vom 14. Novem-

ber 1935," *RGBl. 1935 I*, 1333–4; "Erste Verordnung zur Ausführung des Gesetzes zum Schutze des deutschen Blutes und der deutschen Ehre. Vom 14. November 1935," *RGBl. 1935 I*, 1334–6; "Zweite Verordnung zum Reichsbürgergesetz. Vom 21. Dezember 1935," *RGBl. 1935 I*, 1524–5; "Erste Verordnung zur Durchführung des Gesetzes über die Änderung von Familiennamen und Vornamen. Vom 7. Januar 1938," *RGBl. 1938 I*, 12; "Zweite Verordnung zur Durchführung des Gesetzes über die Änderung von Familiennamen und Vornamen. Vom 17. August 1938," *RGBl. 1938 I*, 1044: "Viertes Gesetz zur Änderung des Gesetzes über das Versteigerergewerbe. Vom 5. Februar 1938," *RGBl. 1938 I*, 115; "Verordnung gegen die Unterstützung der Tarnung jüdischer Gewerbebetriebe. Vom 22. April 1938," *RGBl. 1938 I*, 404; "Verordnung über die Anmeldung des Vermögens von Juden. Vom 26. April 1938," *RGBl. 1938 I*, 414–15; "Dritte Verordnung zum Reichsbürgergesetz. Vom 14. Juni 1938," *RGBl. 1938 I*, 627–8; "Gesetz zur Änderung der Gewerbeordnung für das Deutsche Reich. Vom 6. Juli 1938," *RGBl. 1938 I*, 823–4; "Vierte Verordnung zum Reichsbürgergesetz. Vom 25. Juli 1938," *RGBl. 1938 I*, 969–70; "Verordnung über die Teilnahme von Juden an der kassenärztlichen Versorgung. Vom 6. Oktober 1938," *RGBl. 1938 I*, 1391; "Fünfte Verordnung zum Reichsbürgergesetz. Vom 27. September 1938," *RGBl. 1938 I*, 1403–6; "Erste Verordnung über die berufsmässige Ausübung der Krankenpflege und die Errichtung von Krankenpflegeschulen (Krankenpflegeverordnung – KPflV). Vom 28. September 1938, *RGBl. 1938 I*, 1310; "Verordnung über Reisepässe von Juden. Vom 5. Oktober 1938," *RGBl. 1938 I*, 1342 (alle Pässe ungültig, wieder gültig, "wenn sie von der Passbehörde mit einem vom Reichsminister des Innern bestimmten Merkmal versehen werden, das den Inhaber als Juden kennzeichnet"); "Sechste Verordnung zum Reichsbürgergesetz. Vom 31. Oktober 1938," *RGBl. 1938 I*, 1545–6; "Verordnung gegen den Waffenbesitz der Juden. Vom 11. November 1938," *RGBl. 1938 I*, 1573; "Verordnung zur Ausschaltung der Juden aus dem deutschen Wirtschaftsleben. Vom 12. November 1938," *RGBl. 1938 I*, 1580; "Verordnung zur Wiederherstellung des Strassenbildes bei jüdischen Gewerbebetrieben. Vom 12. November 1938," *RGBl. 1938 I*, 1581 ("§ 1 Alle Schäden, welche durch die Empörung des Volkes über die Hetze des internationalen Judentums gegen das nationalsozialistische Deutschland am 8., 9. und 10. November 1938 an jüdischen Gewerbebetrieben und Wohnungen entstanden sind, sind von dem jüdischen Inhaber oder jüdischen Gewerbetreibenden sofort zu beseitigen."); "Verordnung über eine Sühneleistung der Juden deutscher Staatsangehörigkeit. Vom 12. November 1938," *RGBl. 1938 I*, 1579 ("Juden deutscher Staatsangehörigkeit in ihrer Gesamtheit wird die Zahlung einer Kontribution von 1 000 000 000 Reichsmark an das Deutsche Reich auferlegt."); "Erlass des Führers und Reichskanzlers über die Entziehung des Rechts zum Tragen einer Uniform. Vom 16. November 1938," *RGBl. 1938 I*, 1611; "Verordnung über die öffentliche Fürsorge für Juden. Vom 19. November 1938," *RGBl. 1938 I*, 1649; "Verordnung zur Durchführung der Verordnung zur Ausschaltung der Juden aus dem deutschen Wirtschaftsleben. Vom 23. November 1938," *RGBl. 1938 I*, 1642; "Polizeiverordnung über das Auftreten der Juden in der Öffentlichkeit. Vom 28. November 1938," *RGBl. 1938 I*, 1676; "Verordnung über den Einsatz des jüdischen Vermögens. Vom 3. Dezember 1938," *RGBl. 1938 I*, 1709–12; "Siebente Verordnung zum Reichsbürgergesetz. Vom 5. Dezember 1938," *RGBl. 1938 I*, 1751; "Zweite Verordnung zur Durchführung der Verordnung zur Ausschaltung der Juden aus dem deutschen Wirtschaftsleben. Vom 14. Dezember 1938," *RGBl. 1938 I*, 1902; "Hebammengesetz. Vom 21. Dezember 1938," *RGBl. 1938 I*, 1893–4; "Zweite Verordnung über Mietbeihilfen. Vom 31. Dezember 1938," *RGBl. 1938 I*, 2017; "Achte Verordnung zum Reichsbürgergesetz. Vom 17. Januar 1939," *RGBl. 1939 I*, 47–8; "Neunte Verordnung zum Reichsbürgergesetz. Vom 5. Mai 1939," *RGBl. 1939 I*, 891; "Zehnte Verordnung zum Reichsbürgergesetz. Vom 4. Juli 1939," *RGBl. 1939 I*, 1097–9; "Polizeiverordnung über die Kennzeichnung der Juden. Vom 1. September 1941," *RGBl. 1941 I*, 547 (Star of David with inscription "Jude" mandatory for all Jews older than six years); "Elfte Verordnung zum Reichsbürgergesetz. Vom 25. November 1941," *RGBl. 1941 I*, 722–4; "Zwölfte Verordnung zum Reichsbürgergesetz. Vom 25. April 1943," *RGBl. 1943 I*, 268–9; "Dreizehnte Verordnung zum Reichsbürgergesetz. Vom 1. Juli 1943," *RGBl. 1943 I*, 372.

38 Hassell, *Die Hassell-Tagebücher*, 290.

39 Kieffer, "Carl Friedrich Goerdelers Vorschlag," 474–500, has examined the legal implications of Goerdeler's proposals concerning the position of the Jews in the world.

40 See Egmont Zechlin, *Die deutsche Politik und die Juden im Ersten Weltkrieg*, (Göttingen: Vandenhoeck & Ruprecht 1969), 516–67: Kapitel "Juden und Antisemitismus im Weltkrieg." Prüfung der Klagen, dass "eine grosse Zahl im Heeresdienst stehender Juden verstanden haben, eine Verwendung ausserhalb der vordersten Front, als in dem Etappen- und Heimatgebiet und in Beamten- und Schreibstellen zu finden." (527) On 30 October 1916, the Prussian War Ministry ordered the statistical analysis of the Jews' part in the war as at 1 November 1916. Weiteres: Jacob Segall, *Die deutschen Juden als Soldaten im Kriege 1914–1918* (Berlin: Philo-Verlag 1921); *Statistik der Juden* (Vorwort vom 1. Mai 1917), Berlin 1918, bes., 152 et seq. Results: Segall, *Die deutschen Juden als Soldaten im Kriege 1914–18. Eine statistische Studie* (Berlin: Philo-Verlag 1922), esp. 38; Reichsbund jüdischer Frontsoldaten, Hrsg., *Die jüdischen Gefallenen des deutschen Heeres, der deutschen Marine und der deutschen Schutztruppen 1914–1918* (Berlin: Verlag "Der Schild" 1932), esp. 419. See also Werner T. Angress, "The German Army's 'Judenzählung' of 916. Genesis – Consequences – Significance" (*Leo Baeck Institute Year Book* XXIII 1978): 117–37. The number of those in military service during the First World War, of the entire population in Germany (67,790,000), is 13,250,000 = 19.5 percent.

41 *RGBl. 1913*, § 12, 585–6. The residency requirement was increased to twenty years in 1931; see *Niederschriften über die Vollsitzungen des Reichsrats. Jahrgang 1931* (Berlin: Carl Heymanns Verlag 1931), 19–29 ("Niederschrift der vierten Sitzung (§§ 38 bis 56). Geschehen Berlin, den 5. Februar 1931." "Niederschrift der fünften Sitzung," 12 Feb. 1931, 33; "Niederschrift der vierunddreißigsten Sitzung," 26 Nov. 1931, 394); on 26 November 1933 ("Niederschrift der vierunddreißigsten Sitzung," 394) the requested consultations between the national and Länder governments had not yet taken place and the Reichsrat now agreed "to treat the cases before it on that day on the basis of those provisional principles."

42 *Vierteljahreshefte zur Statistik des Deutschen Reichs für das Jahr 1873. Zweites Heft, erste Abtheilung*. Herausgegeben vom Kaiserlichen Statistischen Amt. [Erster Jahrgang.] Band II. Heft II. Abtheil. 1 der Statistik des Deutschen Reichs (Berlin: Verlag des Königlich Statistischen Bureaus (Dr Engel), 1873 [sic, title-page has 1874]), 122, 144.

43 *Statistik des Deutschen Reichs, Band 451, [no] 4. Volks-, Berufs- und Betriebszählung vom 16. Juni 1933. Volkszählung. Die Bevölkerung des Deutschen Reichs nach den Ergebnissen der Volkszählung 1933. Heft 4. Die Ausländer im Deutschen Reich. Die Bevölkerung einiger Gebiete des Deutschen Reichs nach der Muttersprache. Bearbeitet im Statistischen Reichsamt* (Berlin: Verlag für Sozialpolitik, Wirtschaft und Statistik, Paul Schmidt 1936), no. 5, 13: Of the 499,682 religious Jews counted in Germany on 16 June 1933 (without Saarland), 400,935 were German citizens, 98,747 were foreign citizens or without citizenship. *Statistik des Deutschen Reichs. Band 470, [no] 1. Die Hauptergebnisse der Volks-, Berufs- und Betriebszählung im Deutschen Reich (einschl. Saarland) auf Grund der Zählung vom 16. Juni 1933 und der Ergänzungszählung im Saarland vom 25. Juni 1935. Bearbeitet im Statistischen Reichsamt* (Berlin: Verlag für Sozialpolitik, Wirtschaft und Statistik, Paul Schmidt 1937), 7, has 502,799 as the total, and lists 403,432 with German citizenship and 99,367 foreigners of the Jewish religion [Glaubensjuden].

44 See note 41 above.

45 *Niederschriften über die Vollsitzungen des Reichsrats. Jahrgang 1931* (Berlin: Carl Heymanns Verlag, Berlin W8 1931), 19–29 ("Niederschrift der vierten Sitzung [§§ 38 bis 56]. Geschehen Berlin, den 5. Februar 1931."); on 26 November 1933 ("Niederschrift der vierunddreißigsten Sitzung," 394) the requested consultations between the national and Länder governments had not yet taken place and the Reichsrat now agreed "to treat the cases before it on that day on the basis of those provisional principles."

46 Glaubensjuden.

47 There are no national statistics available for naturalizations after 1 July 1871. They could be researched in the archives of the individual states (Länder). Fritz Kieffer, "Auszug aus dem Entwurf vom Dezember 2005: Carl Friedrich Goerdelers Vorschlag zur Gründung eines jüdischen Staates," 4, based on Adler-Rudel, *Ostjuden in Deutschland 1889–1940* (Tübingen: J.C.B. Mohr [Paul Siebeck] 1959), 20–1 (citing *Allgemeine Zeitung des Judentums* [22 and 29 Sept. 1885]: 149).

48 *Statistik des Deutschen Reichs 451* (5): 8.

49 Ibid.

50 Source: Carl Goerdeler, Papers, Bundesarchiv, Koblenz, N 1113/53. The present English translation of this central document is the first one ever published. The most recent publication of the German text of "Das Ziel" was edited by Gillmann and Mommsen in *Politische Schriften*, 873–4; they say that their edition was based on another version than Schramm's, that Schramm had made "stylistic and text-forming changes" (stilistische und textgestalterische Korrekturen) that he (Schramm) did not indicate and that raise "source-critical concerns" (Gillmann/Mommsen, lxxix) about his edition, and that the text from which they were printing was in private

hands. According to information from the Bundesarchiv, Hans Mommsen, in 2004, turned over to the Bundesarchiv this and other documents from which Gillmann/Mommsen had produced their edition. But when the editor of the present collection asked for a copy of this version of the text, the Bundesarchiv could not find it. The passage below is identical, however, in both Gillmann/Mommsen and the copy that the Bundesarchiv does own.

11. Eine Neuordnung der Stellung der J u d e n erscheint in der ganzen Welt erforderlich; denn überall sind Bewegungen im Gange, die sich ohne organische Ordnung nicht aufhalten lassen und die ohne eine solche Ordnung nur zu Ungerechtigkeiten, Unmenschlichkeiten und mindestens zur unbefriedigenden Unordnung führen. Daß das jüdische Volk einer anderen Rasse angehört, ist eine Binsenweisheit. Im jüdischen Volke selbst sind die Meinungen geteilt, ob es eine staatliche Selbständigkeit erstreben soll oder nicht. Die Zionisten haben schon seit jeher einen eigenen jüdischen Staat verlangt und vorbereitet. Eine bedeutende Rolle haben sie bis 1933 nicht gespielt. Zur Ruhe wird die Welt aber doch nur kommen, wenn das jüdische Volk eine wirklich ausnützbare Möglichkeit erhält, einen eigenen Staat zu gründen und zu erhalten. Ein solches Gebiet läßt sich auf jeden Fall unter durchaus lebenswerten Umständen entweder in Teilen Canadas oder Südamerikas finden. Ist diese Frage durch Zusammenwirken der Mächte gelöst, so ergibt sich für die deutschen Verhältnisse folgende natürliche Regelung: Der Jude ist Staatsbürger seines jüdischen Staates, er hat, wie jeder andere Fremdbürger in Deutschland, nach den für jeden anderen geltenden Gesetzen das Recht der gewerblichen Betätigung. Dagegen scheidet, wie für jeden Engländer, Franzosen usw. aus, öffentlicher Beamter zu werden, in die Volksvertretungen zu wählen oder gewählt zu werden. Auf der anderen Seite genießt er genau die gleichen Rechte wie jeder andere Ausländer, der in Deutschland wohnt und Vermögen hat oder nicht. Was die sogenannten Nürnberger Rassegesetze betrifft, so erledigen sie sich durch diese Regelung auch vollkommen. Die Frage der Rassenvermischung muß stets dem gesunden Sinn des Volkes überlassen bleiben. Eine Ehe zwischen einem Juden und einer Nichtjüdin zwingt diese, der Staatsangehörigkeit des Mannes zu folgen, wie wenn sie Französin oder Engländerin werden wollte! Auch umgekehrt tritt diese Rechtsfolge ein, aber nur wenn die Ehe vor den Nürnberger Gesetzen geschlossen war; andernfalls erhalten erst die Enkel deutsche Staatsangehörigkeit. Keine Regel ohne Ausnahme! Deutsche Staatsangehörige sind Juden

a) die als deutsche Soldaten am Kriege teilgenommen haben und ihre direkten Nachkommen,

b) die oder deren direkte Vorfahren am 1.7.1871 deutsche Reichsangehörigkeit besaßen und ihre direkten Nachkommen,

c) die am 1.8.1914 die deutsche Staatsangehörigkeit besaßen und christlichen Religionsgemeinschaften angehörten und noch angehören, sowie ihre direkten Nachkommen,

d) Abkömmlinge einer Mischehe, die vor dem 1.2.1933 geschlossen ist, sofern sie einer christlichen Religionsgemeinschaft angehören.

In den vergangenen Jahren ist zweifellos ein Unrecht durch Enteignung, Zerstörung usw. jüdischen Besitzes und Lebens in Deutschland großgezogen, das wir vor unserem Gewissen und der Geschichte nicht verantworten können. Hier werden die Möglichkeiten einer Neuordnung erst dann geprüft und gelöst werden können, wenn der ganze Umfang des Geschehens feststeht. Es wird sich dann ergeben, daß wir im Hinblick auf unsere Stellung in der Welt und auf unser eigenes Gewissen aus eigenem Antrieb den Weg zur Heilung beschreiten müssen. Neben der Verfolgung dieses Zieles müssen diejenigen

S o f o r t maßnahmen ergriffen werden, die aus außenpolitischen Gründen zur Entgiftung der öffentlichen Meinung notwendig, zur Wiederherstellung der deutschen Selbstachtung unerläßlich und aus klaren [sic] und uns vollkommen bewusstem Gerechtigkeitsgefühl geboten sind:

a) die Beschränkungen der Juden auf dem Gebiete des Ernährungs-, des Wohnungs- und des Fernsprechwesens, der kulturellen Betätigung, der Gesundheitspflege, der Namensgestaltung sind aufzuheben;

die Ghettos in den besetzten Gebieten sind menschenwürdig zu gestalten; über ihr weiteres Schicksal bestimmen die zuständigen einheimischen Behörden mit Genehmigung der Militärgouverneure, da z.B. die Polen zu der Frage anders stehen wie die Holländer.

51 Goerdeler's term is "Unmenschlichkeiten," literally, "inhumanities"; in the context of the time in which he wrote, the word means "atrocities."

52 Goerdeler's word is "Volk," which may be translated "people" or "nation"; "nation" is the translation used throughout here for "Volk," as it approximates more closely what Goerdeler was advocating: a Jewish national state. Today, the contention that the Jews belonged to another race may not be acceptable, but in Goerdeler's time, it was a commonplace, everywhere, not merely in Germany.

53 Goerdeler's term is "Regelung."

54 Goerdelers's term is "Recht der gewerblichen Betätigung"; Reich law included in the term "Gewerbe" all occupations including those of physicians, pharmacists, advocates, lawyers; see "Gewerbeordnung für den Norddeutschen Bund. Vom 21. Juni 1869," 245–82.

55 "Reichsbürgergesetz. Vom 15. September 1935," *RGBl. I 1935*, *RGBl. I 1935*, 1146; "Gesetz zum Schutze des deutschen Blutes und der deutschen Ehre. Vom 15. September 1935," *RGBl. I 1935*, 1146–7; "Erste Verordnung zum Reichsbürgergesetz. Vom 14. November 1935," *RGBl. I 1935*, 1333–4; "Erste Verordnung zur Ausführung des Gesetzes zum Schutze des deutschen Blutes und der deutschen Ehre. Vom 14. November 1935," *RGBl. I 1935*, 1334–6; "Zweite Verordnung zum Reichsbürgergesetz. Vom 21. Dezember 1935," *RGBl. I 1935*, 1524–5; cf. Lothar Gruchmann, "'Blutschutzgesetz' und Justiz. Zur Entstehung und Auswirkung des Nürnberger Gesetzes vom 15. September 1935," *Vierteljahreshefte für Zeitgeschichte* 31 (1983): 418–42; Jeremy Noakes and Geoffrey Pridham, *Documents on Nazism*, 463–7. Goerdeler apparently referred to the "Erste Verordnung zum Reichsbürgergesetz. Vom 14. November 1935," *RGBl. I 1935*, 1333–4, § 5 Abs. 2c, but he erred; the Nürnberg racial laws had no bearing upon

citizenship; contemporary commentary declared that the principles of the *Reichs-und Staatsangehörigkeitsgesetz* about acquisition and loss of German citizenship "[were] in no way affected"; Kieffer, "Carl Friedrich Goerdelers Vorschlag," 491; the *RuStAG* did not stipulate that a husband's citizenship followed that of his wife, but the opposite.

56 Goerdeler's term is "christlichen Religionsgemeinschaften."

57 The reference "des Geschehens," meaning "events," can only be to that which preceded the phrase: "expropriation, destruction, etc., of Jewish property and life in Germany," thus including mass murder.

58 "Gesetz über die Änderung von Familiennamen und Vornamen. Vom 5. Januar 1938," *RGBl. 1938 I*, 9–10; "Zweite Verordnung zur Durchführung des Gesetzes über die Änderung von Familiennamen und Vornamen. Vom 17. August 1938," *RGBl. 1938 I*, 1044.

17

Sermon of Clemens August Graf von Galen, Bishop of Münster, 3 August 1941

Adolf Hitler, Leader of the National Socialist German Workers' Party, ordered sterilization measures against handicapped patients in state hospitals and nursing homes as soon as he had taken office as Reich Chancellor in 1933. In 1935 he told Gerhard Wagner, the Reich Physicians Leader, that he would initiate euthanasia for the handicapped as soon as war began. By that time, the details of the program had been prepared.[1] In October 1939, Hitler signed an authorization charging the head of the Party chancellery, Reich Leader Philipp Bouhler, and his personal physician, Dr Karl Brandt, with the implementation of the program. He dated the order 1 September 1939, the date when the German invasion of Poland began.[2] Hitler claimed to be the ultimate legislator in Germany, but there was uneasiness among bureaucrats and caregivers about the lack of a proper legal basis for "euthanasia." By 1941, 70,273 victims had been murdered according to the SS' own statistics.

Neither the Catholic nor the Lutheran churches' position toward "euthanasia" was unambiguous before the practice began and during, at least, its initial stages. There were discussions about a possible law to regulate "euthanasia," which caused uncertainty among opponents and supporters of it. In 1940 and 1941, members of the German Catholic hierarchy were negotiating with government agencies about the practice as a whole and also about modalities.[3] The phase of cautious contacts and negotiations ended only in November 1940 and after the Vatican had issued to the German Catholic bishops, on 27 November 1940, a decretal that strictly condemned the destruction of "so-called life not worth living."[4] Still, it took German

Catholic bishops until spring 1941 to openly voice their opposition to "euthanasia." Bishop Preysing of Munich did so in a sermon on 9 March 1941. But the collective of German Catholic bishops in the Fulda Conference of Bishops decided only on 26 June 1941 to issue a pastoral letter, and it was read from pulpits on 6 July 1941.[5]

The suspicious deaths in sanatoriums and asylums were first questioned in March 1940 in Württemberg, where the first killing centre, Grafeneck, was located. Pastor Friedrich von Bodelschwingh tried to refuse handing over his wards.[6] He did resist and protest as much as he could, but was forced to co-operate when he believed it legally inevitable. On 9 July 1940, Paul Braune, a member of the Central Committee of Innere Mission (Home Mission, the Protestant social-welfare organization in Germany), completed a memorandum about the murder of handicapped patients that was immediately conveyed to the Justice Minister, Franz Gürtner.[7] On 12 July 1940, Pastor Paul Braune; Pastor Friedrich von Bodelschwingh, the director of the asylum of Bethel; and Dr Ferdinand Sauerbruch, Chief Surgeon of the Berlin Charité Hospital, met with the Reich Minister of Justice, Franz Gürtner, who learned from them, for the first time, about these murders and was utterly shocked.[8] From the summer of 1940, when the full extent of the killings had become apparent, several Catholic and Lutheran organizations – the Protestant Innere Mission and the Catholic Caritasverband (Charity Association) – and Lutheran and Catholic bishops – first, in July 1940, the Lutheran Bishop of Württemberg, Theophil Wurm, and in the following month the chairman of the Catholic Fulda Conference of Bishops, Archbishop Cardinal Adolf Bertram of Breslau – approached the government to protest against the "euthanasia" killings.[9] Gürtner wrote to Reich Minister and Chief of the Reich Chancellery, Hans-Heinrich Lammers, on 24 July 1940: "As you have communicated to me yesterday, the Führer has declined to issue a law. In consequence of this, I am convinced of the necessity to immediately halt the secret killing of mentally ill persons."[10] On 5 September 1940, the Chief of the Chancellery of the Führer, Reichsleiter Philipp Bouhler, wrote to Gürtner that Hitler had authorized him, Bouhler, to carry out these measures, that he had given the necessary instructions to his staff, and that no additional regulations appeared to be required.[11]

On 28 July 1941, Bishop von Galen wrote to the President of Police in Münster. He had learned that during the current week a large number of patients of the provincial sanatorium, Marienthal, were to be transported to the sanatorium at Eichberg in order to be killed; this violated divine and natural law; it carried the death penalty under § 211 of the Penal Code. He was hereby bringing charges against those responsible and demanded an immediate halt to the proposed removal of the patients.[12] Bishop von Galen also protested publicly in the form of sermons he delivered in Münster's St Lambert's Church on 13 and 20 July, and on 3 August 1941. The 3 August 1941 sermon in particular was distributed to the parishes with the instruction to read it from the pulpit. This protest, printed below, had the greatest impact on the German public.[13] With the exception of the Provost of St Hedwig's Cathedral in Berlin, Bernhard Lichtenberg, who lost his life in custody, "virtually no church leader suffered serious consequences for opposition to the euthanasia killings."[14] Hitler ordered Gauleiters to stop confiscations of church and monastic property.[15] The regime did not arrest any bishops but sent many pastors, including twenty-two priests and seven monastic clergymen, from the Münster diocese to concentration camps.[16] A member of Goebbels' staff demanded that the Bishop be hanged,[17] but Galen was not harmed. The regime sought to avoid confrontation with the higher clergy during the war.[18]

On 24 August 1941, Hitler ordered a stop to the murders in the killing centres then in operation because of public knowledge of the killings and the resulting disquiet.[19] But the killings continued in concentration camps, and more of the handicapped were killed after the "stop order."[20]

The total killed in the "euthanasia" program in German institutions, including "euthanasia" victims in concentrations camps, reached 216,400. In addition, Germans killed an estimated 40,000 "euthanasia" victims in France, 20,000 in Poland, and 20,000 in the USSR.[21]

It should be added that the German Catholic hierarchy made no official protest against the persecution and killing of the Jews.[22] There is evidence that Galen harboured rather strong anti-Jewish sentiments, although apparently not on "racial" grounds.[23]

Sermon by Bishop Clemens August Graf von Galen in St Lambert's Church, Münster, 3 August 1941[24]

Announcements:
I must unfortunately tell you that again this week the secret state police have continued their struggle of annihilation against the Catholic orders. On Wednesday, July 30, the secret state police occupied and declared dissolved the provincial house of the Sisters of our Beloved Lady in Mülhausen, county Kempen, which formerly belonged

to the Bishopric of Münster. Most of the sisters, many of whom come from our bishopric, were expelled and forced to leave the county on the same day. According to trustworthy reports, the monastery of the Missionaries of Hiltrup in Hamm was also occupied and confiscated by the secret state police on Thursday, July 31. The fathers who were staying there have been expelled.

I already publicly stated here in St Lambert's Church on July 13, after the eviction of the Jesuits and Missionary Clarissens from Münster: None of the inhabitants of the monasteries has been charged with either a misdemeanour or a felony, nor indicted, let alone convicted. As I hear, rumours are now being spread in Münster that these clergy, who are members of orders, especially the Jesuits, had been accused or even convicted of illegal offences, including even treason. I declare: that is a base slander of German citizens, of our brothers, and sisters, that we will not tolerate. I have already pressed criminal charges with the attorney-general against a fellow who dared to make such claims before witnesses. I hereby express my expectation that the man be held accountable most speedily, and that our courts still have the courage to hold accountable and punish slanderers who dare to rob the honour of blameless German citizens after their property has already been taken. I request that of all my hearers – indeed, all reputable citizens – from today, if such accusations against the members of orders exiled from Münster are levelled in their presence, immediately secure the name and address of the accuser and of witnesses who may be present. I hope that in Münster there are still men who have the courage to assist in the judicial clarification of such accusations, which poison the German community, by openly standing up with their person, their name, if need be under oath. I ask these persons, if such accusations against our monastic clergy are pronounced in their presence, to forthwith report this to their priest or the Episcopal Vicariate General and have it put on record. I owe it to the honour of the members of our orders, to the honour of our Catholic Church, and also to the honour of our German nation and our city of Münster, that I see to the judicial clarification of the facts and to the punishment, by means of criminal charges to the attorney-general's office, of common slanderers of members of our orders.

[The Bishop continued in his sermon after the reading of the gospel of the day of the 9th Sunday after Whitsunday: "... as Jesus came near Jerusalem and saw the city, he wept over It ..." (Luke 19:41–47)]

[Sermon:]

My dear diocesans! It is a distressing incident that today's gospel narrates. Jesus weeps! The Son of God weeps! Whoever weeps is suffering pain, pain of the body or of the heart. Jesus did not yet suffer physically, and yet he weeps. How great must have been the pain of his soul, the heartache of this bravest of men, that he wept! Why did he weep? He wept over Jerusalem, over the holy, to him so precious city of God, the capital of his nation. He wept over its inhabitants, his compatriots, because they did not recognize that which alone could avert the punitive judgments foreseen in his omniscience and predetermined by his divine justice: "If only you had recognized that which is in the interest of peace for you!" Why do the citizens of Jerusalem not recognize it? Not long before, Jesus has said: "Jerusalem, Jerusalem! ...[25] how often have I desired to gather your children together, as a hen gathers her chicks under her wings. But you were not willing!" (Luke 13:34) You were not willing! I, your king, your God, I *willed* it. But *you* were not willing. How safe, how protected, how sheltered is the chick under the wings of the hen! She warms, she nurtures, she defends it. So I wanted to protect you, to shelter you, to defend you against all harm. I willed it! You were not willing.

Therefore Jesus weeps, therefore this strong man weeps, therefore God weeps. Over the foolishness, over the injustice, over the crime of *unwillingness*. And over the resulting misfortune, which his omniscience sees coming, which his righteousness must impose, when the human sets his *unwillingness* against the commandments of God, against all warnings of his own conscience, against all the loving invitations of the divine friend, of the *best* father. "If only you recognized, still today, on this day, that which is in the interest of peace for you! But you were not willing!" It is something terrible, something outrageously unjust and pernicious, when the human sets his will against God's will! I willed it! You were not willing. Therefore Jesus weeps over Jerusalem.

Devout Christians! In the common pastoral letter of the German bishops of 26 June 1941, read out in all Catholic churches of Germany on 6 July of this year, it said, among other things: "Certainly, there are, according to Catholic moral teaching, positive commandments that would no longer be binding if their fulfillment would bring with it difficulties all too great. But there are also sacred duties of conscience, from which no one can release us, that we must fulfill, whatever the cost, even if it were to cost our life: Never, under no circumstances, may the human being, except in war and in just self-defense, kill an innocent person." I had occasion already, on 6 July, to add to these words of the common pastoral letter the following explanation:

> For some months we have been hearing reports that out of sanatoriums and nursing institutions for the mentally ill, on orders from Berlin, wards who had been ill for a long time and who perhaps appear incurable were forcibly taken away. Regularly, the relatives then received, after a short time, the notification that the patient had died, the body had been cremated, and the ashes could be delivered. Commonly the suspicion bordering on certainty prevails that these numerous, unexpected deaths of mentally ill persons did not just occur but had been intentionally brought about, that thereby that doctrine was followed that asserts that one may destroy so-called "lives unworthy of living," that is, to kill innocent people if one considered their lives no longer of any value for the nation and the state, a terrible doctrine that seeks to justify the murder of innocent persons, that allows as a matter of principle the forcible killing of invalids no longer able to work, of cripples, of the incurably ill, and of persons weakened by age!

As I have learned reliably, lists are now also being drawn up in the sanatoriums and nursing homes of the province of Westphalia, lists of patients who, as so-called "unproductive citizens," are to be transported away and shortly to be killed. The first transport departed from the Marienthal Institution near Münster during the course of this week!

German men and women! Paragraph 211 of the Reich Penal Code is still in force; it stipulates: "Whoever intentionally kills a person, if he has carried out the killing with deliberation, shall be punished by death for murder." Presumably in order to shield from this legal penalty those who deliberately kill the poor people, relatives of our families, the patients destined to be put to death are transported from their home area to a remote institution. Some disease is then given as the cause of death. Since the body is cremated immediately, neither the relatives nor the criminal police can establish subsequently whether the disease really was present and what was the cause of death.

I have been assured, however, that in the Reich Ministry of the Interior, and in the office of the Reich Physicians Leader, Dr Conti,[26] no secret is made of the fact that indeed a large number of mentally ill in Germany already have intentionally been put to death and [a large number] shall be put to death in future.

The Reich Penal Code stipulates in paragraph 139: "Whosoever receives credible knowledge of the intention ... to commit a crime against life ... and fails to notify the authorities or the endangered person in due course, shall be ... punished."[27]

When I learned of the intention to take patients from Marienthal away in order to put them to death, I pressed charges on 28 July and by registered letter with the attorney-general at the state court of Münster and with the President of Police in Münster, in the following terms:

> According to information having reached me, in the course of this week (one speaks of 31 July), a great number of wards of the Provincial Nursing Home Marienthal, near Münster, were to be transported, as so-called "unproductive citizens," to the Eichberg Nursing Home, in order, as it has happened according to general persuasion after such transports from other nursing homes, forthwith deliberately to be put to death. Since such an action not only contradicts the divine and natural moral code, but also is, according to § 211 of the Reich Penal Code, murder, and to be punished by death, I am bringing charges, duty-bound in accordance with § 139 of the Reich Penal Code, and I request that the thus-endangered citizens be protected at once, through prosecution, against the authorities intending the transport and murder, and that they inform me of the measures taken.

I have not been notified of any intervention by the attorney-general or the police. As early as 26 July, I had, in writing, raised the most serious objection with the Provincial Administration of the Province of Westphalia, to which the institutions are subordinate, to which the patients' *care* and *cure* are entrusted. To no avail! The first transport of innocent persons condemned to death has left Marienthal! And from the sanatorium and nursing home of Warstein, as I hear, 800 patients have already been transported away. So we must reckon that the poor, defenceless patients will be put to death sooner or later.

Why? Not because they committed a crime worthy of death, not because they attacked their warden or nurse so that he had no choice but to resist his attacker with force in order to preserve his own life in justified self-defence. These are cases in which, besides the killing of the armed enemy of the country in a just war, the use of force to the extent of killing is permitted and often necessary.

No, not for such reasons must those unhappy patients die, but because in accordance with the judgment of some physician,[28] in accordance with the expertise of some commission, they have become "unworthy of living"; because, based upon this expertise, they belong to the "unproductive" members of the nation. One judges: they can no longer produce goods; they are like old machines that no longer run; they are like an old horse that has become incurably lame; like a cow that no longer gives milk. What does one do with such an old machine? It is scrapped! What does one do with a lame horse, with such an unproductive head of livestock?

No, I do not want to take the comparison to the end – terrible though its warrant and its luminous power may be!

It is, of course, not a question here of machines; it is not a question of a horse or cow, whose only purpose is to serve human beings, to produce goods for human beings! One may smash them, one may slaughter them, as soon as they no longer fulfill this purpose! No, here it is a question of human beings, our fellow humans, our brothers and sisters! Poor, sick human beings, unproductive human beings if you like. But have they thereby forfeited the right to life? Have you, have I, the right to live only as long as we are productive, as long as we are recognized by others as productive?

If one establishes and applies the principle that one may kill "unproductive fellow humans," then woe to us all when we become old and infirm by age! If one may kill unproductive fellow humans, then woe to the invalids who gave, sacrificed, and lost, in the productive process, their strength, their healthy bones! If one may forcibly eliminate unproductive humans, then woe to our brave soldiers who return home seriously wounded in war, as cripples, as invalids!

Once it is conceded that human beings have the right to kill "unproductive" fellow humans – and even if now, for the time being, only the wretched and defenceless mentally ill are targeted – then, *in principle*, the *murder* of all unproductive people, that is the incurably ill, the disabled cripples, the invalids of labour and war, then the murder of all of us will be permitted when we become old and infirm and thereby unproductive. Then some secret edict need only order that the procedure tested with the mentally ill be extended to other "unproductives," that it be applied also to those with incurable lung diseases, to those weakened by age, to the labour invalids, and to the soldiers seriously wounded in war. Then none of us is certain to keep his life any longer. Any commission can place him on the list of the "unproductive" who, according to the judgment, have become "unworthy of life!"

And no police will protect him, and no court of law will avenge his murder and deliver up the murderer to his deserved penalty! Who then can still have confidence in a physician? Perhaps he will report the patient as "unproductive" and receive the instruction to kill him! Unimaginable are the barbarization of morals, the general mutual mistrust that will intrude into families, if this terrible doctrine is tolerated, adopted, and observed! Woe to humans, woe to our German nation, if the holy commandment of God, "You shall not kill," that the Lord proclaimed amid thunder and lightning from Sinai, that God, as creator, from the beginning has written into the conscience of humans, if this commandment is not merely violated, but if this violation is also tolerated and practised with impunity!

I will tell you an example of what is now happening. In Marienthal, there was a man of about fifty-five years of age, a farmer from a rural parish of Münsterland – I could tell you his name – who for some years had been suffering from mental disorders and who had therefore been entrusted to the *care* of the Provincial Asylum of Marienthal. He was not completely deranged; he could receive visits, and he was always happy when his relatives came. Only fourteen days ago, he had a visit from his wife and from one of his sons, a soldier serving on the front and who had home leave. The son was very attached to his ailing father. So the parting was difficult. Who knows if the soldier will return, will see his father again, because he could fall in the struggle for the German nation. Now the son, the soldier, will quite certainly on this earth not see his father again, for he has since then been placed on the list of the unproductive. A relative who wanted to visit the father in Marienthal this week was refused with the information that the patient had been transported away from here on the order of the land ministerial defence council.[29] Where to, could not be said. The next of kin would be notified in a few days.

What will this notice say? Just as in other cases. That the man died, that the body was cremated, that the ashes could be delivered upon the payment of a fee!³⁰ Then the soldier in the field who stakes his life for the German nation will not see his father again here on earth, because fellow Germans at home have taken his life!

The facts stated by me are confirmed. I can name the sick man, his wife, his son who is a soldier, and the place where they live!

"You shall not kill!" God wrote this commandment into the conscience of humans long before a penal code threatened a penalty for murder, long before the public prosecutor's office and court of law pursued and avenged murder. Cain, who slew his brother, was a murderer long before there were states and courts of law. And he confessed, pressed by the accusation of his conscience: "My misdeed is greater than one for which I could find forgiveness! ... Whoever finds me will kill me, the murderer." (Genesis 4:13)[31]

"You shall not kill!" This commandment of God, the only Lord who has the right to decide over life and death, was written into the hearts of humans from the beginning, long before God proclaimed his moral law to the children of Israel on Mount Sinai with those lapidary, short sentences etched in stone that have been recorded for us in the Holy Scriptures, which as children we learned by heart from the catechism.

"I am the Lord your God!" Thus begins this unalterable law. "You shall have no other gods beside me." The only, eternal, transcendental, omnipotent, omniscient, infinitely holy and just God has given these commandments. Our creator and future judge! Out of love for us, he has inscribed these commandments in our hearts and proclaimed them to us for they correspond to the requirement of our nature that God created; they are the unalterable norms of a rational and God-pleasing, a beneficial and holy human and social life.

God our Father, with these commandments, wants to gather us, his children, as the hen gathers her chicks under her wings. When we humans follow these commands, these invitations, this call of God, then we are guarded, protected, preserved from harm, defended against the menace of destruction, like the chicks under the wings of the hen.

"Jerusalem, Jerusalem, how often have I desired to gather your children together as a hen gathers her chicks under her wings, but you were not willing!"[32] Shall that again become true in our German Fatherland, in our Westphalian homeland, in our city of Münster? How is it in Germany, how is it here among us with obedience to the divine commandments?

The eighth commandment: "You shall not bear false witness, you shall not lie!" How often is it violated insolently, even publicly!

The seventh commandment: "You shall not steal!" Whose possessions are still secure after the arbitrary and ruthless expropriation of the property of our brothers and sisters who belong to Catholic orders. Whose property is protected, if this illegally confiscated property will not be restored?

The sixth commandment: "You shall not commit adultery!" Think of the instructions and assurances given in the notorious Open Letter of Rudolf Hess, who has since disappeared, published in all the newspapers, about free intercourse and unmarried motherhood.[33] And all the other shameless and base things one can read, observe, and learn on this point, here in Münster, too! What shamelessness in clothing have the youth had to accustom themselves to. Preparation for future adultery! Because modesty, the protective cell of chastity, is being destroyed.

Now the fifth commandment: "You shall not kill" is also being set aside and violated under the very eyes of the authorities who are obliged to protect the judicial order of life, while one presumes deliberately to kill innocent, although sick, fellow humans only because they are "unproductive," can produce no more goods.

How is it with the observance of the fourth commandment, which demands reverence and obedience to parents and superiors? The position and the authority of parents is already widely undermined, and becomes ever more shaken, with all the requirements that are being imposed upon youth against the will of parents. Does one believe that sincere reverence and conscientious obedience to the *state's* authority will be preserved if one continues to violate the commandments of the highest authority, the commandments of God, when one combats, nay attempts to eradicate even the belief in the only true, transcendent God, the Lord of heaven and earth?

The observance of the first three commandments has indeed already, for a long time, been widely discontinued in public in Germany and also in Münster. How many desecrate and withdraw from God's service the Sabbath, along with the holidays! How the name of God is misused, dishonoured, and blasphemed!

And the first commandment: "You shall have no other gods before me!" Instead of the only true eternal God, one makes one's own idols according to one's pleasure, in order to worship them: nature or state or nation or race. And how many are there, whose God is in reality, according to the word of Saint Paul, "the belly" (Phil. 3:19), their own well-being, to which they sacrifice all, even honour and conscience, sensuality, lust for money, lust for power! Then one may also try to appropriate divine authority, to make oneself Lord over life and death of fellow humans.

"When Jesus came near Jerusalem and saw the city, he wept over it and said: 'Would that even today you recognized the things that make for peace. But now they are hidden from your eyes. Behold, the days will come upon you when your enemies will dash you to the ground, you and your children, and within you leave no stone upon another, because you did not recognize the days of your affliction.'"[34]

With his bodily eyes, Jesus then saw only the walls and towers of the city of Jerusalem, but his divine omniscience saw more deeply, recognized how it was within the city and with its inhabitants: "Jerusalem, I desired to gather your children together, as a hen gathers her chicks under her wings. But you were not willing!" That is the great sorrow that weighs upon Jesus' heart, that brings tears to his eyes: I wanted the best for you, but *you* are not willing! Jesus sees the sinfulness, the terrible, the criminal, the destructiveness of this *unwillingness*! The little man, the frail creature, sets his created will against God's will! Jerusalem and its inhabitants, His chosen and favoured people, set its will against God's will! Foolishly and criminally it defies the will of God! Therefore, Jesus weeps over the abominable sin and over the inevitable punishment: God will not tolerate derision!

Christians of Münster! Has the Son of God in his omniscience seen only Jerusalem and its people at that time? Has he wept only over Jerusalem? Is the nation Israel the only nation that God has enveloped with fatherly concern and motherly love, guarded, drawn to himself? And has that not been willing? That has refused God's truth, has cast away God's law, and so plunged itself into destruction?

Has Jesus, the omniscient God, beheld then also our German nation? Also our Westphalia, our Münsterland, the Lower Rhine? And has he wept over us also? Wept over Münster? For a thousand years, he has taught our forefathers and us with his truth, guided us with his law, nurtured us with his grace, gathered us as the hen gathers her chicks under her wings. Has the omniscient Son of God seen at that time, that in our time, too, he must pronounce the judgment over us: "You were not willing. See, your house will be laid waste to!" How terrible that would be!

My Christians! I hope there is yet time. But it is high time! That we understand, still today, on this day, the things that make for peace for us, that alone can save us, can preserve us from the divine punishment:

That we, without any reservation or reduction, accept the truth revealed by God and confess it through our lives.

That we make the divine commandments the guideline of our lives and take seriously the word: Rather die than sin! That we, in prayer and honest atonement, implore God for forgiveness and pity for ourselves, for our city, for our country, for our whole beloved German nation!

But whoever wants to continue provoking God's chastisement, whoever blasphemes our faith, whoever despises God's commandments, whoever makes common cause with those who alienate our youth from Christendom, whoever robs and drives away our members of orders, with those who deliver to their deaths innocent people, our brothers and sisters, with him we want to avoid all intimate contact, from his influence we want to withdraw ourselves and ours, so that we shall not become infected by his impious thoughts and deeds, so that we shall not become accomplices and consequently fall under the chastisement that the just God must inflict and will inflict over all who, like the ungrateful city Jerusalem, do not want what God wants.

Oh God, let us all today, on this day, before it is too late, recognize the things that make for peace for us!

Oh most sacred heart of Jesus, grieved to tears over the blindness and misdeeds of humans, help us with your grace, so that we shall continually strive for that which pleases you and abstain from that which displeases you, so that we remain in your love and find rest for our souls.

Amen!

Let us pray for the poor patients who are threatened with death, for our exiled members of orders, for all the destitute, for our soldiers, for our nation and fatherland and its Führer.

Our father ...[35]

NOTES

1 Henry Friedlander, *The Origins of Nazi Genocide. From Euthanasia to the Final Solution*, 39–45.

2 Ibid., 67.

3 Martin Höllen, "Katholische Kirche und NS-'Euthanasie,'" *Zeitschrift für Kirchengeschichte* 91 (1980): 53–82.

4 Ibid., 78.

5 Ibid., 78–9.

6 Eberhard Bethge, *Dietrich Bonhoeffer. A Biography*, revised ed., 688: "In the summer of 1940, on behalf of Fritz von Bodelschwingh of the Bethel institutions and Pastor Paul Braune of the Lobethal institution, Bonhoeffer spoke with his father about giving them authoritative medical documents that they could use as grounds for refusing to hand their patients over." Bethge, *Bonhoeffer. Theologe, Christ, Zeitgenosse. Eine Biographie*, 773, mentions Bodelschwingh's and Braune's refusal to hand over patients ("Weigerung, Patienten auszuliefern"); Leroy Walters, "Paul Braune Confronts the National Socialists' 'Euthanasia' Program," 476. Bodelschwingh was forced to co-operate; he noted: "Mit dem Regierungspräsidenten in Minden, der im Auftrag des Ministeriums in Berlin mit uns verhandelte, ist folgendes vereinbart worden: Es bleibt dabei, dass wir die Fragebogen selbst nicht ausfüllen. Das wird vermutlich durch eine von Berlin entsandte Kommission geschehen. Dieser stellen wir pflichtgemäss Akten und mündliche Auskünfte zur Verfügung. Um der Kommission die rein technische Arbeit zu erleichtern – es handelt sich dabei um die ersten 7–8 Zeilen der Fragebogen – werden wir ausser den Akten Kartothekblätter für jeden einzelnen Kranken bereithalten, aus denen die Angaben abgelesen oder abgeschrieben werden können." Anneliese Hochmuth, *Spurensuche. Eugenik, Sterilisation, Patientenmorde und die v.Bodelschwinghschen Anstalten Bethel 1929–1945* (Bielefeld: Bethel-Verlag 1997), 96–111 quotes Pastor F.v.Bodelschwingh to Pastor Walther Zilz, Bethel 27 Jan. 1941, HAB (Hauptarchiv Bethel) 2/65-58.

7 Marikje Smid, *Hans von Dohnanyi – Christine Bonhoeffer. Eine Ehe im Widerstand gegen Hitler* (Gütersloh: Gütersloher Verlagshaus 2002), 249–50; Walters, "Paul Braune," 454–87; Walters, "Der Widerstand Paul Braunes und des Bonhoefferkreises gegen das 'Euthanasie'-Programm der Nationalsozialisten," in Christof Gestrich and Johannes Neugebauer, eds., *Der Wert menschlichen Lebens. Medizinische Ethik bei Karl Bonhoeffer und Dietrich Bonhoeffer* (Berlin: Wichern-Verlag 2006), 98–146.

8 Lothar Gruchmann, *Justiz im Dritten Reich 1933–1940. Anpassung und Unterwerfung in der Ära Gürtner*, 505–14; Walters, "Paul Braune," 472–3.

9 Cf. Martin Höllen, "Katholische Kirche und NS-'Euthanasie'"; Georg Schwaiger, "Kardinal Michael von Faulhaber," *Zeitschrift für Kirchengeschichte* 80 (1969): 359–74.

10 Gruchmann, *Justiz im Dritten Reich*, 507–8.

11 Ibid., 513–14.

12 Bischof Clemens August Graf von Galen, *Akten, Briefe und Predigten 1933–1946*, 869.

13 See Ulrich von Hassell, *The von Hassell Diaries 1938–1944* (1948 ed.), 191, 198, 203, 216; Joseph Goebbels, *Die Tagebücher, Teil II*, vol. 1, 232.

14 H. Friedlander, *The Origins of Nazi Genocide*, 115–16.

15 J.S. Conway, *The Nazi Persecution of the Churches 1933–45*, 279, cites *Documents on German Foreign Policy 1918–1945 (Series D 1937–1945)*, vol. 13, no. 340, encl. 2 (London: Her Majesty's Stationery Office 1964), 536–7: Bormann an Gauleiter, FHQ 30.7.41: "The Führer has ordered: The confiscations of church and monastic property shall be halted immediately until further notice. Independent measures may not be taken by the Gauleiters in any circumstances even if special circumstances in individual cases urgently require the utilization of church or monastic property on the basis of the legal regulations."

16 Rudolf Morsey, "Clemens August Kardinal von Galen. Versuch einer historischen Würdigung," *Jahrbuch des Instituts für christliche Sozialwissenschaften* 7/8 (1966/67): 367–82, here 375.

17 Noakes and Pridham, *Documents on Nazism, 1919–1945*, 308–9.

18 Joseph Goebbels, *Die Tagebücher, Teil II*, Band 3 (Munich: K.G. Saur 1994), entries 11 and 26 March 1942, 455, 555.

19 Gruchmann, *Justiz*, 533

20 Heinz Faulstich, "Die Zahl der 'Euthanasie'-Opfer," in Andreas Frewer, Clemens Eickhoff, eds., *"Euthanasie" und die aktuelle Sterbehilfe-Debatte. Die historischen Hintergründe medizinischer Ethik* (Frankfurt, New York: Campus 2000), 218–34, esp. 227–8; Friedlander, *The Origins of Nazi Genocide*, 109, 113–15, 151; Balfour, *Withstanding Hitler*, 228; Ian Kershaw, *Popular Opinion and Political Dissent in the Third Reich. Bavaria 1933–1945* (Oxford: Clarendon Press 1983; New York: Oxford University Press 1983), 272, 334: "The halting of the 'action' was the direct consequence of the pressure of 'public opinion.'" However, it was not halted.

21 Faulstich, "Die Zahl der 'Euthanasie'-Opfer," 218–34, esp. 227–8.

22 Concerning Faulhaber's failure, cf. Schwaiger, "Kardinal Michael von Faulhaber," 371–2.

23 Beth A. Griech-Polelle, *Bishop von Galen. German Catholicism and National Socialism*, 96–135, esp. 108–9.

24 Source: Copy in the Münster Episcopal Archive, A8 and another numbered A9. The printed version in Peter Löffler, ed., *Bischof Clemens August Graf von Galen. Akten, Briefe und Predigten 1933–1946*, vol. 2 (Mainz: Matthias-Grünewald-Verlag 1988), 869, 874–83, is described as based on A8 but is inaccurate in comparison with both A8 and A9; it also includes the "Announcements," which are not in either A8 or A9, but appeared in a contemporary printing in the Swiss paper *Das Neue Volk* 8 (November 1941). The translation that follows keeps as close as possible to the original archival text. The translation by Patrick Smith in *The Bishop of Münster and the Nazis. The Documents in the Case* is imprecise. See also Beth A. Griech-Polelle, *Bishop von Galen*; Heinrich Portmann, *Cardinal von Galen*.

25 Ellipsis are in the archive copy.

26 Leonardo Conti, MD.

27 Ellipses are in the archive copy.

28 Löffler misread "Amtes" for "Arztes."

29 "Ministerrat für Landesverteidigung" suggests a national authority, although the context makes a regional authority more likely. In fact, patients were transferred to other institutions by order of the Reichsverteidigungskommissare (Reich Defence Commissars).

30 On 12 August 1941 Galen ordered all priests and rectors of Münster Diocese to send him a list, by 1 September 1941, of all cases of burials of ashes with the names, ages, causes of death, places and dates of death of the deceased and to report equally all future cases of Catholics who were cremated against their will; Löffler, *Bischof Clemens*, 879.

31 Bishop von Galen's quotation is close to Luther's translation; the revised German version and *The New Oxford Annotated Bible with the Apocrypha* (New York: Oxford University Press 1977) are in agreement about the meaning in the English version: "My punishment is greater than I can bear ... whoever finds me will slay me." The ellipsis is in the archive copy.

32 Matthew 23:37.

33 The letter was dated 23 December 1939 and appeared in print in the entire German press.

34 Luke 19:41; Galen's quotation has an ellipsis and some slight changes.

35 Ellipsis in archive copy.

18

Ulrich von Hassell on Bishop von Galen's Sermons, August 1941[1]

Ebenhausen, 30 August 1941[2]

In July and August, Bishop Graf von Galen of Münster preached three courageous sermons against the persecution of the churches and the murder of the mentally feeble, speaking with hitherto unheard-of openness about the lawlessness and the methods of the Gestapo. Himmler was seething and demanded the most drastic action immediately (allegedly by shooting). Meanwhile, poor Kerrl[3] became rather frightened during the entire Bormann (= Hitler) campaign and implored Hitler to stop the fight against the churches during the war. Hitler sent for Bormann and, according to the oft-proven method for success, considered it tactically correct to retreat a few steps, as in the Echternach dancing procession, that is, to order the Gauleiters to stop. Himmler, on the other hand, declared that for him this was not a matter of church questions, but that, in the interest of state (read: the system's) security, he must proceed further, having the impudence to plead the interests of the Wehrmacht. Until now, Galen had been confined only to Münster. Why did Rome let Galen fight it out alone? And what did *our* exalted princes of the church? Hannah Nathusius[4] was there and described the methods applied in Neinstedt against the mentally feeble, who were working there wholly commendably, and who had been marched in formation through the town to the train station.[5] Some had asked her why they were not at least given the "injection" right there in Neinstedt. The poor souls, therefore, knew exactly what was happening. The citizens were so agitated that a Party speaker was sent to calm them with the shameless argument that they, the citizens, would now get better rations after the share for the mentally feeble was cancelled.

NOTES

1 For background on Hassell, see document no. 15; for Galen, see introduction to document no. 17.
2 Source: The translation follows the new German edition: Hassell, *Die Hassell-Tagebücher 1938–1944*, 269–70; cf. Hassell, *The Von Hassell Diaries 1938–1944* (Hamish Hamilton edition 1948), 191.
3 Hanns Kerrl (1887–1941), from 1935 Reich Minister for Church Affairs.
4 Hannah von Nathusius (1875–1946), painter, a cousin of Hassell. Her father, the theology professor Martin von Nathusius, had a farm in Neinstedt.
5 Neinstedt, in the Harz district of Quedlinburg, had institutions for the care of the mentally ill and for epileptics.

FOREIGN POLICY

19

Lieutenant-General Ludwig Beck, Chief of the General Staff of the Army, on an Unofficial Visit to Paris, 16–20 June 1937

Ludwig Beck was born in Biebrich on the Rhine on 29 June 1880, the son of a successful industrialist who came from a family of Hessian army officers. He joined an artillery regiment in 1898 and rose through the ranks of the Prussian Army and Reichswehr to brigadier[1] and divisional commander by 1932. From 1 October 1933 to 27 August 1938, he was Chief of the General Staff of the Army (until 1 July 1935 the position was called "Chief of Troop Office" because the Treaty of Versailles forbade a General Staff). He resigned his post on 19 August 1938 in protest against Hitler's war policy and became the leading elder statesman of the German resistance to Hitler. He committed suicide after the failure of the insurrection on 20 July 1944.

Beck welcomed the rise of the National Socialists in the years 1930–32 and Hitler's appointment as Chancellor in 1933.[2] As Chief of the General Staff of the Army, he presided over German rearmament. At the same time, he became concerned about Hitler's belligerence and the danger of war, to say nothing of the political and racial repression and persecution at home. His position was conflicted: he agreed with the general aim of restoring Germany's proper position in Europe, but he deplored the means the regime employed. In 1934 he objected to the speed of rearmament, which increased the danger of war,[3] and criticized Hitler for not seeking international agreements for rearmament within reasonable limits.[4] In March 1935 he argued for a rearmament ratio of 1:3 to 1:2 between Germany and her potential opponents – France, Czechoslovakia, Belgium, and Poland; the key term in his memorandum was "defence."[5] He appeared still to agree with what he perceived to be the aims of Hitler's policy, quarrelling only with the methods.[6] But two months later, he refused to lay plans for any operations against Czechoslovakia except in the case of a French attack upon Germany (since France and Czechoslovakia were allies).[7] An attack upon Czechoslovakia to solve the Sudeten Question would be possible only if France, Britain, and the United States did not object, which was to say, in Beck's view, never.[8] He noted that the only reasonable "military-political" maxim was to maintain good relations with all powers. If a war of aggression was intended, he would resign.[9] Beck was moderately successful. No plans for an attack against Czechoslovakia were laid until 1937.

Beck insisted that the Chief of the General Staff of the Army must be heard by the political leadership on strategic and "military-political" issues.[10] He demanded precisely the role that the British Chiefs of Staff had when they advised Prime Minister Neville Chamberlain, in March 1938, concerning the German threat to Czechoslovakia:

> We conclude that no pressure that we and our possible Allies can bring to bear, either by sea or land or in the air, could prevent Germany from invading and overrunning Bohemia and from inflicting a decisive defeat on the Czechoslovakian Army. We should then be faced with the necessity of undertaking a war against Germany for the purpose of restoring Czechoslovakia's lost integrity, and this object would only be achieved by the defeat of Germany and as the outcome of a prolonged struggle. In the world situation today, it seems to us that if such a struggle were to take place it is more than probable that both Italy and Japan would seize the opportunity to further their own ends, and that in consequence the problem we have to envisage is not that of a limited European war only, but of a world war.[11]

In March 1937 Beck published a letter by Carl von Clausewitz in which Clausewitz had warned: "The obligation and the right of the art of war vis-à-vis policy is mainly to prevent policy from demanding things *that are contrary to the nature of war*, so that it [policy] will not, from ignorance of the effects of the instrument, commit errors in using it."[12]

In May 1937 the War Minister, Field Marshal Werner von Blomberg, ordered the preparation of plans for a German military intervention in Austria in case the Habsburg monarchy was restored. Beck demurred and argued that the Austrian army would put up resistance, as his Austrian counterpart, General Alfred Jansa, had told him, and that a German intervention would only damage the case for German-Austrian union.[13] No plans had been made when Hitler ordered the invasion of Austria in March 1938.[14] In June 1937, during a visit to Paris, Beck addressed warnings of Hitler's intentions to the governments of Britain and France.

The British Ambassador in Berlin, Sir Eric Phipps, reported about Gerneral Beck to the Secretary of State for Foreign Affairs, Anthony Eden, on 7 January 1937: "He is not in sympathy with the present regime and regrets that the 'revolution' is not yet over."[15]

The British Military Attaché in Berlin, Colonel F. Noel Mason-Macfarlane, noted: "On the surface it might well appear that Beck's very marked anti-war attitude might have been connected with the unpreparedness at that moment of the Wehrmacht for war. But those of us who had had the good fortune to get to know him and to appreciate the integrity of his character and his dislike and mistrust of Hitler and the Nazis realized that he was actuated primarily by his genuine determination to do all he could to prevent the horrors of a second world conflict."[16]

General Gamelin and the Military Attaché in the German Embassy at Paris, Major-General Erich Kühlenthal, invited the German War Minister, Field Marshal Werner von Blomberg, to visit France for the purpose of stabilizing peaceful relations between the two countries. Blomberg was unable to accept, and he sent Lieutenant-General Ludwig Beck, Chief of the General Staff of the Army (1 July 1933–27 August 1938), to unofficially visit his French counterpart, General Maurice Gamelin, in Paris. They met from 16–20 June 1937.

The meeting was disguised as a visit on the occasion of the World's Fair. In Paris, Beck met Gamelin; the French Minister of Defence, Édouard Daladier; and Marshal Philippe Pétain.[17] Beck was reported by the retired British Air Attaché, Group-Captain M.G. Christie, to have made the remarks reproduced below at a social occasion that included the German Military Attaché and his Assistant, General-Staff Captain Hans Ritter, who reported the remarks to Christie. Ritter had close ties to Beck. Christie was financially independent and used his many connections to supply the Head of the British Foreign Office, Robert Vansittart, with information. Christie identified Ritter as "Knight," or "Kn." in his reports.[18]

Very secret[19]
Gist of Conversation between General Beck, Chief of the German Army general staff, and one or two *intimate* friends (officers) on his visit to Paris. June/1937.

There is no political meaning in my visit to the French Army. I came as a gentleman to talk with gentlemen to try & improve the atmosphere of our relations. The Press has reported that I have made certain proposals: that is absolutely untrue: I have made none, & I had no mandate for any political proposals. Of course I could have touched upon a theoretical agreement for the limitation of armaments, but I did not do so, because I know that the German Govt/ would most certainly break any such agreement; indeed from the start *neither* Gen. Goering for the Air Force *nor* Admiral Raeder for the Navy would keep to it. As to the Army's attitude Fritsch & I could vouch for that, but to what purpose, when we know that Himmler & the Party Leaders would get round it by persuading Adolf Hitler to form & equip several new divisions of SS. troops: the Führer would never include his SS troops in any Limitation of Armaments Pact.

N.B. At present there is one Division of Blackshirts SS in the Reich, picked men, equipped as an Infantry Division with the most modern weapons etc; term of service = four years in the ranks: SS troops are quartered in proper barracks.

Beck went on to say:

The financial & commercial outlook is very depressing: the Stimmung im Volke sehr gespannt u. nicht zuletzt durch den Kirchenkampf.[20] The Radicals of the Nazi Party, Goebbels, Himmler, Heydrich, Ley, Rosenberg & sometimes Göring[21] keep impressing upon Hitler that in order to counter internal discontent (zur Behebung der inneren Lage)[22] a success in the field of foreign politics is necessary. We military men, with the main exception of Marshal Blomberg, are opposed to any such adventure but we can no longer guarantee against it. Since March 7th/36 (Rheinlandbesetzung[23]) our position has become so much weaker morally. In the case of *Spain*, we (the Gen Staff) wanted to keep absolutely clear, but we only managed to prevent direct intervention by the Reich. Again as regards *Austria*, Himmler & Party drew up a plan last month (May) *with* the consent (Zustimmung) of Hitler but *without* the knowledge of the Kriegsministerium[24] to march into Austria with ss Blackshirt troops, occupy the country (reckoning upon no resistance on part of the Austrian Army) & compel (erzwingen) a plebiscite on the issue of the Anschluss. Fortunately Papen & Gen Muff, our Military Attaché in Vienna, got wind of the plan & together with ourselves persuaded Hitler to withdraw his approval. We must however realise that the whole of the Party Radicals are pressing the Führer for a Heldentat.

In a still smaller circle of friends Beck spoke of Hitler & Blomberg. Of the former he said "pathologisch u. völlig unberechenbar"[25]; of the latter he said approx as follows, "Blomberg is absolutely a Phantast."[26] "He is completely eingefangen,["][27] ie under the spell of Hitler & Rosenberg. In a recent talk with me Blomberg spoke of the likelihood of war between Russia & Germany. I said I could see no grounds whatever for such a war. He replied, "War against USSR seems to be unavoidable because Communism & Natl Socialism can never both exist alongside each other." I asked him "Has mankind really gone back to the Religious Wars of the Middle Ages?" Blomberg answered "Doch, so ähnlich denke ich mir den Verlauf der zukünftigen Politik."[28]

NOTES

1 British/Canadian/American equivalent rank for Generalmajor. German military ranks are given as their British/Canadian/American equivalents: Generalmajor thus becomes brigadier; Generalleutnant major-general, General lieutenant-general.

2 Kunrat Freiherr von Hammerstein, *Spähtrupp* (Stuttgart: Henry Goverts Verlag 1963), 16, 19; Nicholas Reynolds, *Treason Was No Crime*, 42–3; Alexander [Freiherr] von Falkenhausen, Bericht über meine Stellung zur N.S.D.A.P. und ihrem Regime, typescript (no place, 15 Nov. 1946), National Archives, Washington, DC, Record Group 338, MS no. B-289; Max von Viebahn, Generaloberst Ludwig Beck 29.6.1880–20.7.1944, signed typescript (no place, 29 June 1948), in the editor's possession.

3 Beck's draft of a memorandum of 20 May 1934 in Bundesarchiv-Militärarchiv (BA-MA), N 28/1.

4 Klaus-Jürgen Müller, *General Ludwig Beck. Studien und Dokumente*, 166, 171, 350–4. Britain and France had been inclined in 1932 to concede to Germany, not military "equality," which Reichswehr Minister Brigadier Kurt von Schleicher had demanded in a radio address in July 1932 and in an interview with the *New York Times*

in August 1932, but an increase of the limit the Treaty of Versailles had put upon the strength of Germany's armed forces. After Hitler had been appointed chancellor, they delayed their agreement and at the Disarmament Conference in Geneva in October 1933 they proposed a waiting period of four years. The French government insisted that Germany must show good behaviour for an indefinite time before armaments negotiations would be resumed. This gave Hitler the opportunity to claim unfair discrimination of Germany as a nation of lesser rights, and he withdrew Germany from the Disarmament Conference and from the League of Nations. See Peter Hoffmann, *Stauffenberg. A Family History, 1905–1944*, 57–8, 62.

5 Müller, *General Ludwig Beck*, 415–26 (docs. no. 24, 25).

6 [Colonel Carl-Heinrich von Stülpnagel, head of Troop Office section T3 (foreign armies)], Notizen zur augenblicklichen militärpolitischen Lage, typescript, [Berlin], 11 April 1935, BA-MA N 28/2.

7 Beck to Fritsch, 3 May 1935, BA-MA N 28/2; Müller, *General Ludwig Beck*, 438–45 (docs. 28–30).

8 Reynolds, *Treason Was No Crime,* 99–100, suppressing Beck's qualifications for the future; Müller, *General Ludwig Beck*, 150, 152–3, 155–9.

9 Notes by Beck, spring 1935, Müller, *Beck,* 444–5 (doc. no. 30); Wolfgang Foerster, *Generaloberst Ludwig Beck,* 29; Beck to Fritsch 3 May 1935, MS draft, BA-MA N 28/2; Müller, *General Ludwig Beck,* 438–9 (doc. no. 28).

10 Der Oberbefehlshaber des Heeres, Dienstanweisung für den Chef des Generalstabes des Heeres im Frieden, typescript, Berlin, 31 May 1935, BA-MA RH 2/v. 195; Müller, *General Ludwig Beck,* 530 (doc. no. 47).

11 N.H. Gibbs, *Grand Strategy. Volume I: Rearmament Policy,* 642.

12 "Zwei Briefe des Generals von Clausewitz. Gedanken zur Abwehr," *Militärwissenschaftliche Rundschau* 2 (1937), Sonderheft: 8–9.

13 Beck's MS draft and typed carbon copy in BA-MA N 28/2; Müller, *Das Heer und Hitler. Armee und nationalsozialistisches Regime 1933–1940,* 235; Müller, *General Ludwig Beck,* 438–9 (doc. no. 28). Cf. Janice Festa, Anschluss 1938. Austria's Potential for Military Resistance, M.A. thesis, McGill University, Montreal, 1998.

14 Wilhelm Keitel in *Der Prozess gegen die Hauptkriegsverbrecher vor dem Internationalen Militärgerichtshof Nürnberg 14. November 1945-1. Oktober 1946,* vol. 10 (Nuremberg 1947): 566; [Keitel], in Walter Görlitz, ed., *Generalfeldmarschall Keitel: Verbrecher oder Offizier? Erinnerungen, Briefe, Dokumente des Chefs OKW* (Göttingen: Musterschmidt-Verlag [1961]), 95, 178.

15 UK National Archives FO 371/20732/C 163/163/18.

16 N.F. Mason MacFarlane, Papers, Imperial War Museum, London, MM 28.

17 Müller, *General Ludwig Beck,* 248–56; minute by Rintelen, 17 June 1937, Auswärtiges Amt/Politisches Archiv, Berlin, Pol. II 1723 I.

18 On the Christie-Ritter connection see T.P. Conwell-Evans, *None So Blind. A Study of the Crisis Years, 1930–1939,* 91–2; Reynolds, *Treason,* 111–15; Auswärtiges Amt/Politisches Archiv, Berlin, to the editor 5 Sept. 2007; Kühlenthal, Papers, Bundesarchiv-Militärarchiv, Freiburg i.Br., MS 109/1472. See also Patricia Meehan, *The Unneces-*

sary War, 276; Klemens von Klemperer, *German Resistance against Hitler. The Search for Allies Abroad, 1938–1945*, 53, 85–6.

19 Source: Christie Papers, Churchill College, Cambridge, CHRS 1/21A. The entire note with quotations is in Christie's handwriting.

20 Translation: the mood among the people is very tense, and not least due to the church struggle.

21 General Hermann Göring, Hitler's designated successor, C-in-C Air Force, Minister for Air Transport, Plenipotentiary for the Four Year Plan.

22 Translation: remedying the internal situation.

23 Translation: occupation of the Rhineland.

24 Translation: War Ministry.

25 Translation: pathological and wholly unpredictable.

26 Translation: fantast.

27 Translation: captivated.

28 Translation: Yes, I see the course of future policy as similar to that.

20

Ulrich von Hassell's Statement on Conditions of Peace, February 1940

As the former German Ambassador in Rome, Hassell was a personage with international standing. He could still expect his views to carry weight. On 23 February 1940, he wrote the following statement of conditions of peace that a German anti-Hitler government would require. It appears to have been elicited by a feeler from the British Foreign Secretary, Lord Halifax, through an intermediary, James Lonsdale Bryans.[1] It reached Lord Halifax's desk, but it was soon filed away in a Foreign Office ragbag entitled "Private Office papers from various sources 1940."[2]

The context is this. Halifax had, in 1939, followed Prime Minister Neville Chamberlain's lead in seeking contacts with dissident "generals" in Germany in the hope of "a German revolution."[3] Despite some failures (Venlo Incident[4]), Halifax pursued this line until the end of February 1940. On the German side, the Beck-Oster group sought to secure British assurances for an acceptable post-war settlement so that the Army High Command (General Walther von Brauchitsch, Commander-in-Chief of the Army; General Franz Halder, Chief of the General Staff of the Army) might be persuaded to support a coup. Messages between the German underground group and the British government were transmitted by Pope Pius XII personally.[5] Beck and Hassell were in continuous contact in those months.[6] Although Hassell seemed to have been unaware of the German underground-British government contacts when he met with Halifax's intermediary, James Lonsdale Bryans, and to have learned of them only after 15 March, the "Statement" expresses views that were shared, at least in part, by Beck and

Oster, possibly less so by Goerdeler.[7] But it appears that Hassell was not told all that had been in the British response conveyed through Pius XII. On 13 February 1940, Foreign Secretary Halifax wrote to Prime Minister Chamberlain: "If we could get such an internal disruption of Germany, it would, I imagine, be what we want – and I should be inclined to feel that we could get the German creators of a South Germany to agree to an Austrian plebiscite, and that we on our side could agree that the Sudetenland should be a matter for negotiation or perhaps dealt with by way of population transfer."[8] From Halifax's point of view, Hassell's "Statement" belonged in the context of the British government's contacts with the Beck-Oster group, although Halifax knew little about the identity of the group. Hassell's "Statement" followed his view, which he mentioned repeatedly in his diaries, that any enemy demands for regime change in Germany would be the wrong tactic; German regime change had to be Germany's business.[9] Halifax's and Hassell's concepts of a settlement, however, were incompatible. This is most striking in their references to Austria and the Sudeten. In the matter of disarmament, the British government and Hassell also had very different views.[10]

Hassell's Italian son-in-law, Detalmo Pirzio-Biroli, wrote to Halifax from Rome on 10 February 1940, referring to a previous communication of 28 December 1939 that, to his great satisfaction, had been given full consideration by Lord Halifax.[11] Pirzio-Biroli's second letter is printed below. The circumstances of Hassell's meetings with Bryans in Arosa are described in Hassell's diary.[12] He declared that he was seeking to convey to Halifax the views of "many good people in Germany, the best of the Germans and the true Europeans," who had confidence in Halifax's good will and ability to help bring the new Europe into existence. A comparison of Pirzio-Biroli's letter with Hassell's statement, and with views expressed in the same context and in the same months, suggests that Pirzio-Biroli was putting forward Hassell's essential views, with a few variations with which Hassell might not have wished to be directly identified, such as a strong tendency among oppositional conservatives or, as Biroli also called them, "German Nationalists," to keep Göring in a transition government.

Pirzio-Biroli argued in favour of efforts to defuse the crisis before major combat between the Great Powers had been joined by describing the shifting internal situation in Germany: Hitler had gained some ground through propaganda and through the "Bolsheviks" in the NSDAP having had to retreat in the face of Russia's war against Finland. But in other respects Hitler was losing ground: The General Staff of the Army had become more independent, since November, by successfully dragging its feet on two occasions when Hitler had set dates (one for mid-December 1939 and the other for 3 January 1940) for an offensive in the west.

Detalmo Pirzio-Biroli's Letter to Foreign Secretary Lord Halifax[13]

To the Right Honourable Viscount Halifax, K.G.
His Majesty's Secretary of State for Foreign Affairs.
Rome, Feb. 10, 1940

My Lord,

I hear with great satisfaction that my report of Dec. 28, 1939 on Germany was given full consideration by your Lordship on Jan. 8, 1940.

I have returned to Germany for one week during the first part of January and I therefore wish now to have the honour to submit to your Lordship a few more observations and information which should be considered as standing complementary to what I had the honour to write the previous time.

In my last paper I pointed out to your Lordship some aspects of the situation which existed in Germany at the end of November last year and I had reported the views of some of the leading German Nationalists, especially in regard to the chances and means of averting the major world crisis which they feel would inevitably derive from a long and deadly war among the great European Powers. This time, if I may, I shall relate the new developments which the situation in Germany has undergone and I shall transmit the latest message which all people of good will from that country send to your Lordship.

During January the internal political front in Germany showed pretty much the same face it showed in November. Only for certain aspects was the situation at all changed. The aggressive action of Soviet Russia against Finland had caused Herr Hitler to realize, for the first time, the dangers which laid at the bottom of his Soviet policy, and Herr Hitler has been in fact since "marking his step." The Bolshevik faction within the Nazi Party, which highly encouraged by the German-Soviet Pact had hitherto come out into the open, was forced to retreat to the former underground positions. The Bolsheviks, in other words, were forced once more to disguise themselves as "extremist Nazis," with a general advantage for the position of Herr Hitler in the eyes of his people. The success of the thoroughly conducted anti-British press campaign and the slight increase in the supply of food-stuff must of course also be held to account for the renewed power of Nazism over Germany. Such renewed power of Hitler, especially over Northern Germany, was in fact quite visible. If in this respect however the position of Hitler has gained, for certain other respects we can say it has lost ground. The independence and authority of the General Staff of the Army have considerably grown since November. The best proof of this fact can be found in the events which occurred round Christmas time. The Government, encouraged by its renewed power and urged by its impatience, had insisted on an immediate offensive, which was supposed to serve both the political purpose of a "demonstrative action" and the strategical purpose of performing a "test" on the Allied land forces. The first date suggested was Dec. 18 (I think), the second date was Jan. 3 (this last one I know for sure). Both these times the General Staff, not wanting to seem too disregarding of Herr Hitler's will, first replied a half-hearted "yes," but then, at the last moment, declared flatly that the offensive could not be carried out, owing to "technical reasons." After the second rebuff, the Government did no longer ask for an offensive, but resigned itself to postpone it indefinitely. From these facts it appears quite plainly how great the conflict is today between Hitler and his General Staff. The German General Staff is still made up mainly of old Nationalists, sons of their military tradition, and it is by no means an easy instrument in the hands of Herr Hitler's Government.

On this second visit I have again had the chance to talk with several of the most eminent German Nationalists. I have found them more convinced than ever of the fact that an immediate peace is the only alternative to the total destruction of Europe and the downfall of our Western civilization. I have already related to your Lordship, in my previous report, the peace terms which a new Nationalist Government in Germany would be glad to agree to. On this visit I made it my principal object to discuss with those people the exact shape which an eventual new Government in Germany would take. According to the opinion of the leading German conservatives, the best man one can think of is undoubtedly Field-Marshall Goering. It is quite understood of course that Herr Goering in any case could never be more than a merely transitional measure, he would be just "means to an end." As such they rightly consider him as invaluable, owing to his unique popularity among all German classes, and owing furthermore to his background and tradition, which make of him a man who can very easily be influenced by good and intelligent collaborators. I have personally had a chance of having a talk with Herr Goering's sister (Fraulein Ilse Goering), and I was thus enabled to test myself the sound, cultured, intelligent, conservative background of Field-Marshall Goering's family. I have tried several times to make clear what the British point of view would be in connection with any eventual new Government in Germany. I insisted on the fact that Great Britain would never be able to accept any Government which included Herr Hitler or any of his friends and which did not have a sound constitutional basis and an entirely different mentality. Every time I stated this fact, I was answered that no one of the actual Nazi leaders would survive in the new Government, except Goering, and that Goering himself would have as his exclusive function that of operating the "transition." The Government would possibly be made of all those people who (like Schacht, Neurath, etc.) actually represent the best Germany can produce. The ground would also be prepared for a future eventual restoration of the monarchy, although it is too soon now to state how much could be done in this direction. The course which I have just described is, in the mind of all the German Nationalists, the only one which can save Europe from the final catastrophe and restore collaboration and good will. Among all intelligent people in Germany there are today absolutely no illusions as to the future prospects of the present war. Every intelligent German sees quite clearly that this war is already potentially lost for his country. But still, everyone feels that, if the real fighting actually comes, Germany will, despite everything, put up a stern resistence and fight to the end. This is why among all enlighted people there is such a strong desire for peace: because peace seems the only course which can save Germany and Europe at large. From a larger point of view in fact, intelligent Germans feel that, if the war was allowed to progress, it will undoubtedly be a long war, at the end of which, even if the military victory be British, the real final victory can only be commu[nist] with the result of the total destruction of our civilization.

Coming finally to the problem of "action," I have asked those people what could be done on the British side in order to help their struggle for peace, for a renewed Germany, and for an organized Europe. The answer I received can be condensed in the following points.

1) The Germans need from Great Britain some sort of assurance that no military advantage would be taken in case a changement of Government would be carried out. They are quite aware of the difficulties of such a problem, still I have had the impression that even a very simple thing could be of great help to them. It has to be something though which reaches them directly from England and that bore a sufficient amount of authenticity and authority. How can such an assurance be given to them, I am not in a position to know. I nevertheless wish to relate this matter to your Lordship, because it is of the utmost importance and because I do not despair that your Lordship at some future time may find the way of giving it effect.

2) The British propaganda, both on the wireless and by panphlets, should be amended in its psychological key. I have already made some suggestions to this effect in my previous report and I shall therefore not amplify [this] point any further. I feel convinced that the more such campaign is intensified the better. Many Germans keep on listening to the British wireless stations, despite the heavy penalties for such an action, and, if the k[ey] of the propaganda was amended in the right direction, it could turn out to be very effective.

3) The action of the opposition in Germany has often been checked and disturbed by the unrestrained publicity which the British and French press have given to those internal struggles and dissensions. It is not even impossible that most drastic measures on the part of the Nazi Government might follow such ill-timed publicity, entailing even the internment of leaders whose loss to the cause might well prove irreparable. The result of such publicity is practically always to the entire disadvantage of the opposition, in the lines of which fight the best of the Germans and the true Europeans. (Eg. the issue of the Daily Mail, Paris Edition, for Feb. 5th, 1940.)

4) It would be of extreme use and importance if some sort of connection could be established between some eminent representative of the Nationalist party and your Lordship. Such thing would certainly not fail to produce on both sides a better understanding of the situation.

If I, for the second time, do address my words to your Lordship, it is because I feel it my duty to convey to you these messages which come from so many good people in Germany. People who live and strive for a new Europe and who see in your Lordship one of the very few men who today can be fully trusted and who have clear views as to the spirit in which the new Europe must be built.

(a pro-British neutral)
[signed] D.C.P.B.

Ulrich von Hassell's "Statement"

"Confidential!   22-2-40[14]
Dear Mr. Bryans, according to your wishes I beg to include a note on the principles considered to be essential for the establishment of permanent peace.

With kindest regards
Yours very sincerely
Ulrich v. Hassell."

Confidential[15]

I All serious-minded people in Germany consider it as of utmost importance to stop this mad war as soon as possible.

II They consider this because the danger of a complete destruction and particularly a bolshevisation of Europe is rapidly growing.

III "Europe" does not mean for us a chessboard of political and military action or a base of power but it has "la valeur d'une patrie" in the frame of which a healthy Germany in sound conditions of life is an indispensable factor.

IV The purpose of a peace treaty ought to be a permanent pacification and restablishment of Europe on a solid base and a security against a renewal of warlike tendencies.

V Condition, necessary for this result, is to leave the union of Austria and the Sudeten with the Reich out of any discussion. In the same way there would be excluded a renewed discussion of occidental frontier questions of the Reich (f.e.[16] Alsace-Lorraine). On the other hand the germano-polish frontier will have to be more or less identical with the german frontier in 1914.[17]

VI The treaty of peace and the reconstruction of Europe ought to be based on certain principles that will have to be universally accepted.

VII Such principles are the following:

1) The principle of nationality with certain modifications deriving from history.
   Therefore f.e.[18]
2) Restablishment of an independent Poland and of a Czech Republic.
3) General reduction of armaments.
4) Restablishment of free international economical cooperation.
5) Recognition of certain leading ideas by all European states, such as

    a The principles of Christian ethics.
    b Justice and law as fundamental elements of public life.
    c Social welfare as leitmotiv.
    d Effective control of the executive power of state by the people, adapted to the special character of every nation.
    e Liberty of thought, conscience, and intellectual activity.

NOTES

1 J. Lonsdale Bryans, *Blind Victory (Secret Communications Halifax-Hassell)*, 36–81; Bryans, "Zur britischen amtlichen Haltung gegenüber der deutschen Widerstandsbewegung," 347–56; Ulrich von Hassell, *Die Hassell-Tagebücher 1938–1944. Aufzeichnungen vom Andern Deutschland*, 179, 187.

2 Hassell, *The Von Hassell Diaries 1938–1944* (1948), 124; Hassell, *Die Hassell-Tagebücher*, 189; cf. Patricia Meehan, *The Unnecessary War. Whitehall and the German Resistance to Hitler*, 275.

3 Peter W. Ludlow, "The Unwinding of Appeasement," 40.

4 See Peter Hoffmann, "The Question of Western Allied Co-operation with the German Anti-Nazi Conspiracy, 1938–1944," 437–64.

5 See Ludlow, "Papst Pius XII., die britische Regierung und die deutsche Opposition im Winter 1939/40," *Vierteljahrshefte für Zeitgeschichte* 22 (1974): 299–341; Lothar Kettenacker, ed., *Das "Andere Deutschland" im Zweiten Weltkrieg. Emigration und Widerstand in internationaler Perspektive. The "Other Germany" in the Second World War. Emigration and Resistance in International Perspective*; Kettenacker, *Krieg zur Friedenssicherung. Die Deutschlandplanung der britischen Regierung während des Zweiten Weltkrieges* (Göttingen: Vandenhoeck & Ruprecht 1989), 51–67; Hoffmann, *The History of the German Resistance 1933–1945*, 155–8.

6 Cf. Hassell, *Die Hassell-Tagebücher*, e.g. 161, 167–8.

7 Hassell, *Diaries* (1948), 117, 122–3; Hassell, *Die Hassell-Tagebücher*, 179, 187.

8 Ludlow, *Unwinding*, 40.

9 Hassell, *Die Hassell-Tagebücher*, 161, 180.

10 See Hoffmann, "The Question," 437–64; Hoffmann, *The History of the German Resistance*.

11 Detalmo Pirzio-Biroli to Viscount Halifax 10 Feb. 1940, UK National Archives (formerly PRO), FO 800/398 XC/A 56297; cf. Alexander Cadogan, *The Diaries of Sir Alexander Cadogan O.M. 1938–1945* (London: Cassell 1971), 256–7, 263.

12 Hassell, *Diaries* (1948), 108–11, 117, 119–20, 122–5; Hassell, *Die Hassell-Tagebücher*, 168–71, 182, 189–91.

13 Source: Original in UK National Archives, FO 371/34427 XC6694; the letter was written in English and is rendered here orthographically, grammatically, and stylistically unchanged.

14 Source: Hassell's handwritten covering note to Bryans, in UK National Archives, FO 800/398 56034.

15 Source: Hassell's handwritten statement in UK National Archives, FO 800/398 56034, rendered here orthographically, grammatically, and stylistically unchanged.

16 For example.

17 This would help to explain the terms in Hans von Dohnanyi's "X Report" for Halder, which did not reflect the views of the British Foreign Office as conveyed to the German conspirators through Josef Müller and of which Hassell may have been uninformed. See Hoffmann, *History*, 163–8.

18 For example.

21

Foreign-policy Objectives of the
Kreisau Circle, April 1941[1]

Moltke presented the foreign policy objectives of the Kreisau Circle in the following first draft of a memorandum. It combines internal-policy reform with European integration. There also survives in Moltke's papers a shorter summary of the same ideas, dated 20 June 1941.

The proposals in this memorandum were drafted in reaction to the National Socialist foreign policy that had led to the outbreak of the Second World War. These proposals promoted the principles of integrating Europe into a federal state and emphasized European international co-operation to ensure future peace and stability. This entailed eliminating nationalism and integrating the separate national economies, which would also accelerate the post-war reconstruction of Europe. European integration and unity were to be extended to the political sphere through the establishment of a common executive and legislative authority, staffed by representatives of the European states.

The document is a typescript with amendments in Moltke's hand and marginalia in Peter Count von Yorck's hand.

STARTING POINT, GOALS, AND TASKS

I

Starting Position

The analysis of the position in which we find ourselves can be easily endangered and falsified by the goals that we are striving for. It is difficult to ascertain which factual conditions really exist objectively. The following is an attempt to provide an outline of the basic position as it presents itself to me.

1   The individual is unfettered but unfree.

The commitments that have obligated the individual have changed. All adaptations have at some time occurred, from the bare herd instinct and regional cohesion to the full community based on deep religious foundations. One can find the culmination of commitment in the early Middle Ages, when every individual felt attached to the church, when, by comparison, all other relationships were secondary. One can imagine it as individuals represented by small metal sticks that lie scattered across the entire then-known world, in the middle of which stands a powerful magnet to which all are oriented, regardless of whether they have any particular connection or particular detachment tendencies: friendship and enmity are dominated and regulated by common orientation.

As this magnet weakens, the European world disintegrates into smaller groups, until finally the Reformation makes the neutralization of the great magnet manifest. The former universally obligatory commitment is replaced by a number of diverse obligations; this is a development that ultimately has led to the emergence of sovereign states as equivalent, supreme centres of obligation for limited purposes.[3] This development initially left in place and tolerated certain lateral connections: the common European experience of the Renaissance and of the Romantic period created[4] lateral connections of varying strength; the international labour movement has sought to create a new commitment that, according to the will of its proponents, was to assert itself against the state. None of these other commitments has been sufficiently consequential to demand the commitment of the whole person, as the state ultimately did, and as it has enforced it in this century.

However, since the state 'is of this world,' its demand for the commitment of the whole person has manifested itself as an abuse of secular authority, and with this abuse of authority the sense of commitment has been lost, even as the abuse of secular authority by the church in the Middle Ages perhaps has led also[5] to the loss of its bonding function. Thus the sense of inner cohesion with the state has been replaced, on the one hand, by a cohesion similar to the herd instinct for mutual protection and, on the other, by force and coercion of the individual. Thereby the individual, who has lost his bond, has been deprived of his freedom. This is true for all of continental Europe, perhaps also for Russia.

2   The responsibility of the individual is in a process of dissolution.

All small communities in which the individual still bears responsibility are in a process of dissolution. All functions of such small, autonomous communities are being gradually taken over by state organizations. This is true of the old, self-government bodies and of cultural, care-giving, and all manner of social organizations. This is a method by which the state, for its own purposes, frees energies that were committed in small communities.[6]

A sense of responsibility for the development of humanity as a whole is almost completely non-existent any longer. It cannot be seen at the moment, to be sure, how such a sense of responsibility could be acted upon.

Individual responsibility for the state as such does not exist anymore, either. The state today can exist only through its organizations; the individual's position in the organization at all times is only one that does not allow him to attain a sense of responsibility for the whole. The organization of the state consists of technicians, of specialists, who work in isolation.

3   Forms of expression are destroyed.

Words have lost their unequivocal meanings; symbols no longer evoke a uniform image; works of art are denuded of their absolute meaning; and they, like all educational values, have become purpose-oriented. They serve the state, have thereby lost their absolute meaning, and have become relative. It is probably no exaggeration if one says that everything that ought to be absolute has become relative, that those forms in which alone we can express absolute values, words, and symbols, including works of art, have been abused, have lost their unequivocal contents, and have thereby ceased to be the messengers of absolute values. Instead things that are entirely lacking in absolute value, like the state, race, and power, have been made absolute.

II

Aims

The aims we are striving for seem to me to be completely unequivocal: in the individual there must be reawakened the sense of inner commitment to values that are not of this world, that alone will make it possible to restore freedom to him;[7] thereby the individual will recover a sense of responsibility that will lead to a flourishing of a true community; this development and the educational work arising from it will only become possible if forms of expression, which are solely at our disposal, once again become generally binding and intelligible.

One must answer for oneself this question: "Are these aims correctly recognized?" before one turns to the next question: "Are these aims attainable?" The distinction between these two questions is so important because one otherwise falls victim to the temptation of considering aims as the right ones that one believes to be the only attainable ones. The consequence is that one loses countless numbers of allies, since every person can justifiably have a different opinion on the question of attainability, which is purely speculative, even when there is agreement on the fundamental position. Among all those who can at all come under consideration as allies, it ought to be possible to achieve agreement on the question of whether the stated goals, apart from their attainability, have been correctly put in the first instance.

1

Are these aims correct? The heart of the matter is the sense of inner commitment to values that are not of this world. The goal is imprecise, as I gladly admit, and I shall be grateful for any improvement. For what is meant is[8] the sense of commitment of all to the *same* values.[9] With this, nationalism and racialism are to be overcome. A situation is to be striven for in which party divisions and conflicts among the people of the globe have only secondary importance, since those who are combined into a party receive their principal orientation from the magnet that attracts and influences everyone equally, and since enemies also agree on the most essential point. I am, however, not able to define these universal values more precisely, because it must be the task of all of humanity to create this magnet, and because it would be presumptuous to say that it was already in place at a specific location and it was merely the obligation of the others to integrate themselves in its sphere of influence.

The second most important point is the attainment of freedom. Freedom is the counterpart of commitment; both belong together. Freedom is the touchstone of commitment, and the commitment is a part of freedom. These two therefore belong together.

The third point is the sense of responsibility. This is a consequence of the certainty of commitment. A sense of responsibility is the outward sign for the existence of commitment. A sense of responsibility presupposes both freedom and commitment. All actions that affect the community, and these are all conceivable actions, must be supported by this sense of responsibility. As soon as this is the case, human communities will again flourish, starting with the family, as the smallest community, to the pursuit of every kind of common interest, to the administration of public affairs and up to the international community. Nothing that happens in the world, or that sometimes must happen, would be destructive to the community if it were clear to all that it would be supported by a sense of responsibility, and if it, in the last resort, stood under the precept of "love thy neighbor as thyself," even if you must cause him grief.

The fourth point is the restoration of the forms of expression. All that has been said can only be achieved with a restoration of forms of expression, and the restoration of forms of expression is a consequence of the achievement of the first three aims. Yes must again be yes, and no must be no, good must again be an absolute, and evil must be, too. If one is unable to communicate, one cannot expect that anything beneficial will result from co-operation.

2

Before I turn to the question of the attainability of these aims, I must, under a subtitle of the question of whether these aims are correct, discuss the question of whether or not the aims are complete and wholly comprehensive. As I see it, everything is contained in these aims. If that is not expressed clearly enough, then I must improve it. I mean the inner disposition (commitment in freedom), the outward action (sense of responsibility in the community), and the form of transmission (word, symbol, and work of art). I do not see what would not be included.

3

The question of whether and to what extent these aims are attainable is necessarily controversial and in doubt. These aims are always attainable by individuals but never by all people. One can consider these aims to have been attained only when such a large proportion of mankind is won over to them, that human affairs are decisively influenced by the disposition ensuing therefrom. The question of attainability is therefore: can a disposition corresponding to the stated aims be achieved with so many people, so that human affairs are thereby decisively influenced? I am prepared to answer yes to this question. In support of this I will present the following intellectual trends, which in my opinion are discernible:

a The end of power politics.
b The end of nationalism.
c The end of the concept of race.
d The end of the power of the state over the individual.

These four connecting links for actions by communities will be confuted by this war. They will lead themselves ad absurdum; they have partially already done so: the greatest expansion of power will not bring peace; nationalism has already proven itself as no longer being an attractive slogan, thus in France, thus in Germany; the racial concept is absurd when the country supposedly protecting and upholding a race associates itself with its stated racial enemies, and when the racially tolerant country protects racial interests; when the greatest power of the state over the individual does not lead to peace, then that will lead to a curtailment of this power.

The following suggests positively that the aims are attainable:

a) The complete shattering of all communities that are smaller than the state, through the destruction of the idol of the state, will leave a vacuum screaming to be filled. It is possible that it will not be filled, and that mankind, at least in Europe, will collapse upon itself like an amorphous crumbling mass. In view of the innate need of people for some kind of bond, it is, however,[10] quite possible that the empty space will be filled out along lines of the aims.

b) The end of the war will find a readiness for introspection and repentance as has never been found since the year 999, when the end of the world was expected.

c) In case the defeated is able to convince the victor of his responsibility, which I consider possible, the victor's example can provide the impetus for a rapid development towards the established aims.

In summary, it is therefore my opinion that the end of the war will offer a chance for a favourable remolding of the world that mankind has not had since the disintegration of the medieval church.

Now the section on the tasks arising from the starting position and aims should follow here. This task-setting, however, must build upon a presumed political and military situation after the end of the war, in order to be tangible and concrete. This presumption must therefore be described beforehand.

III

Presumed Political and Military Situation at the End of the War

A Foreign Policy

1 Germany is defeated, i.e., it is no longer capable of the will to further prosecute the war. This situation can occur as a consequence of the physical exhaustion of the population, as a consequence of industrial exhaustion, as a consequence of internal political upheavals in Germany, and as a consequence of insurrections and revolts in the occupied territories, which, because of the extent of the occupied territories and the manner of their treatment, cannot be stemmed and ultimately will lead to an armed invasion by the Anglo-Saxons. There are a few variants that, however, in my view, have no independent significance.

Note: A German victory implies an armistice, not a peace, because upon it there would have to follow the struggle for the mastery of the seas, which presupposes a decades-long naval building program. This case is of no interest for the task at hand, since it would put into practice the preconditions on which the attainability of the aims depends, only much later in the future. A German victory would deprive this study of every immediate interest and would lead to a completely different task-setting.

2 Peace produces a uniform European sovereignty from Portugal to a point moved as far east as possible, while the entire continent is divided into smaller non-sovereign states that have interlocking political commitments. The following at a minimum would be uniform: customs borders, currency, foreign policy including defence, constitutional legislation, if possible also economic administration.

3 Peace brings an Anglo-Saxon Union whose economic centre of gravity lies on the American continent. Great Britain and the British[11] Empire, particularly the navy, have achieved a prestige that they need not share with any continental power and that gives them the prospect of regaining their former position in relation to the USA. Therefore the emphasis of British interests lies in once more overtaking the USA in the leadership of the Empire, in reasserting its old intellectual claim to leadership. From this results the need to maintain tranquility on the European continent and to keep its rear free for the activity of leading the empire of the Anglo-Saxons.[12] At the same time, the war will have proven that the navy is the greatest instrument of power, so that a "continental sword" is not a vital necessity for Great Britain.

4 The European influence extends to French and Italian North Africa, Russia, the Black Sea, Turkey. The Anglo-Saxon influence extends to India; Africa south of the Congo; South America; the Near East including Egypt, Arabia, and Palestine. The Far East lies in the field of tension of the two combinations – South America and the Far East with a tendency towards the Anglo-Saxon world, the Near East with a tendency towards the European world.

5 This prospect offers not only the possibility of a relatively rapid restoration of the destroyed economic regions, but beyond this offers starting points for co-operation between the European and the Anglo-Saxon world as far as domestic political preconditions for it exist.

6   The military situation is clarified in that the Anglo-Saxon navy is substantially stronger than the navies of Europe, of the Far Eastern states, of Russia, and of South America combined.

B   Domestic Policy

1   From the European demobilization there has emerged a great common economic organization directed by an inter-European economic bureaucracy and by economic bodies of self-administration. Economic policy is unequivocally subordinated to the rest of domestic policy.

2   Europe is divided into historically-grown self-governing bodies that are somewhat adapted to each other in size, but with special relations within groups. Thus the absolute preponderance of the former large states, Germany and France, is broken without leaving lasting resentments.

3   The administration of cultural affairs is decentralized, with the proviso that a continuous exchange between the regions remains possible. The religious communities are denationalized, but have defined claims upon transfer of means.

4   The constitutions of the individual states are entirely different. The consensual position is the furtherance of all small communities, to which public-law authority and certain claims upon transfer of means are conceded.

5   The supreme legislature of the European state is responsible to the individual citizens, not to the self-governing bodies. The active and passive franchise will be acquired in principle, not at a certain age limit, but through engaging in certain activities that advance the community. Whether universal suffrage should ensue from this, or whether the supreme legislature should be formed in another manner is more a question of technique than of principle.

6   Life and limb are to be protected by a process that makes impossible any inception of police methods. Economic existence is to be ensured by property-like structuring of certain work functions. A private-property sphere is to be ensured for dwellings and consumer goods.

7   The non-functional rights to all means of production are to be further restricted, without removing the enjoyment of responsibility and initiative.[13]

8 The supreme government executive authority is to be exercised by a cabinet of five persons: minister-president, foreign minister, defence minister, minister of the interior, economics minister. There are also a number of lesser ministerial posts, each of which is represented in the inner cabinet by one of five senior ministers. Besides the cabinet of these departmental ministers, there will be a lands' cabinet that is formed from representatives of the land governments and that has a permanent consultative function.

IV

Setting the Tasks

1 The intellectual aims are:
   a inner commitment of the individual;
   b freedom of the individual;
   c sense of responsibility of the individual;
   d activation of the sense of responsibility in small communities;
   e restoration of the means of expression.

a The inner commitment of the individual cannot be furthered by third parties. The task that presents itself after the war's end is therefore: through which means can the individual best be caused to become conscious of an inner commitment. It seems to me to be the task of the church to awaken this sense; the only thing the state can do towards this end is to keep the church's space free for the church to be effective – thus, facilitation for the church to administer pastoral care to the troops that will be demobilized, strict observance of Sunday rest, prohibition of all sports and other events during worship hours.

b The freedom of the individual must be an essential part of the program of any political renewal. This freedom must not be represented as an absolute right, however, but only as a correlate of the inner commitment and its outward manifestation. The granting of freedom is therefore to be considered an advance benefit to the individual that obliges him to strive to reciprocate.

In this framework, the aim must be complete freedom of speech, freedom to print[14] within the framework of self-governing controls, and freedom of movement. This freedom would be limited only by criminal and civil laws, but not by police measures.

Freedom of association and assembly for the time being would not exist outside activities in the small communities.

c Sense of responsibility of the individual and activity in small communities. Here is one of the most important starting points for furthering all aims. Everyone must have the opportunity to accomplish something useful for the community. He must be given the opportunity for this. An activity useful to the community at the same time must involve certain political rights, for example active and passive franchise, admission to public office, etc. One will have to examine which functions advancing the community one wishes to recognize and endow with political privileges. In principle, such an activity need not be engaged in the form of full-time civil service. I am thinking of the following functions: voluntary work in labour camps – decisions about political privileges are taken by the camp leader who is himself excluded from these privileges if he is a professional labour-camp leader; municipal administration; administration of social institutions; unremunerated church administration; participation in unremunerated leadership in co-operative associations, in housing co-operatives, study groups, university and school associations, etc.

d Restoration of forms of expression. Only the naturally endowed can create symbols and works of art. But every statesman needs word and action to make himself understood. Words have been robbed of their meaning; actions have become ambiguous. In the place of actions one has now put words, which are followed by contradictory actions for which no explanatory word is offered. The congruence of word and action is essential, action must be unequivocal, and words must be uttered modestly and softly, after the action has taken effect and has been understood as unambiguous.

From the first moment of the New Age, there will be an opportunity to serve the restoration of forms of expression. The stability of the New Age indeed will depend essentially on this occurring from the first moment on. It begins with the membership of the first cabinet; the manner of demobilization is, in quite an essential way, part of it. Thus, for example, if an internal re-script directed that first of all every independent farmer, craftsman, and commercially engaged person with fewer than ten employees were to be discharged, subsequently all employees in enterprises of the crafts, commerce, and agriculture with fewer than ten employees, and after that all who intended to settle as craftsmen in a rural area, this would have a greater effect for the restoration of forms of expression than any national law for the protection of small businesses proclaimed with all the means of propaganda.

Part of this is also the restoration of metal-minting on the basis of metal value.

2 Further tasks arise from the presumed foreign-political situation.

a What must a comprehensive European state look like so that it will convince the members of the European community of states, and so that it will also be acceptable to the victors? Which are its common intellectual foundations?

b Strategic and military minimal requirements of the European state.

c Which proposals for the organization of the planned economy can be put forward?[15] How far can such proposals be realized for individual branches of industry through a self-governing method, even before uniform sovereignty is established? How far can the pan-European demobilization be viewed as a task of the community and lay the cornerstone for co-operation: employment of troops to reconstruct destroyed economic substance, gradual[16] assumption of this work by European labour-camps, and corresponding discharge of troops, etc.?

d How in the general confusion can the capacity to act of the most important cabinets and their co-operation be assured? Use of military command authority and its gradual replacement by civilian authorities; if possible from the beginning a permanent conference of diplomatic envoys of all European states; avoidance of the impasse of armistice commissions; avoidance of various parallel co-ordination systems.

3 It seems to me that, from this, there result quite clear groups of tasks; the solution of the problems put forward at [point] 1 and thus the establishment of principles for the New Age are the most important one. These principles must equip the first stable cabinet with the inner justification to exercise authority and thereby credibility, internally, and confidence and legitimacy externally.

Unless this is achieved and preserved, the finest proposals regarding the questions raised at [point] 2 will be political waste paper.

V
List of Tasks

1   Which tasks can the churches engage in and what are their demands?
    a   ministry for the troops;
    b   making priests available, training new priests, international exchange of priests;
    c   honouring holidays: service and labour, press, radio, sports, artistic and social events;
    d   common themes for certain days, for example special atonement and prayer days;
    e   religious youth education;
    f   avoidance of dogmatic disputes.

2   What can be done to make clear the intention of ensuring life and limb of the individual?
    a   repeal of all police authority for arrests without judicial warrant, except when the arrested person has been apprehended *in flagranti*;
    b   routine review of all arrests;
    c   establishment of a special court of law for the protection of the individual against arbitrary arrest;
    d   which measures must be taken to protect against abuse the basic freedom to print?
    e   to what extent must freedom of movement be curtailed for reasons of a directed economy?

3   Which kinds of community are to be recognized and furnished with political privileges?
    a   Which state agency will approve a community?
    b   Which rights can be granted to a community?
        aa   home rule;
        bb   levying revenues;
        cc   police and surveillance functions;
        dd   sanction rights over members;

  ee the right to grant political privileges to members;
  ff claims upon financial transfers of the state.
 c Which political privileges can be granted to members of such communities?
  aa active and passive franchise;
  bb admission to public political office;
  cc other special prerogatives in the decision-making process of superior state authorities.
 d Who determines the privileges to be granted to a community or its members?
  aa a general state distribution agency?
  bb the regional body immediately above the community?
  cc the community leader?

4 Which measures can be taken at once in order to give an adequate form of expression to the New Thinking?
 a uniform drafting of all laws and ordinances through one agency;
 b reduction of the number of proclamations of state intentions;
 c abolition of the propaganda ministry;
 d centralization of the few important tasks, decentralization of all others.

5 constitution of the European common state?
 a common ideology;
 b common tasks;
 c internal constitutions of the individual states;
 d size of individual states;
 e special relations within certain groups of states (Scandinavian, Baltic, East-European, German, Balkan, West-European, Mediterranean, etc.).

6 Strategic and military requirements of the European state:
 a security of coasts or mobile fleet?
 b security of internal communication arteries;
 c security of supplies through the Mediterranean Sea;
 d security of the Dardanelles and the Baltic Sea;
 e security of North Africa;
 f security of supplies from the region up to the Urals;
 g internal disarmament;

    h   qualitative disarmament;
    i   fleet strength;
    k   air force.

7   Establishment of pan-European planned-economy agencies.
    a   expansion of European cartels into agencies of the economic community;
    b   expansion of pan-European workers' organizations;
    c   establishment of a European agency for the reconstruction of destroyed areas, with authority to distribute burdens;
    d   establishment of a European agency for large tasks of the common economy;
    e   organization of demobilization;
    f   establishment of a European economic[17] co-ordination authority;
    g   establishment of a European currency and consideration to what extent a return to coinage is possible.

8   Establishment of European political co-ordination authorities.
    a   substitution of civil agencies for military authority;
    b   prevention of the forming of borders;
    c   introduction of scheduled conferences of diplomatic envoys from all European states;
    d   introduction of a permanent pan-European secretariat;
    e   introduction of a pan-European supreme[18] court of law.

NOTES

1 See introduction and sources in document no. 4; Hans Mommsen, "Der Kreisauer Kreis und die künftige Neuordnung Deutschlands und Europas," *Vierteljahrshefte für Zeitgeschichte* 42 (1994): 361–77.

2 Source: Freya von Moltke, Papers; Bundesarchiv, Koblenz, N 1750 Bd. 1; date in Moltke's hand; the document is printed, with some variations, in Ger van Roon, *Neuordnung im Widerstand. Der Kreisauer Kreis innerhalb der deutschen Widerstandsbewegung,* 507–17; see also Roon, *German Resistance to Hitler.*

3 This word inserted in Moltke's hand. Obvious typing errors, such as a missing letter, are corrected without annotation.

4 This word in Moltke's hand, replacing "left in place."

5 This word inserted in Moltke's hand.

6   Marginal in Peter Graf von Yorck's hand: "this is certainly true for the workplace, to a certain extent even for the family."

7   Marginal in Yorck's hand: "the values of this world must also [?] without reference" (incomplete comment?).

8   Deleted: "naturally."

9   Marginal in Yorck's hand: "as absolutes."

10   This word inserted in Moltke's hand.

11   This word substituted in Moltke's hand for "old."

12   Inserted in Moltke's hand: "of the Anglo-Saxons."

13   Marginal in Yorck's hand: "socialization."

14   Corrected in Moltke's hand from "think."

15   Marginal in Yorck's hand: "mining union Eur Com."

16   This word inserted in Moltke's hand.

17   This word inserted in Moltke's hand.

18   This word inserted in Moltke's hand.

22

Carl Goerdeler's Peace Plans, 1941–1944

Carl Goerdeler, the Mayor of Leipzig from 1930–37, was the most tireless motor driving the movement to overthrow Hitler. From the first days of Hitler's chancellorship in 1933, he opposed discrimination against Jews.[1] He resigned from office after his Nazi Deputy Mayor had removed, from in front of the Gewandhaus, the statue dedicated to its first Director, Felix Mendelssohn-Bartholdy, whom the Nazis considered a Jew. The deputy mayor complained to the regional Nazi Chief, Reichsstatthalter Martin Mutschmann, of Goerdeler's having resisted from 1933 every single renaming of a street that bore the name of a Jew; of having obstructed every effort to remove the Mendelssohn-Bartholdy statue; that "the real cause [of the conflict] lay in Dr Goerdeler's world view, which was the opposite of National Socialism"; and that "Dr Goerdeler's attitude in the Jewish Question had been revealed particularly clearly in the matter of the Mendelssohn-Bartholdy statue." Goerdeler involved himself in efforts to win military support for a coup d'état, to prepare concepts for Germany's internal political reorganization afterward (see document no. 16) and to solicit support abroad early in the development of the Resistance in Germany. He was particularly concerned about the persecution of the Jews in Germany, and sought to work against it where he could, protecting Jews in Leipzig in every possible way, and seeking to induce the western powers to impose sanctions upon Germany, coupled with a demand that the persecutions cease.

On 6 and 7 August 1938, at the request of Robert Vansittart – until January 1938 the Permanent Undersecretary of State for Foreign Affairs and now Chief Diplomatic Advisor to the British government – A.P. Young, an industrialist, met with Goerdeler at his vacation place in Rauschen Dune. Goerdeler urged the British government to refuse any further discussions of vital issues that the German government was interested in until their practices against the Jews had been discontinued. Young's representative, Dr Reinhold Schairer, and Goerdeler met on 6 and 7 November 1938, after 10,000 Jews from the territory of Poland but without either German or Polish citizenship had been driven across the German-Polish border into Poland. Goerdeler predicted "a great increase in the persecution of the Jews and Christians" and, as Young wrote for Vansittart, declared himself "greatly perturbed that there is not yet in evidence any strong reaction throughout the democracies, in the Press, the Church, and in Parliament, against the barbaric, sadistic, and cruel persecution of 10,000 Polish Jews in Germany." Between 4 December 1938 and 15 January 1939, Goerdeler again provided information to A.P. Young and deplored "the cruel and senseless persecution of the Jews"; warned that Hitler was determined to conquer the world, and that he had "decided to destroy the Jews – Christianity – Capitalism"; and urged the British government to exert strong pressure upon the German government "to save the world from this terrible catastrophe."[2]

With the beginning and progress of the war, Goerdeler concentrated more and more on methods to remove Hitler and his government. This was not possible as long as Hitler commanded the loyalty of the army. When in November 1939 an officer tried to convince General Franz Halder (Chief of the General Staff of the Army from 1938 to 1942) to lead a coup d'état, Halder's answer was characteristic of the attitude of many of the most senior commanders of the army: "1. It violates tradition. 2. There is no successor. 3. The young officer corps is not reliable. 4. The mood in the interior is not ripe. 5. 'It really cannot be tolerated that Germany is permanently a "people of helots" for England.' 6. Concerning offensive: Ludendorff, too, in 1918, had led the offensive against the advice of everyone, and the historical judgment was not against him. He, Halder, therefore did not fear the later judgment of history either."[3]

Therefore, the only way to win over military leaders for the removal of Hitler seemed to be commitments from Germany's opponents in the war that they would not treat a Germany that had overthrown Hitler as they had done at Versailles. This view led to numerous Resistance contacts abroad with the aim of soliciting support.

Allen Welsh Dulles, the American Office of Strategic Services (intelligence service) resident in Berne, Switzerland, from November 1942 to the summer of 1945, commented on Goerdeler's peace initiatives:[4] The story of

Goerdeler's (and others') peace initiatives "proves that before the plot came to a head a serious effort was made to get in touch with the Allies, that the plotters received no encouragement from the West, and that they were told clearly and repeatedly that we had made common cause with Russia in the determination to continue together to a complete and united victory."

Two of the documents below, 1 and 4, are reproductions in diplomatically accurate English versions; the first is the translation prepared in the Foreign Office in London. Numbers 2, 3, and 5 are the editor's translations from the German. The first is Goerdeler's Peace Plan of 30 May 1941. Its transmission to the British government and its reception there are described in the next part of this introductory commentary. The second document is Goerdeler's peace plan of May 1943; its genesis is described in the fourth document, Jacob Wallenberg's account. The third document contains Goerdeler's views in September 1943. The fifth document gives Goerdeler's views in May 1944.

BACKGROUND OF THE FIRST DOCUMENT

In 1954 Gerhard Ritter first revealed Goerdeler's peace plan of 30 May 1941.[5] He had been informed of it by Professor Friedrich Wilhelm Siegmund-Schultze in Zurich. Siegmund-Schultze was a contact and intermediary in Switzerland for a large number of concerns, including aid for refugees and efforts of the German Resistance to bring about the fall of the Hitler government. The document was drafted in April 1941.[6] In May 1941 Siegmund-Schultze was asked to transmit the peace proposals in the first document. The document carried an initial "B," allegedly indicating the approval of the Commander-in-Chief of the Army, Field Marshal von Brauchitsch.[7] In the same week, Rudolf Hess flew to Scotland, presumably to offer Britain peace as Hitler's attack on the Soviet Union was imminent.[8] The regime appeared to be off balance. Siegmund-Schultze did not have great hopes of a successful appeal to the German people to rise up against the Nazi regime before it was too late, yet he agreed to serve as intermediary. It was essential, of course, for a peace proposal and appeal for British support to reach the British government before Germany invaded the Soviet Union (22 June 1941).

Siegmund-Schultze wrote to William Temple, the Archbishop of York, on 24 May and attempted to have the letter transmitted by the British legation in Berne. The legation refused, and Siegmund-Schultze now sent an open telegram to the Archbishop asking that the Foreign Office instruct the consulate in Zurich to transmit an urgent message from Siegmund-Schultze to him. Archbishop Temple did not know what Siegmund-Schultze was attempting but approached the Foreign Office in London on 4 June and was told that the requested permission to the consulate in Zurich would be granted, although this was delayed until after the German attack on the Soviet Union; Siegmund-Schultze's original project had been overtaken by events. In Siegmund-Schultze's view, the cessation of hostilities now had to have priority. The British government may not, of course, have been interested in preventing the German attack against the Soviet Union, because it was likely to reduce the menace of both – Germany and the Soviet Union – to the balance and to British interests, and it was likely to give Britain a powerful ally against Germany. When Siegmund-Schultze learned on 4 August that the legation in Berne was now ready to co-operate, he handed over a letter, dated 24 July and addressed to Archbishop Temple, that included a memorandum of peace terms drafted by Goerdeler. Siegmund-Schultze stated in his covering letter that he had been asked some weeks ago to transmit the suggestions in the memorandum to the British government, went on to describe the difficulties he encountered with his attempts to make a contact, and said he was now sending the memorandum in the hope that it would "reach you and the British Government in due time." The German Resistance group with which Siegmund-Schultze was in touch hoped, after the moment of crisis in May and June had not been exploited, for another opportunity to act in the autumn. "It would be of great importance for the responsible men,[9] to have some evidence, that the British Government feels still bound by its former declarations to negotiate about peace terms with a German Government that overthrows the National-sozialistic regime. If I could show a document of this kind to a representative of the group who will visit me in the second half of August, it would mean a great step forward to a negotiated peace between free nations."[10]

Siegmund-Schultze's letter and Goerdeler's memorandum, which Siegmund-Schultze handed over in its original German,[11] arrived at the Foreign Office on 23 August and received attention at the highest level. By this time, having been – perhaps intentionally – delayed for months, it had lost any potential usefulness it may be conjectured to have owned. The British government, by this time, had agreed with the American government on common war aims in the "Atlantic Declaration," or "Atlantic Charter"; they had made great strides in bringing the United States into the war; they were allied, by default and by agreement, with the Soviet Union; and they were not going to risk the successful prosecution of the war against Germany.

Frank K. Roberts of the Foreign Office Central Department noted on 24 August, on the Foreign Office form used for the preparation of decisions by the Foreign Secretary:[12]

We do not know who is behind Dr S., but we can hazard a guess that it is our old friends the "reasonable" Generals, Dr Goerdeler & possibly Dr Schacht. The manner of approach is reminiscent of the ecclesiastical approach through Mr Baldwin Raper in March 1940 (see Flag E at attached copy of our memo on peace-feelers).[13]

No doubt there are serious Germans beginning to think of jettisoning Hitler to save Germany, and a very recent red paper suggests that such news are spreading among the army & businessmen.

The terms proposed (translation behind) mark an advance on anything previously suggested (e.g. see the "Dahlerus" terms at Flag F in attached memo. or the "Weissauer" terms at Flag G).[14] In particular Poland & Czechoslovakia are apparently to be allowed an independent national existence. But the arrangements suggested under 2, 3 & 5 seem quite inacceptable. Points 6–15 have a familiar Geneva phraseology & are no doubt designed to appeal to humanitarian instincts here. But 7 would of course mean complete German supremacy at least in Europe. 14 & 15 not unnaturally conflict with the last point in the Atlantic declaration[15] prescribing the *unilateral* disarmament of agressor states.

I think the letter should be passed onto the Archbishop urgently, but it might be accompanied by a letter from the S. of S.[16] reminding His Grace that the attitude of H.M.G. was laid down in the S. of S.'s speech of July 29 & in the Atlantic Declaration and that no more detailed reply on behalf of HMG. can be returned to these anonymous German peace-feelers.

William Strang, head of the Foreign Office Central Department, commented on 25 August:[17]

I agree.

In sending on the message to the Archbishop, we should, I think, say that while we should be willing to let Dr Schultze know through Mr Kelly[18] that the Archbishop had received the message, we would strongly advice His Grace not to send any further acknowledgment.

We might also repeat what was said in the last paragraph of Sir A. Cadogan's[19] letter to the Archbishop of June 9th in C 6320/6320/18, namely that he should ensure that the message is not made public and that no use is made of it.

There are, I suspect, people in the church (e.g. the Bishop of Chichester) who might like to think of making peace on these insidious and disastrous terms.

Sir Alexander Cadogan noted on 26 August:[20] "I agree. In the first place there is no indication as to who these 'German personalities' are, or whether there is the least likelihood of their forming a Gov. In the second place the terms are unacceptable anyhow."

The Secretary of State for Foreign Affairs, Antony Eden, consulted Prime Minister Winston Churchill and received this reply:[21]

Prime Minister's Personal Minute
Most Secret. In a locked box.
Foreign Secretary:
I am sure we should not depart from our policy of absolute silence. Nothing would be more disturbing to our friends in the United States or more damaging with our new ally, Russia, than the suggestion that we were entertaining such ideas. I am absolutely opposed to the slightest contact. If you do not agree, the matter should be raised before the War Cabinet sitting alone.

The message from Siegmund-Schultze was sent on to the Archbishop but with the renewed request that he keep it confidential and make no use of it. Cadogan's draft of his letter to the Archbishop of York of 20 September 1941 follows:[22]

With reference to my letter of June 9th, we have now received, through our legation in Berne, the annexed letter, with enclosures, from Doctor Ziegmund Schultze.

I have felt bound to show this correspondence to the Secretary of State,[23] who desires me, in forwarding this letter, to renew to you the request, made in my former letter, that you will ensure that it is not made public in any way or any use made of it.

Mr Eden assumes that you would readily accept this condition, seeing that, to note one point only, the "peace aims" outlined in the enclosure would appear (§ 3) to involve the incorporation of Alsace and Lorraine in the Reich.

There are other points that will probably strike you as equally unacceptable and others again which, though specious, would require elucidation.

I may say that these proposals are not unlike others which have reached us by various channels from sources that do not inspire great confidence.

1

Memorandum by Carl Goerdeler, May 1941[24]

A group of German personalities, to which leading men of all professions belong, is ready to undertake responsibility for the establishment of a government which, at the appropriate time, would seek confirmation of its position through a free expression of the will of the German people. All measures relating to this would be exclusively a matter of German internal politics. The leading personalities concerned meanwhile wish at this stage to be clear whether peace negotiations could be taken up immediately[25] after the successful establishment of such a government repudiating National Socialism, in accordance with earlier assurances from the British Government.

The following peace aims planned by the German group are proposed as a basis for negotiations:

(1) The restoration of the complete sovereignty of neutral countries occupied during the war by the belligerents.

(2) Confirmation of the Anschluss[26] of Austria, Sudetenland, and the Memelland, which took place before the war.

(3) The restoration of the 1914 German frontiers with Belgium, France, and Poland.[27]

(4) The establishment of European frontiers on the basis of national right of self-determination at a peace conference of the various states.

(5) The return of German colonies or of equally valuable colonial territory, coupled with the simultaneous creation of an international mandatory system for all colonies.

(6) No war reparations – reconstruction in common.

(7) Abolition of customs frontiers.

(8) The establishment of a world economic council, provided with full powers.

(9) International control of currencies.

(10) Resumption of the work of the International Labour Office.

(11) Restoration of justice[28] – punishment of the guilty.

(12) Development of the activities of the International Court of Justice.[29]

(13) Establishment of a regular conference of European states and of corresponding arrangements on a regional basis.

(14) The general limitation and decrease of armaments.

(15) International control of armaments and of the armaments industry.

2

Goerdeler's Peace Plan of May 1943[30]

1 The German nation must and will liberate itself from a system that commits horrifying crimes under cover of terror and has destroyed the laws, the honour, and the liberty of the German nation.

2 In the interest of all of mankind, the removal of this system must take place as soon as possible. Attempts thus far have failed. Thousands of Germans have been executed and tortured to death; many tens of thousands are languishing in concentration camps and penitentiaries.

3 It is therefore important that the act of liberation not be interfered with; otherwise it is hardly executable during the war. Troops of the liberator[31] must not be bombed; no bombs must be dropped in areas that he has liberated. Thus the air war must cease in some areas for the time being. The liberator will order the illumination of the cities.

4 As soon as the action will have been concluded, a civilian government will be established. It will order the cessation of submarine operations.

5 All of this is possible only if the liberator can presume that he will not be met with a call for unconditional surrender.

6 The government will represent all social strata, all confessions, all German lands.

7   A regent will be at the head of the Reich.

8   The Reich will have a constitution. The nation will elect a Reichstag. The German lands and occupational and professional groups will form an upper house.

9   Since elections during war and before calm prevails are not possible, there will be formed a temporary Reich council[32] to which the government submits declarations, laws, etc.

10   The basis of law and tranquility in Germany is home rule.[33] The centralization forced by the Dictate of Versailles will be abolished. The German lands, districts, and communities again receive the greatest [measure of] home rule. The Prussian provinces become German lands.

11   The first task is the restoration of the law, decency, and liberty. All criminals, where ever the crimes have been committed, shall be punished by the German nation itself. The world will receive sufficient knowledge of this. Lynch justice[34] will not be tolerated. The Party disappears.

12   Purity and conscientiousness in the administration will be restored; the civil servants have only to implement the laws with justice.

13   In the occupied territories, the national authorities will be restored. The evacuation will take place with utmost speed, with consideration of the situation, the maintenance of order, etc.

14   The full independence of all European nations will be restored and guaranteed.

   The German frontier against Poland is to be set by negotiation. If there is agreement, Germany guarantees the existence of Poland and supports a state union of Poland-Lithuania. To the east of Poland, the Russian territory of 1938 will be evacuated.[35] Further evacuations only in consultation with Poland and her allies.

   In the west, the linguistic frontier is the one that is just and promises tranquility.

15   Poland and Czecho-Slovakia become completely free; their political and economic future is to be shaped according to their interests.

16   Germany desires the continued existence of Finland and is prepared to fight for it just as for the Polish eastern frontier.

17   For west of this frontier, the European community of interests and culture must form itself, among whose members there must

never again be a war. What position Russia will take in these matters depends on negotiations.

17 [sic] The first step in Europe is a European economic union with a permanent economic council and clear practical goals. (Traffic, justice, currency, customs, etc.)

A European reconstruction agency be established in the framework of this union, in which Germany will selflessly employ all its resources, but on the basis of rational economic points of view.

18 This union shall have a judicial system for the adjudication of conflicts of every kind, and a police force.

19 Germany joins a regionally structured world league whose aims are clear and pragmatic and which establishes an arbitration procedure. The main task is the establishment of a world-currency bank.

20 Germany's financial situation demands the utmost disarmament. The possible limits will be adjusted according to Europe's relationship with Russia and to the situation in the Far East, where common European interests are at stake. Naval armament is renounced. Germany is prepared to internationalize the air force.

21 The German economic policy will aim against autarchy, against *any* state-planned economy,[36] for freedom of the individual, for private enterprise, for free competition and performance. Controls over prices, wages, and goods must continue for a transition period. The state is to ensure only the rule of law, decency, and social justice, as well as sound finances. This is the principal contribution it can make toward the happiness of human beings. It will have to leave much to the religious organizations.

The nationalization of mineral resources will take place. The methods for its best implementation are being examined.

22 The best contribution toward the stabilization of the currencies and toward the restoration of the exchange of goods in the world is the ordering of the public budget. It enforces the utmost disarmament.

23 German social policy will attach great importance to cooperation with other nations. It will determine insurance for sickness, invalidism, old age, and accident. But the unionized workers will themselves administer these institutions; they will delegate members to the economic chamber and they will be informed in the shops equally as the board members. Therefore it

is necessary to raise the level of economic education. The workers will be able to operate economic enterprises as co-operatives on the basis of competition.

24 Unemployment will not be combated with artificial credits; they ruin finances. Insofar as subsidies are necessary, they will be financed so that responsibility is increased, and the will to work and to take correct measures is strengthened.

25 Social policy should not have the effect of decreasing the responsibility of parents and families, of the individual for his fate. The opposite is necessary. For this the sanctity of matrimony and the purity of family life are the indispensable foundation.

26 Education will again be aimed at comprehensive general education and at strengthening religious forces, without which a noble humanity is not possible.

This is the plan. Germany possesses a sufficient number of people who are capable of carrying it out.

But especially these people, who respect and desire the independence of all other nations, reject passionately the interference of other nations in German affairs.

If one hears therefore that Poland, East Prussia, and parts of Silesia are being demanded, that one wishes to intervene in the German education system, that it is intended to do in Germany what Germans themselves must do and what they alone can successfully do, then one must take a dark view of the future of Europe and of the white nations. For it can be founded only upon their free association, upon independence and respect, not upon a new degradation.

We alone shall call Hitler and his fellow criminals to account because they have tarnished our good name. But behind it we shall defend our independence.

3

Goerdeler's views on terms of peace as explained to
Field Marshal von Kluge and as reported by the
Gestapo after interrogating Goerdeler[37]

The Gestapo report quotes from Goerdeler's testimony:
Kluge expressed his deep concern about the prospects of the war. He made clear that Germany's resources were insufficient to hold the

front in the east [...], much less an imminent new front in the west, [...] and that the war was lost if great decisions were not taken. These had to consist in shortening and relieving the fronts by retreating to natural, easily defensible positions [...] It was therefore a question of which foreign-policy opportunities could be created or which necessities would arise from such a decision. He asked me for information about this. I gave it to him. [...] The fact that dominated the foreign-political position was that Russia and Britain were fighting a joint war against National-Socialist Germany; however, they had been brought together by Germany's policy, that is to say accidentally, not on the basis of a premeditated political plan. There existed between them the same profound conflict of interests that had evolved from 1815. For Britain, a strong Russia was the only but deadly serious threat, nay endangerment of her Empire [...] There was only one source of security for Britain in Europe, namely a sufficiently strong Germany in a healthy Europe [...]

Kluge suggested that the British might treat us again as they had done in 1918. I countered that they would then with certainty have to decide their own demise if they wished to act so foolishly. In 1919 they could presume to do this because not only we were beaten down, but Russia too [...] A wise British foreign policy could not permit the war to result in the sole presence of a Russian giant on the continent. To be sure, we needed to be prudent enough to arrange our policy so that the English and the German line converged [...]

Kluge asked me what kind of agreement with Britain I thought possible. I was able to tell him what Wallenberg[38] told me a month later, in October 1943, as the British view [as follows]:

In the east, the frontier of 1914; east of it, Poland-Lithuania as a united state, independent but, through their anti-Bolshevist vital interests, driven to Germany's side; Austria and the Sudeten region remain German; South Tyrol to Bozen-Meran becomes German again; Eupen-Malmady remains German; on Alsace-Lorraine, Germany and France will negotiate directly; here various solutions were conceivable that would eliminate this conflict once and for all; no infringements upon German sovereignty; no reparations, but joint reconstruction of Europe; economic union of the European states without Russia.

With this question there would, after all, erupt a profound conflict of interests between England and the U.S.A., which I explained to Herr Kluge in detail. I informed him that I had spoken with Wallenberg and that he proposed to suggest to the English to end the air war against [German] domestic regions as it threatened Europe's future, but that I as yet had not heard from Wallenberg as to the thoughts of the English. But that I was in this regard very confident, since I knew the English, their interests, their policy, and their methods very accurately through their history, and that I had the best personal relations with leading English politicians of nearly all parties.

Kluge then asked me for my domestic-policy views, which I developed for him:
Strengthening home rule to balance the strong leadership powers that the nation always needed;
better protection of certain rights of the individual;
absolutely independent judges;
as soon as possible a free economy, integrated into guiding principles and planning of the state;
clarification of the position of the churches;
simplification of the education system and raising of standards; and finally a comprehensive balancing of interests[39] without the formation of parties.

Thereafter, Kluge and Beck had a private consultation; then I was brought in again, and Kluge said to me that it was now most urgent to act in order to exploit the military situation in timely fashion. It was still possible [Kluge said], with a timely agreement with the Anglo-Saxons, to stabilize and make impregnable the Eastern Front east of the old eastern frontier of Poland, which I had demanded as the utmost. He was convinced, however, that the Führer was not ready to take such decisions and in particular to give the military experts the opportunity of wide-ranging providential retreats, quite apart from the fact that according to his [Kluge's] information the Anglo-Saxons would not concede the basis for peace I had outlined to him. The interests of the nation therefore demanded an independent action of the military, but this was possible only if the Führer's person were eliminated, if necessary by force. When Kluge hinted in response to my question that one must not shy away from the use of the utmost force, I declared to him that I considered this method wrong; it was necessary to speak quite openly with the Führer; the commanders-in-chief and the Chief of the General Staff were obligated to do this; from such a dialogue, conducted with clarity, candour, and courage, all else would by itself result. A good cause would make its way vis-à-vis everyone.

Since Herr von Kluge was not to be convinced, I said to him finally that I could advise him only politically; that we were already informed through Tresckow; [I asked him] whether he could say to me that I had an opportunity as a politician to take the initiative. This question he had to answer in the negative, whereupon I said, then the military leaders whose lack of candour vis-à-vis Hitler had allowed things to go as far as they had come must themselves find the right method to obtain a good peace instead of a lost war. Herr von Kluge acknowledged that and said he would discuss anything further with his comrades. I should only see to it that the Anglo-Saxons later behaved correctly, and with that this conversation closed.

4

Jacob Wallenberg's Account[40]

Very early, probably in 1940, we discussed the possibilities of a coup d'état in Germany. I often stressed the surprise abroad that there was no organized anti-Nazi movement in Germany, especially as it was known that large sections of the German population and many leading personalities were opposed to Nazism. Goerdeler replied that this criticism was partly unfounded as close to 200,000 Germans were or had been in prison or concentration camps because they had opposed the regime. No coup d'état was possible without the aid of the military, and military help was difficult to secure as long as military successes continued.

In November 1941, Goerdeler informed me of the German defeat outside Moscow. During a visit in February 1942, he told me that Hitler had discharged and court-martialed a number of officers because of this crucial defeat, although everyone knew Hitler himself was responsible. Most of the officers were exonerated by the court martial, but after this a bitter feeling against Hitler developed within high officers' circles. Goerdeler was more hopeful about the possibilities.

In April 1942, Goerdeler again came to Stockholm and suggested that we [the Wallenbergs] should get in touch with Churchill, whom Goerdeler said he had contacted personally before the outbreak of the war. He wanted to have in advance the Allies' consent to peace in case he and his fellow conspirators succeeded in making Hitler a prisoner and overthrowing the Nazi regime. This was not the first time Goerdeler had broached this subject. I always tried to make it clear to him that no advance promises would be forthcoming and, in order to convince him, I arranged a meeting between him and my brother, Marc Wallenberg, who had intimate contact with the British. My brother also categorically declared to Goerdeler that advance promises could not be obtained.

During my later visits to Berlin Goerdeler reverted to this point, and in November 1942 we had several long discussions. I impressed on him the risks to which he and his associates would expose themselves, as such a matter would be handled by so many in England and the United States that there would always be the danger of a leak. This did not frighten him. I then tried to make it clear that he and his friends should try to bring about a change irrespective of the attitude of London or Washington. I believe this argument had more effect on him than the risks involved in trying to get Allied encouragement. He said he would discuss it with his friends and let me know. A few days later he told me that they were convinced that it was right to act without promises from the Allies. On the other hand, he requested that I be available to get in touch with the Allies as soon as the Hitler regime had been overthrown. This I promised to do.

I next met Goerdeler in February 1943. He said the decision of the Casablanca Conference[41] for unconditional surrender made his work with the German militarists more difficult since some of the military insisted that if the German forces had to capitulate, they wanted Hitler to bear the responsibility for it. On the other hand, the catastrophe at Stalingrad had occurred and this had made some of the military realize something would have to be done to remove Hitler. Goerdeler told me they had plans for a coup in March of 1943 but that he was not sure that it could be carried through because Hitler was taking all precautions and was surrounded by a bodyguard of 3,000 people and hardly dared to appear at the front any more.

In May 1943, Goerdeler again came to Stockholm. He knew that my brother was in London and asked that he should immediately get in touch with Churchill. I asked him to draw up a memorandum regarding all the points that the new regime would accept, such as punishment of war criminals, war damages, disarmament, democratic regime, etc. Goerdeler gave me such a detailed memorandum. He also requested that as soon as the coup occurred the Allies discontinue bombing German cities in order to show the German people they were well disposed toward the new regime. Furthermore, he desired that as far as possible Berlin and Leipzig be spared during the next few days as the central organizations of the anti-Nazi movement were located at those points and a disruption of communications would make a coup more difficult. I got in touch with my brother, who passed the information on to the British.

In August I received word that Goerdeler wanted me to go to Berlin. I arranged a reason for such a trip and had several conferences with him. His main points were that all preparations were now ready for a coup in September[42] and that the intention was to send a certain Fabian von Schlabrendorff immediately to Stockholm. He asked me to persuade the British to send a suitable contact man to meet Schlabrendorff. I replied that I should be glad to do this as soon as the coup occurred and that I would inform the Allies that a German, representing the new leaders, was in Stockholm not to negotiate but merely to obtain Allied advice as to how the new government should go about obtaining peace. On these conditions I accepted the assignment.

On this occasion, as many times before, Goerdeler mentioned certain personnel questions. He was especially interested in knowing about Schacht's[43] position. Schacht apparently wished to play a leading role and considered himself suitable for Foreign Minister, not realizing that he had no standing with the Allies and the people were critically disposed toward him. Goerdeler told me that Social Democratic circles in Germany were against including Schacht in the new government, but that he might be made head of the Reichsbank. Goerdeler had already informed me that the intention was, if the coup succeeded, to make General Beck head of the state and that an interim government would be formed with some military men, civil servants, and representatives of labour unions and local interests. As soon as possible elections would be held, and Goerdeler thought it likely that the Social Democrats would take the lead. Goerdeler never told me what his own position would be in the new government.

On this and on previous occasions Goerdeler said that advances had been made to them on behalf of Himmler. No reliance was placed on these advances, and it was their intention to take him into custody at the same time as Hitler.

I was awaiting the month of September with great suspense. It passed without anything happening. I had no opportunity of contacting Goerdeler before the end of November 1943, when I again visited Berlin. Goerdeler declared that two assassination attempts had been made. He said the plans were in no way dropped but that they had been changed in one particular. The original intention was to take both Hitler and Himmler into custody and put them before a 'summary' court. But it had become clear that it would be necessary to assassinate them.

This was the last time I visited Berlin and the last time I met Goerdeler. During the winter, spring, and summer of 1944 I received several communications from him to the effect that the plans were still alive, that the assassination would certainly take place, and requesting me to abide by the previous agreement. At the beginning of July I received a telegram that State Secretary Planck[44] wished to visit me in Stockholm about July 20, to which I replied that I was away on vacation and would only return the beginning of August. I then received a further message that it was of importance that he have an opportunity to meet me. I agreed to meet him on the morning of July 22. On July 20 the coup took place. Planck, who for some reason had taken over the place of Schlabrendorff, never came. He was arrested and executed. Goerdeler was arrested when he was about to flee to Sweden, subjected to questioning and torture, and executed. Many people, it is said, were arrested on account of memoranda and notes found in his belongings.

I was warned from several quarters not to go to Germany, as my intimate co-operation with Goerdeler was known. In the month of November I received an invitation to visit Himmler, which I did not accept. I do not believe that anything would have happened to me, but I do not consider it entirely unlikely that Himmler might have asked me to perform for his account the assignment that I had accepted for Goerdeler. The fact that I was, of course, not willing to do anything of the sort reinforced my decision not to go.

5

Goerdeler's Views in May 1944[45]

1   Immediate cessation of the air war;
2   abandonment of invasion plans;
3   avoiding further sacrifices of blood;
4   permanent defensive capacity in the East, evacuation of all occupied territories in the North, West, and South;
5   abstaining from every occupation;

6   free government, independently chosen constitution;

7   full participation in the implementation of the armistice condi-
    tions, in preparing the shaping of the peace;

8   national frontiers of 1914 in the East, continued union of Austria
    and Sudeten with the Reich, autonomy for Alsace-Lorraine, ac-
    quisition of Tyrol to Bozen, Meran;

9   active reconstruction with participation in the reconstruction of
    Europe;

10 independent settling of accounts with criminals in the nation;

11 recovery of honour, self-esteem, and respect.

NOTES

1   See Peter Hoffmann, "The German Resistance to Hitler and the Jews: The Case of
    Carl Goerdeler," 277–90.

2   A.P. Young, The "X" Documents, 45–9, 59, 136, 154–62, 177.

3   Helmuth Groscurth, Tagebücher eines Abwehroffiziers 1938–1940 (Stuttgart:
    Deutsche Verlags-Anstalt 1970), 236; also recorded by Hassell, as related by Goer-
    deler in Ulrich von Hassell, Die Hassell-Tagebücher 1938–1944. Aufzeichnungen vom
    Andern Deutschland, 144–5; Ulrich von Hassell, The Von Hassell Diaries 1938–1944
    (1948 ed.), 88–9.

4   Source: Allen Welsh Dulles, Germany's Underground, 140.

5   Ritter, Carl Goerdeler und die deutsche Widerstandsbewegung, 322, 585.

6   "Around Easter": Easter was 13 April 1941. Klemens von Klemperer, German Resist-
    ance against Hitler. The Search for Allies Abroad, 1938–1945, 227. The date 30 May 1941,
    the Friday before Pentecost (1 June 1941), is the date when Goerdeler's intermedi-
    ary, the Robert Bosch executive Willy Schlossstein, brought Siegmund-Schultze in
    Zurich the document.

7   On this and the following, see Gerhard Ritter, Carl Goerdeler und die deutsche Wider-
    standsbewegung, 322–5; 527, n. 9; 585; Klemperer, German Resistance against Hitler,
    227–9; John S. Conway, "Between Pacifism and Patriotism – A Protestant Dilemma:
    The Case of Friedrich Siegmund-Schultze," in Francis R. Nicosia and Lawrence D.
    Stokes, eds., Germans Against Nazism, 99–102; a typed copy of the correspondence
    of Siegmund-Schultze with Archbishop Temple is in Public Record Office (PRO),
    London (Kew), FO 371/26543/XC 4461 and FO 371/26543/C9472/610/G.

8   Cf. Winston S. Churchill, The Second World War, vol. 3 (Boston: Houghton Mifflin
    Co. 1950), 48–55; Martin Gilbert, Road to Victory. Winston S. Churchill 1941–1945, vol.
    VI (London: Heinemann 1983), 1087–8; id., Winston S. Churchill, vol. VII (Toronto:
    Stoddart 1986), 243.

9 The Resistance principals in Germany.

10 PRO, FO 371/26453/XC 4461.

11 Typed copy in German and in English translation in PRO, FO 371/26453/XC 4461; German version printed in Ritter, *Carl Goerdeler und die deutsche Widerstandsbewegung*, 585; not in Gillmann/Mommsen, *Politische Schriften und Briefe Carl Friedrich Goerdelers*; Gillmann/Mommsen do not even mention Siegmund-Schultze and his mediation, which is now well documented by Conway.

12 PRO, FO 371/26543/XC 4461; the quotation below follows the spelling in the original in Roberts' hand.

13 Lothar Kettenacker, ed., *Das "Andere Deutschland" im Zweiten Weltkrieg. Emigration und Widerstand in internationaler Perspektive. The "Other Germany" in the Second World War. Emigration and Resistance in International Perspective*, 164, 174–5.

14 Ibid., 141–4, 164–8.

15 Point 8 of the "Atlantic Charter," signed by Prime Minister Churchill and President Roosevelt on 14 August 1941, demanded the disarmament of "nations that threaten, or may threaten, aggression"; Churchill said in Cabinet on 19 August 1941 that Britain's war aim regarding Germany was that nation's effective disarmament; United States No. 3 (1941), Joint Declaration by the President of the United States of America and Mr Winston Churchill, representing His Majesty's Government in the United Kingdom, Known as the Atlantic Charter, August 14, 1941, Cmd. 6321, accounts and papers, London 1941; War Cabinet 84 (41), Conclusions of a Meeting of the War Cabinet held at 10 Downing Street, S.W.1, on Tuesday, 19 August 1941, at 11:30 a.m., PRO, Cab. 65/19. See also Peter Hoffmann, "The Question of Western Allied Co-operation with the German Anti-Nazi Conspiracy, 1938–1944," 437–64.

16 Secretary of State.

17 PRO, FO 371/26543/XC 4461.

18 David Kelly, British Minister in Berne.

19 Permanent Undersecretary of State in the Foreign Office.

20 PRO, FO 371/26543/XC 4461.

21 PRO, FO 371/26542/[C 610], FO 371/26543/C10855, PREMIER 4/100/8. *Dokumente zur Deutschlandpolitik, I. Reihe*, vol. 1, ed. Rainer A. Blasius (Frankfurt am Main 1984), 269 and note 3; Klemens von Klemperer, *German Resistance against Hitler*, 228–9.

22 PRO, FO 371/26543/XC 4461.

23 Anthony Eden.

24 Source: PRO, file FO 371/26543/XC 4461, and FO 371/26543/C9472/610/G. The document was drafted and agreed on around Easter 1941. It bears the date of 30 May 1941. A copy reached the British government through the Wallenbergs. The document was handed over in the German original; it is reproduced here from its English translation in the British Foreign Office files.

25 FO note: "The translation of 'alsbald' has already caused difficulty in connexion with one of Hitler's speeches, but this seems to be the sense in this connexion."

26 German version (Ritter, *Goerdeler*, 585): "Anschlüsse ... an Deutschland."

27 FO note in margin: "i.e. no Alsace-Lorraine for France no corridor or Posnania for Poland."

28 FO note: "the German word can mean law and/or right."

29 The German word here is "Schiedsgerichtsbarkeit" meaning, more literally, "court-of-arbitration system."

30 Source: Bundesarchiv, Koblenz, Goerdeler Papers, N 1113/23, in German; included here in English translation. Gerhard Ritter noted on his copy by hand: "Von Herrn Bankdirektor Jakob Wallenberg – Stockholm 'vertraulich' übersandt 5/4.52. Auf Verlangen Wallenbergs schrieb *Goerdeler* das Nachfolgende in Stockholm *19.–20/V.43* nieder für London." The typescript, in German, appears to be a copy of a manuscript draft by Goerdeler, since there are corrections in two different hands, one of them Ritter's, the other not Goerdeler's. The paper is printed in Sabine Gillmann und Hans Mommsen, eds., *Politische Schriften und Briefe Carl Friedrich Goerdelers*, 945–9. See also Goerdeler's 26 March 1943 memorandum in Ritter, *Goerdeler*, 593–611; referred to but not included in Gillmann/Mommsen, 868.

31 The German Resistance government.

32 Reichsrat.

33 The German term for home rule is Selbstverwaltung.

34 The word "Lynchjustiz" is inserted in ( ) by hand; above it another hand wrote "Lynchjustice."

35 1938 means the territory east of what was then Poland, implying that the territories occupied by the Soviet Union in September 1939, essentially those east of the Curzon Line, would be returned to Poland, and that no German troops would remain stationed east of Poland. In view of Soviet expectations and plans, this would contradict the German guarantee to Poland. See Hoffmann, "The Question of Western Allied Co-operation with the German Anti-Nazi Conspiracy, 1938–1944," 453–7.

36 "(planwirtschaft)" is entered by hand.

37 Source: US National Archives, College Park, Maryland, Microcopy T-84 rolls 21; Hans-Adolf Jacobsen, ed., *"Spiegelbild einer Verschwörung." Die Opposition gegen Hitler und der Staatsstreich vom 20. Juli 1944 in der SD-Berichterstattung. Geheime Dokumente aus dem ehemaligen Reichssicherheitshauptamt.* (Stuttgart: Seewald 1984), 410–12: Der Chef der Sicherheitspolizei und des SD, SS-Obergruppenführer Ernst Kaltenbrunner, Berlin, 21 September 1944, to Reichsleiter Martin Bormann (for Hitler), reporting on interrogations of those arrested for involvement in the 20th July 1944 insurrection, enclosure 2/21 September 1944 [h], excerpt from the interrogation of the Lord Mayor Goerdeler (ret.). Goerdeler was interrogated about a meeting with Field Marshal Günther von Kluge and General (Generaloberst) Ludwig Beck, the military head of the conspiracy against Hitler, in the home of General Friedrich Olbricht, Chief of General Army Office in Home Army Command in September 1943. Kluge had commanded Army Group Centre in the campaign against the Soviet Union from 19 December 1941 to 28 October 1943 when he had a car accident; BA-MA RH 19 II/155. Only the main points of the Gestapo summary from

Goerdeler's account are here translated. The numerous digressions and the underlinings are not reproduced.

38 Jacob Wallenberg, Chief Executive Officer of the Enskilda Banken in Stockholm.

39 "Zusammenfassender Ausgleich."

40 Source: Dulles, *Germany's Underground*, 142–6; interview with Jacob Wallenberg, Stockholm, 16 September 1977. Goerdeler was well acquainted with Jacob Wallenberg, the Swedish banker, who was a member of the Swedish government's commission on economic relations between Sweden and Germany. Goerdeler met with Wallenberg several times during the war, on business for Robert Bosch Co. (cloaking operations; see Gerard Aalders and Cees Wiebes, "Stockholm's Enskilda Bank, German Bosch and IG Farben. A Short History of Cloaking," *The Scandinavian Economic History Review* 33 (1985): 25–50) and disclosed to him his plans for the overthrow of Hitler's regime. Jacob Wallenberg summarized his conversations with Goerdeler for Allen Dulles.

41 For the Casablanca Conference, see *Foreign Relations of the United States. The Conferences at Washington, 1941–1942, and Casablanca, 1943* (Washington, DC: US Government Printing Office 1968).

42 For details of the coup plans for September and October 1943, see Hoffmann, *Stauffenberg. A Family History, 1905–1944*, 225–6.

43 Hjalmar Horace Greeley Schacht, Reichsbank President 1923–30, 1933–39; Reich Economics Minister 1934–37. Schacht was involved in coup plans from 1938. Cf. Hoffmann, *The History of the German Resistance 1933–1945*, 69, 82–7, 92, 136.

44 About Erwin Planck, cf. Astrid von Pufendorf, *Die Plancks. Eine Familie zwischen Patriotismus und Widerstand* (Berlin: Propyläen Verlag 2006).

45 Translated from German. Sources: Findings of People's Court on Hermann Kaiser, 17 Jan. 1945, BA EAP 105/30, including extracts from Kaiser's diary; "*Spiegelbild einer Verschwörung*," 118, 126–7, 727–8. On 26 May 1944, Stauffenberg and Goerdeler met in Captain Hermann Kaiser's office at Home Army Command in the Bendlerstrasse in Berlin; Kaiser prepared these notes of Goerdeler's views for Stauffenberg on points for negotiations with the Allies.

23

Adam von Trott zu Solz:
Peace Missions
1939–1944

Adam von Trott zu Solz (9 August 1909–26 August 1944) was born in Potsdam into an old family from the Principality of Hesse-Kassel, which had
become Prussian in 1866, as the son of the Prussian Minister of Culture.
On his mother's side, he was a descendant of John Jay, the first American
Supreme Justice. He was trained in law at the universities of Munich, Göttingen, and Berlin, received a doctorate in law in 1931, and was a Rhodes
Scholar at Oxford 1931–33. From the beginning of Hitler's regime, he was
in a determined opposition that became active in 1939. After a journey
"around the world" (March 1937 to November 1938) to the United States and
the Far East, with an extended stay in China, he returned to Germany "resolved to take an active part in the opposition to Hitler."[1] He travelled to
England in June 1939 and to America in the fall to search for a way to save
the peace. Again he insisted on returning home.[2] From the spring of 1940,
he worked in the German Foreign Office.

On his visit to England in 1939, he was able on 3 June to speak to the
Foreign Secretary, Lord Halifax, and the newly appointed Ambassador to
the United States, Lord Lothian. A few days afterward, he had a meeting
with Prime Minister Neville Chamberlain at No. 10 Downing Street. He
argued in favour of some material gesture of good will toward Hitler's Germany, specifically a solution for Danzig and the Polish Corridor, and economic co-operation to facilitate trade and aid Germany financially. If he
knew that Lord Halifax, who in February 1938 succeeded Anthony Eden
as Secretary of State for Foreign Affairs, had personally offered Hitler con-

cessions on 19 November 1937 regarding peaceful revisions of the Treaty of Versailles concerning Danzig, Austria, Czechoslovakia, armaments, and colonies, he nevertheless felt, in view of the British government's commitment to the defence of Poland (Prime Minister Chamberlain's declaration in the House of Commons on 31 March 1939) that an admittedly desperate effort had to be made to avert war.[3] Trott understood the British position to be even harder and more determined than the guarantee for Poland's independence suggested, and he also anticipated the horror and the enormity of the looming catastrophe of another European war.[4]

During the war, Trott continued his efforts for peace. He travelled abroad, especially to Switzerland (at least six trips) and Sweden (four trips), as well as to France and Italy.[5] He wrote memoranda, always designed to lay the foundations for post-war reconstruction based on mutual understanding and trust, and, where possible, with the participation of those Germans who opposed Hitler and his policies.[6] Some of the memoranda have been published in learned periodicals, starting twelve years after the war; some have become available more recently in the British Foreign Office files. Trott's widow, Clarita von Trott zu Solz, compiled a collection of accounts of Trott's activities.[7] Katharine J. Sams, in her dissertation, examined Trott's efforts in detail to the beginning of 1940 and modified some of Klemperer's findings and conclusions.[8] A full and detailed scholarly account of Trott's wartime activities is still a desideratum.

The first of Trott's wartime memoranda, printed below as "no. I," was one he had written possibly in part during his 1939 voyage across the Atlantic, after which he arrived in New York on 2 October, but certainly before Charles Bosanquet sailed from New York to England on 4 October, because Trott gave it to Bosanquet so that he might convey it to Lord Halifax. The memorandum has been incorrectly dated for December 1939 in the literature on the subject, until Katharine Sams' 1999 dissertation.[9]

There are points that Prime Minister Chamberlain's speech of 12 October, in which he responded to Hitler's peace offers, and the memorandum have in common. But for Chamberlain, the basis for a just post-war settlement was an Allied victory. Trott did not think Britain and France could defeat Germany without Russian support. He believed that the overthrow of Hitler's regime was the most constructive starting point. While Chamberlain did not change his government's official and public position, he did pursue the possibility of a German internal revolt.[10]

A November 1939 memorandum addressed to President Delano Roosevelt has been attributed to Trott by Hans Rothfels. It was, however, originally drafted by Paul Scheffer and German fellow émigrés in New York. The memorandum is not reproduced here; it was written in English, and it is accessible in this form in Rothfels' publication in *Vierteljahrshefte für Zeitgeschichte*.[11]

After successfully having insisted on important revisions, Trott agreed, explicitly risking his life in doing so, to pose as author.[12] He had a passage removed that predicated the future peace upon a German defeat; in an interview with the American Assistant Secretary of State, George S. Messersmith, Trott said the memorandum "represented his views as a whole"; but he still had reservations about calling for "a statement of the Allied peace aims or conditions" at this time because of the danger of a premature settlement leaving the present German government in place.[13] (There is an implication in Trott's reservation that the war had to be prosecuted, not suspended; the continuation of the war was likely to harden Allied insistence on total victory and impose a super Versailles on Germany. But Trott was likely to have understood the British position that victory would have to be part of the basis of a settlement. Trott's emphasis in the changes he demanded and attained was on negotiation, and this would likely have a different character after an internal overthrow of the Hitler regime.) After the changes Trott had insisted upon, the memorandum argued for the Allies to proclaim their desire for a "constructive and fair peace," to declare definite war aims, and to state what "maximum concessions" would be required of Germany, "or to assure that their [the German people's] territorial status of 1933 shall be disputed under no circumstances."[14] Further, there must not be a victors' peace, or a partition of Germany. Such a notion would only drive the German people into the Nazi or Soviet camp and make it impossible for the underground opposition to remove Hitler's or a succeeding similar regime; and it would be "disastrous to the future peace of Europe."[15] Considering that Trott believed Germany could not be defeated by Britain and France alone and without Russia's assistance, his acceptance at this early stage of a territorial settlement based on less than the status quo ante bellum is certainly remarkable.[16]

Although Trott's memorandum was well received at the American Department of State, his mission in America suffered from various suspicions against him, and most disastrously from Maurice Bowra's denouncing him to Justice Felix Frankfurter.[17] Trott attended a conference on "Problems of the Pacific," organized by the New York Institute of Pacific Relations at Virginia Beach in November 1939; he was accompanied by John W. Wheeler-Bennett, a historian assigned by the British Ambassador in Washington,

Lord Lothian, to accompany Trott during the conference – to be his "eyes and ears" in the United States.[18]

Wheeler-Bennett, who had long discussions with Trott about the future of Germany and Europe, supported Trott's resistance efforts. He wrote a "Memorandum" and a "Note on the Restoration of a *Rechtsstaat* in Germany," dated 28 December 1939, signed "JWB"; both are in the British Foreign Office files.[19] The memorandum and note reached Halifax and Chamberlain. They did not generate direct action, but may well have reinforced Chamberlain's and Halifax's resolve to pursue their contacts with the German underground Resistance through the good offices of Pope Pius XII.[20] The memorandum and note are based on Wheeler-Bennett's many conversations and discussions in "length and in detail" with Trott; they also reflect Trott's views, and they show that Trott had made a profound impression upon his new friend and convinced him of the existence in Germany of "high patriots," who were waging a "War for the Liberation of the German People" who were an "ally" of the "Democratic Powers."[21] Wheeler-Bennett argued for a clear public commitment on the part of the Allies to a "just and generous treatment" of a "New Reich" that removed the National-Socialist dictatorship. Later in the war, Wheeler-Bennett changed his position and, on 21 April 1943, he signed a memorandum more critical of Trott than the one of 28 December 1939.[22]

Wheeler-Bennett sent the memorandum of 28 December 1939, reproduced below as "no. 11," to Sir Robert Vansittart. Trott asked Wheeler-Bennett to send a copy of the memorandum to his friend David Astor, to whom he wrote on 26 December 1939 that he considered it *very important* that it should be taken seriously before it is too late." But it was not "taken seriously." Trott's new effort to influence British policy, and his entire mission to America had been a failure.[23] Distrust all round dominated the atmosphere in the months before and after the beginning of the war.

In September 1940, during the Battle of Britain, Trott paid a visit to the Secretary of the World Council of Churches in Geneva, Willem A. Visser 'tHooft. Trott's message, which Visser 'tHooft composed and conveyed to Trott's English friends, was sombre. Trott outlined to Visser 'tHooft, for his friends in England, the situation of the German Resistance, which was "weak and disorganized," yet he emphasized that at this time resistance to Hitler by force was "absolutely necessary." Since it was not a message overtly coming from Trott but from a respected Dutch clergyman, it was also understood "as an unmistakable blueprint for co-operation and close contact [...] between those Germans who are struggling against nihilism and for a European order and those in the occupied and annexed territories who have the same aims and purposes."[24] Trott's message is printed below as "no. III."

In December 1941 in Geneva, Trott had a conversation with A. Roland Eliot, Executive Secretary, Student Division, of the YMCA National Council of the Student Christian Association in New York. This was after the German offensive in the summer had failed to defeat the Soviet Union. Wheeler-Bennett reported on the conversation to the British Embassy in Washington.[25] Trott now believed, and said, that the overthrow of Hitler, which needed the leadership of the army, could succeed only after German military power had been broken. This, again, implied Germany's total defeat, with all its consequences. The document is printed below as "no. IV."

In April 1942 Trott visited Visser 'tHooft in Geneva and handed him a long memorandum for the Lord Privy Seal, Sir Stafford Cripps.[26] This memorandum, printed below as "no. V," was produced by resistance members associated with the Kreisau Circle together with Trott.[27] On 26 September 1942, Trott wrote to Dr Harry Johansson of the Nordic Ecumenical Institute in Sigtuna to thank him for his help: "I feel that you have fully understood that we do *not* intend to plead for support or even encouragement from friends on the other side – but that we wish to deposit our faith in the necessity of some such movement springing from solidaric and representative minds in the whole of Chr. Europe to make salvation possible. Personally, I live with the conviction that a foundation for this exists and we are called upon to build on it now."[28] The British reaction may be found in Foreign Secretary Anthony Eden's speech in Usher Hall, Edinburgh, on 8 May 1942. The Foreign Secretary said the longer the German people supported their regime the heavier grew their own responsibility "for the damage that they are doing to the world [...] Therefore, if any section of the German people really wants to see a return to a German state that is based on respect for law and for the rights of the individual, they must understand that no one will believe them until they have taken active steps to rid themselves of their present régime."[29]

In October 1943, Trott took another trip to Sweden, and in June 1944 still another, from which his last memorandum for the British government, printed below as "no. VI," resulted. It was obviously – and explicitly – incompatible with Allied war aims. How deep the chasm was, not only between the material aims of the resistance and the Allies, but also between their attitudes and mentalities, upon which Trott had always placed the greatest emphasis, is best illustrated by the following quotations.

Sir Ivone Kirkpatrick, 1933–38 in the British Embassy in Berlin; 1939–40 head of the Foreign Office Central Department; at the time of writing the Controller of the BBC European Services, wrote on 6 July 1944 about the German resistance: "[...] the opposition is unlikely to be able to do anything to shorten the war. They are not powerful enough, the terror is too efficient, and moreover they would not act unless we gave them assurances which would gravely embarrass us later. At the worst to give them a glimpse into our minds might drive them into the Nazi camp!"[30]

Wheeler-Bennett wrote after Stauffenberg's failed uprising,[31] in a memorandum of 25 July 1944, which was approved at all levels:

It may now be said with some definiteness that we are better off with things as they are today than if the plot of July 20th had succeeded and Hitler had been assassinated [...] By the failure of the plot we have been spared the embarrassments, both at home and in the United States, that might have resulted from such a move and, moreover, the present purge is presumably removing from the scene numerous individuals which might have caused us difficulty [...] the Gestapo and the S.S. have done us an appreciable service in removing a selection of those who would undoubtedly have posed as 'good' Germans after the war, while preparing for a third World War. It is to our advantage therefore that the purge should continue, since the killing of Germans by Germans will save us from future embarrassments of many kinds.[32]

The Prime Minister said in the House of Commons on 2 August: "The highest personalities in the German Reich are murdering one another, or trying to, while the avenging Armies of the Allies close upon the doomed and ever-narrowing circle of their power."[33]

Adam von Trott was hanged on 26 August 1944.

I

[Memorandum for Lord Halifax[34]]

[before 4 October 1939]

1) Popular opinion in Germany is still convinced that England is fighting another imperialist war. Whatever view is held about the immediate cause of the outbreak it is almost generally believed

that the allies are guilty of the same sinister motives for which they blame Hitler. British radio and leaflet Propaganda has so far been unconvincing in this respect. It has not been able to touch the core of people's bitter grievance against Hitler and this war. Though some leaflets have been reasonably well composed (especially the one ending with "letzte Warnung"),[35] other leaflets have simply been posted in party propaganda boxes without comment. The party can still rely on the simple but penetrating argument: "This is what the allies said about the Kaiser in 1914–18 and see what they did to us then!"

When everything is said and done about the daily growing unpopularity of the Nazi régime in Germany, there is required an element in the English approach to the German mind that has hitherto been lacking, if the German people is to be convinced that Britain, given the chance, will not fall back on the "method of Versailles" or even – as has been argued in some quarters – "to something much more terrible than Versailles."

This for instance is the reason why a thoroughly antinazi general told me the other day that in the end the decent element in Germany may see themselves driven to form the last defence of Nazidom to save Germany from annihilation.

The other recurrent argument runs as follows: (In case of an allied victory)[36] We cannot possibly expect any leniency from Western Europe once the furies of war are really let loose, and (in case of an Allied victory) can only hope to save Germany by opening the floodgates to Russia.[37] Though "National-Bolshevism" is seen as the greatest internal peril for an ordered German future, it is still on balance being preferred to another humiliation by the allies.

All this goes to necessitate that to be convincing your approach to non-nazi opinion must be deepened and intensified.

2) You can win an effective response for a "crusade against Nazi oppression" only if you succeed to clear it from the suspicion of Machiavellian make-believe. This is not a matter of clever propaganda technique of which the German public is sick and tired but of basing your policy on what should strike yourselves and your potential German cooperators as a convincing "change of heart," a real determination to build the peace of Europe on justice and equality.

The sincerity of this conviction must rise above any doubt, it must be spread by a carefully selected network of trustworthy personal relationships over the warring frontiers, and its application to the unsolved problems of Europe must be entrusted to the highest and most disinterested abilities found inside the several countries concerned. Only then will it be possible by mutual consent to arrive at pronouncements of policy which are bound to supersede in effectiveness what is at present rightly branded and dismissed as "mere propaganda"

Our aim must be a popular drive throughout Europe uniting the forces which will save our common traditions from barbarism. Such a popular drive should give a deeper meaning and hope to the present struggle in all the countries concerned, a justification for the heavy sacrifices and a reasonable hope for a constructive European future. In England it would probably have to change the present political pattern considerably. In Germany – where it has to gather its momentum underground – that same popular drive must of necessity rally around the following elements, and it is through them that a convincing approach to the German mind from England should be found at this juncture.

a) *The working classes* are suffering the most intense restriction of living standards (caused by Nazi policy). Though there have been local outbreaks of discontent, it would be wrong to assume that economic pressure will cause anything like a general revolt in a comparatively near future. This possibility seems to be ruled out by most expert observers. Rationing and regimentation can go a good deal further. This, however, does not alter the fact that the working man's existence, i.e. the existence of nine out of ten noncombattant Germans, is becoming increasingly intolerable, especially since the suspension of almost all civil rights is adding a gnawing sense of humiliation to the present stress.

It is in the working classes too that a strong tradition of international cooperation and of rational politics is still lingering, and where the return to self-elected trade unions and other free institutions is most urgently desired.

A clear disillusionment as to the workability of Marxism has been deepened to passionate resentment against a communist régime which for self-interest has allied itself to the fascist tyranny. The German-Russian accord has discredited the extreme left and has consolidated a conception of "socialist unity" which wishes to square the redemption of working class rights with the moral and cultural traditions of Europe which would be finally submerged in a nazi-bolshevic amalgamation. The abandonment of Marxism as a dogmatic creed during the experiences of recent years has opened the working class mind in Germany to the need for close cooperation with other elements in the community on which an effective peace drive must also be based.

b) The official and officer class in Germany have submitted to Nazi rule not – as is often held abroad – because of a mere lack of moral independence, but because the intolerable confusion and disruption which had always threatened the German state since the great war seemed to postulate a régime of stern discipline however unpleasant some of its concomitant features may be. While there has been a great deal of irresponsible craving for power and emoluments, there have also been a large number of officers and officials who in the past have only held on to their positions from a sense of responsibility in spite of most resentful indignation about nazi methods. Their personal reactions are still based on a sense of honour and duty, on a rational patriotism and a high degree of intellectual competence. There will quite clearly come the breaking point when their studied selfrestriction to routine work can no longer be squared with a régime whose policy destroys the fundamental interests of the nation. This realisation – especially in the officer class – cannot happen at the height of a triumphant campaign; but indispensable as they are for setting up an alternative political order of things, they too are intellectually the most restive, critical and to an astonishing degree antagonistic elements within the present régime. To win their confidence in a common attempt at European reconstruction will be indispensable for any effective drive in this direction.

c) Finally there is the personal and human[38] element which is being deeply stirred by present happenings. The religious forces are[39] so far preponderantly allied to a narrower sense of national loyalty as indicated in the case of the officials. The battle of Protestants and Roman Catholics against Nazidom has been fought mainly on ground where an illegitimate invasion of the spiritual domain of the Church was supposed to be taking place. War is generally considered to be an affair of the state, and its command of the supreme sacrifice receives the Churches' ethical approval. The Christian Churches of Europe in the last war failed to give a different ideal of Christian duty, and the Churches this time can hardly be looked for to dissociate themselves from their national loyalties (and to preach self-sacrifice for a Christian régime throughout Europe). And yet some such appeal, cloaked not in theological or ecclesiastic terms but in terms of the essential needs and dignity of human life which are being discarded at present form[s] the final medium which will strike to the roots of all the forces in Europe sincerely willing the change.

II

JWB[40]

MEMORANDUM

The avowed aim with which Great Britain entered upon the present conflict with Germany was to destroy that evil thing called "Hitlerism" which has terrorised Germany and threatened Europe for the past seven years, and in addition, to maintain "the rule of law and the quality of mercy in dealings between man and man, and in the great Society of civilized States" (Lord Halifax, November 7, 1939).

"We are not fighting against you, for whom we have no bitter feelings," said Mr. Chamberlain to the German people at the very outset, "but against a tyrannous and foresworn regime."[41]

In a sense, then, the present struggle is a War for the Liberation of the German People, and in the struggle the Democratic Powers have an ally within Germany itself in those high patriots of every class and calling who reflect the fundamental decency of the German People. These elements, more numerous and powerful than may be supposed, have a common aim with the Democratic Powers in destroying the Nazi régime and in restoring in Germany a Reign of Law (a Rechtsstaat) that will ensure to the German People their ancient liberties. (See attached note on the Rechtsstaat.)

It is, therefore, to the interests of the Democratic Powers that those elements within Germany should be strengthened and encouraged to the point where they themselves can take the initiative, and this point can only be reached when these liberating elements are themselves assured that the New Reich, which it is our common aim to achieve, will meet with just and generous treatment at the hands of the Democratic Powers.

This essential preliminary assurance can only be given by a clarification and reemphasis of the aim with which the Democratic Powers began the war. Progress towards this end has been made in the various declarations of the Allied Statesmen. The world now knows, that while we are fighting for the destruction of Hitlerism and restitution of the wrongs done to Austria, Czecho-Slovakia, and Poland, we do not contemplate either a vindictive peace or a peace dictated to Germany by the victorious Allies. In addition, we are pledged to the principle that under the future peace settlement "each country would have the unfettered right to choose its own form of internal government so long as that government did not pursue an external policy injurious to its neighbours" (Mr. Chamberlain, November 26, 1939).

These general terms, however, are not sufficient to convince completely a German people already rendered incredulous by the memory of what they honestly believe to be the betrayal of the Fourteen Points[42] by the Treaty of Versailles, and, while it is realized that a full statement of peace terms would be inopportune at this moment, it is also true that a more definite assurance is necessary before the elements within Germany antagonistic to the régime can feel themselves justified in taking the momentous and perilous step of rising against their national government. They can not be expected to risk all in the common cause without being 100 percent certain that the new Germany, which they will help fashion, will receive both justice and generosity.

For this purpose, therefore, it is of the utmost importance that, at the earliest possible moment, a Statement should be made by Great Britain, France, Poland, and the British Dominions who are at war, to the effect that:

(1) It is not their intention to impose any political dismemberment upon a Germany in which the *Rechtsstaat* has been restored.

(2) They look forward to collaborating with such a Germany in a new European Order, in which disputes should be settled by sane negotiation and not by violence.

(3) Within the spirit of this New Order, they will immediately resume the method of peace-time trade and industrial negotiations, including financial facilities for fostering exports and imports, and of equal access to raw materials. They will support any move towards greater economic units in Europe if the new German government is prepared to cooperate in such a policy.

(4) They expect the active participation of Germany in a general reduction of armaments.[43]

The urgency for swift action in this matter is occasioned by a number of reasons:

(1) The fact that the German Ministry of Propaganda is already issuing for home consumption a lurid version of the terms which the victorious Allies are alleged to be planning to impose upon Germany. These include the annexation of East Prussia by Poland and of South Saxony by Czecho-Slovakia; the incorporation of Bavaria, Baden, and Wurttemberg in a South German Habsburg State; and the creation of a French Protectorate comprising the Rhineland, Westphalia, and Hesse.

It is clear what effect a statement of this nature will have on the German mind if it once obtains a grip. Even refugees would return from abroad to join in a *guerre à l'outrance* rather than submit to such humiliation.

(2) The danger that delay or failure on the part of the Allies to make clear their intentions towards a Germany purged of the evils of National Socialism – and organized in the form indicated above – may have the effect of destroying the last vestige of hope in the hearts of this element of liberation and of driving them willy-nilly, not necessarily to the support of Hitler, but to the ultimate defence of the Fatherland.

(3) The very real danger that a prolonged war of increasing severity and horror will result in Germany becoming "National Bolshevik," and thereby, in collaboration with the U.S.S.R., constituting an even greater threat to the fabric of European civilization.

It is agreed that peace with a Nazi, or shadow-Nazi, Government in Germany is unthinkable, but for this very reason it is the more necessary to indicate to those elements within the Reich, with whom we *could* negotiate, our desire to conclude a peace of Statesmanship and justice, and thereby hasten the day when this will become possible.

December 28, 1939

This need not in any way entail or involve a return to the Weimar System. What is required of Germany is a clear and unmistakable sign that the evils of the Nazi regime have been abolished for ever.

Steps towards this end might be as follows:

(I)   The resignation of the present Reich and Prussian Governments, and the arrest and exile of the individuals composing them; the appointment of a Provisional Government.

(II)   The abolition of the Secret Police and of arbitrary arrest.

(III) Restoration of the freedom of speech, press, worship, and of public assembly and organisation of Labour.

(IV)   Dissolution of the party "para-military" organisations, S.A. and S.S.

(V)   Abolition of the totalitarian principle of the single party.

(VI)   Dissolution of the present Reichstag and free elections to a Constituent Assembly which shall decide on and organise the future form of Government for Germany.

It would be for the Constituent Assembly to decide between the claims of the monarchy and republicanism, and to amend the constitution accordingly; to appoint commissions to decide upon what should and what should not be retained of the legislation promulgated by decree during the Third Reich; and to organise the liquidation of the Party organisation in all spheres of national life.

In the meantime it would be the task of Provisional Government, supported by the army and police force, to maintain order in the country, to restrain the desire for revenge on the part of the population and to carry on negotiations for a general European agreement on the basis of the accepted formula.

December 28, 1939

III

Trott's Message through W.A. Visser 'tHooft, September 1940

To: Paton[44]

Notes on the situation (September 1940)

1   At the present moment the position of the German Government is exceptionally strong. This is of course due to two factors:

a) that the government has largely succeeded in taking the wind out of the sails of the opposition groups

b) that the government has succeeded in its war policy.

Nothing succeeds like success.[45]

2 All opposition groups have been weakened during the last years.

   a) The *socialists* have been weakened by the fact that certain points of their programme have been carried out by the nazis rather than by themselves. While salaries are on the whole lower today than they were even before 1933 and while trade-unionism is dead, the nazis have succeeded in abolishing un-employment and in abolishing the successes of capitalism and even in commanding the obedience of the former capitalist ruling class. Thus they have effectively billed[46] that kind of so-cialism which was merely based on economic claims. The only kind of socialism which can continue to resist is that which is based on faith in the freedom and dignity of man. This is at the moment only to be found among a small élite. It is import-ant to note that these socialists turn increasingly to Christian-ity, since they have discovered that socialism needs a Chris-tian basis in order to find sufficiently deep and indestructible roots.

   b) The *Catholics* seem to have lost much of their fighting power. Many of the younger clergy are more or less pro-nazi and the hierarchy is hampered by the Vatican-policy which is still based on the hope of some compromise with the totalitarian powers. Little can therefore be expected of the R.C. Church as such. There are however among the R.C.'s a certain number of laymen and priests who are working along independent lines and seek their inspiration in Berdiaeff, Maritain and other writers who point to a spiritual Renaissance which would find expression in a new European order and in social reform.

   c) The *Confessional Church* is largely disorganised. Its members are in danger of turning pietistic and of taking a quietistic and relativistic attitude to the affairs of this world. But here again there are some (not only among the Confessionals but also among Protestants in general) who seek to relate their faith to the situation and are continuing the fight in the political realm.

   d) The *Conservatives* who were always ardent patriots have largely been won over by the recent victories. Nevertheless there is a considerable group among them who hold on to the more chevaleresque traditions of German aristocracy and who are keenly aware of the dangers of a Hitler victory and are waiting for their opportunity to restore the ethical and political traditions of constitutional government. They also seek a revival of religious orientation.

3   But while opposition is at the moment weak and disorganised the chances for a change of the regime are not to be underestimated. For as soon as a set-back would occur the situation might be profoundly modified. The totalitarian regime creates a gigantic vacuum in public opinion and that vacuum[47] might suddenly be filled with a new content, if events take a different turn.

4   At the moment life in Germany, while difficult, is tolerable. Rationing and bombardments are not such that there is general demoralisation. But if the attack on England would fail, if another winter of war would have to be accepted, if there would come complications in other directions (America? Russia?) and if at the right moment a magnanimous peace-offer would be made, a new situation would arise.

5   It is then at the moment necessary to resist Germany by force – for only thus is there hope for the creation of a favourable situation for a change of regime. But it is also necessary to prepare for a peace offer from the right source and at the right moment. The offer should come in such a way that Germans can *trust* it. It should be of such a nature that the Germans can feel that it is neither another Versailles nor a mere return to the status quo ante. It should give Germany a territory which coincides as nearly as possible with its ethnographic frontiers and provide a constructive and daring solution of the European colonial and economic problems. The slightest suggestion that the democratic powers would keep Germany "down" would consolidate the whole of the country behind Hitler. And so would the suggestion that the democratic powers have no constructive ideas as to the future.

6   If on the other hand Britain is defeated, the struggle will have to go on on the interior battle-front. In that case it is of the highest importance that cooperation and close contact should be established between those Germans who are struggling against nihilism and for a European order and those in the occupied or annexed territories who have the same aims and purposes. It is a

false national sentiment which would lead people of the occupied territories to refuse to cooperate with those Germans who are ultimately devoted to the same cause as they are themselves. It is natural that in defeated countries opposition takes a specifically national colouring but this opposition will be utterly ineffective if it does not relate itself to similar groups in other countries which are in the same position and especially to the groups in Germany which alone are in the position to form an effective centre of the whole body of opposition.

7   It is clear that the struggle is in the last resort of a spiritual nature. The Churches as such cannot undertake it. But church members are to be in the forefront of it. They have that rock-bottom under their feet, which is needed to stand firm in the present tempest; they have the close relations with their fellow-Christians in other countries which are now so indispensable for collaboration in mutual confidence. But they will have to cooperate with all those who still have faith in principles of law and liberty, who believe in the spiritual mission of the European nations, and who are therefore willing to collaborate in the struggle against nihilism.

September 1940[48]

IV

NOTE ON THE ELIOT-TROTT CONVERSATIONS
[by John W. Wheeler-Bennett]
GENEVA, DECEMBER 1941[49]

Mr Eliot[50] of the National Council of Student Christian Association, saw Adam von Trott zu Solz in Geneva on December 18–20 – at which time, it will be remembered, he was said to have been in South America – and had in all about ten hours conversation with him.

Trott began by describing his own position. He had, he said, deliberately refused to become an expatriate, and had elected to return to Germany after his visit to America in the winter of 1939, because he believed he could be more useful working within the Reich than outside it. He himself had always been anti-Nazi, but he now found that there was a growing number of people in all classes who were, as it were, catching up with him.

This movement of opposition, though unorganized, was carried along by an irresistible ground swell of feeling, impelled[51] by two motives.

1 The growing realization of the plight into which their early toleration of National Socialism had led them.
2 A deep-seated fear of Bolshevism without and Communism within.

The movement was to be found in all classes but more particularly among the Church, Labour and the Army. Churchmen had disclosed a far greater degree of outspoken criticism of the regime (e.g. Graf Galen's sermons, and the visit of Cardinal Faulhaber, and the Lutheran Bishop of Stuttgart to the Reichskanzlei in December to protest against the depredations of the Gestapo.) But at the same time they were teaching the philosophy of order and responsibility in preparation for the overthrow of the Nazis and the future peace.

Labour was realizing more and more that it had become the dupe of National Socialism and was turning to the Church for guidance not so much in spiritual matters but in the admiration for the stand taken by certain of its leaders. It is said to be a frequent question in Labour circles when a man secretly professed anti-Nazi views: "Is he a member of the 'Fighting Church'?"

It was, however, to the Army, Trott said, that the movement looked for its real leadership. He would name no names but he indicated that there were certain generals and senior officers, both in the field and on the general staff, who were to be counted upon if and when the time came. He also gave certain examples of discontent in the Army as a whole, (e.g. the Moelders incident,[52] and the refusal of certain commands on the Eastern Front to execute orders of great cruelty against the Russian prisoners.) There was a growing feeling that the Army had created in the Party a Frankenstein Monster, which had passed beyond their control and was, by its own blunders, about to plunge both itself and them into complete catastrophe. More specifically he said, that the Japanese alliance was regarded by the Army as unnatural, and was resented. As in the ranks of Labour there was an increasing regard for the Church and for Christian principles. Mimeographed copies of Robert Paton's "The Church and the Post-War World" had been distributed in Norway by German troops. (Incidentally, it was said that this book had had a wide illicit circulation in Germany, especially among the Army.)

Asked whether the object of the movement was a negotiated peace with the Army, Trott was emphatically negative. Peace, he said, and incidentally the success of the movement was only possible after the military power of Germany had been broken. It was hoped, however, that, at an unstated time, it would be possible to stage a coup d'etat and substitute for the present regime a provisional government which could "demand a new deal" from the United Nations for the "decent Germans".

Once established, this government would take certain immediate measures which should serve as acts of good faith vis-a-vis the Allies. These measures would include:

1   The proclamation of the restoration of the *Rechtsstaat*.[53]
2   The rescinding of anti-Jewish legislation.
3   The return of confiscated property to Jews and Gentiles alike.
4   The evacuation of all occupied territory in *Western* Europe.
    (N.B. No provision was made in these "immediate measures" for the evacuation of Czecho-Slovakia, Poland, Austria, Greece and Yugo-Slavia, and though Mr. Eliot was not entirely clear on the point, it was his impression that Trott was unwilling to surrender any territory which would weaken the position of Germany against Russia.)
5   A statement on the position which the new Germany sees for herself in a federated Europe which she would not seek to dominate.
6   A proposal that, in view of the chaos which would exist in Germany after the collapse of the Nazi regime and the consequent danger of Communism, the German Army in a properly reduced form should be permitted to assist and co-operate with the forces of the United Nations in keeping order within the Reich.

It was finally re-emphasised that there should be no let-up in the Allied attacks on Germany, for under this pressure the movement would grow and gather strength. It was, however, felt that Allied propaganda should give some assurance to the German people that a differentiation would be made between themselves and the Nazi Party, and that Germany would not be partitioned as of her former frontiers.[54] At present they were being convinced by Goebbels that defeat would spell extinction.

J.W. W-B.[55]

April 22, 1942

V
Memorandum by Adam von Trott, April 1942

Strictly Private and Confidential[56]

I.

The development of recent weeks and months has not brought us nearer to answering the question, who will be the so-called "victor" in the present struggle. And yet it has become more and more obvious to all thinking people that western civilisation as such is dangerously threatened in its spiritual and material fundaments. The following features which characterize the present European situation should be kept in mind as they may shortly determine conditions in the entire world.

(1) *Intensified mass destruction of life and economic substance*: Economic losses, inescapably bound up with the war, are bringing about such general impoverishment that even victor nations will be grievously affected by them for many decades.

   Human losses will be of a magnitude which threatens the very continuation of civilized society for years after the war. This pertains not only to the powers at war, but to all nations which, although not directly involved in the struggle, suffer from its manifold repercussions (famine, epidemics, etc.).

(2) *Increasingly totalitarian control of national life* everywhere: The absorption[57] of all national reserves and resources, economic as well as human, by total warfare is becoming unavoidable even in countries which by temperament and on principle are opposed to totalitarianism. Restrictions necessary during such a war are bound to thwart the realm of personal freedom, its cultural and economic productiveness to the point of suffocation.

(3) *Trend towards anarchical dissolution*: The general breakdown of personal security and civil life has already created an extremely vulnerable state of affairs all over Europe. It is impossible to ignore the danger of a complete breakdown of the framework of civilized existence. The military and diplomatic achievements of the Soviet Union are giving a strong impetus to illegal cells of the Third International everywhere in Europe. And Soviet methods in Finland, in the Baltic, Poland, and Roumania as applied in 1939–40 do not justify the belief that bolshevism has

as yet changed into a form of government adapted to western standards.

II.

In view of this situation and its potentialities[58] of catastrophe we consider it necessary to address ourselves to all those on this side of the Atlantic and beyond it who can still realize the scope of this danger. We consider it an irrefutable fact that in spite of all differences between individual countries there is as yet such similarity of conditions and community of spiritual heritage between ourselves and the West that the attempt to discuss certain vital dangers which threaten the essence of our common future should be made under all circumstances.

We do not intend to justify our own position, we are ready to accept our due share of responsibility and of guilt. But we feel justified to appeal to the solidarity and fairness which some responsible groups in the West are extending to those forces in Germany which have consistently fought against Nihilism and its national socialist manifestations. The consciousness of this solidarity in thoughts and in deeds seems to us an indispensable condition for continuing this exchange of views. Such solidarity should first express itself in the fact that appeals like this are not flaunted and discredited by wrong use in the press as it has happened in the past. We would particularly ask our friends to do everything in their power to prevent this in the future. Matters which may appear as sensational news on your side of the frontier are often of such a precarious character on ours that a minimum of sympathetic imagination should prevent giving publicity to them. Deliberate attempts to discredit the forces standing behind a message like the present one have been noticeable even in the Christian periodical press. In this respect we can only appeal to your conscience.

III.

The most urgent and immediate task to stave off catastrophe in Europe is the earliest possible overthrow of the Régime in Germany. The change can take place either by way of anarchical dissolution or by the establishment of a Government which would return to the standards of civilized Europe.

The first possibility would be tantamount to a wholesale European Catastrophe.[59] It would be inevitably linked up with Soviet military success and form the first step towards world revolution by military means.

A success of the second possibility is only conceivable if it is also linked up outside Germany with the final overcoming of European nationalism[60] particularly in its military expression.

The forces in Germany striving for the latter possibility are inspired by the ideas and the circles of the Christian opposition which has crystallized in years of struggle against national socialism. Militant Christianism in its widest sense is the only unbroken core of resistance within the Nazi State, and it has now formed powerful contacts with groups hitherto indifferent to Church and Religion. The key to their common efforts is a desperate attempt to rescue the substance of personal human integrity, equally threatened by Nazism and anarchic Bolshevism. Restitution of the unalienable right, divine and natural, of the human person forms their basic aim. The political and constitutional reconstruction, for which they are working, is conceived in terms of a practical application of the Christian European tradition to modern human needs in the social, political, economic and international sphere.

Seizure of power by these forces in Germany is hindered by the following obstacles:

(a) The dire necessity of national defence against the Soviet Union and against anarchical developments on the eastern frontier of Germany as well as in the Balkans.

(b) Existing control of the entire national life by police (Gestapo) and the anticipated difficulty of dealing with Nazi remnants and anarchical outbreaks after the Nazi overthrow.

(c) The complete uncertainty of the British and American attitude towards a change of government in Germany.

(d) The movements of indiscriminate hatred anticipated in the event of a sudden relaxation of German control in the occupied parts of Europe.

The last two problems cannot be overcome without international co-operation even at this stage.

IV.

Without, for obvious reasons, giving further details of names, dates and programme, it can be said here that our support is drawn from the following groups:

(1) Substantial parts of the working class

(2) Influential circles in the army and bureaucracy

(3) The Militant groups in the Churches

These groups agree on the following lines and principles of reconstruction:

(a) Self-government and decentralisation within Germany.

The structure of the State thus achieved, would be characterised as follows: Breaking up the masses by the creation of smaller and greater units of local self-administration.[61] Application of modern socialist principles in all sectors of political and economic life.

(b) Self-government and federalism within Germany should be organically connected with federalism within Europe (including Britain) and close international cooperation with the other Continents.

This European Federalism would have the following results:

Re-establishment of the right of self-determination within the frame of the European Federation for *all* nations, particularly for those actually under Nazi rule.

We[62] believe in the necessity to reconstitute a Free Polish and a Free Czech state within the limits of their ethnographic frontiers.

Progressive achievement of general disarmament, which we consider to be an economic and social problem as much as a problem of national policy.

(c) Renunciation of economic autarchy in exchange for free access to raw materials overseas.

(d) The political and economic reorganisation of Europe must be free of concepts such as 'status quo' and 'status quo ante'. The main emphasis must lie on social and political security.

(e) The New Germany would be willing to cooperate in any international solution of the Jewish problem.[63]

(f) Germany would be willing to cooperate with all other nations in order to overcome the misery existing in the countries now under Nazi rule.

V.

We consider these points a first basis for talks on a wider and more detailed scale and are ready to join in with all those who are determined to halt this tremendous destruction of all human values. An exchange of ideas seems to us hopeless only as long as we are faced with a one-sided tendency to blame and to judge. There is a definite difference between active crime and criminal negligence. But, whatever the responsibilities are, there should be a common recognition of our failure to deal in a Christian manner with the historical, geographic, economic and psychological factors which have brought the world to the present situation.

We sincerely hope that our still unadequate attempt to do so will be met with frank cooperation in the practical task to face a common future beyond the catastrophe now confronting us all.

VI

Memorandum by Adam von Trott, June 1944[64]

I have been asked to name such groups in Germany who have for patriotic reasons opposed Hitler all along and would therefore be able to cooperate later on.

Since it is still not clear, though it is believed in German opposition groups that the official British attitude even towards an antinazi government is expressed by the formula of unconditional surrender, it is unfortunately only possible to give a somewhat qualified answer.

It is necessary also to clear up first what type of "opposition" one is thinking of, if one is to arrive at a realistic view of the situation. There are, no doubt, genuine anti-nazi elements which would for patriotic reasons cooperate under such conditions, if and when they come about, in a nonpolitical capacity in administrative and technical functions etc. Later on it would be comparatively easy to work out a list of these persons. This is, however, a highly precarious procedure considering the hazards to which these will be exposed in the meantime. It is moreover extremely improbable that those who are preserving their cooperation for this eventuality will then[65] be in a strong enough[66] position to exercise any effective public authority when the nazi system actually breaks up. It would then be necessary to wait and rely upon the allied armed forces to suppress nationalist as well as anarchist elements which are bound to arise everywhere in the country.

A distinctly different type of opposition consists of those who are not waiting for outside events but are actually trying all along to remove and replace the present system. It may be difficult to credit these people in spite of their so far invisible achievements from abroad, but it would be a serious mistake to form an estimate of the probable developments on the continent without taking their existence into account. Naturally this type of person will tend in the struggle that he is engaged in to consider cooperation or even communication on the basis of unqualified "unconditional surrender" psychologically and politically impossible.

After the abandonment of the Atlantic Charter for Germany and in the absence of any alternative set of principles according to which a defeated Germany will be treated, "unconditional surrender" is interpreted by this group of people as really implying the surrender of even the most elementary conditions for rebuilding after the war – the deliberate exchange, in fact, of one lawless tyranny for another. The abandonment of the principle of selfdetermination for German populations must, in the absence of any other limitation against complete arbitrariness,[67] to their mind entail the slicing up of national territory at the instigation of uncontrolled passions in neighbouring countries violated by Hitler, an arbitrary slave traffic in German workers and soldiers[68] and denial of the right themselves to mete[69] out justice to Nazi criminals, [a right] which seems to them an indispensable[70] presupposition in the process of regaining a rudimentary sense of national selfrespect.

These people know that in order to establish even a minimum of effective public authority during and after the breaking point, they must – in the face of all material hardships and deprivations which will be inevitable – at least represent a sense of renewed inner integrity and national self respect which, owing to an almost complete ignorance of the real bias and intentions of the Western powers, they feel is being implicitly denied to them[71] at present.

It[72] is, I think, no exaggeration to state that the very persons now most effectively challenging Hitler's[73] command will, if their present conception of Western intentions proves correct, be ultimately driven underground and form the leadership of a German resistance movement.

Some assurance, however, regarding the territorial integrity (or self-determination of the main body of German speaking population, some understanding about the orderly procedure of military demobilisation[74] by the German command in cooperation with Allied control commissions[75] and about the punishment of Nazi criminals by German courts (excepting perhaps those cases of flagrant outrages of a more local character where arrests have been effected on the spot) would remove the worst obstacles now barring confidence and contact between this opposition group[76] and the Western allies.

In order[77] to gain effective control[78] within Germany it is, in turn, necessary for these men to rely on the unreserved cooperation of certain senior[79] personalities in the Oberkommando[80] certain leading elements in the uncorrupted sections[81] of the Ordnungspolizei[82] and the[83] municipal police authorities of several of the larger cities,[84] and certain militant groups formerly belonging to the Social Democratic Party, Reichsbanner, Trade Union movement etc. These individuals are naturally unwilling[85] to shoulder the burden and blame of Hitler's[86] defeat unless[87] they can hope to offer the people some improvement or advantage in their situation compared[88] to what would follow Hitler's – own defeat. Accepting unconditional surrender now, they would feel unable later on to counteract the[89] mass slogan of having "stabbed in the back" our fighting forces – a slogan which is bound to recur even more violently and immediately than it did after 1918. From the start they would prove unable to squash nationalist or anarchist extremism as unpatriotic. The country would inevitably split into a nationalist and a communist camp, possibly an interminable civil war the two sides of which would probably expect and find support from the respective great powers in the east and west. The emergence of two opposing post-nazi Germanies would become irresistible;[90] preponderance under the psychological conditions prevailing at the moment would most likely accrue[91] for the national-bolchevist side, while in the parts occupied by the Western powers nationalist opposition would quite possibly cluster around a new "Hitler legend" to the effect that had he been allowed to continue his delaying fight, the hostile coalition might have broken after all, occupation of German territory prevented etc. etc.

It is held by this group that at present no political support of their effort to prevent this is forthcoming from the Western powers.[92] It is further realized that there are political tendencies among the Western allies to discredit and if possible destroy every, even an anti-nazi nucleus of German political integration as a political danger for the future.

As long as it seems necessary for the Western powers to confine their war policy exclusively to the military aspect of unconditional surrender this group feels that the only alternative to further immense sacrifices of life and to the risk of a completely unmanageable[93] chaos in Europe depends primarily on their own success [to] bring to a head their already advanced preparations[94] to establish an effective and reliable[95] political system,[96] before or at least during the break down of Hitler's[97] military and political machine.[98] They know that this cannot be achieved by a military dictatorship. Though the first phase of taking over can only be effected by armed force, they know that internally and externally all depends[99] on the establishment of a democratic[100] civilian government broadly representative of all genuinely anti-nazi groups within the country, i.e. the two Churches, the moderate as opposed to the violently communist working class organisations, the conservative and progressive elements in the bureaucracy[101] and army. A group of political leaders potentially representative of all these strata has been formed and works in close contact with the military commanders who are engaged in their own[102] preparations.[103] Some of these political leaders are known in England and have been carrying on intermittent contacts with the outside world through neutral countries.[104] But it will, I trust, be considered reasonable that under the present circumstances a strict rule has been accepted that the top figure and the composition of the active inner group is not to be disclosed as long as the attitude of the Allies[105] has not been more clarified. Apart from vital considerations of safety they feel[106] that the giving of names would *under present conditions* serve no other interests but those of war intelligence and propaganda and may thereby destroy the last nucleus by[107] which a minimum of civilized order in the Western sense could be rebuilt in Germany.

It is impossible to give a concrete estimate of the chances of success since this depends on many different and precarious circumstances[108] which it is difficult or impossible to understand from abroad. It is recognized, however, that the opposition[109] must first act[110] and establish itself and then cope with the practical political possibilities on all sides, provided that some qualification of the term "unconditional surrender" is forthcoming.[111]

It is, as I know, a matter of sincere regret to the very men on whose behalf this statement has been written that owing to the present impasse it had to be confined only[112] to an indication of the basic character of the[113] militant type of opposition in Germany. There can be no doubt, however, that if some authoritative understanding were forthcoming regarding the main points and obstacles which appear to bar[114] the way to[115] cooperation, the group in question would supply the information which proves indispensable to bring it [cooperation] about.

It may be permitted in conclusion to emphasize that the utmost possible secrecy is a vital prerequisite, but that a practical advance seems only possible by the mutual dispatch of reliable agents who are personally acquainted with the men, plans and measures the coordination of which is likely to become necessary in this matter.

NOTES

1 Klemens von Klemperer, *German Resistance against Hitler. The Search for Allies Abroad, 1938–1945*, 123.
2 Ibid., 187.
3 *Akten zur deutschen auswärtigen Politik 1918–1945, Series D (1937–1945) (ADAP D)*; The Earl of Birkenhead, *Halifax. The Life of Lord Halifax* (London: Hamish Hamilton 1965), 368–74; *The Parliamentary Debates, fifth series, volume 345, House of Commons, official report* (London: His Majesty's Stationery Office 1939), col. 2415; Alexander Cadogan, *The Diaries of Sir Alexander Cadogan O.M. 1938–1945*, 342.
4 Klemperer, *German Resistance*, 125–6, quotes William Douglas-Home's recollections of the conversation on 3 June 1939.
5 Peter Hoffmann, *The History of the German Resistance 1933–1945*, 114–19, 216–34, 240–5.
6 For overviews of the foreign contacts of the German Resistance, see Hoffmann, *The History*, and Klemperer, *German Resistance*.
7 Clarita von Trott zu Solz, *Adam von Trott zu Solz. An Account*.
8 Katharine J. Sams, Political Thought and Action in the Life of Adam von Trott, 1909–1940, Ph.D. Dissertation (Montreal: McGill University 1999).
9 Ibid., 540–2. The memorandum was published by Hans Rothfels, "Trott und die Aussenpolitik des Widerstandes," *Vierteljahrshefte für Zeitgeschichte* 12 (1964): 300–25, spec. 313–15 (from Trott's typed draft, then in the possession of Julie Braun-Vogelstein in New York), 316–17; Sams uses this publication and the copy from Julie Braun-Vogelstein's papers, now in the Bundesarchiv in Koblenz. Incorrect dating in Rothfels, "Adam von Trott und das State Department," 305, 313, and Christopher Sykes, *Troubled Loyalty. A Biography of Adam von Trott zu Solz*, 314, with consequent misinterpretation of the function of the memorandum in Trott's efforts; equally Klemperer, *German Resistance*, 186 and 212, note 232, incorrectly dating the memo-

randum for Halifax for "late in 1939"; Klemperer could not find it in the Foreign Office files; it is unclear what happened to it: Sams, Political Thought, 547.

10 Sams, Political Thought, 547–9; Hoffmann, "The Question of Western Allied Cooperation with the German Anti-Nazi Conspiracy, 1938–1944," 437–64.

11 Rothfels, "Adam von Trott und das State Department," 318–32.

12 Sams, Political Thought, 570, 572–8; Rothfels, "Adam von Trott," 318–32; Sams, Political Thought, 561–78.

13 Klemperer, *German Resistance*, 182–9, cites a copy of the "Scheffer-Trott Memorandum" in Public Record Office (now The National Archives), Kew, FO 371/34449/C 5218/155/18, reproduced in Rothfels, "Adam von Trott"; Hoffmann, "The Question," 443–51; Callum A. MacDonald, "The Venlo Affair," *European Studies Review* 8 (1978): 443–64.

14 Rothfels, "Adam von Trott," 327.

15 Ibid., 323, 327.

16 Cf. Sams, Political Thought, 572–4.

17 Klemperer, *German Resistance*, 57, 180–9, esp. 185; Sams, Political Thought, 551. In a letter to David Astor, Trott defended himself against the "ill-deserved reputation of an appeaser" who was "out for another Munich"; this may help to explain parts of his memoranda and conversations while in America.

18 Sams, Political Thought, 547.

19 Ibid., 603–11 and 677, note 325, cites Public Record Office (now The National Archives), Kew, FO 71/24363/C1545/267/62 and Rothfels, "Trott und die Aussenpolitik des Widerstandes," *Vierteljahrshefte für Zeitgeschichte* 12 (1964): 316–18.

20 Sams, Political Thought, 610–11.

21 Rothfels, "Trott und die Aussenpolitik," 316.

22 John W. Wheeler-Bennett, "Adam von Trott and Peace Feelers," PRO, FO 371/34449 160116.

23 Klemperer, *German Resistance*, 57, 180–9.

24 Ibid., 268–71 and 299, note 19, cites copies in the archive of the World Council of Churches and Armin Boyens, *Kirchenkampf und Ökumene 1939–1945. Darstellung und Dokumentation unter besonderer Berücksichtigung der Quellen des Ökumenischen Rates der Kirchen* (Munich: C. Kaiser c. 1973), 152–4, 325–6.

25 PRO, FO 371/34449/160116; Klemperer, *German Resistance*, 300, note 34, cites a copy in FO 371/34449/C 5218/155/18.

26 In "Peace Moves Mr Visser 'tHooft," PRO, FO 371/30912/C 5428/48/18; printed in Rothfels, "Zwei aussenpolitische Memoranden der deutschen Opposition (Frühjahr 1942)," 392–5, and Ger van Roon, *Neuordnung im Widerstand. Der Kreisauer Kreis innerhalb der deutschen Widerstandsbewegung*, 572–5; see Klemperer, *German Resistance*, 277–81.

27 Cf. documents 4, 7, and 21; Helmuth James von Moltke, *Letters to Freya 1939–1945*, 229; Klemperer, *German Resistance*, 277–9.

28 Klemperer, *German Resistance*, plate before 241; spelling as ibid.

29 *The Times* (9 May 1942), 5; Eden explicitly refers to Trott's declarations that the Resistance wished to restore the Rechtsstaat.

30 Quoted in Richard Lamb, *The Ghosts of Peace 1935–1945* (Salisbury, England: M. Russel 1987), 283. This may be seen as a reaction to Trott's June 1944 memorandum, at pp. 306–10, this volume.

31 Cf. Hoffmann, *Stauffenberg. A Family History, 1905–1944*, 253–77.

32 Quoted in Lamb, *The Ghosts*, 296–7.

33 Debates, fifth series, vol. 402 (1944), 2 Aug. 1944, col. 1487.

34 Source: Bundesarchiv Koblenz, Nachlass Adam von Trott zu Solz N 1416/31 and N 1416/2; on first page in N 1416/31 MS note "über Charles Bos an Lord Halifax"; on first page in N 1416/2 MS note "Dok. II Denkschrift Adam v. Trott für Lord Halifax (New York, Spätjahr 1939)" by Hans Rothfels who edited the publication of the memorandum with that heading in Rothfels, "Trott und die Aussenpolitik des Widerstandes," *Vierteljahrshefte für Zeitgeschichte* 12 (1964), 313–15. Cf. Sams, Political Thought, 540–2; Rothfels, 305, says only that the document had been in the custody of Julie Braun-Vogelstein in New York but not who had custody of it when he edited it; Rothfels misattributed it to Trott's exclusive authorship; Trott identified himself with the memorandum's contents, but it had been drafted by Paul Scheffer: Sams, Political Thought, 570, 572–8; Rothfels, "Adam von Trott und das State Department," 318–32; Sams, Political Thought, 561–78. The most important primary and secondary sources, in addition to those just listed, are: David Astor, "The German Opposition to Hitler. A Reply to Critics"; Sir Isaiah Berlin, "A Personal Tribute to Adam von Trott (Balliol, 1931)"; Christabel Bielenberg, *The Past is Myself*; C.E. Collins, "Brave against A Tide"; Charles Collins, "Adam von Trott and the German Opposition to Hitler"; Shiela Grant Duff, *The Parting of Ways. A Personal Account of the Thirties;* Hoffmann, *The History of the German Resistance 1933–1945;* Hoffmann, "Oberst i.G. Henning von Tresckow und die Staatsstreichpläne im Jahr 1943"; Klemperer, ed. *A Noble Combat. The Letters of Shiela Grant Duff and Adam von Trott zu Solz 1932–1939;* Klemperer, *German Resistance against Hitler. The Search for Allies Abroad, 1938–1945;* [Clarita von Trott zu Solz], Adam von Trott zu Solz. Eine erste Materialsammlung, Sichtung und Zusammenstellung, mimeographed typescript ([Reinbek 1957]; Clarita von Trott zu Solz, *Adam von Trott zu Solz. An Account;* W.A. Visser 'tHooft, "The View from Geneva"; Hedley Bull, ed., *The Challenge of the Third Reich. The Adam von Trott zu Solz Memorial Lectures*; Henry Ozelle Malone Jr, *Adam von Trott zu Solz: The Road to Conspiracy against Hitler.*

35 "Final warning."

36 These words in parentheses are a MS insertion presumably by Scheffer.

37 Here crossed out: "(by letting in the Russian flood)."

38 MS insertion "personal and human" over crossed-out "religious."

39 MS insertion "The religious forces are" over crossed-out "It too is."

40 Source: Public Record Office (now The National Archives), Kew, FO 371/24363/C1545/267/62 (Sams, 677, note 325); Rothfels, "Trott und die Aussenpolitik," 316–18; "JWB" is in Trott's handwriting; Rothfels, "Trott und die Aussenpolitik," 307.

BEHIND VALKYRIE

41 Cf. for example R.A.C. Parker, *The Second World War*, rev. ed. (Oxford: Oxford University Press 2001), 16, 38.

42 President Woodrow Wilson's peace program proclaimed in his speech to a Joint Session of Congress on 8 January 1918.

43 This point, as several others, conflicted with the policy of the British government as expressed in such phrases as "I didn't see how we could make peace so long as the German military machine remained intact" (the British minister at the Vatican, Sir Francis d'Arcy Osborne, to Lord Halifax, 16 February 1940 in Peter Ludlow, "Papst Pius XII., die britische Regierung und die deutsche Opposition im Winter 1939/40," 337), "complete victory" (Chamberlain in the Supreme War Council meeting of 28 March 1940, in Llewellyn Woodward, *British Foreign Policy in the Second World War*, vol. 1 [London: His Majesty's Stationery Office 1970], 286), and "victory at all costs" (Churchill in the House of Commons on 13 May 1940, in *The Parliamentary Debates, Fifth Series, Volume 345, House of Commons, Official Report, Volume 360* [London: His Majesty's Stationery Office 1940], col. 1501–2).

44 Source: World Council of Churches, Geneva, Library & Archives: Paper, 994.2.07/22: VtH 342a; printed in Boyens, 325–6 from a copy in Archive of the Ecumenical Council of Churches (Geneva), Box WCC ipof VII. Paton was the Reverend William Paton, Secretary of the International Missionary Council, and Associate Secretary General of the World Council of Churches.

45 This sentence is omitted in Boyens, 325.

46 Meaning obscure; error for "killed"?

47 The document has "cauum."

48 The document has no signature; Boyens, 326, inserted "<W. A. Visser 'tHooft>" before "September 1940."

49 Source: Public Record Office (now The National Archives), Kew, FO 371/34449/160116; Klemperer, *German Resistance*, 300, note 34, cites another copy in FO 371/34449/C 5218/155/18. The reproduction here follows the spelling in the document, except for two errors indicated in notes 51 and 53.

50 A. Roland Elliot is the correct name; he was Executive Secretary, Student Division, of the YMCA in New York.

51 The original has the typing error "imprelled."

52 Moelders incident: Air Force Colonel Werner Mölders, ordered to attend the funeral of Air Force General Ernst Udet in Berlin, died on his way there in the crash of an airplane in which he was a passenger on 22 November 1941; these deaths shocked the German public, and rumours were circulating; Nicolaus v. Below, *Als Hitlers Adjutant 1937–45* (Mainz: v. Hase & Koehler Verlag 1980), 295; Joseph Goebbels, *Die Tagebücher. Teil II. Diktate 1941–1945. Band 2. Oktober–Dezember 1941* (Munich, New Providence, London, Paris 1996), 351–2.

53 The original has the typing error "Rechtsstadt."

54 Cf. Hoffmann, "The Question," 437–64.

55 John W. Wheeler-Bennett.

56 Source: Typed memorandum, unsigned, undated, in "Peace Moves Mr Visser 'tHooft," Public Record Office (now The National Archives), Kew, FO 371/30912/C 5428/48/18; Trott handed the memorandum to Willem Visser 'tHooft, Secretary-General of the Ecumenical Council of Churches, in Geneva, shortly before Visser 'tHooft's departure to London, and Visser 'tHooft transmitted the memorandum to Sir Stafford Cripps, who showed it to Churchill; Churchill commented "very encouraging"; the reproduction here follows the spelling of the archive document unless otherwise indicated; introduced in Rothfels, "Zwei aussenpolitische Memoranden der deutschen Opposition (Frühjahr 1942)," 390–2, and printed ibid. 392–5; Rothfels had available for his publication a copy (Abschrift) provided by Visser 'tHooft; cf. Roon, *Neuordnung im Widerstand*, 572–5; see also Pastor Hans Schönfeld's "Statement by a German Pastor at Stockholm, 31st May 1942"; Rothfels, "Zwei aussenpolitische," 395–7; and George Kennedy Allen Bell, in George Cicestr [Bell], "The Background of the Hitler Plot," *The Contemporary Review* (October 1945): 203–8; George Kennedy Allen Bell, *The Church and Humanity (1939–1946)* (London: Longmans Green 1946), 165–7; Klemperer, *German Resistance*, 277–81.

57 Spelling in the document "absorbtion."

58 In the document "potentiallties."

59 In the document "catastrophy."

60 Cf. Moltke, document no. 21.

61 Cf. Moltke, document no. 4.

62 "We" indicates, as is already apparent, that Trott is speaking also for the Kreisau group.

63 Cf. Goerdeler, no. 16.

64 Source: Copy in Bundesarchiv, Koblenz, Nachlass Adam von Trott N 1416/2; this appears to be a xerox of the copy with MS corrections in Trott's hand in Archive of the Nordic Ecumenical Institute, Sigtuna, Sweden; introduced and printed in Henrik Lindgren, "Adam von Trotts Reisen nach Schweden 1942-1944 – Ein Beitrag zur Frage der Auslandsverbindungen des deutschen Widerstands," 274–91; the copy that is considered to have reached the British government could not be found in the Foreign Office files: Klemperer, *German Resistance*, 408, note 178. The reproduction here follows the spelling of the document, including inconsistencies, unless otherwise annotated; Lindgren does not mention Trott's many MS changes and insertions.

65 "then" inserted in Trott's handwriting.

66 "strong enough" inserted in Trott's handwriting.

67 The document has "arbitraryness."

68 Cf. Henry Morgenthau, *Germany Is Our Problem* (New York: Harper & Brothers 1945); *Foreign Relations of the United States. The Conference at Quebec 1944* (Washington: United States Printing Office 1972), 390.

69 The document has "meat."

70 The document has "indispensible."

71 "to" inserted in Trott's handwriting over crossed-out "by"; "the" amended in Trott's handwriting as "them."

72 This paragraph is inserted, typed, at the bottom of the page.

73 The document has "Hitlers."

74 "demobilisation" inserted in Trott's handwriting over crossed-out "procedure."

75 "in cooperation with Allied control commissions" inserted in Trott's handwriting at the bottom of the page.

76 "this opposition group" inserted in Trott's handwriting over crossed-out "the more serious type of an alternative leadership in Germany."

77 "In order" inserted in Trott's handwriting.

78 "control" inserted in Trott's handwriting.

79 "senior" inserted in Trott's handwriting.

80 "Oberkommando" inserted in Trott's handwriting over crossed-out "High command of both field and home forces."

81 "sections" inserted in Trott's handwriting over crossed-out "parts."

82 "the Ordnungspolizei" inserted in Trott's handwriting over crossed-out "administrative."

83 "the" inserted in Trott's handwriting.

84 "authorities of several of the larger cities" inserted in Trott's handwriting.

85 After "unwilling," the words "and unable" are crossed out.

86 The document has "Hitlers."

87 The document has "unders."

88 "compased" corrected in Trott's handwriting to "compared."

89 "counteract the" inserted in Trott's handwriting.

90 The document has "irresistible."

91 The document has "acrue."

92 Crossed out: "however desirable and helpful it eventually be," with "eventually" in Trott's handwriting.

93 The document has "unmanagable."

94 "bring to a head their already advanced preparations" inserted in Trott's handwriting.

95 Corrected by hand from "relably."

96 "in time" after "system" is crossed out.

97 The document has "Hitlers."

98 Either the Resistance was largely ignorant of the fairly elaborate Allied preparations for the post-war administration of Germany, or, more likely, Trott tried to have the Resistance seize the initiative.

99 "all depends" inserted in Trott's handwriting.

100 "democratic" inserted in Trott's handwriting.

101 The document has "burocracy" in Trott's handwriting over crossed-out "administration."

102 "their own" inserted in Trott's handwriting.

103 "of a different kind" crossed out.

104 "through neutral countries" inserted in Trott's handwriting.

105 "attitude of the Allies" inserted in Trott's handwriting over crossed-out "international position."

106 "they feel" inserted in Trott's handwriting.

107 "and around" crossed out.

108 "many different and precarious circumstances" inserted in Trott's handwriting over crossed-out "a kind and number of hazards."

109 "the opposition" inserted in Trott's handwriting over crossed-out "it."

110 "act" inserted in Trott's handwriting.

111 "provided that some qualification of the term 'unconditional surrender' is forthcoming" added in Trott's handwriting.

112 "only" inserted in Trott's handwriting.

113 "othe" corrected by "of" in Trott's handwriting over crossed-out "o."

114 "appear to bar" inserted in Trott's handwriting over crossed-out "have been shown to lie in."

115 "to" inserted in Trott's handwriting over crossed-out "of."

MILITARY RESISTANCE

24

Claus Schenk Graf von Stauffenberg
to His Father, April 1926

Claus Schenk Graf von Stauffenberg (15 November 1907–20 July 1944), son of Alfred Schenk Graf von Stauffenberg, Lord Chamberlain to King William II of Württemberg, joined a cavalry regiment in 1926 and became a career and general-staff officer.[1] He served in an armoured division in the Polish and French campaigns in 1939 and 1940. From the beginning of June 1940, he was a section head in the Army High Command. From 15 February 1943 he served as senior staff officer in the 10th Panzer Division in Tunesia until he was severely wounded in combat on 7 April, losing his right hand, two fingers on the other hand, and an eye. He recovered and served in the Home Army High Command. His career prospects were brilliant; in the summer of 1944 he was due for promotion to general rank. On 20 July 1944 he placed a briefcase with explosives next to Hitler during a briefing in Hitler's Wolf's Lair headquarters in East Prussia, flew back to Berlin, and launched Operation "Valkyrie" to overthrow Hitler and the National Socialist regime. Since the explosion had not killed Hitler, the coup collapsed, and the leaders, including Stauffenberg, were shot during the night of 20/21 July 1944. Some 700 were arrested in connection with the coup; about 180 of them were hanged.[2]

In August 1942 Stauffenberg had told a fellow general-staff officer that his motives for attempting to assassinate Hitler were the criminal policies of the regime, "the treatment of the population [in the Soviet Union] by the German civil administration, the lack of political planning for the occupied countries, the treatment of the Jews." Therefore, he said, the war was a monstrous crime, and Hitler, the chief criminal, must be forcibly removed.[3]

Before Stauffenberg graduated from secondary school in Stuttgart in 1926, he had considered a career as an architect. This was at the time of the military occupation by French and Belgian forces of Germany's industrial heartland on the Ruhr in January 1923. At the time, Stauffenberg was much influenced by poetry and the arts; he did not enjoy very robust health; and, while his elder brothers Berthold and Alexander volunteered for military service, Claus was too young.

The document below, as do also documents nos. 26, 27, and 28 in this volume, illustrates Stauffenberg's convictions of human decency, public service, and family honour as the chief motivations for his idealism.

Bamberg Tuesday[4]
[27 April 1926]

My Father!

Many· many thanks for your letter· to my dismay I hear that Duli[5] has broken her foot· I hope that it is nothing serious. The death of Otto Tessin[6] grieves me very much· especially when I think how your best friends are passing away: Stuttgart is changing more and more. – That the first years of my profession would not be very pleasant was always clear to me: it is after all not easy for one of us to act the commoner for a long time and to forgo all things intellectual almost completely· perhaps it is not easy either to keep focusing on the more ideal goals and motivations· the consciousness of which would make the unbearable bearable. I am now, as I was before, convinced that my decision was right, and if only the smallest hint of a benefit can accrue to the fatherland when more intellectual persons make themselves available (not merely the sporting and those who seek military service because they are keen on steel helmets and marching) I am richly rewarded for the sacrifice of a few years of my youth. Your confidence and acceptance of my choice· like that of my brothers and friends is infinitely valuable to me in this respect since I myself indeed easily tend towards pessimism with regard to the future we have to live through· not, however, that I lacked self-confidence! I thank you for your advice: I am in any case exceedingly cautious and reserved with people who do not possess my full confidence· my real self is in fact no one else's concern.

On 6 June we go to Grafenwöhr.[7] I do not yet know anything for certain about leave at Whitsuntide· if you can send me 50 marks for this month I can get by well for leave and purchases· if it is now inconvenient to you it will be all right. Please send me pictures: I was thinking of the two Dürer engravings in our room· also Berthold could select some of their pictures brought back from Italy· then also photographs of Duli· Berth. Alex and us together with you[.] I have one of you. Thanks for the laundry basket.

Kiss Duli and tell her to get well. Regards to Mika.

I most cordially kiss your hand

your grateful son

Claus.

Money please in registered sealed letter

NOTES

1 See Peter Hoffmann, *Stauffenberg. A Family History, 1905–1944.*

2 Peter Hoffmann, *The History of the German Resistance*, 712–13, note 21; 719–20, note 25.

3 Peter Hoffmann, "Major Joachim Kuhn: Explosives Purveyor to Stauffenberg and Stalin's Prisoner," *German Studies Review* 28 (2005): 521; see document no. 27.

4 Source: MS, ink-pencil, editor's archive; Stauffenberg used Stefan George's script, spelling, and punctuation; German in Hoffmann, *Claus Schenk Graf von Stauffenberg. Die Biographie*, 486.

5 The Stauffenberg brothers' nickname for their mother.

6 Colonel (Ret.) Otto Freiherr von Tessin, Royal Chamberlain in Württemberg.

7 Military training grounds near Hof.

25

Lieutenant-General Ludwig Beck's Coup Preparations, July 1938

In his last two years in office as Chief of the General Staff of the Army, Lieutenant-General Beck focused his energies upon the prevention of war. His publication in March 1937 of General Carl von Clausewitz's letter of 22 December 1827, with his warning against misuse of the military instrument, his refusal to lay plans for an intervention in Austria, his warnings to the French and British governments in June 1937, his insistence that peaceful means to address Germany's vital interests were available and had not been exhausted all served the same purpose. On 5 November 1937 Hitler convened a meeting of the War Minister, Field Marshal Werner von Blomberg; the Commander-in-Chief of the Army, General Werner Freiherr von Fritsch; Grand Admiral Erich Raeder, Commander-in-Chief of the Navy; General Hermann Göring, Commander-in-Chief of the Air Force; and Konstantin Freiherr von Neurath, the Foreign Minister, in the Reich Chancellery, and spoke to them at length about his plans to conquer Czechoslovakia, to annex Austria, and generally to expand German Lebensraum. Blomberg, Fritsch, Neurath, and even Göring raised objections, but Hitler was undeterred. Hitler's Wehrmacht aide, Colonel (General Staff) Friedrich Hossbach, communicated the substance of the meeting to Beck.[1] On 12 November, Beck noted that Hitler's statements revealed a shocking ignorance: France's and Britain's opposition to an expansion of German space must not be considered immutable before peaceful means had been exhausted.[2] On 19 November, Lord Halifax, Anthony Eden's designated successor as the British Secretary of State for Foreign Affairs, visited Hitler at Berchtesgaden with the message that Britain would not oppose revisions of the Treaty of Versailles concerning Danzig, Austria, Czechoslovakia, colonies, and armaments, provided any revisions resulted from friendly negotiations.[3] This only emboldened Hitler. On 13 December 1937, Hitler approved a directive for an unprovoked attack upon Czechoslovakia; Blomberg issued it on 21 December 1937.[4] On 14 December 1937, Beck noted that the planned peacetime German army would not be ready before 1 October 1942 and that a wartime army could not be ready before 1 April 1943.[5] Beck believed that France would honour her alliance obligations to Czechoslovakia, that Britain would support France, and that Britain herself would not lack allies. He resolved to demonstrate, through a General Staff exercise, that German forces might succeed in a campaign against Czechia but would lose a war against the western powers.[6] From then on, in a series of memoranda of increasing urgency dated 5 May, 29 May, 3 June, 15 July, 16 July, 19 July, and 29 July 1938, Beck impressed upon the Commander-in-Chief of the Army, General von Brauchitsch, that the Czech question could be resolved peacefully if Germany accepted conditions that Britain could support, but that if Germany attempted an aggression against Czechia, then France, Britain, the Soviet Union, and ultimately the United States would intervene and prosecute "a war to the death against Germany."[7] Beck requested that the Commander-in-Chief of the Army prevail upon "the Supreme Commander of the Wehrmacht [Hitler] to halt the war preparations he has ordered and to postpone his proposed solution of the Czech question by force until the military conditions for it have changed radically."[8]

Beck's dissent was noticed by foreign diplomatic envoys in Berlin. The British Military Attaché, Colonel F. Noel Mason-Macfarlane, reported "outspoken criticism of Nazi Party by General Beck at a small dinner party" at General Beck's on 18 January 1938. "2 I had a long talk with the General after dinner. He spoke in very general terms, but made no effort to disguise the fact that he views many of the activities of the Government with profound mistrust and disapproval. He was particularly emphatic on the evil which is accruing from the Government's Economic policy and its treatment of the religious question. 3 In discussing the general world situation on very broad and superficial lines, the General expressed his profound concern over the trend of events and became quite despondent."[9]

Briefing notes 16 July 38[10]

The Führer apparently considers inevitable a solution by force of the Sudeten German question by invading Czechia; he is confirmed in this view by an entourage of irresponsible, radical elements. Opinions are divided regarding Göring's position. Some believe that he recognizes the seriousness of the situation and is attempting to have a calming influence upon the Führer; others think that he is playing a duplicitous game, as in the case of Blomberg and Fritsch, and will cave in when he faces the Führer.

All upright and serious German men in positions of responsibility in the state must feel called upon and duty-bound to use all conceivable means and ways down to the ultimate consequence, in order to avert a war against Czechia, which in its consequences must lead to a world war, which would mean finis Germaniae.

The most senior leaders of the armed forces are called and qualified for this first and foremost, because the armed forces are the executive instrument of force of the state leadership in the prosecution of a war.

The ultimate decisions about the existence of the nation are at stake here; history will indict these commanders of blood guilt if they do not act according to their professional and political knowledge and conscience.

The soldier's duty to obey ends when his knowledge, his conscience, and his sense of responsibility forbid him to carry out a certain order.

If their [the military commanders'] advice and warnings in such a situation are not heard, then they have the right and the duty before the nation and before history to resign from their posts.

If they all act thus with a common will, the execution of an act of war will be impossible. They will have thereby protected their Fatherland from the worst, from its ruin.

It is a lack of greatness and of a comprehension of the task if a soldier in the highest position in such times only sees his duties and tasks confined to his military instructions, without becoming conscious of the highest responsibility before the entire nation.

Extraordinary times require extraordinary actions!

Other upright men in positions of responsibility in the state outside the armed forces will join them on their way.

If one keeps one's eyes and ears open, if one does not deceive oneself with false figures, if one does not live in the intoxication of an ideology, then one can come only to the realization that, in military-political terms (leadership, training, and equipment), in economic terms, and in terms of public opinion, we are *not* prepared for war at this time.

The thought of a "Blitzkrieg" (in Prague after two days?) is a non-sensical dream; one should have learned from the history of modern warfare that ambush-like surprises have hardly ever led to lasting success.

Our preparations (west) are or will be so clearly recognizable that preventive measures by the enemy will have to be reckoned with. The war propaganda in the foreign press has already begun (Article Konrad-Reichenau-Pierre Cot).[11]

In the case the objections of men with standing were to succeed in preventing war, considerable internal political tensions [would] have to be reckoned with.

The radical side will declare that the execution of the Führer's intentions failed because of the incompetence of the armed forces and its commanders. Renewed and intensified defamations will begin. It will be necessary to keep a vigilant eye and ear.

The Führer is said to have declared in a small gathering: I must conduct the war against Czechia with the old generals; the war against England and France I shall conduct with a new group of commanders.

It will therefore be necessary to take a decision to bring about a clarifying showdown between the armed forces and the SS immediately with or subsequently to a protest.

It would also be appropriate at the same time to give a brutally clear description of the true opinions of the people, which very essentially have been called into being by the rising rule of bigwigs in the Third Reich.

Concerning the timing of these measures:

One can probably expect that in the course of the summer months (August) an English and French note will arrive, perhaps still in a conciliatory tone, which will be followed after a certain interval by one written in the form of an ultimatum that will no longer allow the leadership of state any room for evasion or yielding, if the opponent does not take preventive measures regardless.

Consequently, the timing – *immediately after arrival* of the first note – appears as the most favourable one for any measures.

Finally, one other consideration may be suggested: whether one ought not consciously to take the position that the Führer's current attitude and the measures he ordered are to be seen only as an intended great bluff vis-à-vis the opponent, and whether one ought not to adapt one's conduct to this: i.e., that one cannot believe that the measures ordered are really intended to lead to war, but that one considers them only an ingenious bluff.

This position, however, could mean playing a dangerous game.

[signed] B

Addendum on 19 July 1938

If a démarche in the form of an objection with all of its consequences is decided upon, and if thereby the outbreak of a war can still be prevented, the question must be explored whether one ought not to activate this step to bring about a showdown with the SS and the party bosses, which is unavoidable in order to restore law and order.

Probably for the last time, fate offers the opportunity to free the German nation and the Führer himself from the nightmare of a Cheka and from the manifestations of party bigwigism, which, by influencing the attitude of the people, will destroy the existence and the welfare of the Reich and enable communism to revive.

In this regard, the following points of view, among others, must be prominent:

1 There can and must be no doubt that this struggle is conducted for the Führer.
2 Upright and capable men of the Party must be informed in factual terms of the seriousness of the situation, must be convinced of the necessity of such a step and to support it. E.g. Gauleiter Wagner[12] in Silesia, Reichsstatthalter Bürckel[13] in Vienna.

The Army Group Commander in Vienna[14] and the Commanding General of VIIIth Army Corps[15] (on the occasion of the track-and-field games in Breslau) could be employed for this.

There must not arise the slightest suspicion of a plot and yet the most senior military leaders must *stand united* behind this step under all circumstances. Such generals will also be found in the air force.

Short, clear slogans:

For the Führer!
Against the war!
Against the tyranny of the Party bosses!
Peace with the church!
Freedom of expression!
Away with Cheka methods!
The rule of law in the Reich restored!
Reduction of all levies by half!
No building of palaces!

Housing for the people!
Prussian simplicity and honesty!

[signed] B

Briefing notes of 29 July 1938

The interview with W.[16] on 28 July 1938 corresponded in all essential points to the tenets in the briefing notes of 16 July 1938 and the addendum of 19 July 1938.

The Führer continues to insist that a war must be prosecuted against Czechia, even if France and England intervene, which he does not actually expect. The time appears to have passed for dissuading him from this view through factual reasons and warnings, or at least that has become considerably more difficult. Apparently he is confirmed in his view only by Ribbentrop (who then speaks of the dynamism of the Third Reich) and in the second place by Himmler, insofar as the latter is at all consulted on such issues.

W. asserts once more that Göring is in no way one of the warmongers, as recent conversations with him are said to indicate.

Therefore it is becoming ever more urgent to examine the question if and when the Commander-in-Chief of the Army with the generals of the Army united behind him (army group commanders and [army corps] commanding generals) confront the Führer and declare to him in the most pointed form that we are currently not prepared for a war against Czechia and its consequences in terms military (leadership, training, and equipment), economic, particularly however financially, and in terms of public opinion. This fact has been repeatedly substantiated in detail by competent military persons, without any success. The Commander-in-Chief of the Army together with his most senior commanding generals regret that they cannot assume responsibility for the conduct of a war of this nature without incurring a share of the guilt for it before the nation and before history. They will therefore resign from their posts, should the Führer insist on the prosecution of this war.

The form of this declaration cannot be made in impressive, hard, and brutal enough terms.

The suitable timing for this démarche probably will be the second half of September. By then the intoxication of the Party Convention will have abated. Moreover, the arrival of notes from the French and British governments may be expected from August, which will produce greater clarity about the situation.

At the same time, the Minister of Finance will have to launch a similar démarche, since the situation of the Treasury will force him to do so at that time.

Halifax asked W., when he was taking his leave, to give the Führer regards and declared that for him it would be the finest conclusion of his life if he saw Hitler, at the side of the King of England, enter London greeted enthusiastically by the people. That phrase was actually suggested by Princess Hohenlohe, but in any case formulated impressively.

Halifax remarked further that it ought to be possible to induce the Führer to a declaration that the Czech Question, having presented a problem in Europe for centuries, would not be solved violently in a short span of time.

W. hardly thought it possible that such a declaration would be made.

W. had no sort of brief to deliver a message in London, but had merely received from the Führer instructions for his conduct.

While the Führer had been quite approachable in his interview with Wiedemann before the latter's departure, he was brusquely rejecting at the report after his return.

As indicated in the briefing notes of 16 July 1938, internal tensions have to be reckoned with in any case; it will therefore be necessary for the Army to be prepared, not only for a potential war, but also for an internal showdown at home, which needs to take place only in Berlin. Issue orders accordingly. Get Witzleben[17] together with Helldorf.[18]

[signed] B

NOTES

1 *Documents on German Foreign Policy, 1918–1945. From the Archives of the German Foreign Ministry, Series D*, vol. 1, no. 19 (London: His Majesty's Stationery Office 1949), 29–39; Friedrich Hossbach, *Zwischen Wehrmacht und Hitler 1934–1938* (Wolfenbüttel: Wolfenbütteler Verlag 1949), 181–92.

2 Klaus-Jürgen Müller, *General Ludwig Beck. Studien und Dokumente zur politisch-militärischen Vorstellungswelt und Tätigkeit des Generalstabschefs des deutschen Heeres 1933–1938*, 498–501 (doc. no. 43).

3 *Akten zur deutschen auswärtigen Politik 1918–1945. Serie D (1937–1945) (ADAP D)*; The Earl of Birkenhead, *Halifax. The Life of Lord Halifax* (London: Hamish Hamilton 1965), 368–74.

4 *ADAP D*, vol. VII, 1956, Anhang III K, 547–51; Jodl diary 13 Dec. 1937, *Trial of the Major War Criminals before the International Military Tribunal Nuremberg 14 November 1945–1 October 1946*, vol. 28 (Nuremberg 1948), 355–6.

5 Müller, *General Ludwig Beck*, 266.

6 Ibid., 500 (doc. no. 43); Beck's memorandum for Fritsch of 3 June 1938, MS draft in Bundesarchiv-Militärarchiv, Freiburg i.Br. (BA-MA), N 28/3; Müller, *General Ludwig Beck*, 528–37 (doc. no. 47); BA-MA Wi/IF 5.1502.

7 Beck's MS notes and drafts in BA-MA N 28/4; Müller, *General Ludwig Beck*, 502–12, 521–60 (docs. no. 44, 46–52). In March and September 1938, the British Chiefs of Staff advised Prime Minister Neville Chamberlain (and acted responsibly in "military-political" matters, as Beck demanded that the Chief of the General Staff must do) "that no pressure that we and our possible Allies can bring to bear, either by sea, or land, or in the air, could prevent Germany from invading and overrunning Bohemia and from inflicting a decisive defeat on the Czechoslovakian Army." The object of restoring Czechoslovakia's lost integrity "would only be achieved by the defeat of Germany and as the outcome of a prolonged struggle." If such a struggle were to occur in the current world situation, it was "more than probable that both Italy and Japan would seize the opportunity to further their own ends, and that in consequence the problem we have to envisage is not that of a limited European war only, but of a world war." N.H. Gibbs, *Grand Strategy, Volume I: Rearmament Policy*, 642.

8 Müller, *General Ludwig Beck*, 549 (doc. no. 49).

9 Public Record Office (now UK National Archives), Kew, FO 371/21660/C 580/62/18.

10 Source: Bundesarchiv-Militärarchiv, Freiburg i.Br., N 28/4. The principal primary and secondary sources in print are: Müller, *The Army, Politics and Society in Germany, 1933–45*; Müller, *Generaloberst Ludwig Beck. Eine Biographie*; Nicholas Reynolds, *Treason Was No Crime. Ludwig Beck, Chief of the German General Staff*.

11 "Konrad" may be Colonel (GS) Rudolf Konrad in XVIII Army Corps command at Salzburg. Lieutenant-General Walter von Reichenau was the Commander of Army Group Command 4 in Leipzig. Pierre Cot (1895–1976) was a French politician (radical socialist), Air Transport Minister 1933–34 and 1936–38, as well as Trade Minister in 1938; he advocated a hard line against Hitler's policies and opposed the government's "Munich Policy."

12 Josef Wagner, 1898–1945, a miner's son, a Catholic, former school teacher, 1928 NSDAP Gauleiter of Westphalia, 1935 Gauleiter of Silesia, 1938 Oberpräsident (governor) of Upper and Lower Silesia, Reich Prices Commissioner under the Four Year Plan, January 1941 resigned as Gauleiter and Oberpräsident; in October 1942, he was expelled from the NSDAP, in part because his wife opposed the marriage of their daughter to a member of Hitler's SS bodyguard regiment who was not a member of the Church; probably murdered by the SS at the end of the war. See Peter Hüttenberger, *Die Gauleiter. Studie zum Wandel des Machtgefüges in der NSDAP*; Karl Höffkes, *Hitlers politische Generale. Die Gauleiter des Dritten Reiches. Ein biographisches Nachschlagewerk*.

13 Josef Bürckel, 1895–1944, a labourer's son, a former school teacher, 1926 NSDAP Gauleiter of Rheinpfalz, 1935 Saarpfalz, 1939–40 Vienna. See Höffkes, *Hitlers politische*; Hüttenberger, *Die Gauleiter*.

14 Lieutenant-General Wilhelm List.

15 Lieutenant-General (Am.) Ernst Busch. Cf. Müller, *Das Heer und Hitler. Armee und nationalsozialistisches Regime 1933–1940*, 335–6.

16 Captain Fritz Wiedemann, Hitler's Personal Aide.

17 Lieutenant-General Erwin von Witzleben, Commanding IIIrd Army Corps (Berlin).

18 Wolf Heinrich, Count von Helldorf, Berlin President of Police.

19 See note 1.

26

Captain Claus Schenk Graf von Stauffenberg to Brigadier Georg von Sodenstern, February–March 1939

Cavalry Captain Claus Schenk Graf von Stauffenberg wrote to Brigadier Georg von Sodenstern, Chief of the General Staff of Army Group 2 at Frankfurt on Main, to express support for views Sodenstern had set out in an article on "The Essence of Being a Soldier" in the *Militärwissenschaftliche Rundschau* of January 1939, which was edited in the 7th Section of the General Staff of the Army. The French military periodical *Cyrano* said Sodenstern had openly taken a position against the National Socialist ideological infiltration of the Army. Stauffenberg had to phrase carefully what he could not say in plain words in the police-state conditions of Hitler's Germany.[1]

Wuppertal-Barmen, 6.2.39[2]
Lönsstr. 25.

Highly esteemed General!

As a reader of the *Militärwissenschaftliche Rundschau,* may I be permitted to express, Sir, the gratitude of a younger man for the essay "On the essence of being a soldier." Not that the General's words had presented us with something new or unknown, for it would be a sad thing if we based ourselves – even if unconsciously – so little upon the permanent foundations of the soldier's ethos; nor is something aroused here that made us see for the first time a great question of our era, for every soldier who is worth a mention must today constantly strive, with open eyes or instinctively, after the guiding thoughts in the General's essay; your ideas are expressed so felicitously, with the honourable fire of our martial profession, and at the same time with such sharply measured intellectual clarity, that they help drown out the always audible clamour of our day. It is this that moves me, Sir, to write this letter of thanks.

I know well how unbecoming it is in me to address "praise" or "approval" to the General. All the more do I hope that the General will receive these lines as the thanks of a junior who was in harmony with the General's words and who wants "to be led by men whose bearing commands his respect,"
and who remains ever
the General's
obedient
Graf Stauffenberg.
Captain (Cav.).

Wuppertal, 13.3.39[3]

Highly esteemed General!

An answer from the General to my letter is more than I had expected. I must be all the more grateful for the General's kind letter in that it again addresses *the*[4] question that ought, more than any other, to arouse the whole officer corps and particularly those in my cohorts, whom one could call the "link in the chain"; and which – I verily believe – consciously or unconsciously, clear-sightedly or rather more dimly, does stir them emotionally.

In the phrase about the danger "of the universalization of the soldier's life into something commonplace," the General has put his finger on the critical point – the position of the military and its responsible support, the officer corps, in the life of the nation – with such precision that, in view of the further deductions the General has made,[5] to address a personal assurance and a general request by the younger officer to the older, and in this I am assuredly not speaking only for myself.

The request: at the end of your letter, Sir, you express the fear that the admonitions of a generation that obviously provides the leadership of today's Armed Forces no longer find the right echo among the young. I know that, coming from the General's mouth, this does not signify resignation, as is already proved by the publication in the *Rundschau*. But the General will perhaps understand that I see here an inchoate distancing from the younger generation that must ultimately end by hampering the active effectiveness of the very men who represent that great heritage – the men who have been purged of the dross of the merely conventional, the mere superficial everyday appearances, by the trial of the World War they fought through. I have encountered essentially the same attitude several times, and particularly among the officers of whom – the General will not take this to be an inappropriate value judgment! – we younger ones are accustomed to say, "a splendid soldier, a true leader"! This attitude is more than comprehensible in face of the widely propagated and idolized losing of the self in the masses. But if there is any danger that the confidence in the absolute validity of the aristocratic foundation of the soldier's concept of the state and life, the validity that spans the most diverse eras, may be lost to its best-qualified spokesmen and transmitters, then the crisis of which the General speaks and in which we already find ourselves becomes a grave danger.

No doubt we too, the officer corps, have already had to pay our tribute to the masses, and we ourselves have already partly become mass, at least in the younger generation: a mass with all its suffocating dangers, but also with its weaknesses. If some of us – even if we are imperceptibly few in number – succeed in awakening the incorruptible perception of the genuine and essential, and confirm the immortal bearing of the officer and gentleman, then we shall have won half the battle.

In this connection another thing is close to my heart. Although I am rather suspicious of the catchword "total," and although this catchword has been misused everywhere in our military environment, it is highly appropriate to the concept of the officer. We cannot afford to withdraw into the purely military, meaning purely professional environment, although the best of us are particularly inclined to do so in view of the situation and because of the tremendous effectiveness of forces outside our ranks that have expanded the Reich and put us in the saddle, seemingly by themselves, without any contribution from us. To be a soldier, especially a military leader, an officer, means to be a servant of the state, to be part of the state, and that includes overall responsibility. The sense of this must not be lost. To preserve and teach this comprehensive concept of the soldier's mission seems to me today our greatest task. What can be accomplished by an unshakable faith and a focussed determination that does not shy away from anything: that is before all our eyes. That we or our sons and grandsons should not have to begin anew here; that the link should not be broken here; that a generation that has not allowed itself to be distracted from the essence of being a soldier by the superficialities of the pre-war era, or by four years of war, or by the dislocations and confusions of the post-war era should not deny itself: that is my request. I believe my line of thinking is sufficiently consistent to allow a judgment of what this means: we must know not only how to fight for the Army itself, no, we must fight for our nation, for the state itself, in the knowledge that the military forces and its pillar, the officer corps, represent the most essential support of the state and the true embodiment of the nation.

I may hope not to be misunderstood by the General as I naturally often am by others: I am not concerned with this or that point of view, nor with opposition arising from personal background or education or profession, only with the Reich. For however one may twist and turn things, in the end, in the great battle, the national battle that will decide upon the existence or non-existence of the nation, responsibility will fall to the military forces; whether or not we are "reserved" today, in the true fateful moments no political or other organization could relieve us of so much as an iota of responsibility. Again, if today's propaganda slogan, to the effect that we failed to "toe the line" sufficiently before the Munich Agreement, seems to be justified, it must nonetheless be said that the caution displayed by a large part of the officer corps, while it was surely politically inexpedient, actually corresponded to a very true inner instinct. And if it revealed a disharmony between political leadership and its resonance in the military forces, then perhaps it was due less to a lack of true soldierly attitudes among the officer corps than to the fact that the position of the officer corps within the state is purely professional and task-oriented, since the political leadership had not managed to concede to it the indispensable measure of confidence and co-responsibility that is, after all, indispensable for the leadership of the nation in arms, which will as ever fall to it in war.

The assurance of which I spoke at the beginning, Sir, is really contained in the preceding. It means the will, in spite of all dubious appearances and in spite of the nearly overwhelming force of a contrary line of development, to fight for the whole and not for a part. It

means faith in a generation of leaders and teachers who represent for us more than merely the embodiment of a venerable tradition.
With German Greeting[6] I am
the General's ever
grateful and obedient
Graf Stauffenberg.

NOTES

1 See Peter Hoffmann, *Claus Schenk Graf von Stauffenberg*, 107–10.
2 Source: Bundesarchiv-Militärarchiv, Freiburg i.Br., Sodenstern Papers, N 594, MS, ink; for the German, see Hoffmann, *Stauffenberg*, 487–90; cf. Hoffmann, *Stauffenberg* (English ed.), 107–10.
3 Ibid.
4 Underlined in MS.
5 There are words missing in Stauffenberg's sentence here, perhaps "I beg."
6 An approved substitute for "Heil Hitler."

27

Major Claus Schenk Graf von Stauffenberg on War Crimes, August 1942

In the months following 20 July 1944, the arrested conspirators were questioned about their attitude to the National Socialist racial policies. Some said they had supported limitations upon the influence of Jews in the professions, in the media, and in the cultural fields, but disagreed with the regime's methods. Others merely declared the persecution of the Jews too harsh. Berthold Graf Stauffenberg said to his interrogators in the days before his execution that he and his brother Claus had initially approved of the greater part of National Socialist internal policies, among them "the racial principle." But he meant nothing more sinister than to deprecate racial mixing, for he concluded that "the fundamental ideas of National Socialism had in practice all been perverted into their opposites."[1]

Some combined their condemnations of the regime's actions with the concession that they had initially greeted the National Socialists with approval; others honestly revealed their personal anti-Jewish bias while condemning the regime's crimes.[2] Some of the interrogators endeavoured to help their charges in exchange for exculpatory affidavits after the Allied victory.[3] Given that there was much that was suppressed or bent to suit the situation, the comprehensive conclusion the Gestapo reached and submitted to Hitler is the more remarkable. The summary of the Secret State Police investigation on this subject, written at the end of October 1944, after more than three months of cruel interrogations and torture of approximately 700 persons arrested in connection with the conspiracy, reached a shattering conclusion. On 28 October 1944, the Gestapo

reported: "The entire inner alienation from the ideas of National Socialism that characterized the men of the reactionary conspiratorial circle expresses itself above all in their position on the Jewish Question. [...] they
stubbornly take the liberal position of granting to the Jews in principle the
same status as to every German."[4]

In the first months of the campaign against the Soviet Union in 1941,
Stauffenberg's attention was drawn to the crimes committed by SS and
police units behind the front lines. Only weeks after the beginning of
the campaign in the summer of 1941, Stauffenberg asked 2nd Lieutenant
Walther Bussmann, in the High-Command Quartermaster War Administration Branch, "to collect everything that implicated the SS." Bussmann
informed Stauffenberg, from the summer months of 1941, of the reports
of the mobile killing forces (Einsatzgruppen), and Stauffenberg saw the figures of those killed that these forces reported and that ran to hundreds of
thousands.[5] As German operations against the Red Army, after spectacular
initial successes, began to falter and, in autumn 1941, the situation became
precarious, Stauffenberg's energies were absorbed by the desperate efforts
of the General Staff to keep the front supplied. From the beginning of 1942,
Stauffenberg's verdicts against the mass murder of the Jews accumulated.
In a conversation with a fellow general-staff officer in April 1942, Stauffenberg expressed his outrage at the mass murder of Jews and non-Jews and
the mass starvation of Soviet prisoners of war in German custody – two
million had died before 28 February 1942. A similar conversation is recorded for May 1942, when Stauffenberg received an eye-witness account
of a mass killing. In August 1942, Stauffenberg told a fellow general-staff
officer, suddenly and out of context: "They are shooting Jews in masses.
These crimes must not be allowed to continue." During a night in the same
month, at the General-Staff Headquarters compound near Vynnitsa in
Ukraine, Stauffenberg had a conversation with another general-staff officer
and co-worker, Captain Joachim Kuhn, about the subject. Kuhn recorded
this conversation in Soviet captivity in August 1944.[6]

Major Joachim Kuhn Quoting
Major Claus Schenk Graf von Stauffenberg[7]

If one can give any meaning to a war of aggression, then it is this:
that it shall clear the way for a policy that will be fruitful for the largest possible part of mankind.

The daily staff reports about the treatment of the population by the German civil administration, the lack of political planning for the occupied countries, the treatment of the Jews prove that Hitler falsely claimed that he was conducting the war for the reorganization of Europe.

Therefore this war is monstrous; if it is also conducted in such manner that for operational and organizational reasons it cannot even be won, then it is to be termed a senseless crime, quite apart from the fact that from the moment when we made the mistake of attacking Russia, Germany could not sustain it in terms of personnel or materiel, even with the best leadership. But merely remarking this will not do. One must firstly ask about the ultimate cause and secondly about the consequence. Ultimate cause lies, I am now quite clear about this, in the Führer's person and in National Socialism. Consequence is to ask[8] what the German General Staff must do in consequence of this situation. As a General-Staff officer and soldier who has to some extent already made a name for himself [Stauffenberg was considered "the coming man" in OKH[9]], I believe to have the right and the duty, to search for precisely that. The General Staff is not a congregation of trained craftsmen, but it is decisively taking part in leadership. "To lead" means also to bear responsibility and to make one's active influence felt. Influence upon what? If the war can no longer be won, this can only be influence upon the preservation of the German people. That is only possible through the speediest conclusion of peace, now, while we still have our strength. Have we made our influence felt thus far other than through criticism and words? No! So our thinking, day and night, has to be directed upon this our only duty today – as long as it is not yet too late.

On 3 February 1943, Stauffenberg added in a conversation with Kuhn:[10] "The consequence about which we often asked is the establishment of a temporary military dictatorship." And in May 1943, while recovering from having been severely wounded in Tunisia, he clarified:[11] "The successful struggle against National Socialism and its fanatical theories and aims, thus the way to the preservation of the people, goes only through the removal of Hitler's person and of what surrounds him."

NOTES

1 *Spiegelbild einer Verschwörung*, 447–57, 471–4; Peter Hoffmann, *Stauffenberg. A Family History, 1905–1944*, 92, 190, 211–12; Hoffmann, *The History of the German Resistance*, chapter 12.

2 See Hoffmann, "The German Resistance, the Jews, and Daniel Goldhagen," 73–88.

3 Rudolf Fahrner to the author, 9 May 1977.

4 *Spiegelbild*, 449–50, 457, 471.

5 Hoffmann, *Stauffenberg*, 133.

6 Ibid., 133, 151–2; record of interrogation of Major Joachim Kuhn, 2 Sept. 1944, Central Archives of the Federal Security Service (FSB) of the Russian Federation, Moscow; facsimile printed in Hoffmann, *Stauffenbergs Freund. Die tragische Geschichte des Widerstandskämpfers Joachim Kuhn*, 190–1.

7 Source: Record of interrogation of Major Joachim Kuhn, 2 Sept. 1944, Central Archives of the Federal Security Service (FSB) of the Russian Federation, Moscow; facsimile printed in Hoffmann, *Stauffenbergs Freund*, 186–210, excerpts here translated at 190–1.

8 Syntax reflects military style.

9 Oberkommando des Heeres, Army High Command; Kuhn's insertion in his quotation is in parentheses.

10 Source: as in *Stauffenbergs Freund*, 191, note 7.

11 Source: as in *Stauffenbergs Freund*, 191, note 7.

Colonel Claus Schenk Graf von Stauffenberg's Programmatic Statement, July 1944

Of the few who participated in the writing of these sententia, Claus Schenk Graf von Stauffenberg, his brother Berthold, and Rudolf Fahrner, only Fahrner testified on their origins. Claus and Berthold Schenk Graf Stauffenberg were executed on 20 July and 10 August 1944, respectively; their brother Alexander was in Athens and did not participate in the composition of the document or learn of it until much later; the Gestapo never became aware of its existence. Rudolf Fahrner, a friend of the Stauffenberg brothers, retained a copy with corrections in Claus Stauffenberg's handwriting and survived to testify to the drafting of the "oath."[1]

According to Rudolf Fahrner's evidence, Claus Stauffenberg requested that Berthold Stauffenberg and Rudolf Fahrner draft the document, which they did in the first days of July 1944. Fahrner has stated consistently that Claus Stauffenberg was the author of all or almost all of the ideas in the document. Fahrner referred to it as an "oath."[2]

Berthold's secretary, Maria Appel, typed it under Fahrner's dictation at Naval High Command, where Berthold was a judge in the international-law department of 1st Section, Supreme Naval Command. Claus made some changes in the carbon copy with his left hand and gave it to Fahrner on 4 July with the assignment to hide it. Maria Appel destroyed Berthold Stauffenberg's papers after his arrest on 20 July 1944.

Evidence for Claus Stauffenberg's authorship of the Oath comes also from a conversation between Fritz-Dietlof Count Schulenburg and Axel Baron von dem Bussche. The endeavour is consistent with Claus Stauffenberg's sense of the ceremonial.

The idea of a manifesto, for the keepers of the friends' legacy after the probable demise of the principals, is found in Rudolf Fahrner's books on Arndt and Gneisenau, and Stauffenberg may have had his impulse from reading them. Stauffenberg wrote to a friend in 1942 that he often referred to Fahrner's *Gneisenau* for his official duties. In both his works, Fahrner stated that at the beginning of March 1812, when Napoleon prepared his campaign against Russia, the emperor had forced Prussia to participate in the campaign, to accept French occupation of Prussia except Silesia, and to allow free passage for and the provisioning of the Grande Armée. Fahrner wrote: "The King surrenders. Gneisenau receives the discharge which he has repeatedly demanded; Scharnhorst goes on indefinite leave; Clausewitz, Groeben and others – in all 300 officers – demand and receive their discharge. Gneisenau and the friends feel sacred honour desecrated, the very germ of future growth endangered. Fearing the spread of a slavish mentality and its distortions of history, they set down their views in a common secret confession so that future times may learn, even if they themselves were to perish, that there had been men alive who had seen and felt the whole disgrace."[3]

Gneisenau's biographer Pertz, whose work Fahrner evidently used, describes the taking of vows in the spring of 1811 (not 1812) only as a project of Gneisenau's that came to naught.[4] Fahrner dramatized the story.

A comparison of the Oath with Claus Stauffenberg's independently documented views reveals a thoroughgoing correspondence between these views and the ideas in the Oath.

In his poem "Abendland I" ("Occident I") of 1923, Stauffenberg wrote of Germany's mission to the west as a continuation of Germany's role in the universal Christian empire of the Middle Ages. He mentioned the same ideas in a letter of 1936: for a German, the sublime heights of culture were always a linked "universal effectiveness: the Holy Empire, humanism, the Klassik."[5] The reference to the "equality lie" coincided with Stauffenberg's own view.

The Oath[6]

We believe in the future of the Germans.
We know that the German has powers that designate him to lead
   the community of the occidental nations to a more beautiful life.

We acknowledge in spirit and in deed the great traditions of our
nation that, through the amalgamation of Hellenic and Christian
origins in the Germanic character, created western man.

We want a New Order that makes all Germans supporters of the
state and guarantees them law and justice, but we scorn the lie
of equality, and we bow before the hierarchies established by
nature.

We want a nation that will remain rooted in the soil of the
homeland close to the powers of nature, that will find its
happiness and its satisfaction in its given surroundings, free and
proud, and will overcome the low passions of envy and jealous
resentment.

We want leaders who, coming from all classes of the nation, in
harmony with the divine powers, high-minded, lead others high-
mindedly, with discipline and sacrifice.

We unite in an inseparable community that through its bearing and
actions serves the New Order and forms for the leaders of the
future the fighters whom they will need.

> We pledge
>> to live blamelessly,
>> to serve in obedience,
>> to keep silent unswervingly,
>> and to stand for each other.

NOTES

1 On the provenance and drafting of the oath, and for the comments in this introduction, see Peter Hoffmann, *Stauffenberg. A Family History, 1905-1944*, 242, 246,
293–5.

2 In German, "Schwur" or "Eid."

3 Rudolf Fahrner, *Gneisenau* (Munich: Delfinverlag 1942), 56–7.

4 G.H. Pertz, *Das Leben des Feldmarschalls Grafen Neithardt von Gneisenau*, vol. 2
(Berlin: Georg Reimer 1865), 89–91.

5 Hoffmann, "Claus Graf Stauffenberg und Stefan George: Der Weg zur Tat," *Jahrbuch der Deutschen Schillergesellschaft* 12 (1968): 522–3; Claus Stauffenberg to Erffa,
22 Nov. 1936, typed, copy in the papers of Nina Schenk Gräfin von Stauffenberg.

6 Source: Typed carbon copy with Claus Stauffenberg's MS changes in Stefan George
Archiv, Stuttgart. First publication in full, in facsimile, in Hoffmann, *Claus Schenk
Graf von Stauffenberg und seine Brüder*, 396–7; also in Hoffmann, *Stauffenberg* (Eng-
lish ed.), 244–5, translation 293–4 (here slightly altered).

29

Field Marshal Erwin Rommel's Report, July 1944

Field Marshal Erwin Rommel, professional soldier, decorated veteran of the First World War, was well liked by the National Socialist leadership and for a time commanded Hitler's headquarters military guard. In the Second World War he acquired fame as commander of 7th Panzer Division in the campaign in the west in 1940. From 1941 he was the best known general in the German forces fighting in North Africa, and he finally commanded Army Group B in France when Allied forces had landed there in 1944. By this time, he was a sworn enemy of Hitler and ready to collaborate with the conspirators who planned the uprising of 20 July 1944. The events of that day might have taken a different turn had Rommel not been severely wounded on 17 July 1944. When Rommel's involvement in the conspiracy was revealed, Hitler gave him the choice of suicide, or a trial followed by kith-and-kin imprisonment of his family.[1]

In the document printed below, Rommel confronted Hitler with an ultimatum. He did so through proper channels, that is to say, through his superior, Field Marshal Günther von Kluge, Supreme Commander West. Kluge sent the ultimatum to Hitler and addressed to the Führer his own assessment of the situation, which fully supported and partially repeated that of Rommel.[2]

The Commander-in-Chief
of Army Group B   H.Q., 15.7.44

Considerations of the Situation

The situation on the Normandy front grows more difficult daily and is approaching a severe crisis.

Due to the severity of the fighting, the enemy's enormous use of material, above all artillery and tanks, and the effect of the enemy's unrestricted command of the air over the battle area, our own casualties are so high that the fighting strength of the divisions is rapidly diminishing. Replacements from home come only very sparingly and, with the difficult transport situation, take weeks to reach the front. As against casualties of around 97,000 men (including 2,360 officers) – that is, on average 2,500 to 3,000 men per day – replacements to date number 10,000 (of which around 6,000 have actually arrived).

Material losses the deployed troops have incurred are also uncommonly large and could be replaced up to now on only a very small scale, for example, so far 17 tanks as against losses of 225.

The newly arrived infantry divisions are raw, unused to battle, and – with their small establishment of artillery, armour-piercing guns, and close-combat anti-tank guns – not in a state, after hours of barrage and heavy bombing, to successfully repulse major enemy offensives for any length of time. As the fighting has shown, with this use of material by the enemy, even the bravest troops will be smashed piece by piece, losing men, arms, and territory.

Through the destruction of the railway system and the threat of the enemy air force to roads and tracks up to 150 km behind the front, supply conditions are so difficult that only the barest essentials can be brought up, and it is necessary to exercise the greatest economy in everything, above all in artillery and mortar ammunition. These conditions are not likely to improve, as enemy action is steadily reducing available transport capacities, and enemy activity in the air is likely to become more effective as the many airfields in the bridgehead area are taken into use.

No new forces of any consequence can be brought into the Normandy front without weakening the front of the 15th Army [on the Channel] or the Mediterranean front in southern France. The front of the 7th Army alone urgently needs 2 fresh divisions, since the troops there are exhausted.

On the enemy's side, fresh forces and quantities of war materiel flow to the front every day. The enemy supplies are undisturbed by our air force. Enemy pressure is becoming steadily stronger.

In these circumstances, we must expect that the enemy in the foreseeable future will succeed in breaking through our thin front, especially that of the 7th Army, and thrust deep into France. I may refer to the enclosed reports of the 7th Army and the 2nd Paratrooper Corps. Apart from the Panzer Group West's sector reserves, which for the time being are tied down by the fighting on their own front and, due to the enemy's command in the air, can only move by night, no mobile reserves are available at 7th Army for defence against such a break-through. Action by our air force will have, as before, very little effect.

The troops are everywhere fighting heroically, but the uneven struggle is nearing its end. In my opinion, it is necessary to draw conclusions from this situation. As Army Group Commander-in-Chief I feel myself in duty bound to speak plainly on this point.

[F.d.R.d.A.]   signed Rommel
signed signature   General Field Marshal.
Lieutenant.

NOTES

1 Hans Speidel, *Invasion. Ein Beitrag zu Rommels und des Reiches Schicksal* (Tübingen and Stuttgart: Rainer Wunderlich Verlag Hermann Leins 1949), 133-75-85; Speidel, *Aus unserer Zeit. Erinnerungen*, 168–89, 211–13; H. Liddell Hart, ed., *The Rommel Papers*, 493–506; Dieter Ose, *Entscheidung im Westen 1944. Der Oberbefehlshaber West und die Abwehr der alliierten Invasion*, 186–93; cf. Speidel, *Invasion 1944. Rommel and the Normandy Campaign*; Speidel, *Invasion 1944. Le destin de Rommel et du Reich.*
2 Ose, *Entscheidung*, 336.
3 Source: Typed copy of Rommel's report in Bundesarchiv-Militärarchiv, Freiburg i.Br., RH 19 IX/8, 21 et seq.; the original teletypescript in the papers of Army Group B command, with Rommel's MS marginals, "had to be destroyed on the occasion of the later arrest of the Army Group Chief of the General Staff [General Speidel]"; Speidel, *Invasion. Ein Beitrag*, 138–9; printed in Ose, *Entscheidung*, 334–5; a translation appeared in Liddell Hart, *The Rommel Papers*, 486–7. See also Speidel, *Invasion 1944. Le destin de Rommel et du Reich*; Desmond Young, *Rommel*; Dennis E. Showalter, *Patton and Rommel. Men of War in the Twentieth Century.*

BIBLIOGRAPHY

Adolph, H.J.L. *Otto Wels und die Politik der deutschen Sozialdemokratie 1894–1939.* Berlin: de Gruyter 1971

Akten zur deutschen auswärtigen Politik 1918–1945. Series D (1937–1945). Vol. I, no. 31. Baden-Baden: Imprimerie Nationale 1950

Albrecht, Richard. *Der militante Sozialdemokrat. Carlo Mierendorff 1897 bis 1943.* Berlin: J.H.W. Dietz Nachf 1987

Arad, Yitzhak, Israel Gutman, and Abraham Margaliot, eds. *Documents on the Holocaust. Selected Sources on the Destruction of the Jews in Germany and Austria, Poland and the Soviet Union.* 8th ed. Lincoln: University of Nebraska Press; Jerusalem: Yad Vashem 1999

Arndt, Ino. *Die Judenfrage im Licht der evangelischen Sonntagsblätter von 1918–1933.* Dissertation, Universität Tübingen 1960. Typescript

Arndt, Ino. "Machtübernahme und Judenboykott in der Sicht evangelischer Sonntagsblätter." Wolfgang Benz, ed. *Festschrift für Helmut Krausnick zum 75. Geburtstag.* Stuttgart: Deutsche Verlags-Anstalt 1980

Astor, David. "The German Opposition to Hitler. A Reply to Critics." *Encounter* 33, no. 4 (1969): 96

Balfour, Michael. *Withstanding Hitler in Germany 1933–45.* London, New York: Routledge 1988

Balfour, Michael, and Julian Frisby. *Helmuth von Moltke. A Leader Against Hitler.* London and Basingstoke: Macmillan 1972

Barkai, Avraham. *From Boycott to Annihilation. The Economic Struggle of German Jews, 1933–1943.* Hanover and London: University Press of New England 1989

Barkai, Avraham. *Vom Boykott zur "Entjudung." Der wirtschaftliche Existenzkampf der Juden im Dritten Reich 1933–1943.* Frankfurt am Main: Fischer Taschenbuch Verlag 1987

Beck, Ludwig. *Studien.* Stuttgart: K.F. Koehler Verlag 1955

Bentin, Lutz-Arwed. *Johannes Popitz und Carl Schmitt. Zur wirtschaftlichen Theorie des totalen Staates in Deutschland.* Munich: C.H. Beck 1972

Benz, Wolfgang and Walter H. Pehle, eds. *Encyclopedia of German Resistance to the Nazi Movement.* New York: The Continuous Publishing Company 1997

Berlin, Sir Isaiah. "A Personal Tribute to Adam von Trott (Balliol, 1931)." *Balliol College Annual Record* (1986): 61–2

Besier, Gerhard, and Gerhard Ringshausen. *Bekenntnis, Widerstand, Martyrium. Von Barmen 1934 bis Plötzensee 1944.* Göttingen: Vandenhoeck & Ruprecht 1986

Bethge, Eberhard. *Dietrich Bonhoeffer. Theologe, Christ, Zeitgenosse. Eine Biographie.* Munich: Chr. Kaiser Verlag 1970

– *Dietrich Bonhoeffer. A Biography.* Rev. and ed. by Victoria Barnett, based on the 7th German edition. Minneapolis: Fortress Press 2000

Bielenberg, Christabel. *The Past is Myself.* London: Chatto & Windus 1968

Blasius, Rainer A., ed. *Dokumente zur Deutschlandpolitik*, 1. Reihe/Vol. 1. Frankfurt am Main: Alfred Metzner Verlag 1984

Bleistein, Roman. *Alfred Delp. Geschichte eines Zeugen.* Frankfurt am Main: Josef Knecht 1989

Bödeker, Johanna. "Johannes Popitz: Auf der Suche nach einer neuen Wirtschaftsordnung." *Der Staat. Zeitschrift für Staatslehre, öffentliches Recht und Verfassungsgeschichte* 24 (1985): 513–25

Bonhoeffer, Dietrich. *Dietrich Bonhoeffer Werke.* 17 vols. Ed. Eberhard Bethge, et al. Munich: Chr. Kaiser-Gütersloher Verlagshaus 1986–1999

– *Dietrich Bonhoeffer Works.* 17 vols. Minneapolis: Fortress Press 1996–

– *Gesammelte Schriften.* 6 vols. Ed. Eberhard Bethge. Munich: Chr. Kaiser Verlag 1965–74

– "Die Kirche vor der Judenfrage." *Der Vormarsch. Evangelische Monatsschrift für Politik und Kultur* 3 (1933): 171–6

– "Wandlungen des Führerbegriffs in der jungen Generation," *Kreuz Zeitung* 26 February 1933

Bracher, Karl Dietrich, Wolfgang Sauer, and Gerhard Schulz. *Die nationalsozialistische Machtergreifung. Studien zur Errichtung des totalitären Herrschaftssystems in Deutschland 1933/34.* 2nd ed. Cologne: Westdeutscher Verlag 1960

Breitman, Richard. "A Deal with the Nazi Dictatorship? Himmler's Alleged Peace Emissaries in Autumn 1943." *Journal of Contemporary History* 30 (1995): 411–30

Bryans, J. Lonsdale. *Blind Victory (Secret Communications Halifax-Hassell).* London: Skeffington 1951

– "Zur britischen amtlichen Haltung gegenüber der deutschen Widerstandsbewegung." *Vierteljahrshefte für Zeitgeschichte* 1 (1953): 347–51

Bull, Hedley, ed. *The Challenge of the Third Reich. The Adam von Trott zu Solz Memorial Lectures.* Oxford: Clarendon Press; New York: Oxford University Press 1986

Cadogan, Alexander. *The Diaries of Sir Alexander Cadogan O.M. 1938–1945.* London: Cassell 1971

Calvacoressi, Peter. "On the Difficulties of Being an Anti-Nazi." *Encounter* 33, no. 2 (1969): 93–4

– "The Brink of Catastrophe." *Balliol College Annual Record.* (1986): 93–6

Clements, K.W. *Bonhoeffer and Britain.* London: Churches Together in Britain and Ireland 2006

Coady, Mary Frances. *With Bound Hands. A Jesuit in Nazi Germany. The Life and Selected Prison Letters of Alfred Delp*. Chicago: Loyola Press 2003

Collins, C.E. "Brave against a Tide." *Balliol College Annual Record* (1986): 87–90

Collins, Charles. "Adam von Trott and the German Opposition to Hitler." *The Folio Society Prospectus 1990*. London: The Folio Society 1990

Conway, John S. *The Nazi Persecution of the Churches, 1933–45*. New York: Basic Books 1968

Conwell-Evans, T.P. *None So Blind. A Study of the Crisis Years, 1930–1939*. London: Harrison & Sons 1947

Delp SJ, P. Alfred, SJ Papers. Arch. Prov. Germ. SJ, Munich. Abt. 47 Nr. 23, 3

– *The Prison Meditations of Father Alfred Delp*. Montreal: Palm Publishers 1956

– *Im Angesicht des Todes*. Frankfurt am Main: Josef Knecht Carolusdruckerei 1961

– *Gesammelte Schriften*. 5 vols. Ed. Roman Bleistein. Frankfurt am Main: Josef Knecht 1982–1988

– *Advent of the Heart. Seasonal Sermons and Prison Writings 1941–1944*. San Francisco: Ignatius Press 2006

Dietrich, Donald J. "Catholic Resistance in the Third Reich." *Holocaust and Genocide Studies* 3 (1988): 117–86

Dulles, Allen Welsh. *Germany's Underground*. New York: Macmillan 1947. New edition, n.p.: Da Capo Press 2000

Ehrle, Gertrud, ed. *Licht über dem Abgrund. Aufzeichnungen und Erlebnisse christlicher Frauen 1933–1945*. Freiburg: Herder 1951

Endrass, Elke. *Gemeinsam gegen Hitler. Pater Alfred Delp und Helmuth James Graf von Moltke*. Stuttgart: Kreuz 2007

Erhardt, Helmut. *Euthanasie und Vernichtung "lebensunwerten" Lebens*. Stuttgart: Enke 1965

Foerster, Wolfgang. *Generaloberst Ludwig Beck. Sein Kampf gegen den Krieg. Aus den nachgelassenen Papieren des Generalstabschefs*. Munich: Isar-Verlag 1953

Friedländer, Henry. *The Origins of Nazi Genocide. From Euthanasia to the Final Solution*. Chapel Hill: The University of North Carolina Press 1995

Friedländer, Saul. *The Years of Extermination. Nazi Germany and the Jews, 1939–1945*. New York: HarperCollins 2006

Galen, Bischof Clemens August Graf von. *Akten, Briefe und Predigten 1933–1946, II, 1939–1946 (Veröffentlichungen der Kommission für Zeitgeschichte, Reihe A: Quellen, Band 42)*. Mainz: Matthias-Grünewald-Verlag 1988

Gamelin, Maurice. *Servir*. 3 vols. Paris: Plon 1946–47

Gerstenmaier, Eugen. *Streit und Friede hat seine Zeit. Ein Lebensbericht*. Frankfurt: Propyläen Verlag 1981

– "Der Kreisauer Kreis: Zu dem Buch Gerrit van Roons 'Neuordnung im Widerstand.'" *Vierteljahrshefte für Zeitgeschichte* 15 (1967): 221–46

Gibbs, N. H. *Grand Strategy. Volume I: Rearmament Policy*. London: Her Majesty's Stationery Office 1976

Gillmann, Sabine, and Hans Mommsen, eds. *Politische Schriften und Briefe Carl Friedrich Goerdelers*. 2 vols. Munich: K.G. Saur 2003

Gisevius, Hans Bernd. *Bis zum bittern Ende*. Zurich: Fretz & Wasmuth 1946

– *To the Bitter End*. Trans. by Richard and Clara Winston. Boston: Houghton Mifflin Co. 1947

– *To the Bitter End*. New introduction by Peter Hoffmann. New York: Da Capo Press 1998

[Goebbels, Joseph]. *Die Tagebücher von Joseph Goebbels. Sämtliche Fragmente*. 23 vols. Munich, New Providence, London, Paris: K.G. Saur 1987–2008

Graham, Robert A. "The Right to Kill in the Third Reich. Prelude to Genocide." *Catholic Historical Review* 62 (1976): 56–76

Graml, Hermann, et al. *The German Resistance to Hitler*. London: B.T. Batsford 1970

Grant Duff, Shiela. *The Parting of Ways. A Personal Account of the Thirties*. London: Peter Owen 1982

Greschat, Martin, ed. *Zwischen Widerspruch und Widerstand. Texte zur Denkschrift der Bekennenden Kirche an Hitler (1936)*. Munich: Chr. Kaiser 1987

Griech-Polelle, Beth A. *Bishop von Galen. German Catholicism and National Socialism*. New Haven: Yale University Press 2002

Gruchmann, Lothar. *Justiz im Dritten Reich 1933–1940. Anpassung und Unterwerfung in der Ära Gürtner*. 2nd printing. Munich: R. Oldenbourg Verlag 1990

Hapig, Marianne. *Tagebuch und Erinnerung*. Ed. Elisabeth Prégardier. Edition Mooshausen. Annweiler: Plöger 2007. Based upon Gertrud Ehrle, ed. *Licht über dem Abgrund. Aufzeichnungen und Erlebnisse christlicher Frauen 1933–1945*. Freiburg: Herder 1951

Hassell, Fey von. *Hostage of the Third Reich. The Story of My Imprisonment and Rescue from the SS*. Ed. David Forbes-Watt. New York: Charles Scribner's Sons 1989

– *A Mother's War*. Ed. David Forbes-Watt. London: John Murray 1990

Hassell, Ulrich von. *Vom Andern Deutschland. Aus den nachgelassenen Tagebüchern 1938–1944*. Zurich: Atlantis Verlag 1946. 1988 German edition more complete.

– *The Von Hassell Diaries 1938–1944: The Story of the Forces Against Hitler Inside Germany, as Recorded by Ambassador Ulrich von Hassell*. Garden City, NY: Doubleday 1947

– *The Von Hassell Diaries 1938–1944. The Story of the Forces against Hitler inside Germany, as Recorded by Ambassador Ulrich von Hassell, A Leader of the Movement*. London: Hamish Hamilton 1948

– *The Von Hassell Diaries, 1938–1944*. Westport, CT: Greenwood Press 1971

– *Die Hassell-Tagebücher 1938–1944. Aufzeichnungen vom Andern Deutschland*. Eds. Friedrich Freiherr Hiller von Gaertringen and Klaus Peter Reiss. Berlin: Siedler Verlag 1988

– *Der Kreis schliesst sich. Aufzeichnungen in der Haft 1944*. Ed. Malve von Hassell. Berlin: Propyläen 1994

– *Journal d'un conjuré 1938–1944. L'insurrection de la conscience*. Paris: Berlin 1996

– *Römische Tagebücher und Briefe 1932–1938*. Ed. Ulrich Schlie. Munich: Herbig 2004

Helmreich, Ernst Christian. *The German Churches under Hitler. Background, Struggle, and Epilogue*. Detroit: Wayne State University Press 1979

Höffkes, Karl. *Hitlers politische Generale. Die Gauleiter des Dritten Reiches. Ein biographisches Nachschlagewerk*. Tübingen: Grabert-Verlag 1986

Hoffmann, Peter. *German Resistance to Hitler*. Cambridge, Massachusetts: Harvard University Press 1988

– *The History of the German Resistance to Hitler, 1933–1945*. Cambridge: MIT Press 1977; 3rd. Eng. ed. Montreal: McGill-Queen's University Press 1996

– *Stauffenbergs Freund. Die tragische Geschichte des Widerstandskämpfers Joachim Kuhn*. Munich: C.H. Beck 2007

– *Claus Schenk Graf von Stauffenberg. Die Biographie*. 3rd edition. Munich: Pantheon 2009.

– *Stauffenberg. A Family History, 1905–1944*. 3rd ed. Montreal: McGill-Queen's University Press 2009

– "Beck, Rommel and the Nazis: The Dilemma of the German Army." *Limits of Loyalty*, ed. by Edgar Denton III, 101–25. Waterloo, ON: Wilfrid Laurier University Press 1980

– "The German Resistance, the Jews, and Daniel Goldhagen." *Hyping the Holocaust. Scholars Answer Goldhagen*, ed. by Franklin H. Littell, 73–88. East Rockaway, NY: Cummings & Hathaway

– "The German Resistance to Hitler and the Jews: The Case of Carl Goerdeler." *The Genocidal Mind. Selected Papers from the 32nd Annual Scholars' Conference on the Holocaust and the Churches*, ed. by Dennis B. Klein, Richard Libowitz, Marcia Sachs Littell, Sharon Steeley, 277–90. St Paul, MN: Paragon House 2005

– "Ludwig Beck: Loyalty and Resistance." *Central European History* 14 (1981): 332–50

– "The Question of Western Allied Co-operation with the German Anti-Nazi Conspiracy, 1938–1944." *The Historical Journal* 34 (1991): 437–64

– "Ludwig Beck: Soldatentum und Verantwortung. Ein Widerstandskämpfer aus Hessen." *Polis* 42 (2005): 19–36

– "Oberst i.G. Henning von Tresckow und die Staatsstreichpläne im Jahr 1943." *Vierteljahrshefte für Zeitgeschichte* 55 (2007): 331–64

Höllen, Martin. "Katholische Kirche und NS-'Euthenasie.'" *Zeitschrift für Kirchengeschichte* 91 (1980): 53–82

Huber, Ernst Rudolf. *Staat und Kirche im 19. und 20. Jahrhundert: Dokumente zur Geschichte des deutschen Staatskirchenrechts*. 5 vols. Berlin: Duncker und Humblot 1973–95

Hunt, Richard N. *German Social Democracy 1918–1933*. New Haven: Yale University Press 1964

Hüttenberger, Peter. *Die Gauleiter. Studie zum Wandel des Machtgefüges in der NSDAP*. Stuttgart: Deutsche Verlags-Anstalt 1969

Italiaander, Rolf. *Besiegeltes Leben. Begegnungen auf vollendeten Wegen. Gerhart Hauptmann, Ulrich v. Hassell, Albrecht Haushofer. Drei Erinnerungsblätter*. Goslar: Deutsche Volksbücherei 1949

Jan, Julius von, pastor. Personnel file A 227. Landeskirchliches Archiv, Stuttgart

Kempner, Benedicta Maria. *Priester vor Hitlers Tribunalen*. Gütersloh: Bertelsmann, Reinhard Mohn, n.d.

Kettenacker, Lothar, ed. *Das "Andere Deutschland" im Zweiten Weltkrieg. Emigration und Widerstand in internationaler Perspektive. The "Other Germany" in the Second World War. Emigration and Resistance in International Perspective*. Stuttgart: Ernst Klett Verlag 1977

Kieffer, Fritz. *Judenverfolgung in Deutschland – eine innere Angelegenheit? Internationale Reaktionen auf die Flüchtlingsproblematik 1933–1939*. Stuttgart: Franz Steiner Verlag 2002

– "Carl Friedrich Goerdelers Vorschlag zur Gründung eines jüdischen Staates." *Zeitschrift der Savigny-Stiftung für Rechtsgeschichte* 125 (2008): 474–500

Klemperer, Klemens von, ed. *A Noble Combat. The Letters of Shiela Grant Duff and Adam von Trott zu Solz 1932–1939*. Oxford: Clarendon Press 1988

– *German Resistance against Hitler. The Search for Allies Abroad, 1938–1945*. Oxford: Clarendon Press 1992

Koch, Lutz. *Erwin Rommel. Die Wandlung eines grossen Soldaten*. Stuttgart: Walter Gebauer 1950

Krausnick, Helmut. "Ludwig Beck." *Widerstand im Dritten Reich. Probleme, Ereignisse, Gestalten*, ed. by Hermann Graml. Frankfurt am Main: Fischer Taschenbuch 1984

– ed. "Goerdeler und die Deportation der Leipziger Juden." *Vierteljahrshefte für Zeitgeschichte* 13 (1965): 338–9

Kurtz, Harold. "David Astor & the German Opposition." *Encounter* 33, no. 3 (1969): 89–90

Leber, Annedore. *Conscience in Revolt*. London: Valentine Mitchell 1957

– "Ulrich von Hassel[l]." *Das Gewissen entscheidet*, 198–201. Berlin: Mosaik-Verlag-Annedore Leber 1957

– *Das Gewissen entscheidet*. Berlin: Mosaik-Verlag-Annedore Leber 1960

Lewy, Günther. *The Catholic Church and Nazi Germany*. New York: McGraw-Hill 1964

Liddell Hart, B.H., ed. *The Rommel Papers*. London: Collins 1953

Lindgren, Henrik. "Adam von Trotts Reisen nach Schweden 1942–1944 – Ein Beitrag zur Frage der Auslandsverbindungen des deutschen Widerstands." *Vierteljahrshefte für Zeitgeschichte* 18 (1970): 274–91

Littell, Franklin H., and Hubert G. Locke, eds. *The German Church Struggle and the Holocaust*. Detroit: Wayne State University Press 1974

Ludlow, Peter W. "The Unwinding of Appeasement." In Lothar Kettenacker, ed. *The 'Other Germany' in the Second World War: Emigration and Resistance in International Perspective*. Stuttgart: Klett 1977

Ludlow, Peter. "Papst Pius XII., die britische Regierung und die deutsche Opposition im Winter 1939/40." *Vierteljahrshefte für Zeitgeschichte* 22 (1974)

MacDonogh, Giles. *A Good German. Adam von Trott zu Solz*. London: Quartet Books 1989

Magas, Gregory. Nazi Crimes and German Reactions: An Analysis of Reactions and Attitudes within the German Resistance to the Persecution of Jews in German-controlled Lands, 1933–1944, with a focus on the writings of Carl Goerdeler, Ulrich von Hassell, and Helmuth von Moltke. M.A. thesis. Montreal: McGill University 1999

Malone, Henry O. *Adam von Trott zu Solz. Werdegang eines Verschwörers 1909–1938*. Berlin: Siedler Verlag 1986

– Adam von Trott zu Solz: The Road to Conspiracy against Hitler. Ph.D. dissertation. Austin, Texas: University of Texas at Austin 1980

Matheson, Peter, ed. *The Third Reich and the Christian Churches*. Edinburgh, Scotland: T. & T. Clark 1981

Meehan, Patricia. *The Unnecessary War. Whitehall and the German Resistance to Hitler*. London: Sinclair-Stevenson 1992

Meier, Kurt. *Der evangelische Kirchenkampf*. 3 vols. Göttingen: Vandenhoeck & Ruprecht 1976–84

Meier-Benneckenstein, Paul, and Arel Friedrichs, eds. *Dokumente der deutschen Politik. Bd.I: Die nationalsozialistische Revolution 1933*. 5th ed. Berlin: Junker und Dünnhaupt Verlag 1939

Meyer-Krahmer, Marianne. *Carl Goerdeler und sein Weg in den Widerstand. Eine Reise in die Welt meines Vaters*. Freiburg im Breisgau: Herder Taschenbuch Verlag 1989

Militärgeschichtliches Forschungsamt, ed. *Germany and the Second World War*. Vols. 1–10. English trans. Oxford: Clarendon Press; New York: Oxford University Press 1990–

Minuth, Karl-Heinz, ed. *Akten der Reichskanzlei. Regierung Hitler 1933–1938. Teil I: 1933/34*. Vol. 2. Boppard am Rhein: Harald Boldt Verlag 1983

Mohr, Philipp Caspar. *Kein Recht zur Einmischung? Die politische und völkerrechtliche Reaktion Großbritanniens auf Hitlers "Machtergreifung" und die einsetzende Judenverfolgung*. Tübingen: Mohr Siebeck 2002

Moltke, Helmuth James von. *Briefe an Freya 1939–1945*. Ed. by Beate Ruhm von Oppen. Munich: C.H. Beck 1988

– *Letters to Freya 1939–1945*. Ed. and trans. by Beate Ruhm von Oppen. New York: Alfred A. Knopf 1990

Mommsen, Hans. *Beamtentum im Dritten Reich*. Stuttgart: Deutsche Verlags-Anstalt 1966

– "Gesellschaftsbild und Verfassungspläne des deutschen Widerstandes." *Der deutsche Widerstand gegen Hitler. Vier historisch-kritische Studien*. Ed. by Walter Schmitthenner and Hans Buchheim. Cologne: Kiepenheuer & Witsch 1966

– "Social Views and Constitutional Plans of the Resistance." *The German Resistance to Hitler*. Ed. by Hermann Graml, et al. London: B.T. Batsford 1970

– "Der Kreisauer Kreis und die künftige Neuordnung Deutschlands und Europas." *Vierteljahrshefte für Zeitgeschichte* 42 (1994): 361–77

- *Alternatives to Hitler. German Resistance under the Third Reich.* London, New York: I.B. Tauris 2003

Müller, Klaus-Jürgen. *Das Heer und Hitler. Armee und nationalsozialistisches Regime 1933–1940.* Stuttgart: Deutsche Verlags-Anstalt 1969

- *General Ludwig Beck. Studien und Dokumente zur politisch–militärischen Vorstellungswelt und Tätigkeit des Generalstabschefs des deutschen Heeres 1933–1938.* Boppard am Rhein: Harald Boldt Verlag 1980

- *The Army, Politics and Society in Germany, 1933–45. Studies in the Army's Relation to Nazism.* Manchester: Manchester University Press 1987

- *Generaloberst Ludwig Beck. Eine Biographie.* Paderborn: Ferdinand Schöningh 2007

Nazi Conspiracy and Aggression. 8 vols. Washington, DC: U.S. Government Printing Office 1946–48

Nicosia, Francis R. and Stokes, Lawrence D., eds. *Germans Against Nazism. Nonconformity, Opposition and Resistance in the Third Reich. Essays in Honour of Peter Hoffmann.* New York: Berg 1990

Niebuhr, Reinhold. "The Death of a Martyr." *Christianity and Crisis* 5, no. 11 (25 June 1945): 6–7

Noakes, Jeremy, and Geoffrey Pridham. *Documents on Nazism, 1919–1945.* New York: The Viking Press 1974

Nowak, Kurt. *"Euthanasie" und Sterilisierung im "Dritten Reich." Die Konfrontation der evangelischen und katholischen Kirche mit dem "Gesetz zur Verhütung erbkranken Nachwuchses" und der "Euthanasie"-Aktion.* Göttingen: Vandenhoeck & Ruprecht 1978

Ose, Dieter. *Entscheidung im Westen 1944. Der Oberbefehlshaber West und die Abwehr der alliierten Invasion.* Stuttgart: Deutsche Verlags-Anstalt 1982

Phayer, Michael. "Questions about Catholic Resistance." *Church History* 70, no. 2 (2001)

Pope, Michael. *Alfred Delp S.J. im Kreisauer Kreis. Die rechts- und sozialphilosophischen Grundlagen in seinen Konzeptionen für eine Neuordnung Deutschlands.* Mainz: Matthias-Grünewald-Verlag 1994

Portmann, Heinrich. *Cardinal von Galen.* London: Jarrolds 1957

Reich, Ines. *Carl Friedrich Goerdeler. Ein Oberbürgermeister gegen den NS-Staat.* Cologne: Böhlau Verlag 1997

Reynolds, Nicholas. *Treason Was No Crime. Ludwig Beck, Chief of the German General Staff.* London: William Kimber 1976

Ritter, Gerhard. *Carl Goerdeler und die deutsche Widerstandsbewegung.* 2nd ed. Stuttgart: Deutsche Verlags-Anstalt 1956

- *The German Resistance: Carl Goerdeler's Struggle Against Tyranny.* Trans. by R.T. Clark. London: George Allen & Unwin 1958

Roijen, J.H. van. "Adam von Trott in Holland." *Encounter* 33, no. 3 (1969): 91

Roon, Ger van. *Neuordnung im Widerstand. Der Kreisauer Kreis innerhalb der deutschen Widerstandsbewegung.* Munich: R. Oldenbourg Verlag 1967

- *German Resistance to Hitler. Count von Moltke and the Kreisau Circle.* Trans. by Peter Ludlow. London: Van Nostrand Reinhold 1971
-, ed. *Helmuth James Graf von Moltke. Völkerrecht im Dienste der Menschen.* Berlin: Siedler Verlag 1986
Rothfels, Hans. *The German Opposition to Hitler. An Appraisal.* Hinsdale, Illinois: Henry Regnery Company 1948; London: Oswald Wolff 1961
- *Die deutsche Opposition gegen Hitler. Eine Würdigung.* Neue, erweiterte Ausgabe. Frankfurt am Main: Fischer Taschenbuchverlag 1977
- "Zwei aussenpolitische Memoranden der deutschen Opposition (Frühjahr 1942)." *Vierteljahrshefte für Zeitgeschichte* 5 (1957): 388–97
- "Adam von Trott und das State Department." *Vierteljahrshefte für Zeitgeschichte* 7 (1959)
Ruge, Friedrich. *Rommel und die Invasion. Erinnerungen.* Stuttgart: K.F. Koehler 1959
Sams, Katharine J. Political Thought and Action in the Life of Adam von Trott, 1909–1940. Ph.D. dissertation. Montreal: McGill University 1999
Schäfer, Gerhard. *Landesbischof D. Wurm und der nationalsozialistische Staat 1940–1945. Eine Dokumentation.* Stuttgart: Calwer Verlag 1968
-, ed. *Die Evangelische Landeskirche in Württemberg und der Nationalsozialismus. Eine Dokumentation zum Kirchenkampf.* 6 vols. Stuttgart: Calwer Verlag 1972–86
Schlabrendorff, Fabian von. *The Secret War Against Hitler.* London: Hodder & Stoughton 1966
Schmidt, Heinz Werner. *With Rommel in the Desert.* London: Harrap 1951
Schmidt, Kurt Dietrich, ed. *Dokumente des Kirchenkampfes II. Die Zeit des Reichskirchenausschusses 1935–1937. Erster Teil (1935 bis 28. Mai 1936).* Göttingen: Vandenhoeck & Ruprecht 1934
Schmitthenner, Walter, and Hans Buchheim, eds. *Der deutsche Widerstand gegen Hitler. Vier historisch-kritische Studien.* Cologne: Kiepenheuer & Witsch 1966
Scholder, Klaus, ed. *Die Mittwochs-Gesellschaft. Protokolle aus dem geistigen Deutschland 1932 bis 1944.* Berlin: Severin und Siedler 1982
- *The Churches and the Third Reich.* 2 vols. Philadelphia: Fortress Press 1987–88
- "Die Kapitulation der evangelischen Kirche vor dem nationalsozialistischen Staat." *Zeitschrift für Kirchengeschichte* 80 (1969): 182–206
Schöllgen, Gregor. *Ulrich von Hassell 1881–1944. Ein Konservativer in der Opposition.* Munich: C.H. Beck 1990
- *A Conservative Against Hitler. Ulrich von Hassell: Diplomat in Imperial Germany, the Weimar Republic and the Third Reich, 1881–1944.* New York: St Martin's Press 1991
- "'Another' Germany: The Secret Foreign Contacts of Ulrich von Hassell During the Second World War." *International Historical Review* 11 (1989): 648–67
Scholtyseck, Joachim. *Robert Bosch und der liberale Widerstand gegen Hitler 1933 bis 1945.* Munich: C.H. Beck Verlag 1999
Schulz, Gerhard. "Über Johannes Popitz (1884–1945)." *Der Staat. Zeitschrift für Staatslehre, öffentliches Recht und Verfassungsgeschichte* 24 (1985): 485–511

Schwaiger, Georg. "Kardinal Michael von Faulhaber." *Zeitschrift für Kirchengeschichte* 80 (1969): 359–74

Showalter, Dennis E. *Patton and Rommel: Men of War in the Twentieth Century.* New York: Berkley Caliber 2005

Smith, Patrick, ed. and trans. *The Bishop of Münster and the Nazis. The Documents in the Case.* London: Burns Oates 1942

Speidel, Hans. *Invasion 1944. Le destin de Rommel et du Reich.* Paris: Berger-Levrault 1950

– *Invasion 1944: Rommel and the Normandy Campaign.* Chicago: Regnery 1950

– *Aus unserer Zeit. Erinnerungen.* Berlin: Propyläen 1977

"Spiegelbild einer Verschwörung." Die Opposition gegen Hitler und der Staatsstreich vom 20. Juli 1944 in der SD-Berichterstattung. Geheime Dokumente aus dem ehemaligen Reichssicherheitshauptamt. Ed. Hans-Adolf Jacobsen. Stuttgart: Seewald 1984

Steltzer, Theodor. *Von deutscher Politik. Dokumente, Aufsätze und Vorträge.* Ed. by Friedrich Minssen. Frankfurt am Main: Josef Knecht Carolusdruckerei 1949

Stoll, Gerhard E. *Die evangelische Zeitschriftenpresse im Jahre 1933.* Witten: Luther-Verlag 1963

Sykes, Christopher. *Troubled Loyalty. A Biography of Adam von Trott zu Solz.* London: Collins 1968

Trial of the Major War Criminals before the Nuremberg Military Tribunal. Nuremberg 14 November 1945–1 October 1946. 42 vols. Nuremberg: Secretariat of the Tribunal 1947–49

Trott zu Solz, Clarita von. *Adam von Trott zu Solz. An Account.* Trans. by Elke Langbehn. CD. ca. 2002. From the original German: Clarita von Trott zu Solz. *Adam von Trott zu Solz. Eine erste Materialsammlung, Sichtung und Zusammenstellung.* Reinbek, Germany: 1957. Mimeographed.

Twitchell, H. Kenaston. "Contacts with the German Resistance." *Balliol College Annual Record* (1986)

Usinger, Fritz, ed. *Carlo Mierendorff. Ein Einführung in sein Werk und eine Auswahl.* Wiesbaden: F. Steiner 1965

Vassiltchikov, Marie 'Missie.' *The Berlin Diaries 1940–1945.* London: Chatto & Windus 1985

Verhandlungen des Reichstags. VIII. Wahlperiode 1933. Band 457. Berlin: Reichsdruckerei 1934

Visser 'tHooft, W.A. "The View from Geneva." *Encounter* 33, no. 3 (1969): 92–4

Volk, Ludwig, ed. *Akten Deutschen Bischöfe über die Lage der Kirche 1933–1945. Band 5 (Veröffentlichungen der Kommission für Zeitgeschichte, Reihe A, Nr. 34).* Mainz: Matthias-Grünewald 1983

– *Katholische Kirche und Nationalsozialismus. Ausgewählte Aufsätze. (Veröffentlichungen der Kommission für Zeitgeschichte, Reihe B Band 46).* Mainz: Matthias-Grünewald 1987

Wagner, Walter. *Der Volksgerichtshof im nationalsozialistischen Staat. (Quellen und Darstellungen zur Zeitgeschichte, Band 16/III.)* Stuttgart: Deutsche Verlags-Anstalt 1974

Walters, LeRoy. "Paul Braune Confronts the National Socialists' 'Euthanasia' Program." *Holocaust and Genocide Studies* 21, no. 3 (2000): 454–87

Weisenborn, Günther. *Der lautlose Aufstand. Bericht über die Widerstandsbewegung des deutschen Volkes 1933–1945.* Hamburg: Rowohlt Verlag 1962

Winterhager, Wilhelm Ernst. *Der Kreisauer Kreis. Porträt einer Widerstandsgruppe.* Berlin: Stiftung Preußischer Kulturbesitz 1985

Wuermeling, Henric L. *"Doppelspiel." Adam von Trott zu Solz im Widerstand gegen Hitler.* Munich: Deutsche Verlags-Anstalt 2004

Young, A.P. *The 'X' Documents.* Ed. by Sidney Aster. London: Andre Deutsch 1974

Young, Desmond. *Rommel.* London: St James Place 1950

Zimmermann, Erich, and Hans-Adolf Jacobsen, eds. *Germans against Hitler, July 20, 1944.* 4th ed. Bonn: Press and Information Office of the Federal Government of Germany 1964

Zipfel, Friedrich. *Kirchenkampf in Deutschland 1933–1945.* Berlin: de Gruyter 1964

INDEX

Casablanca Conference, 277, 283
Catholic Church: and euthanasia, 211–12; and Jews, 213. *See also* Vatican
census, 198–9
Chamberlain, Neville: on countries' choice of internal governments, 294; commitment to Poland, 285; and Czechoslovakia, 232, 329n7; and dissident German generals, 238; and German people, 293; and Halifax on internal disruption of Germany, 59, 239, 285; and Hitler's peace offer, 285; Trott and, 284–5; and Wheeler-Bennett's memorandum and note, 287, 293–4
Chancellor: Confessing Church memorandum to, 101–16; Goerdeler as candidate for, 66; Hitler as, 13, 20–2, 35, 60, 156, 196, 211, 231, 236n4, 263; Kreisau Circle on, 81–2, 95n11; in "Provisional Basic Constitutional Law," 31–3, 35; treason against, 203n28
Christianity: anti-Christianity, 108–10, 161, 172, 174, 176–7, 264; de-Christianization, 103–10; education in, 86; ethics of, 245; freedom of, 119, 153–4n48; in Kreisau Circle, 43, 50–2, 76–7, 82–3; and Mierendorff, 99; morality, 58; in opposition, 304; people, 120, 131; press, 303; principles, 300; in "Provisional Basic Constitutional Law," 28; re-Christianization, 127; and socialism, 297; and the state, 51, 76, 113n22, 113n24, 113–14n26, 123–4, 141–2, 156, 293, 341
Christie, M.G., 233, 236n18
churches, Christian, 86, 293; destruction of order, 105–6; freedom of, 105–6, 111; and Jews, 141–7, 150n8, 150n15, 154n61, 155n65, 155n67, 157, 199–200, 264; Kreisau Circle on, 82, 259; labour and, 300; persecution of, 227; and state, 63, 142, 293; Trott on, 299–300, 304. *See also* Catholic Church; Christianity; clergy; Evangelical Church; German Christians; Lutheran Church; Protestantism

Churchill, Winston: and Atlantic Charter, 281n15; on failure of Stauffenberg's uprising, 289; and German Resistance feelers, 268, 276–7; and Trott's memorandum through Visser 'tHooft, 314n56
citizenship, 65n31, 152n33; of Jews, 94, 156, 182, 192–4, 197–200, 207n43, 209–10n55, 264
Citizenship Law (1913), 192, 194, 197
civil service: in Hassell's "Programme," 61, 63; in Law for the Restoration of the Professional Civil Service, 34–5, 41n19, 137–8, 147–8n3, 156–7, 182; in "Provisional Basic Constitutional Law," 28–9, 37
Clausewitz, Carl von, 232, 322, 341
clergy, 66, 83, 138, 149n6, 156–8, 176–7, 297; in concentration camps, 114–15n27, 213–14; Lutheran ministers and Confessing Church memorandum to Hitler, 101–3; and "muzzling decree," 179n12; in "Provisional Basic Constitutional Law," 29. *See also* churches
Coffin, Henry Sloan, 118, 120
commerce, 30, 41n14, 84, 258
communications facilities, 38, 278
Communists, 20, 99, 100n2, 101, 182, 235, 291, 300–1, 308–9, 326
concentration camps, 35, 39, 94, 98, 102, 110, 115n2, 160–1, 172, 174, 213, 270, 276; Auschwitz, 194; clergymen in, 115n2, 174, 213; in Confessing Church's memorandum, 110; euthanasia victims in, 213; Germans in, 160, 172, 270, 276; Jews in, 161, 172, 174, 194; Lutherans in, 102; in "Provisional Basic Constitutional Law," 35, 39; Sachsenhausen, 102
Concordat, 82, 157
Confessing Church, 115, 119, 297; and Aryan paragraph, 140, 157; circulation of Dibelius's message, 102–3; and de-confessionalization, 106–8; formation of, 13, 157; memorandum to Hitler, 101–11, 157; and National Socialism, 113; and Niemöller, 13, 180n31; Trott on, 297

Constitution, 95n11; and Enabling Act, 22; European, 254–5, 260; and freedom of expression, 65n31; German, post-1945, 65, 95n11; in Goerdeler's plans, 193, 271, 280; and Hitler's Chancellorship, 60; Kreisau Circle and, 78–9, 254–5, 260; and "Programme," 60–1, 62–4; and Popitz's "Provisional Basic Constitutional Law," 26–40, 56–7; Moltke's concepts for reconstruction of Germany and, 42–53; and National Socialist Party, 60; proportional electoral system under, 58; and rise of Hitler, 58, 60; treason against, 203n28; Trott on, 296, 298, 304; Weimar, 22, 24, 58, 60; and Wels, 22, 24

Conti, Leonardo, 217

Cot, Pierre, 325, 329n11

coup d'état, 3, 59, 66, 75–6, 100n2, 124, 202–3, 231, 238, 283, 298, 319, 322–8, 336–7, 343; Beck and, 67, 238, 278, 322–8; Gerstenmaier and, 135n40; Goerdeler and, 263–4; Goerdeler/ Wallenberg discussions on, 276–9; Halder and, 264; imminent 1943, 43; Mierendorff and, 100n2; Moltke and, 43, 75; Operation Valkyrie (Walküre) or 20 July plot, 70–1, 124, 135n40, 231, 319, 336–7, 343; Schacht and, 283n42; Trott and, 301

Cour permanente de justice internationale, 91

Cripps, Sir Stafford, 288, 314n56

Cuhorst, Hermann, 158, 169, 178

Czechia, 245, 305; invasion of, 323–5, 327–8; occupation of, 58–9

Czechoslovakia, 295; Beck and, 231–2, 322–5, 327–8; Britain and, 59, 232, 285, 294, 323, 329n7; Chamberlain and, 294; France and, 232, 323; in Goerdeler's peace initiatives, 267, 271; in Hassell's peace plans, 245; Hitler and, 285, 322–5, 327–8; invasion of, 232, 295, 322–3, 327–8, 329n7; occupation of Czechia, 58–9; Trott on, 285, 301, 305. *See also* Sudetenland

Daladier, Édouard, 233

defence: Beck on, 231; commissars, 226; in Hassell's "Programme," 63; Kreisau Circle on, 91, 254, 256; ministerial council, 219; in "Provisional Basic Constitutional Law," 28, 34, 37, 39, 41n19; Trott on, 295, 304

Defence Law, 35, 41n19

Delp, Alfred, 122–4; arrest and trial of, 124–9, 135n43; as Catholic, 122–4; and euthanasia, 123, 132n12; execution of, 124, 128–9; help to Jews, 123–4; and Kreisau Circle, 123–4, 135n43; letter to Jesuit friends, 125–31; and National Socialism, 123–4

Delp, Ewald, 123

Delp, Johann Adam Friedrich, 122

Delp, Maria (née Bernauer), 122

Denmark, 58

Dibelius, Otto, 102

"Directives for the Application of the Law on the State of Siege," 56–7

disarmament, 239, 260–1, 267, 272, 277, 281n15, 305

Disarmament Conference, 236n4

Doehle, Heinrich, 101

Dohnanyi, Hans von: Goerdeler's memorandum and, 195; "X Report," 246n17

domestic policy, Kreisau Circle on, 255–60

Dulles, Allen Welsh, 264

Ecclesiastical Decree Office, 110, 116n38

economy: European economic union, 261, 272, 274, 295; Beck and, 323–4; freedom of, 48–9, 275; in Goerdeler's peace plans, 270, 272–5; in Hassell's "Programme," 60–3; and individual, 49–50; international cooperation, 245, 247, 254–5, 261, 270, 272, 284, 295, 298; Jews in, 183; Kreisau Circle on, 77–8, 81, 83–6, 88, 254–5, 258–9, 261; in Mierendorff's proclamation, 99; Moltke on, 44–5, 48–50; in "Provisional Basic Constitutional Law," 28–30, 35; self-government in, 99; socialist organization of, 99; and society, 187; state and, 44–5, 48–50, 63, 272, 275; in Trott memorandum, 302–6

Eden, Anthony, 233, 268, 284, 288, 312n29, 322

Eichberg, 212, 217

Einsatzgruppen, 194, 337

Eliot, A. Roland, 288, 299–301

Enabling Act, 20–4

England. *See* Britain

ethics, 50–2, 61, 77, 82–3, 93–4, 99, 108, 110–11, 217, 219, 292; Christian, 28, 53, 58, 76, 104, 108, 110, 215, 245; and individual, 51; international, 90–1; and justice, 108, 110; and state, 51, 141–2, 298

Europe, Christian, 288, 293, 299, 304; bolshevization, 244; cooperation within, 76, 99, 193, 245, 247, 270–2, 288, 291, 296, 305; criminal law, 94; demobilization, 255, 258, 261; as economic union, 261, 272, 295; Germany's position in, 43, 78, 231–2, 244, 267, 274, 286–7, 301; in Moltke's Constitutional Concepts, 43; new, 239, 244, 288, 290, 294–5, 297, 305, 338; postwar integration of, 291, 301, 305; postwar reconstruction of, 76–7, 242, 244–5, 247, 272, 274, 280, 292; and Russia, 61, 99, 272, 274; union, 43, 247, 254–5, 258, 260–1, 272, 274, 301, 305; and the war, 120, 285, 290, 329n7, 338

euthanasia: Catholic Church and, 211–12; Delp and, 123; Galen and, 211–26; of handicapped persons, 211–23; Hassell and, 227–8; Lichtenberg and, 213; Lutheran Church and, 211–12; of mentally ill, 211–13, 216–19, 227–8; number of victims of, 213

Evangelical (Lutheran) Church, *evangelisch*, 82, 96n12, 101, 103–11, 113–14n26, 114n27, 115n32, 138, 144, 149–50n6, 179n12

Fahrner, Rudolf, 340–1; *Gneisenau,* 341

Falkenhausen, Alexander von, 69, 71, 195

family, 28, 77–9, 82–3, 152n25, 251, 262n6, 273, 320

Faulhaber, Michael, 123, 225n22, 300

federalism, 305

Fellgiebel, Erich, 70

finance, 30, 106, 272–3

Finland, 239–40, 271, 302

Forck, Bernhard Heinrich, 101, 111

foreign affairs, 44

Forell, Birger, 102

France: anti-war agreement with Germany, 188; and Czechoslovakia, 232, 323, 325, 327; deportation of Jews from, 194; euthanasia victims in, 213; in German propaganda, 295; invasion of, 58, 76; in Moltke's plans, 76; and nationalism, 252; in postwar Europe, 255, 269, 274, 282n27; and rearmament, 231, 235–6n4; and Ruhr occupation, 320; threat of war, 233, 325

Frank, Reinhold, 125, 134n26

Frankfurter, Felix, 286

freedom: of association, 257, 297; and Christianity, 119, 129, 153–4n48; Church and, 105–6, 111, 143, 256, 296; economic, 48–9, 245, 272, 275, 305; of expression, 60, 65n31, 256–7, 296, 326; of faith and conscience, 77; of Germany, 99, 111, 119, 177–8, 326; individual, 31, 45–7, 54n20, 61n4, 78, 87, 100, 248–52, 256, 272, 297, 302; of movement, 256, 259; political power and, 46, 99; of the press, 64, 256, 259, 296; of prisoners, 87; and socialism, 24, 99; in Wels's speech, 22, 24

Freisler, Roland, 124, 126–7, 129, 135n43, 135n46

Frick, Wilhelm, 21, 24n3, 158

Fricke, Otto, 101, 111

Fritsch, Werner, Freiherr von, 234, 322, 324

Führer. *See* Hitler

Galen, August, Graf von, 211–13, 226n30; and Jews, 217; sermons, 213–23, 227–8, 300

Gamelin, Maurice, 233

Gauleiter, 37, 184, 190, 213, 225n15, 227, 329n12, 330n13

General Staff, 239–41, 338

George, Stefan, 321nn4–5
German Christians, 103, 114n27, 117,
   137–8, 150, 152n25, 157, 171
German National People's Party
   (*Deutschnationale Volkspartei, DNVP*),
   24n4, 24–5n6, 186
Gerstenmaier, Eugen, 72n1; on co-
   ordination meeting of anti-Hitler
   plotters, 68; Hassell on, 69; and Hitler,
   135n40; in Kreisau Circle, 66, 68; trial
   of, 126, 135n40, 135n43
Gestapo (Secret State Police, Geheime
   Staatspolizei), 35, 37, 43, 61, 110, 118,
   124–6, 168, 171, 183, 191, 289, 304;
   on conspirators' attitudes toward
   National Socialist racial policies,
   336–7; Galen and, 213–14, 227; on
   Goerdeler's peace terms, 273–6; in
   Hassell's "Programme," 61
Gillmann, Sabine, 201–2n5, 203n24,
   207–8n50
Gisevius, Hans Bernd, 70–2
Gneisenau, August, Graf Neidhardt von,
   341
Goebbels, Joseph, 102, 113n26, 185n11, 188,
   213, 234, 301
Goerdeler, Carl Friedrich, 72n1, 73n9,
   73n11, 192; "The Aim" ("Das Ziel"),
   193–5, 197, 201, 201n3, 202–3n11,
   202–3n20, 203n24, 204n30, 206n39,
   207–8n50, 209n52, 209n55; and armistice with West, 195; arrest of, 279;
   in Beck-Goerdeler-Hassell-Popitz
   group, 66, 75–6, 193–4, 196; British
   contacts, 196, 264–6, 269, 276–7; at co-
   ordination meeting, 66, 68–9, 73n11;
   Dulles on, 264–5; execution, 183, 279;
   Gestapo and peace terms of, 273–6,
   282–3n37; and Hassell, 68–9, 73n9,
   187, 195; and Hassell's "Programme,"
   56; and Hassell's "Statement," 239; and
   Hitler, 264; and Jews (plan), 192–201,
   203n24, 209n52, 263–4; and Leuschner,
   195; meeting with Beck and Kluge,
   275–6, 282–3n37; meeting with Hassell,
   Popitz, and Jessen, 194; meeting with
   Stauffenberg in Kaiser's office, 283n44;

and Moltke, 75–6, 197; and National
   Socialism, 263, 269; peace plans, 263–
   80, 282n30; and removal of Hitler, 195,
   263–4, 276–9; travels of, 196, 204n30;
   treason of, 196, 264; Wallenberg's account of views, 276–9; and younger
   conspirators, 195
Göring, Hermann, 21, 24n2, 190, 234,
   237n21, 239, 241–2, 324; Beck on, 234,
   324, 327; Hassell and, 69, 185n12, 188;
   Hitler's successor, 237n21; at Hossbach
   conference, 322; and 9 November 1938
   pogrom, 183–4, 190; Popitz and, 69,
   182–4
Göring, Ilse, 184, 185n12, 242
Göring, Karl, 185n12
Grafeneck, 212
Grynszpan (Grünspan), Herschel, 157, 175,
   191n13
Gürtner, Franz, 158, 183, 189, 191n17, 212
Guttenberg, Karl Ludwig Freiherr von
   and zu, 194–5

Habermann, Max, 58, 187
Halder, Franz, 195, 238, 246n17, 264
Halifax, Edward Frederick Lindley Wood,
   1st earl of: and German resistance
   movements, 59, 238–40, 284–5, 287–9,
   293, 310–11n9, 312n34; and Hitler, 322–3,
   328; and Wiedemann, 328
Hamburg, fire bombing of, 67, 76
Hamerow, Theodore S., 120–1n1
handicapped persons: euthanasia of,
   211–26; sterilization of, 211
Hanover, 157
Hapig, Marianne, 124, 133n22
Harris, Arthur T., 76
Hassell, Fey, 188
Hassell, Ilse von (née von Tirpitz), 26–7,
   56–7, 186–7
Hassell, Johann Dietrich von, 57
Hassell, Margarete von (née Stosch), 186
Hassell, Ulrich von, 26, 66, 73n11, 186–8;
   arrest, 187; and Austria, 239; and Beck,
   195, 238–9; in Beck-Goerdeler-Hassell-
   Popitz group, 26, 56, 66–7, 75–6, 194–5;
   and co-ordination meeting of plotters,

Church and, 213; churches and, 101, 137–47, 150n7, 151–2n24, 174; citizenship, 192–4, 196–201, 209n52, 264; conversion, 138; Delp and, 123; deportations, 42, 124, 194, 196, 198, 264; DNVP and, 186; Galen and, 213; Goerdeler and, 192–210, 263–4; Grynszpan, 191; Hassell on, 186, 188–90, 194; and Jan, 156–81; Jewish state, 51, 192, 196–200, 204n30, 209n52; Kreisau Circle (and Moltke) and, 77, 87, 250, 252; legislation against, 63, 138, 156, 197–210, 301; marriage of, 197, 199–200; Moltke and, 42–3; murder of, 42, 123, 158, 193–4, 196–8, 200, 210n57, 213, 337; NSDAP and, 61, 63, 108, 137–8, 156, 157–8, 163, 175–6, 182–4, 189, 196–8, 264, 336; numbers in Germany, 198–9, 207n43; outrages against, 61, 101, 123–4, 137–8, 156–7, 163, 173; pogrom of 9 November 1938, 156–62, 163, 165–78, 183–4, 188–90, 191n13, 196; in Poland, 194, 196–8; Polish, in Germany, 196, 264; Popitz and, 182–4; in "Provisional Basic Constitutional Law," 35–6, 41n19; religion, 145, 199, 207n43; Stauffenberg and, 319, 337–8; Trott and, 301, 305; views of 20 July 1944 conspirators, 336–7. See also Kreisau; "Law for the Restoration of the Professional Civil Service"; Nürnberg Racial Laws

Johansson, Harry, 288

justice: Bonhoeffer and, 152n33; Christianity and, 108–11, 126, 142, 159–61, 171–3, 215; Delp and, 126–7; Gerstenmaier and, 135n43; Goerdeler and, 192, 199–201, 270–2; Hassell and, 245; and the international community, 92, 272, 294–5, 307; Jan and, 159–61, 167, 171–6; judges and, 63; people's sense, 24, 201; Stauffenberg and, 342; system, 63–4, 99–100, 108–11, 126, 142, 176, 186, 245, 270–1, 290, 342; Trott and, 290; violation, 39, 43, 60–1, 92, 110–11, 127, 152n33, 159, 161, 167, 172, 174–6, 192, 199–200, 215, 271

Kaiser, Hermann, 67, 283n44
Kaiser, Jakob, 58, 187
Kapp, Wolfgang, 186
Kelly, David, 267, 281n18
Kerensky, Alexander, 68, 73n10, 75
Kerrl, Hans, 105, 113n26, 158, 184n3, 227, 228n3
Kieffer, Fritz, 203n24
Kirkpatrick, Sir Ivone, 289
Kluge, Günther von, 70–1, 273–6, 282n37, 343
Koch, Werner, 102
Konrad, Rudolf, 325, 329n11
Kötzschke, Hermann, 102, 112n7
Kreisau: and Beck-Goerdeler-Hassell-Popitz group, 66–8, 75; on Britain, 92, 254; on Catholic Church, 82; and civil service, 257; and Christianity, 43, 50–2, 54n23, 76–7, 82–3, 87–97; and concentration camps, 94; Circle, 66, 75, 95, 98, 123–4, 126, 134, 187, 247, 288, 314n62; constitutional concepts, 42–55; formation, 42–3; members in Tegel Prison, 124; Mierendorff and, 98; Moltke and, 42–3, 66–8; and postwar reconstruction, 76–9, 187, 247; preparations for Hitler's overthrow, 75–6, 97; rejection of "racial concept," 43, 77, 87, 250, 252; and socialism, 66; "Special Directive" regarding enemy occupation, 88–9; and Trott's memorandum of April 1942, 288, 302–6

Kreuz Zeitung, 14, 19nn1–2, 156–7
Krosigk, Lutz, Graf Schwerin von, 183, 185n9, 188–9, 191n18
Kühlenthal, Erich, 233
Kuhn, Joachim, 337–8

labour, labourers, 83–4, 86, 88, 99, 218–19, 257–9, 300
Labour Front, 62, 107
labour legislation, 23, 30, 41
Labour Movement, 248, 270
labour unions, 278, 296. See also trades unions
Lammers, Hans-Heinrich, 212

43, 76; trial, 124, 126–7; and Weimar multi-party system, 187

Mommsen, Hans: and Goerdeler's "Das Ziel," 193, 201–2n5, 202–3n20, 203n24, 207–8n50; and Hassell, 57, 193

Montgomery, Bernard, 43–4

morality. See ethics

Moscow, battle of, 194, 276

motives: Bonhoeffer, 139; Delp, 122–31; Kreisau circle, 52, 89–95; Popitz, 183; Stauffenberg, 319–20; Trott, 290, 300

Muff, Wolfgang, 235

Müller, Fritz, 101, 111

Müller, Josef, 246n17

Müller, Ludwig, 106, 174, 179n12

municipalities, 78–80, 113n19

Mussolini, Benito, 67

Mutschmann, Martin, 263

Nathusius, Hannah von, 227–8, 228n4

Nathusius, Martin von, 228n4

nationalism, 13, 27, 88, 239–43, 247, 250, 252, 304, 306, 308

National Socialism, 27, 42, 60, 98, 100–1, 113n24, 123, 183, 189, 192, 295, 300, 304, 336–8; and Christianity, 115n35; and Confessing Church, 101, 108, 157; laws against, 65n31

National Socialist German Workers' Party (NSDAP), 24n2, 62–3, 113n21, 123, 156, 239, 329n12; and Christianity, 105; and churches, 13, 113n24, 115n32; and the Constitution, 60; and German Christians, 13; and Jews, 61, 123, 137–8, 156, 189, 196–8; and pogrom, 156, 164; and socialism, 23–4

natural order, 45–54

Navy, 198, 234, 254–5, 322

Near East, 254

Neinstedt, 227–8nn4–5

Neurath, Konstantin, Freiherr von, 183, 185n10, 242, 322

New Order, 43, 76–7, 142, 192–3, 199, 295; Stauffenberg and, 342

New York Herald Tribune, The, 102, 112n18, 157

Niebuhr, Reinhold, 117, 120–1

Niederdeutsche Kirchenzeitung, 137, 147–8n3, 153n46, 154n62

Niemöller, Martin, 13, 167, 170, 174, 176, 180n31; and Confessing Church, 13; and Confessing Church memorandum to Hitler, 101, 111

NSFK (National Socialist Flying Corps), 62, 65n25

NSKK (National Socialist Motoring Corps), 62, 65n25

NSV (National Socialist People's Welfare), 38, 62, 170

Nürnberg Racial Laws, 156, 183, 188, 193, 197–200, 209–10n55

OKW. See Armed Forces Supreme Command

Olbricht, Friedrich, 67, 70, 282n37

Olympic Games, Berlin, 1936, 102, 157

Operation Gomorrha, 76

Operation Valkyrie (Walküre), 319. See also coup d'état

Osborne, Francis d'Arcy, 313n43

Oster, Hans, 195, 238–9

Östreicher, Luise, 134n33

Palestine, 196, 204n30, 254

Papen, Franz von, 182, 235

Pastors' Emergency League, 13, 113n26, 180n31

Paton, Robert, "The Church and the Post-War World," 300

Paton, William, 296, 313n44

Paulus, Friedrich, 71

peace aims, peace terms. See Goerdeler; Hassell; Trott; war aims

Penal Code, 175, 177–8, 212, 216–17, 220

People's Court (Volksgerichtshof), 124, 126–7, 135n49, 179n11, 183

Pertz, G.H., 341

Pétain, Philippe, 233

Phipps, Sir Eric, 233

Pirzio-Biroli, Detalmo, 239; letter to Halifax, 240–4

Pius XI, Pope, 43

Pius XII, Pope, 238–9, 287
Planck, Erwin, 26, 195, 279, 283n43
Plötzensee Prison, 125, 127, 134n25, 135n49
Poelchau, Harald, 124
Poland, 34, 44, 58, 60, 157, 231, 244–5, 295, 319; Britain and, 284–5, 294; euthanasia victims in, 213; in Goerdeler's peace initiatives, 267, 269, 271, 273–5, 282n27, 282n35; in Hassell's "Statement," 245; invasion of, 211; Jews in, 194, 196, 198; return of Jews to, 196, 264; Trott on, 301–2, 305
police, 34–5, 37, 39, 62, 72n1, 93, 110, 126, 135n38, 135n43, 158, 165–6, 168, 171, 183, 191nn22–3, 196, 212–14, 216–17, 219, 255–6, 259, 272, 296, 304, 308, 330n18, 331, 336–7. See also Gestapo (Geheime Staatspolizei); security police
political prisoners, 39
Popitz, Cornelia Schulz, 26, 41n14, 57
Popitz, Johannes, 26, 41n14, 56–8, 73n11, 182; arrest, 183; in Beck-Goerdeler-Hassell-Popitz group, 66, 68, 75–6; at co-ordination meeting, 66, 68–9, 73n11; execution of, 183; and Goerdeler, 187, 193–5; and Hassell, 185, 187–8, 195; and Hassell's "Programme," 56–8; and Hitler, 183–4; and Jews, 182–4; and "Law for the Restoration of the Professional Civil Service," 182–3; and National Socialism, 35, 183; and parliamentary system, 58; and pogrom, 183–4; on post-Hitler governance, 58; and "Provisional Basic Constitutional Law," 26–7, 27–40, 73n11
power: and the churches, 77, 82, 108, 131, 133–4n23, 297, 304; consolidation of NSDAP, 20; and the economy, 99; and freedom, 46; and the Gestapo, 35; of the Head of State, 35, 100, 241; and law, 46, 293; of the masses, 15; and the military, 27, 29, 58, 63, 87–8, 254, 288, 292, 301; NSDAP and, 20, 23–4, 61, 241; and perception, 46–7; politics, 24, 252; of the resistance, 289; state and, 27, 46–7, 58, 252

Preachers' Seminary, 118, 140, 169
press: censorship of, 14, 64
Preysing, Konrad, Cardinal Graf von, 212
Prinz-Albrecht-Strasse Prison, 124–5
prisoners of war, 39, 300, 337
propaganda: Allied, 301, 325; British, 243, 290–1, 309; against Christianity, 105; and Jews, 137, 157–8; Kreisau Circle on, 258, 260; Mierendorff and, 98; National-Socialist, 98, 239, 290, 295, 334; Pirzio-Biroli on, 239, 243; in "Provisional Basic Constitutional Law," 37; socialist, 98; Trott on, 290–1, 295, 309
Prussia, 26, 29–30, 36–7, 63, 66, 73, 107, 114–15n27, 115n33, 138–9, 150n13, 182, 186, 188, 193, 195, 206n40, 231, 271, 273, 284, 295–6, 319, 327, 341

race, 182–3, 193, 197, 200, 213, 231; Bonhoeffer and, 13, 138, 141, 145–6, 155n62, 155n65; in Confessing Church memorandum, 108; Galen and, 221; German Christians and, 157; Goerdeler and, 200, 209n52; Jan and, 161, 172, 174–5; Kreisau Circle and, 43, 77, 87, 250, 252; Mierendorff and, 99; Stauffenbergs and, 336. See also Nürnberg Racial Laws
Raeder, Erich, 234, 322
Raper, Baldwin, 267
Rasmussen, Larry L., 120–1n1, 152n25, 152n33, 153n45, 153n46, 154–5n62, 155n68, 155n69
Rath, Ernst vom, 175, 188, 191n13
ration cards, 39, 88, 123
Realpolitik, 61, 69
rearmament, 231
Rechtsstaat, 287, 293–4, 296, 301, 312n29
reconstruction: Bonhoeffer and, 119–20; and Christianity, 76–7, 86, 304; church constitution, 147–8n3; economic, 83, 258; Goerdeler on, 269, 272, 274, 280; Hassell on, 244; Kreisau Circle on, 43, 76, 86, 247–61; Moltke on, 42–53; post-